**Coping with city growth during the
British industrial revolution**

Coping with city growth during the British industrial revolution

JEFFREY G. WILLIAMSON
Department of Economics, Harvard University

The right of the
University of Cambridge
to print and sell
all manner of books
was granted by
Henry VIII in 1534.
The University has printed
and published continuously
since 1584.

Cambridge University Press

Cambridge

New York   Port Chester   Melbourne   Sydney

Published by the Press Syndicate of the University of Cambridge
The Pitt Building, Trumpington Street, Cambridge CB2 1RP
40 West 20th Street, New York, NY 10011, USA
10 Stamford Road, Oakleigh, Melbourne 3166, Australia

First published 1990

Printed in the United States of America

Library of Congress Cataloging-in-Publication Data
Williamson, Jeffrey G., 1935–
  Coping with city growth during the British industrial revolution /
by Jeffrey G. Williamson.
      p.   cm.
  Includes bibliographical references.
  ISBN 0-521-36480-9
  1. Cities and towns – Great Britain – Growth – History – 19th century.
2. Great Britain – Economic Conditions – 1760–1860.   I. Title.
  HT384.G7W54   1990
  307.76′0941′09033 – dc20   *b7300*   89-27453
                                                            CIP

British Library Cataloguing in Publication Data
Williamson, Jeffrey G. (Jeffrey Gale) 1935–
  Coping with city growth during the British Industrial
  Revolution.
  1. Great Britain. Cities. Growth, history
  I. Title
  307.7′64′0941

ISBN 0-521-36480-9

Contents

v

Tables

Figures

Acknowledgments

The idea for this book began to sprout in the summer of 1982, when I returned to the University of Wisconsin from a year's leave at the World Bank. Two different research projects seemed to converge at that time. Allen Kelley and I had almost finished another fruitful collaboration, this one to be published in 1984 as *What Drives Third World City Growth?* The collaboration entailed an ambitious effort (too ambitious, we sometimes thought) to model Third World urbanization experience from the early 1960s to the 1980s, during a period of spectacular progress and enormous problems in cities throughout Asia, Africa, and Latin America. Fresh from studying these contemporary industrial revolutions, I then resumed work on the First Industrial Revolution, which had been left brewing on the back burner, an effort that eventually appeared in 1985 as *Did British Capitalism Breed Inequality?*

It occurred to me that these two interests might be merged with profit. That is, the book with Allen Kelley suffered from ignoring historical precedents while my work on the British industrial revolution had ignored the urban dimensions that attracted so much contemporary interest in the nineteenth century, long before the same debates resumed in the 1960s. Indeed, *Coping with City Growth* makes extensive use of contemporary Third World experience. It exploits the contemporary Third World literature to help sharpen the historical issues, and it also uses Third World evidence to help form comparative judgments of city-growth performance and problems during the First Industrial Revolution. I hope the reader finds some value in writing history backwards in this way. I certainly have.

I have accumulated many intellectual obligations along the way. Although Allen Kelley has never seen this book, my collaborative work with him in the past has had a clear impact on it. He has my belated thanks. Others have read bits and pieces of this book along the way, and have been otherwise helpful in sharing their data and expertise. I feel extraordinarily fortunate to have so many friends to thank, and here they are: David Bloom,

George Boyer, Lou Cain, Alec Cairncross, Brad DeLong, Jan DeVries, Barry Eichengreen, Stan Engerman, Bob Fogel, Carol Heim, Paul Hohenberg, Lynn Lees, Frank Lewis, Peter Lindert, Don McCloskey, David Mitch, Joel Mokyr, Cynthia Morris, Larry Neal, Cormac O'Grada, Sidney Pollard, Sam Preston, Andrei Rogers, Ken Snowden, Rick Steckel, Carolyn Tuttle, David Weir, and Tony Wrigley. Apart from her many virtues, I am also lucky to have a wife, Nancy Williamson, who shares her computer skills with me.

I have been blessed with some terrific graduate research assistants since the project started in earnest during the summer of 1984: Chris Hanes, Miles Kimball (assistant professor at Northwestern), Tim McBride (The Urban Institute), Tom Mondschean (assistant professor at DePaul), Erin Page, and Andy Warner. In addition, classroom battles with a generation of outstanding Harvard graduate students have sharpened the arguments, and made me more aware of the flaws still remaining. My deepest thanks to them all.

The project has benefited by funding from the National Science Foundation (NSF) and the National Institutes of Health (NIH). National agencies like the NSF and the NIH have played critical roles in fostering quantitative research by cliometricians. A lot of good cliometric work could not be done without their support. Whether *Coping* is "good work" I leave for the critics to judge, but I am pleased to thank both agencies.

I would also like to thank the Economic History Association and the editors of *Explorations in Economic History, Oxford Economic Papers,* and the *Population and Development Review* for permission to reproduce here some of my work that has appeared in the following publications: "Urban Disamenities, Dark Satanic Mills and the British Standard of Living Debate," *Journal of Economic History* (March 1981), 75–84; "Was the Industrial Revolution Worth It? Disamenities and Death in 19th Century British Towns," *Explorations in Economic History* (July 1982), 221–45; "The Historical Content of the Classical Labor Surplus Model," *Population and Development Review* (June 1985), 171–91; "The Impact of the Irish on British Labor Markets During the Industrial Revolution," *Journal of Economic History* (September 1986), 693–720; "Did English Factor Markets Fail During the Industrial Revolution?" *Oxford Economic Papers* (December 1987), 641–78; and "Migrant Selectivity, Urbanization, and Industrial Revolutions," *Population and Development Review* (June 1988), 287–314.

Most important, I want to thank my children for putting up with my compulsiveness over the years. Apparently it did them little harm, since Amy, Kirk, Hilary, and Megan have all turned out to be marvelous adults, and they are great company besides. This book is dedicated to them.

Cambridge, Massachusetts

1. Coping with city growth, past and present

1.1   Looking backward from the present[1]

The past quarter century witnessed unprecedented economic progress in the Third World as gauged by the standards of the First Industrial Revolution. Economic success of that magnitude has always created problems of dislocation and structural adjustment. City growth is one such problem, and given the unprecedented progress in the Third World, their city growth problems seem, at least to those who ignore history, unprecedented as well. By the end of this century, the United Nations forecasts urban population growth rates three times those of rural areas. Two billion people, exceeding 40 percent of the Third World population, will live in cities; some cities will have reached extremely large size – Mexico City at 31.6 million, São Paulo at 26 million, and Cairo, Jakarta, Seoul, and Karachi, each exceeding 15 million. Current rates of Third World city growth border on the spectacular, averaging between 4 and 5 percent per annum.

Analysts and policymakers are sharply divided on the city-growth problem. Pessimists stress the Third World's inability to cope with the social overhead requirements of rapid urban growth and high urban densities, citing ugly squatter settlements, pollution, environmental decay, and planning failure as evidence of their inability to cope. Third World city growth is viewed by the pessimists as another example of the "tragedy of the commons," a classic example of overuse of a collective resource. In contrast, optimists view city growth as a central force raising average living standards. They view urbanization as the natural outcome of economic development, and a requisite for the more rational use of economic resources. To the optimist, the tragedy of the commons is really nothing more than an example of poor economic planning and inappropriate prices. Debate over public options remains intense, the optimists favoring

1 The first three paragraphs of this section draw on Kelley and Williamson (1984), pp. 3–4.

1

an open-city approach and the pessimists searching for ways to close the cities down.

Economic success breeds problems of adjustment, and they certainly seem severe in Third World cities. Development economists have spent almost three decades debating urban unemployment, underemployment and the alleged failure to absorb the flood of rural emigrants into city labor markets; the persistent influx of newcomers makes it extremely difficult for municipal planners to improve the quality of social overhead; the migrants crowd into densely packed urban slums, jammed into primitive dwellings with little or no social services; and the rising density and size of the city augments pollution while lowering the quality of the city environment.

None of this would sound unfamiliar to Victorians coping with city growth in the middle third of the nineteenth century. They too were overwhelmed by the same "success." They too took innumerable surveys, held countless parliamentary hearings, published one official document after another, searched for scapegoats, and struggled with reform. Thus, the debate between the Third World city-growth optimists and pessimists is hardly new, and can be found in the British *Parliamentary Papers* as early as the 1830s, in treatises by political economists, and in the British press.

1.2   Placing Britain's city growth in perspective

During the Reform Debates of the 1830s and 1840s, the conventional wisdom had it that Britain was undergoing unusually rapid city growth. This characterization is embedded in the historiography even today. To offer one example, Michael Flinn (1965, p. 4) cites census data to show that some nineteenth-century towns grew at rates "that would bring cold sweat to the brows of twentieth-century housing committees." Thus, Glasgow grew at 3.2 percent per annum in the 1830s, Manchester and Salford at 3.9 percent in the 1820s, Bradford at 5.9 percent in the 1830s, West Bromwich at 4.8 and 5.4 percent in the 1820s and 1830s, and Dukinfield nearly trebled in the 1820s. These were the fast-growing cities and towns in the industrializing North, of course, and, as it turns out, these were the decades of most rapid growth. On average, Britain's cities grew somewhat slower than the previous examples suggest, about 2.5 percent per annum in the 1820s. Furthermore, these rates were almost half of those for the Third World in the 1960s (Table 1.1).

Table 1.1. *A comparative assessment of city-growth performance*

| Country | Date maximum city growth reached | | | Maximum rate of city growth (% per an-num) |
	Early 1800–1850	Middle 1850–1900	Late post-1900	
England & Wales	1821–1831			2.50
France	1830–1850			1.58
Germany	1830–1850			3.43
Austria		1800–1900		2.10
Belgium		1880–1900		1.95
Denmark		1880–1900		3.22
Finland		1880–1900		4.00
Italy		1880–1900		1.86
Norway		1850–1870		2.94
Sweden		1850–1900		2.91
Netherlands			1900–1910	1.93
Spain			1900–1910	1.82
Switzerland			1900–1910	3.22
Europe (excluding England & Wales)		1880–1900		2.58
Third World (excluding China)			1960–1970	4.21

Sources: All European estimates but England and Wales are derived by applying Bairoch and Goertz (1986, p. 288) urban shares to Mitchell's (1978, pp. 3–8) population figures. England and Wales are derived from Table 2.4 below. (It should be noted that Bairoch's implied city-growth rates are considerably higher.) The Third World estimate is from UN (1987, pp. 70 and 75).

However, contemporary observers living during the First Industrial Revolution had reason to view Britain's city growth as being unusually fast. After all, they had no previous industrialized country experience with which to gauge their own. They had only the evidence that city growth was faster in the early nineteenth century than it was in the previous one. Looking backward from the vantage point of the 1980s, we do not suffer the same limited vision of history. The Victorians were unable to make comparative assessments, but we can.

So, was Britain's city growth rapid by the standards of the "typical" European industrial revolution? As Table 1.1 shows, there was little that was unusual about Britain's city growth during the First Industrial Revo-

Table 1.2. *A comparative assessment of urbanization levels*

Country	Date	Income per capita in 1970 $	Level of urbanization (%)
Belgium	1850	584	31.8
Denmark	1870	563	20.2
Italy	1910	548	40.5
Norway	1890	548	20.5
Sweden	1900	616	19.3
France	1870	567	25.0
Germany	1870	579	24.4
Unweighted average of above seven countries	1850–1910	572	26.0
England & Wales	1840	567	48.3

Sources: Derived from Crafts (1985), Tables 3.2 and 3.3, pp. 54–5 and Bairoch and Goertz (1986), p. 288.

lution. The rest of Europe reached its peak rate of city growth much later in the nineteenth century, of course. Whereas the peak rate for England and Wales occurred in the 1820s, the peak rate for the rest of western and southern Europe was during the last two decades of the nineteenth century. Yet, the rate of city growth at their respective maxima were almost identical: 2.5 percent per annum for England in the 1820s versus a little less than 2.6 percent per annum for the rest of Europe between 1880 and 1900. The key message emerging from Table 1.1, therefore, is that Britain's city growth at her peak in the 1820s was no different from the rates achieved in the rest of Europe at its peak.

The level of urbanization is a different story. Table 1.2 relies on N. F. R. Crafts's book (1985, chp. 3) to assess Britain's urbanization levels relative to the rest of nineteenth-century Europe and the contemporary Third World. In 1970 dollars, Britain's per capita income was $567 in 1840. Because urbanization is highly correlated with per capita income, we want to compare levels of urbanization between countries of comparable incomes. Table 1.2 offers that evidence for England and seven other European countries. At roughly the same per capita income, England in 1840 had a much higher urban share, 48.3 percent, than did the rest of Europe in the mid-to-late nineteenth century, 26 percent, or even the contemporary Third World, 26.4 percent. Yet, this comparison tells us far more about British comparative advantage and eighteenth-century preconditions than it does about its alleged "unusual" city growth in the early nineteenth century, and it is the latter that is at issue in this book.

1.3   The issues

Exploring how Britain coped with city growth during the First Industrial Revolution is useful for four reasons: first, because its urban transition was completed long ago, while it is ongoing in the Third World; second, because Britain underwent the first urban transition and thus had to search for novel ways to cope with what was a singular event at that time; third, because Britain's urban transition can be well documented (it cannot for most of the countries listed in Table 1.1); and fourth, because Britain's experience was fairly typical.

How, then, did Britain cope with city growth during the First Industrial Revolution?

We begin the search for answers in Chapter 2 with a demographic reconstruction of what I call the urban transition. Here, I offer decadal estimates of emigration from the lagging countryside, immigration into the booming cities, and city growth. We discover that immigration played a much bigger role that did natural increase compared with the contemporary Third World. This seems to be explained in large part by the far higher rates of natural increase in the countryside than in the city. In contrast, the Third World has never had to cope with Britain's problem; namely, excess labor demands centered in cities where the rates of natural increase were lowest. We also discover that the rate of rural emigration was very rapid long before "rural depopulation" became a popular issue in the late nineteenth century, and that there is no evidence to support the view that potential rural emigrants were reluctant to leave. And the immigrants self-selected; the flows were dominated by young adults, and this had important implications for city pauperism, dependency burdens, accumulation, and the evolution of the excess labor demands, which immigration satisfied.

Chapter 3 pursues the migrant-selectivity theme and develops an estimate of the human capital transfer implied by the rural emigration. The numbers are very large, suggesting that human capital flows between countryside and city were far more important than financial flows. This event served to ease the pressure on city capital markets as they tried to cope with the investment requirements of rapid city growth.

Chapter 4 turns from the supply of city labor to the demand for city labor and its absorption. In contrast with the "overurbanization" thesis so popular in the Third World literature, urbanization did not outpace industrialization during the First Industrial Revolution. Furthermore, it appears that the demand for labor in the cities was fairly elastic and shifted to the right at very bouyant rates during the four critical decades, 1821–61, when city growth problems were said to have reached their peak.

Chapter 5 turns from a macro assessment of city labor absorption to micro issues. One of the most popular paradigms of city labor markets in the Third World literature is the so-called Todaro model. It implies "failure" in labor markets, "irrational" immigrants, and that immigrants do badly relative to the native-born. It turns out that the evidence from 1851 fails to support this view. Instead, immigrants responded to current job prospects, achieved economic success on par with the native-born, and were absorbed by the city labor market quite easily.

Chapter 6 looks at the experience of one important group of immigrants that has gotten so much attention since the 1820s – the Irish. It offers answers to three questions: Was the standard of living of British labor significantly depressed by the Irish influx? Were potential emigrants from Britain's countryside crowded out? Did "elastic" Irish labor supplies foster industrialization? The answers are surprising and revisionist.

Although the preceding chapters appear to take a benign neoclassical view of the operation of British labor markets during the First Industrial Revolution, Chapter 7 points out that there were large and rising wage gaps between city and countryside. These gaps are common during industrial revolutions, but they seem to have been especially large in Britain in the early 1830s. This was partly due to cost-of-living differentials, quality-of-life differentials, and rural poor relief. It was also due to labor-market failure. This chapter assesses the impact of the labor-market failure, explores who gained and who lost from the failure, and then traces out the accumulation implications.

Chapter 7 argues that Britain's cities were starved for labor and capital, and thus that city growth was too slow. The Third World literature on city growth takes quite a different position, and the British evidence seems to be inconsistent with it. Chapter 8 shows that Britain did not overurbanize, that there was an antiurban bias (rather than a prourban bias, as argued for the Third World), but that wage gaps overstate the benefits to additional immigration. The latter had its source in high city death and sickness rates associated with crowding and disease. That is, the marginal social costs of city growth were likely to have exceeded the marginal private costs.

Chapter 9 explores this theme in greater detail. It describes the perils of early nineteenth-century city life, and relates them to crowding and the high cost of urban housing. Inelastic supplies of housing and city space played a key role in creating the high mortality, which led Engels to call immigration to Victorian cities "social murder." Yet, wages reflected the perils of city life, clean and less crowded cities paying lower wages than dirty and crowded ones. The chapter offers an estimate of the value workers placed on the better quality of life they gave up when they migrated from the countryside to the city, and it turns out that the deterioration in the quality of life facing the average laborer – more of whom were in the dirty cities – did little to erase the income gains associated with industrialization and urbanization up to the 1850s.

The key question, however, is whether Britain could have done better for her working classes in the cities. It appears that it could. In fact, Britain underinvested in her cities. Although much has been made of the "modest investment requirements" associated with the British industrial revolution, that fact does not offer support for the smug conclusion that Britain pursued some optimal labor-intensive policy. On the contrary, what it reflects is that Britain underinvested in her city infrastructure. Chapter 10 attempts to estimate the magnitude of that underinvestment by exploring the costs of two counterfactual policies: a city decrowding policy introduced after the French War, when new war debt was no longer a crushing financial burden; and a regime in which sanitary reform was introduced faster and sooner. It turns out that understanding why Britain underinvested in city social overhead is crucial to making sense out of the sharp difference with the Third World, where it is argued that there is overinvestment in cities.

These, then, are the main questions raised in this book. Now I must show how I got my answers.

2. The urban demographic transition: Births, deaths, and immigration

2.1 Why do we care about the urban demographic transition?

A reconstruction of the demographic dimensions of the urban transition should help improve our understanding of the First Industrial Revolution.

Certainly it is essential in searching for answers to any of the following questions: Did English cities grow more by natural increase than by migration? Did city immigration rates rise as industrialization accelerated? Did rural emigration rates respond vigorously to the employment demands of rapid city growth, or were rural Englishmen more attached to the land than has been true of other industrial revolutions? Was migration selective? If so, what was the impact of the selectivity on the city economy? What role did push and pull forces play in rural and urban labor markets? These questions have always been at center stage in debates about the First Industrial Revolution. The answers will hinge on an assessment of those forces creating and displacing jobs in the two labor markets, as well as on the migration behavior thought to link them, assessments which cannot be made without the prior demographic reconstruction performed in this chapter.

Consider, for example, the Third World overurbanization debate which was initiated by Bert Hoselitz in the 1950s. His thesis was that urbanization was outpacing industrialization in the sense that urban populations were large relative to industrial jobs, at least when compared with late nineteenth-century experience (Hoselitz 1955, 1957). The implication was that urban labor was moving into low-wage, residual service underemployment by default. Hoselitz's thesis reinforced the belief that industrial employment growth in Third World cities was disappointing, that the cities were being swamped by workers pushed off the land, and that city immigrants were accepting unemployment or marginal service sector underemployment while waiting for the good industrial jobs (Todaro 1969). This debate has important implications for understanding how urban

8

labor markets worked in Britain (Chapter 5) as well as how the cities coped with social overhead requirements (Chapter 10).

Resolution of the British push versus pull debate also hinges on an evaluation of the role of the Poor Laws, the enclosures, and the demise of rural cottage industry in the face of cheaper urban factory production. In addition, the answers hinge on an assessment of cost-of-living in the two locations, house rents and crowding-related disamenities playing a critical role (Chapter 9). And if the Irish immigrant was a serious competitor with the potential English rural emigrant, than we need better estimates of the rural-urban migration flows to explore the crowding-out phenomenon properly (Chapter 6). More generally, any assessment of the efficient operation of labor markets in Britain during the industrial revolution (Chapter 7) will hinge at least in part on the size of the rural-urban migrations that helped to satisfy excess labor demands in the cities.

2.2   Reconstructing rural emigration, city immigration, and the urban transition

The 1841 census added birth-place to birth and death-rate information by registration districts. Although these data are certainly useful for understanding the composition of England's cities at that date, the census takers never asked when the respondent moved to the city. Thus, the 1841 Census does not document migrant flows. Fortunately, however, subsequent censuses also reported birth and death rates by registration districts, so it is a simple (but time-consuming) matter to reconstruct migration flows by comparing actual population totals by location with those predicted from the location-specific birth and death rates. While H. A. Shannon and E. Grebenik (1943) pioneered this methodology with an application to Bristol, Alec Cairncross (1949, 1953, chp. 4) expanded the application to England as a whole for the postcensus period. Dov Friedlander (1969) extended Cairncross's efforts back even further in time to 1800.

Friedlander's method of reconstructing the precensus decades is simple enough (which, for the moment, we make simpler by ignoring external migration and taking the system to be closed):

$$C(t) - C(t-1) = CCBR(t-1)C(t-1) - CCDR(t-1)C(t-1) + M(t-1) \quad (2.1)$$

$$R(t) - R(t-1) = RCBR(t-1)R(t-1) - RCDR(t-1)R(t-1) - M(t-1) \qquad (2.2)$$

where urban (C) and rural (R) populations are known. Four parameters must be estimated – crude birth rates (CBR) and crude death rates (CDR) in city and countryside. With this information in hand, migration, $M(t-1)$, can be derived from either equation. In addition, of course, the migration estimates in (2.1) and (2.2) must be consistent, so we must search for values of those parameters on the right-hand side (the two death rates and the two birth rates) that preserve the equality. Because there are many demographic parameters that would satisfy that equality, we need more information. Given estimates of crude birth rates and crude death rates for England as a whole, and given estimates of the share of the urban population, then the only additional information we require are the relative urban and rural rates. Friedlander solved the problem by assuming that British urban-rural death-rate differentials followed Swedish experience, thus yielding a unique estimate of rural-urban migration and the two birth rates.[1]

Friedlander's estimates for 1801–41 filled a gap in our knowledge about the English urban transition and his estimates for the post-1841 period appear at first sight to be superior to those offered by Cairncross, because, for example, Friedlander's city immigration rates for the 1840s are much more like those found in the contemporary Third World (Kelley and Williamson, 1984, chp. 3) than Cairncross's far lower estimates. But Friedlander's estimates of rural-urban migration can be greatly improved and extended. First, we now have the superior Wrigley and Schofield (1981) aggregate quinquennial population estimates that were unavailable to Friedlander. Second, we have the superior quinquennial nationwide crude birth rates and crude death rates also available in Wrigley and Schofield, rates quite different from those utilized by Friedlander. Third, while Friedlander relied on Adna Weber's (1899) urbanization estimates for 1841–91 and his own guesses for 1801–41, we now have available the far superior estimates of C. M. Law (1967, 1972) from 1750 onward. Fourth, there is absolutely no reason why the English urban transition cannot be disaggregated by region. Because it has been argued that the North and the South of England were likely to have been driven by quite different demographic and economic forces during the industrial revolu-

---

1 Given birth rates for England as a whole, one of these birth rates in equations (2.1) and (2.2) implies the other.

tion, the suggestion is attractive and we shall pursue it. Fifth, there is absolutely no reason why the English urban transition cannot be disaggregated by age and sex. This suggestion turns out to be especially fruitful because many debates about city growth during the First Industrial Revolution appear to hinge on age and sex composition of city immigrations. Finally, if we are willing to make some plausible assumptions, there is absolutely no reason why the analysis cannot be extended back into the eighteenth century.

This chapter will, in fact, offer a complete reconstruction of the demographic dimensions of the English urban transition over the century from 1776 to 1871, pursuing all of these suggestions. As Appendix 2.1 indicates, the reconstruction should be treated with caution in that it relies on some critical assumptions and some questionable data. I believe the issues are important enough, however, to report this tentative reconstruction at this time.

2.3   Fertility and mortality in city and countryside

Table 2.1 supplies estimates of crude birth rates, crude death rates, and crude rates of natural increase for England and Wales across the middle third of the nineteenth century, calculated from the Registrar General's *Annual Reports*, but adjusted by Wrigley and Schofield's (1981, p. 636) undercount ratio. The estimates are supplied for three dates, although each is actually an average over much longer periods: "1841" covers 1838–44, "1856" covers 1851–60, and "1866" covers 1861–70. As the sources and notes to the table indicate, "Urban" refers to urban registration districts plus London and "Rural" is a residual. These urban registration districts correspond to what the census authorities called England's principal cities and towns. In addition, the tables report a breakdown between North and South where the regional classification offered by Phyllis Deane and W. A. Cole (1962, p. 131) is followed with only slight modification.

Although these estimated rates have been calculated as an intermediate step toward learning more about city immigration patterns, it might be useful to pause and note some of the more interesting findings that emerge from the exercise, especially given that mid nineteenth-century England exhibits vital rates in sharp contrast with the contemporary Third World. That is, rural birth rates exceed urban in the Third World: The opposite was true in England. Rural death rates exceed urban death rates

Table 2.1. *Crude birth rates (CBR), crude death rates (CDR), and crude rates of natural increase (CRNI) in various regions of England and Wales, 1838 to 1870 (per 000)*

Region	"1841"			"1856"			"1866"		
	CBR	CDR	CRNI	CBR	CDR	CRNI	CBR	CDR	CRNI
England and Wales									
Total	36.24	22.29	13.95	35.73	22.17	13.56	36.22	22.42	13.80
Urban	37.86	25.96	11.90	37.22	24.82	12.40	37.58	25.10	12.48
Rural	35.41	20.39	15.02	34.86	20.62	14.24	35.39	20.77	14.62
Urban Detail									
London	34.75	25.86	8.89	35.10	23.63	11.47	36.42	24.31	12.11
4 largest cities	36.55	27.34	9.21	36.12	25.17	10.95	37.06	26.00	11.06
Cities ≥ 100,000	37.50	27.16	10.34	36.70	25.42	11.28	37.71	26.20	11.51
Cities < 100,000	38.35	24.30	14.05	37.93	24.00	13.93	37.39	23.64	13.75
Southern cities	34.39	25.23	9.16	34.58	23.36	11.22	35.87	23.82	12.05
Northern cities	41.12	26.64	14.48	39.79	26.25	13.54	39.23	26.33	12.90
All cities	37.86	25.96	11.90	37.22	24.82	12.40	37.58	25.10	12.48

Sources and notes: "1841" refers to total births, 1839–1844, and total deaths, 1838–1844, converted into annual averages, and the rates calculated relative to 1841 populations: from *Registrar General Annual Reports, PP* 1847–8 (v. 25) and 1849 (v. 21). "1856" refers to total births and total deaths, 1851–60, converted into annual averages, and the rates calculated relative to 1851 and 1861 average populations: from *Registrar General Annual Reports, PP* 1862 (v. 17) and 1865 (v. 13). "1866" refers to total births and total deaths, 1861–1870, converted into annual averages, and the rates calculated relative to 1861 and 1871 average populations: from *Registrar General Annual Reports, PP* 1872 (v. 17) and 1875 (v. 18). In Appendix 8 (pp. 631–7) of Wrigley and Schofield's *The Population History of England, 1541–1871* (Cambridge, Mass.: Harvard, 1981), the authors argue that the Registrar General undercounted births and deaths, especially births and especially early in the period 1841–1871. Their Table A8.5 (p. 636) shows exactly the extent of the undercount which they assumed was the case. Their "adjustment ratio" of revised to reported is also applied to the Registrar General's data we have collected here, and the adjustment ratios are:

	Births	Deaths
1841	1.1200009	1.0200012
1856	1.0488000	1
1866	1.0330000	1

We have, like Wrigley and Schofield, assumed that the undercount ratios apply everywhere in England the same. The undercount problem is an old one in the literature, and while we have applied the Wrigley and Schofield rates uniformly throughout rural and urban England, in fact it varied from region to region. Teitlebaum has, in fact, estimated the fertility undercount ratio by country for 1841–1891. Fortunately for us, there seems to be no correlation between urbanization and the undercount. Indeed, for the 1840s "the adjustment factor in London is very close to that of England and Wales as a whole. The same is the case for 1851–1860" (Teitlebaum, 1984. p. 63).

The "South" of England follows the classification suggested by Deane and Cole (*British Economic Growth, 1688–1959* (Cambridge: Cambridge University Press, 1962), pp. 122–35, especially Table 29, p. 131), with a slight modification. Thus

South of England		North of England	
Division I	London	Division VI	West Midland Counties
II	Southeastern Counties	VII	North Midland Counties
III	South Midland Counties	VIII	North Western Counties
IV	Eastern Counties	IX	Yorkshire
V	Southwestern Counties	XI	Wales

Under urban, the "4 largest cities" are, of course, London, Liverpool, Manchester, and Birmingham; those cities (in 1861) greater than or equal to 100,000 and those less than 100,000 is self-explanatory. The unit of observation reported in the *Registrar General Reports* is the District. Thus, the 66 urban districts (including London) are the "principal towns and cities" that underlie the urban totals and their component parts in "1841." "Rural" is simply the residual.

CRNI = CBR − CDR, although reported CRNI may differ due to rounding.

13

in the Third World: The opposite was true in England. Rural rates of natural increase never exceed urban rates by much in the Third World: They exceeded urban rates by a lot in England.[2] As we shall see, these English demographic attributes had very important implications for city immigration, rural emigration, and labor-market behavior during the First Industrial Revolution. They are summarized in Table 2.1.[3]

Crude death rates were much higher in the cities. This well-known attribute of English urbanization appears here as a systematic ordering of CDRs, which was quite stable throughout the mid nineteenth century. They were highest in large cities (although London was an important exception), somewhat lower in small cities, and lowest in rural areas. In addition, the South of England tended to have lower mortality rates than the North, even in the cities. These urban-rural CDR differentials declined some after 1841 but they were still pronounced in 1866. They continued to decline during the remainder of the nineteenth century, but the switch to a regime of relatively benign city mortality environments did not take place until around World War I. Thus, the role of public-health and sanitation reform in making the city a relatively benign mortality environment, even in the Third World, is a twentieth-century phenomenon. In nineteenth-century Europe, the cities were killers, a very important fact in understanding the operation of urban labor markets during the First Industrial Revolution.

In contrast with the contemporary Third World, crude rates of natural increase were considerably higher in England's countryside, espe-

2 Rogers and Williamson (1982, p. 469). Rogers (1984, Table 4, p. 288) offers a convenient summary of Third World experience in 1960 (per thousand):

	Growth rate	Crude birth rate	Crude death rate	Rate of natural increase
Urban	45.5	37.9	15.4	22.5
Rural	16.5	44.1	21.7	22.4

3 It should be pointed out that Cairncross's urban classification of the Registrar General's districts differs from that underlying Table 2.1. As Appendix 2.2 indicates, only forty-nine urban districts are common to the two studies. We include 17 additional urban districts that Cairncross appears to exclude (like Cardiff, Gateshead, Newcastle-upon-Tyne and South Shields), while Cairncross includes sixty-two urban districts that fail to make Law's urban list or, for that matter, the census's list of chief cities and towns in 1841 (*PP*, 1843, vol. 22, p. 10). The difference may be explained by the fact that Cairncross was looking forward to 1911, and we will be looking back toward 1776.

cially in 1841. Furthermore, the differential was due entirely to the lower crude death rates there because the crude birth rates were actually quite a bit higher in the cities, the only exceptions being southern cities in 1841 and 1856. The higher rates of natural increase in the countryside must have placed even greater stress on rural-urban labor markets in Britain as booming labor demands in the cities were distant from booming labor supplies in the countryside. The Third World has never had to cope with England's poor match between excess city labor demands and excess rural labor supplies. Perhaps this is one reason why, as we shall see, city immigration rates were so high in England even though the rate of industrialization was so modest compared with Third World standards.

Rates of natural increase were much lower in southern cities in the 1840s and 1850s than in northern cities (Table 2.3), and it had important implications for migration and labor market behavior. Although labor demand grew somewhat more slowly in the South, immigration still accounted for a larger share of city population growth there. In spite of the fact that the industrial revolution was largely centered in the North, migration seems to have played a greater role in satisfying excess city labor demands in the South of England. This fact also implies that urban labor markets must have been harder pressed to achieve an efficient labor allocation in the South than in the North, a prediction confirmed by evidence on rural-urban wage gaps (Chapter 9).

Natural increase in the cities was sufficiently small to suggest that immigration must have been an important source of city growth throughout the period. However, rates of natural increase in the cities rose between 1841 and 1856, implying a diminution in the relative importance of city immigration over time, and the trend was due entirely to a fall in the city death rates.

Much of this variety in crude birth and crude death rates may be a result of differentials in age distributions, rather than solely a result of differentials in age-specific demographic behavior. Fast-growing areas that absorb immigrants tend to have large proportions of young adults. Thus, to the extent that the cities tended to have a higher proportion of young adults, the crude death rate differentials between urban and rural areas understate age-adjusted mortality-rate differentials, a prediction borne out by the far higher infant-mortality rates in the cities (Chapter 9). Similarly, the higher crude birth rates in the cities may be attributable in large part to the fact that young adults comprised a high proportion of urban populations. We shall return to this issue below. It was central to urban immigration and labor-market behavior during the First Industrial Revolution.

2.4   Rural emigration and city immigration, 1776–1871

1841–71: A reconstruction based on the Registrar General

Tables 2.2 and 2.3 offer a tentative reconstruction of city immigration and rural emigration based on the Registrar General's Reports. Table 2.2 presents these estimates for England and Wales as a whole, and Table 2.3 breaks these aggregates down into the North and South of England. Each table reports decade averages for the 1840s, 1850s, and 1860s.

Consider first the striking similarities by city size. Except for the 1860s, big cities relied on immigration no more heavily than did small cities. In the 1840s, for example, immigration was responsible for about 56 percent of the population increase in London, 60 percent in the four biggest cities (London, Birmingham, Liverpool, and Manchester), 54 percent in major cities (greater than or equal to 100,000 in 1861), and 61 percent in small cities. If anything, it appears that smaller cities were less able to satisfy their labor-force requirements by relying on natural rates of increase, and this was true of both the 1840s and 1850s. The explanation lies in the fact that small cities enjoyed relatively fast growth over these two decades, and even high rates of natural increase could not match the booming demand for labor there. However, this differential between large and small cities reverses in the 1860s, when small cities underwent a striking population slowdown.

Immigration rates declined dramatically from the 1840s to the 1860s among cities of all sizes. For all cities in England and Wales the rate of city immigration declined from 1.44 percent per annum in the 1840s, to .81 percent per annum in the 1850s, and to .23 percent per annum in the 1860s. The decline in these city immigration rates was pronounced everywhere, but it was most dramatic in small cities. As seen in Appendix 2.1 and in the section below, the Registrar General's data tend to introduce a downward bias to city growth and urban immigration estimates. Nevertheless, the declines in city immigration rates are reproduced in what follows below and they offer an intriguing puzzle: Why did city immigration rates fall off when the derived demand for urban labor was booming?

Table 2.3 explores regional attributes. Similarities outweigh differences. First, the rate of city population growth in the North of England was distinctly higher in the 1840s, thereafter it was roughly the same as in the South. Second, the rate of city immigration was much the same in the two regions, slightly higher in the North in the 1840s and 1860s, but distinctly lower in the 1850s.

The big regional differences highlighted in Table 2.3 center on rural areas. Although natural rates of population increase in the rural North were slightly higher than in the rural South, the rates of rural emigration in the North were far lower. The differences are striking: In the 1840s, the rural emigration rate was 1.30 percent per annum down South while only .87 percent per annum up North. Presumably, these regional differences in rural emigration rates reflect lagging demand for farm labor in grain districts in the South of England, thus pushing labor into the southern cities, where demand pull was almost as strong as it was in northern urban labor markets. It also reflects greater excess demands for labor in southern cities, which had lower rates of natural increase. In any case, it cannot be explained by higher rates of rural natural increase in the South pushing labor to the cities in response to some Malthusian glut. The rates of natural increase were, in fact, lower in the rural South than in the rural North.

1776–1871: A long-run reconstruction based on Wrigley, Schofield, and Law

Demographers refer to the urban tra·sition with the same casual familiarity as the demographic transition, but the best they can offer for the former is a stylized pattern – more a hypothesis – like that for the contemporary Third World reproduced in Figure 2.1. (See Zelinksy, 1971; Rogers, 1978; Ledent, 1982; Keyfitz, 1980.) We need some well-documented cases, however, if the urban transition is to have a solid empirical base on which city growth problems can be analyzed. Such cases are hard to come by. Samuel Preston (UN, 1980) and others have been able to reconstruct Third World urbanization and city growth experience since the 1950s (see the survey in Kelley and Williamson, 1984, chps. 3 and 9), yet no similar estimates have been offered for any historical cases. Obviously, this literature should welcome a demographic reconstruction of the urban transition during the British industrial revolution.

Table 2.2. *Urban immigration and rural emigration, England and Wales, 1841 to 1871: Based on Registrar General's registration districts*

	Population at decade starting year (000) (1)	Population increase (000)			Percent Population Increase		Annual percent rates		
		Total (2)	Due to natural increase (3)	Due to immigration (4)	Due to natural increase (5)	Due to immigration (6)	Population increase (7)	Natural increase (8)	Immigration (9)
Rural									
1841–1851	11,193	693	1,814	–1,121	261.76	–161.76	.60	1.50	–1.06
1851–1861	11,886	832	1,819	–987	218.63	–118.63	.68	1.42	–.87
1861–1871	12,718	1,498	2,002	–504	133.66	–33.66	1.11	1.46	–.40
Urban									
1841–1851	4,716	1,326	596	730	44.94	55.06	2.48	1.19	1.44
1851–1861	6,042	1,306	798	508	61.08	38.92	1.96	1.24	.87
1861–1871	7,348	1,148	977	171	85.08	14.92	1.45	1.25	.23
London									
1841–1851	1,948	414	181	233	43.75	56.25	1.93	.89	1.13
1851–1861	2,362	442	287	155	64.95	35.05	1.72	1.15	.64
1861–1871	2,804	450	361	89	80.22	19.78	1.49	1.21	.31
4 Biggest Cities									
1841–1851	2,719	653	262	391	40.17	59.83	2.15	.92	1.34
1851–1861	3,372	632	390	242	61.74	38.26	1.72	1.10	.69
1861–1871	4,004	601	468	133	77.81	22.09	1.40	1.11	.33

Major Cities								
1841–1851	3,315	785	361	424	46.00	54.00	2.13	1.03	1.20
1851–1861	4,100	799	490	289	62.85	37.15	1.74	1.13	.68
1861–1871	4,879	800	595	205	74.40	25.60	1.52	1.15	.41
Small Cities								
1841–1851	1,401	540	211	329	39.14	60.86	3.26	1.41	2.11
1851–1861	1,941	528	290	238	54.95	45.05	2.41	1.39	1.16
1861–1871	2,469	348	364	−16	104.58	−4.58	1.32	1.38	−.06

Sources and notes: The natural increase in population is derived by the crude birth rates (CBR) and crude death rates (CDR) reported in Table 2.1, adjusted by the Wrigley-Schofield "undercount ratio." The CBRs, CDRs and population figures are aggregated over registration districts reported by the Registrar General (*Parliamentary Papers* 1847–48, v. 25; *Parliamentary Papers* 1849, v. 21). The CBRs and CDRs are average rates for three periods: "1841" = 1838/ 39–1844, "1856" = 1851–1861, and "1866" = 1861–1871. In the decade reconstructions reported above, the "1841" parameters are applied to the decade 1841–1851, the "1856" parameters to 1851–1861, and the "1866" parameters to 1861–1871. The "Four biggest cities" refer to London, Liverpool, Birmingham, and Manchester; the "Major cities" refer to all cities ≥ 100,000 in 1861; the "Small cities" are those < 100,000 in 1861. "Urban" includes urban districts plus London which the census identified as the "principal cities and towns" of England and Wales. "Rural" is the difference between aggregate England and Wales, and "Urban." The definition of "city" used here is dictated by the fact that the published data is reported by district. The urban population totals therefore differ from those of Law (1967, 1972) and others.

19

Table 2.3. *Urban immigration and rural emigration, the North and South of England, 1841 to 1871: Based on Registrar General's registration districts*

	Population at decade starting year (000) (1)	Population increase (000)			Percentage population increase		Annual percent rates		
		Total (2)	Due to natural increase (3)	Due to immigration (4)	Due to natural increase (5)	Due to immigration (6)	Population increase (7)	Natural increase (8)	Immigration (9)
NORTH OF ENGLAND									
Rural									
1841–1851	6,333	512	1,042	−530	203.46	−103.46	.78	1.52	−.87
1851–1861	6,845	724	1,093	−369	151.02	−51.02	1.01	1.48	−.55
1861–1871	7,569	1,015	1,235	−220	121.65	−21.65	1.26	1.51	−.29
Urban									
1841–1851	2,228	712	347	365	48.76	51.24	2.77	1.45	1.52
1851–1861	2,940	631	426	205	67.56	32.44	1.94	1.35	.67
1861–1871	3,571	593	492	101	82.92	17.08	1.54	1.29	.28
Major Cities									
1841–1851	1,291	356	174	182	48.98	51.02	2.44	1.27	1.32
1851–1861	1,647	315	191	124	60.51	39.49	1.75	1.10	.73
1861–1871	1,962	344	213	132	61.78	38.22	1.62	1.03	.65
Small Cities									
1841–1851	937	356	160	196	44.85	55.15	3.22	1.57	1.90
1851–1861	1,293	316	212	104	67.15	32.85	2.19	1.52	0.77
1861–1871	1,609	249	250	−1	100.32	−.32	1.44	1.44	0

SOUTH OF ENGLAND

Rural									
1841–1851	4,859	182	774	−592	425.18	−325.18	.38	1.48	−1.30
1851–1861	5,041	108	726	−618	672.18	−572.18	.21	1.35	−1.31
1861–1871	5,149	484	769	−285	158.84	−58.84	.90	1.39	−.57
Urban									
1841–1851	2,488	613	239	374	38.93	61.07	2.20	.92	1.40
1851–1861	3,101	676	368	309	54.47	45.53	1.97	1.12	.95
1861–1871	3,777	555	484	71	87.15	12.85	1.37	1.21	.19
Major Cities									
1841–1851	2,024	429	191	238	44.42	55.58	1.92	.90	1.11
1851–1861	2,453	464	297	167	64.10	35.90	1.73	1.14	.66
1861–1871	2,917	456	376	80	82.46	17.54	1.45	1.21	.27
Small Cities									
1841–1851	464	184	47	137	25.62	74.38	3.34	.97	2.58
1851–1861	648	212	72	140	33.81	66.19	2.83	1.05	1.96
1861–1871	860	99	107	−8	108.42	−8.42	1.09	1.18	−.10

Sources and notes: See Table 2.2. The North and South of England dichotomy follows Deane and Cole (1962, p. 131) with only slight modification, described in Table 2.1.

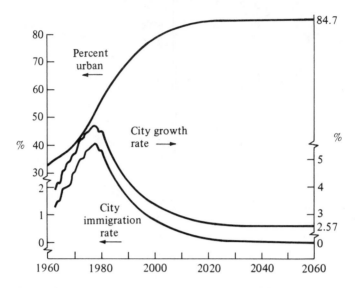

Figure 2.1   The 'stylized' urban transition, based on the contemporary Third World experience of 'fast growth' 1960–2060 (*Source:* Kelley and Williamson, 1984, Figure 6.2, p. 151)

Table 2.4 documents a century of urbanization experience in England.[4] The rate of urbanization was slow but persistent over the century, the share of population urban rising from 25.9 percent in 1776 to 65.2 percent in 1871. In contrast with the stylized urban transition depicted in Figure 2.1, England's urbanization experience during the First Industrial Revolution was more gradualist, an attribute most strikingly revealed by city growth rates. Although there is some evidence of a quickening in city growth rates between 1811 and 1846, which coincides with the acceleration of industrialization after the French wars, one would have expected a more dramatic surge in city growth. The relative stability in city growth rates is surprising. Only in one half-decade (1776–81) did the rate of city growth fall below 2 percent per annum, and it never rose above 3 percent per annum. The average rate of city growth over the thirty-five years of most rapid growth (1811–46) was 2.35 percent per annum, not very much greater than the 2.10 percent per annum rate achieved before and the 2.19 percent per annum rate achieved after. Of course the character of the city growth may have changed significantly over the century – led by old

4 The details of the demographic reconstruction can be found in my working paper (Williamson, 1985b).

Table 2.4. *Urban population shares and city-growth rates England, 1776 to 1871 (in %)*

| Year | Share of population | | City population growth per annum | |
	Urban	Rural		
1776	25.9	74.1	2.10	
1781	(27.5)	(72.5)	1.84	
1786	(29.1)	(70.9)	2.23	1776–1811
1791	(30.6)	(69.4)	2.19	Average 2.10
1796	(32.2)	(67.8)	2.10	
1801	33.8	66.2	2.18	
1806	(35.2)	(64.8)	2.09	
1811	36.6	63.4	2.43	
1816	(38.3)	(61.7)	2.42	
1821	40.0	60.0	2.64	1811–1846
1826	(42.2)	(57.8)	2.36	Average 2.35
1831	44.3	55.7	2.11	
1836	(46.3)	(53.7)	2.06	
1841	48.3	51.7	2.44	
1846	(51.2)	(48.8)	2.07	
1851	54.0	46.0	2.08	
1856	(56.4)	(43.6)	2.10	1846–1871
1861	58.7	41.3	2.38	Average 2.19
1866	(62.0)	(38.0)	2.31	
1871	65.2	34.8	–	

Sources and notes: Interpolated figures in brackets. Based on Law (1967, Table V, p. 130; 1972, p. 22). The city growth rates are for the five years starting with the year listed, calculated as per annum rates, derived by applying the urban share to total population in England less Monmouthshire (Wrigley and Schofield, 1981, Appendix Table A3.3).

versus new towns, by big versus small towns, by manufacturing versus service employment, and satisfied first more by immigration and later more by natural increase, but a remarkably stable growth rate persisted throughout.

Did England's cities grow more by immigration or natural increase? This question is motivated in part by a debate over contemporary Third World experience, where city growth rates have been spectacular, but it also caught Weber's attention almost a century ago (Weber, 1899, chp. 4). Kingsley Davis (1965) and the United Nations (1980) have argued that the rapid expansion of city populations in the Third World is due primarily to natural increase. Michael Todaro (1984) has argued to the contrary. Two demographers, Andrei Rogers (1984, chp. 11) and Nathan

Keyfitz (1980), have shown that the answer depends on which point in the urban transition the assessment is made: At some intermediate point in the urban transition most countries tend to switch from migration-driven to urban-natural-increase-driven city growth. What about English experience?

Table 2.5 shows that the two sources were of about equal importance over the century 1776 to 1871 as a whole.[5] However, immigration's contribution to city growth was considerably greater early in the century, and the crossover point – where the contribution of natural increase begins to exceed immigration – appears in the 1810s and 1820s. This drift away from immigration's importance confirms the Rogers-Keyfitz prediction and it can be seen most clearly when the century is split into three parts:

| | Percent of urban population growth due to: | |
	Natural increase (%)	Immigration (%)
1776–1811	40.3	59.7
1811–1846	54.2	45.8
1846–1871	58.9	41.1

Although some of the diminished importance of immigration can be traced to the decline in the city immigration rate itself, most of it can be attributed to the rise in the rates of natural increase in the cities.

The inverse correlation between city immigration and city natural in-

---

5   The details of the calculation can be found elsewhere (Williamson, 1985b, Appendix C), but the key assumption is that the rural-urban crude birth and crude death rate differentials estimated for 1841 persisted throughout the period from 1776 to 1841. This assumption does *not* impose stability on the urban and rural crude birth and death rates, because we insist that they be consistent with the Wrigley and Schofield nationwide rates. Namely, we infer the city death and birth rates (CCDR and CCBR), and the rural death and birth rates (RCDR and RCBR) from the following (where the urban share in Table 2.4 is denoted as u):

$$CCDR = [z_D (1-u) + u]^{-1} CDR$$
$$RCDR = z_D CCDR$$
$$CCBR = [z_B (1-u) + u]^{-1} CBR$$
$$RCBR = z_B CCBR$$

As we have already indicated, the key assumption is that $z_D = RCDR/CCDR$ and $z_B = RCBR/CCBR$ maintain their "1841" values for the pre-1841 period. It turns out that our estimates of city immigration are relatively insensitive to alternative assumptions regarding trends in the rural-urban differentials.

crease is suggestive. If one caused the other, how did the mechanism work? Did the same favorable labor-market forces that encouraged rapid immigration early in the century also encourage earlier marriage, higher fertility, and more city-born labor-force entrants a couple of decades later, thus in time crowding out potential immigrants? Did exogenous improvements in mortality serve to augment the city labor force, thus crowding out potential immigrants? Did rapid immigration from the Irish and English countryside shift the age distribution of the cities toward young adults so that crude birth rates eventually rose and crude death rates eventually fell, augmenting the ability of the cities to meet their growth requirements through natural increase? These questions can be sharpened by a more careful look at the sources of the city rates of natural increase (Williamson, 1985b, Appendix Table C.1):

| | Average rates per 1,000 City Population | | |
	Crude birth rates	Crude death rates	Crude rates of natural increase
1776–1806	39.0	31.2	7.8
1811–1841	40.0	27.3	12.7
1846–1871	37.2	24.2	13.0

It appears that about 80 percent of the rise in city rates of natural increase between 1776–1806 and 1811–41 was attributable to a decline in city death rates, and all of the rise thereafter was attributable to the same source.

In short, the increased ability of England's cities to satisfy their growth requirements by natural increase over the century 1776–1871 was due to declining crude death rates. This is an important and paradoxical finding in that Wrigley and Schofield have found the opposite to have been the case for England as a whole, where rising fertility was the more important source of population growth acceleration up to the first third of the nineteenth century.

How does this reconstruction of England's urban transition compare with other industrializing countries? Among twenty-nine Third World nations, the rate of urban population growth in the 1960s and 1970s was 4.32 percent per annum (Todaro, 1984, p. 13). Although these city growth rates are double the English rates in Table 2.5, we must remember that every-

Table 2.5. *Urban immigration and rural emigration, England and Wales, 1776 to 1871: Based on Wrigley–Schofield and Law*

A. URBAN

Years	Urban population at starting year (000) (1)	Urban population increase (000)			Percentage urban population increase		Annual percent rates:		
		Total (2)	Due to natural increase (3)	Due to immigration (4)	Due to natural increase (5)	Due to immigration (6)	Urban population increase (7)	Natural increase (8)	City immigration (9)
1776–1781	1,746	191	77	114	40.51	59.49	2.08	0.87	1.26
1781–1786	1,937	184	20	169	11.01	88.99	1.81	0.21	1.62
1786–1791	2,121	247	96	151	38.92	61.08	2.20	0.89	1.37
1791–1796	2,368	272	126	146	46.31	53.69	2.17	1.04	1.20
1796–1801	2,640	289	139	150	48.13	51.87	2.08	1.03	1.10
1801–1806	2,929	333	39	294	11.82	88.18	2.15	0.27	1.91
1806–1811	3,262	356	258	98	72.47	27.53	2.07	1.52	0.59
1811–1816	3,618	462	205	257	44.45	55.55	2.40	1.10	1.37
1816–1821	4,080	517	296	221	57.18	42.82	2.39	1.40	1.06
1821–1826	4,597	640	375	265	58.65	41.35	2.61	1.57	1.12
1826–1831	5,237	648	363	285	56.05	43.95	2.33	1.34	1.06
1831–1836	5,885	646	332	314	51.34	48.66	2.08	1.10	1.04
1836–1841	6,531	700	423	277	60.50	39.50	2.04	1.26	0.83
1841–1846	7,231	927	466	461	50.32	49.68	2.41	1.25	1.23
1846–1851	8,158	880	476	404	54.11	45.89	2.05	1.13	0.97
1851–1856	9,038	981	624	357	63.61	36.39	2.06	1.34	0.77
1856–1861	10,019	1,097	791	306	72.08	27.92	2.08	1.52	0.60
1861–1866	11,116	1,387	781	606	56.33	43.67	2.35	1.36	1.06
1866–1871	12,503	1,516	779	737	51.39	48.63	2.29	1.21	1.15

B. RURAL

Years	Rural population at starting year (000) (10)	Rural population increase (000)			Percentage rural population increase		Annual percent rates:		
		Total (11)	Due to natural increase (12)	Due to immigration (13)	Due to natural increase (14)	Due to immigration (15)	Rural population increase (16)	Natural increase (17)	Rural emigration (18)
1776–1781	4,995	111	322	−211	All	None	0.44	1.25	0.86
1781–1786	5,106	62	187	−125	→	→	0.24	0.72	0.50
1786–1791	5,168	204	347	−143			0.77	1.30	0.56
1791–1796	5,372	187	394	−207			0.68	1.42	0.79
1796–1801	5,559	177	403	−226			0.63	1.40	0.83
1801–1806	5,736	269	216	53	80.30	19.70	0.92	0.74	−0.18
1806–1811	6,005	263	574	−311	All	None	0.86	1.83	1.07
1811–1816	6,268	304	485	−181	→	→	0.95	1.49	0.59
1816–1821	6,572	323	604	−281			0.96	1.76	0.87
1821–1826	6,895	279	676	−397			0.79	1.87	1.19
1826–1831	7,174	225	624	−399			0.62	1.67	1.14
1831–1836	7,399	176	540	−364			0.47	1.41	1.01
1836–1841	7,575	165	607	−442			0.43	1.54	1.20
1841–1846	7,740	36	619	−583			0.09	1.54	1.57
1846–1851	7,776	−77	569	−646			−0.20	1.41	1.73
1851–1856	7,699	46	617	−571			0.12	1.54	1.54
1856–1861	7,745	76	670	−594			0.20	1.66	1.60
1861–1866	7,821	−158	622	−780			−0.41	1.53	2.10
1866–1871	7,663	−181	565	−746			−0.48	1.42	2.05

Sources and notes: The urban and rural populations are derived by applying the share urban to English population totals, the latter taken from Wrigley and Schofield (1981, Table A.3.3, pp. 534–5). The urban share is based on Law (1967, 1972), reproduced in Table 2.4. The CBR and CDR underlying the natural increase estimates in Columns (3) and (12) are described in footnote 5, and they are consistent with the economy-wide CBR and CDR in Wrigley and Schofield. Immigration (+) or emigration (−) is derived as a residual. The remaining columns should be self-explanatory. Numbers of rural emigrants (col. 4) need not be equal to numbers of urban immigrants (col. 13) in the presence of external migration, like the Irish.

thing was growing more rapidly in the Third World. Indeed, the overall population growth rate in the Third World (2.33 percent per annum: Todaro, 1984, pp. 10–11) was also about double that of England over the century 1776–1871 (1.23 percent per annum: Wrigley and Schofield, 1981, p. 529), implying comparable rates of urbanization. In any case, city immigration rates in England during the three decades 1776 to 1806 – ranging between 1.10 and 1.91 – were similar to those recorded in the Third World, averaging 1.79. Given that England's rate of city growth was only half that of the Third World, its city immigration rates are really quite spectacular. Furthermore, these population immigration rates understate labor immigration rates, because the immigrants had far higher participation rates. The next section will pursue the migrant young-adult-selectivity bias in detail, but it implies that rates of labor immigration may have ranged between 1.5 and 2.5 over the three decades 1776–1806.[6]

As it turns out, England's cities relied far more heavily on immigration than has the Third World. Although immigration accounted for 45.8 percent of city population growth in England between 1811 and 1846, it accounted for only 39.3 percent in the Third World in the 1960s and 1970s. The relative importance of immigration to English city growth is even greater if the early years of the First Industrial Revolution are used in the comparison: between 1776 and 1811 immigration accounted for a whopping 59.7 percent of city growth in England.[7] In short, immigration was a much more important source of city growth during the First Industrial Revolution than it is in the contemporary Third World.[8]

6 The conversion of these city immigrants from population to labor force are based on the activity rates implied by the age distributions in Table 2.6.

7 Malcolm Gray (1977, Table 3, p. 112) guesses that immigration was 60.8 percent of town growth in Scotland 1801–51.

8 How do our estimates of the English urban transition compare with those of Friedlander? When Friedlander (1969, Table 4, p. 372) reconstructed the urban transition for 1801 to 1871 he did not have the Wrigley and Schofield nation-wide crude birth and death rates (he used Brownlee and Glass), nor did he have Law's estimates of urbanization (he applied "almost guess work" (p. 378) to the 1801–50 period). Furthermore, he assumed that rural-urban differentials in England followed those in Sweden, making no use of the Registrar General's reports. These steps all matter a great deal to the quantitative dimensions of the English urban transition that Friedlander reconstructs. His assumptions about rates of urbanization 1801–51 far exceed those implied by Law's estimates. His estimated city growth rates are therefore far higher over those five decades. It appears that the English urban transition was far more "gradualist" than Fried-lander's guesses implied. Furthermore, the Brownlee-Glass demographic rates

It was not always so, because there were some episodes of rather modest city immigration rates. Some of these episodes are rather surprising too. For example, the city immigration (and rural emigration) rates in the 1820s were rather ordinary given all the talk of agricultural depression (especially in the South) following the Napoleonic Wars. One would have expected more evidence of a big rural "push." Another surprising example is offered by the late 1840s, when the rate of city immigration appears to have been relatively low. One would have expected more evidence of the Irish famine flooding English cities, unless, of course, potential English rural out-migrants found themselves crowded out by the Irish (Chapter 6).

Let us now turn to rural emigration. With the exception of the war-induced good times for English agriculture between 1801 and 1806, rural emigration took place at every point over the century. Furthermore, the rate of emigration about doubled over the century. That rural emigration rates rose while urban immigration rates fell may seem odd, but the arithmetic was almost inevitable. After all, these rates are calculated as the ratio of migration flows to a population base, and because the urban population base enjoyed fast growth (augmented by immigrants) while the rural population base did not (depleted by emigrants) city immigration and rural emigration rates would have moved in opposite directions almost inevitably.

These measured rates of rural emigration appear to be inconsistent with the allegation that English farm laborers were reluctant to move, and that the agricultural counties were full of "a vast, inert mass of redundant labor" who were "immobile" (Redford, 1926, pp. 84 and 94). On the contrary, these are quite impressive emigration rates by almost any standard. Between 1816 and 1871, the rural emigration rate ranged between .87 and 2.10 percent per annum. The rates for the Third World range between .97 and 1.21 (Kelley and Williamson, 1984, Table 3–13, p. 93). The comparison suggests that rural Englishmen were no more reluctant

---

implied far higher city death rates than do the new Wrigley-Schofield estimates, so that Friedlander has natural rates of increase contributing very little to city growth while city immigration is doing all the work. In contrast, our reconstruction suggests that England was much more like contemporary developing countries than Friedlander's early estimates led us to believe. (See Williamson, 1985b, Table 6 and pp. 29–30.)

to leave agricultural parishes than were rural populations in the Third World, although that judgment should await evidence on the size of the earnings differentials between city and countryside which were necessary to induce the emigration (Chapter 7).

2.5   Were Britain's cities full of young adults?

Cities were prime movers during the industrial revolution, but how much of that dynamism was attributable to the fact that cities were full of young adults, a demographic fact which would have had advantageous economic consequences? If so, was it caused by a migrant-selectivity bias, young adults favoring the cities and shunning the countryside?

To help get an answer to these questions, this section will summarize data from four censuses: 1821, 1841, 1851, and 1861. The choice of these dates makes sense because it will allow a comparison at various critical points on the urban transition, the first two in which city growth rates were rising to a peak and immigration was vigorous, and the second two in which both rates had settled down to more sedate levels. Of course, a comparison of the age distribution in English cities between the 1780s and the 1820s would be even more informative given that city immigration rates were even higher in the late nineteenth century. Alas, census data is not available to make that assessment.

Consider the 1861 data in Table 2.6. Cities had a significantly larger share of people in their twenties and thirties than the countryside: These two groups combined accounted for about 33 percent of the urban population but only about 28 percent of the rural population. The opposite was true, of course, of the tails of the age distribution: The countryside had more old people and children. What was true of the cities in general was even truer of big cities. London, for example, had almost 34 percent of its population in their twenties and thirties. Nor is this young-adult bias small by the standards of the contemporary Third World. On the contrary, although the urban share of those in their twenties and thirties exceeded the rural share by about 4.7 percentage points in 1861 England, Table 2.7 shows the figure to have been 3.4 percentage points in the Third World in 1970. The same contrast emerges when Latin American data is used in the comparison. The young-adult bias during the First Industrial Revolution was stronger than it is today in the Third World.

Table 2.6. *Age distributions in England and Wales: Males and females combined, 1861 (in %)*

Age class (years)	Total	All cities	Rural	Big cities	Small cities	Northern cities	Southern cities	London
0–4	13.46	13.22	13.60	13.25	13.16	13.75	12.71	12.92
5–14	22.17	20.74	23.00	20.52	21.19	21.32	20.20	20.14
15–19	9.63	9.58	9.66	9.41	9.91	9.71	9.46	9.24
20–29	16.94	18.72	15.91	18.99	18.18	18.66	18.77	18.88
30–39	13.01	14.24	12.31	14.59	13.56	14.00	14.47	14.81
40–49	10.29	10.70	10.06	10.88	10.34	10.46	10.91	11.06
50–59	7.08	6.74	7.28	6.67	6.88	6.58	6.89	6.81
60+	7.42	6.02	8.23	5.70	6.64	5.44	6.57	6.14
Total	100.00	99.96	100.05	100.01	99.86	99.92	99.98	100.00
20–39	29.95	32.96	28.22	33.58	31.74	32.66	33.24	33.69

Sources and notes: For definitions of "big," "small," "northern," and "southern" cities see sources and notes to Table 2.1. "Rural" is simply the residual between total England and Wales and her cities. The 1861 census data is taken from *Parliamentary Papers* 1863, vol. 53, pt. 1.

Table 2.7. *Age distributions in the contemporary Third World, 1970: Urban and rural (in %)*

Age class	Less developed regions		Latin America	
	Urban	Rural	Urban	Rural
0–4 yrs.	14.4	16.5	14.4	18.4
5–14	24.3	25.4	24.8	28.5
15–19	11.1	10.1	10.6	10.1
20–29	17.0	14.5	16.2	14.3
30–39	12.4	11.5	11.8	10.3
40–49	9.0	8.7	9.2	7.7
50–59	6.0	6.2	6.3	5.3
60+	5.8	6.0	6.6	5.3
Total	99.7	99.9	99.9	99.9
20–39	29.4	26.0	28.0	24.6
Dependency rate	42.4	46.7	43.5	50.3

Source: UN (1982), Table 5, pp. 35 and 42.

Table 2.8. *Age distributions in England and Wales: Males and females compared, 1861 (in %)*

Age (years)	Total		All cities		Rural	
	Male	Female	Male	Female	Male	Female
<5	13.86	13.08	13.95	12.55	13.81	13.40
5–14	22.84	21.54	21.73	19.85	23.45	22.56
15–19	9.80	9.47	9.54	9.61	9.94	9.39
20–29	16.31	17.53	17.97	19.39	15.39	16.42
30–39	12.81	13.21	14.09	14.38	12.10	12.51
40–49	10.27	10.31	10.67	10.72	10.06	10.06
50–59	7.07	7.09	6.57	6.89	7.35	7.21
60+	7.04	7.77	5.36	6.61	7.98	8.47
Total	100.00	100.00	99.88	100.00	100.08	100.02
20–39	29.12	30.74	32.06	33.77	27.49	28.93

Sources and notes: See Table 2.6.

Furthermore, Table 2.8 documents that the female young-adult bias did not exceed that of males by much. When we compare the share of populations in their twenties and thirties, the cities exceeded the countryside by about 4.6 percent for males and 4.8 percent for females. Thus, while the demographic impact of "the heavy nineteenth-century migration of males to the Empire and to the United States" (Teitelbaum, 1984, p. 77) is revealed in the Table 2.8 totals for England and Wales (females in their twenties and thirties account for 30.7 percent of their totals and males of the same age account for only 29.1 percent of their totals), a similar sex differential is revealed in both city and countryside. The implication seems to be that rural-urban migration within England did not exhibit the same male-adult bias that international emigration did. Were that not so, we would have found a greater imbalance favoring females in the countryside over those in the cities.

If the cities were full of young adults in 1861, we would expect them to have been more so a few decades earlier. After all, the cities were absorbing immigrants at a more rapid rate early in the century, and because immigrants tend to be young adults (see Section 2.7 below), the cities ought to have contained even larger proportions of young adults earlier in the urban transition.

Table 2.9 summarizes the young-adult bias for those early years, and it confirms that the urban young-adult bias was even greater early in the

Table 2.9. *Changing age distributions in England and Wales by location, 1821 to 1861 (in %)*

Year	Total	All cities	Big cities	Small cities	London	Rural	Differences between urban and rural			
							All cities	Big cities	Small cities	London
A. Percent of population aged 20–39										
1821	27.55	31.98	33.73	29.43	34.60	26.59	+ 5.39	+ 7.14	+ 2.84	+ 8.01
1841	30.72	35.04	35.91	33.00	36.42	28.86	+ 6.18	+ 7.55	+ 4.14	+ 7.05
1851	30.69	34.34	35.04	32.86	35.31	28.84	+ 5.50	+ 6.20	+ 4.02	+ 6.47
1861	29.95	32.96	33.57	31.74	33.69	28.21	+ 4.75	+ 3.53	+ 3.53	+ 5.48
B. Dependency rate										
1821	44.30	38.80	37.00	41.50	35.85	45.50	− 6.70	− 8.50	− 4.00	− 9.65
1841	40.66	36.33	35.63	38.01	35.36	42.49	− 6.19	− 6.86	− 4.48	− 7.13
1851	40.08	36.61	36.07	37.76	35.51	41.84	− 5.23	− 5.77	− 4.08	− 6.33
1861	43.00	40.00	39.50	41.00	36.66	44.80	− 4.80	− 5.30	− 3.80	− 8.14

Sources and notes. See Table 2.6 for definitions of urban aggregates. The underlying census data is taken from: *Parliamentary Papers*, 1822, vol. 15; *Parliamentary Papers*, 1843, vol. 22; *Parliamentary Papers*, 1852–1853, vol. 8; and *Parliamentary Papers*, 1863, vol. 53, pt. 1. The number of cities underlying these calculations increases over time, of course, as small towns graduate to city status, and as small cities graduate to large. The dependency rate is defined as the percent aged 0–14 and above 64 in total population.

century. Two summary statistics are reported in the table: the percent of the population aged twenty to thirty-nine, a statistic we have already used for 1861, and the dependency rate, or the share of the population below age fifteen and above age sixty-four. The two statistics tell the same tale: The young-adult bias reaches its peak in 1821–41. For example, while the dependency rate was 4.8 percentage points higher in the countryside than the cities in 1861, it was 6.7 percentage points higher in 1821. Indeed, the young-adult bias was really quite enormous in 1821, especially for the big cities: The dependency rate in London, for example, was almost 10 percentage points lower than it was in rural England in that year.

In short, cities were even more crowded with young adults in the 1820s and 1840s than in the 1860s. Children and old people were even scarcer in the cities early in the urban transition.

2.6   The importance of being a young adult

Although English cities certainly exhibited dynamic economic attributes for other reasons, part of that dynamism must have been due solely to their lower dependency rates and young-adult abundance.

As a result of these favorable demographic features, cities would have had higher per capita incomes. Per capita income gaps favoring the city has always been a stylized fact of modern economic growth. Part of the explanation may lie simply with higher city labor participation rates, and they were 3.2 percentage points higher in the cities than in the country-side in 1821 (Williamson, 1985b, Appendix Tables D.1 and D.2). Of course these higher labor-participation rates also made it easier for any city to satisfy its employment requirements, thus reducing its demand for immigrants.

As a result of these favorable demographic features, cities would also have had lower relief burdens. There is a very extensive literature that explores the sources and impact of the old Poor Laws in England (Blaugh, 1963; McCloskey, 1973; Boyer, 1985, 1986), and all of it stresses the fact that Speenhamland was an agricultural relief scheme. Yet, how much of this fact might have been due simply to demography – young adults select-ing cities and shunning the countryside, leaving behind dependents who were more vulnerable to pauperism? It certainly was true that the inci-dence of pauperism was higher in the countryside than in the cities. This can be seen from county data for 1851 (Boyer and Williamson, 1987). If we array counties by the share of population urban, we get the following:

Sample	Number of counties	PAUPC	OLDPC	KIDSPC
urban = 0	16	.0591	.0846	.3630
urban = 1–19%	12	.0553	.0826	.3604
urban = 20–35%	7	.0527	.0786	.3598
urban = 36–65%	7	.0397	.0684	.3523
London	1	.0258	.0611	.3191

where PAUPC are numbers relieved per capita, OLDPC is the share of the population sixty and above, and KIDSPC is the share of children aged 0–14. Note that the pauper rate falls with urbanization as does the dependency rate. That is, while 8.5 percent of the rural counties were elderly, London's figure was only 6.1 percent, and while 36.3 percent of the rural counties were less than age fifteen, London's figure was only 31.9 percent. The correlation suggests that the dependency burden should help explain high pauper rates in the countryside and low pauper rates in the cities. When a simple OLS regression is estimated on this data, strong dependency rate effects do indeed emerge:

X Variables	Estimated coefficient	t-statistic	
Constant	−0.192	1.444	
OLDPC	+0.755	2.021	
RVPROP	−0.001	0.566	R^2 = .494
IRISH	+0.100	0.656	N = 43
URBAN	+0.027	1.413	Mean PAUPC = .053
AGRIC	+0.088	2.770	F-statistic = 7.824
KIDSPC	+0.437	1.459	

where IRISH is the percent of the population Irish, AGRIC is the employment share in agriculture, URBAN is the share in urban areas, and RVPROP is the rateable value of property. The demographic variables perform well, especially the share elderly. Furthermore, when the regression is used to ask how much of the difference in the predicted PAUPC between rural counties and London is explained by the demographic variables in 1851, the answer is all of it. Irish presence didn't matter, and after controlling for the impact of demography, urban counties had higher pauper rates, not lower. The AGRIC variable also helps to account for the high rate of pauperism in the countryside, presumably a result of the relief of the able-bodied during slack seasons. But the key finding is that the young-adult bias accounts for most of the variance in pauperism between city and countryside in 1851.

As a result of these favorable demographic features, the cities should also have had higher saving and accumulation rates. This follows directly from the life-cycle and dependency hypotheses. These hypotheses – associated with Ansley Coale, Edgar Hoover, and Paul Demeny (see the summary in Bilsborrow, 1980) – argue that high dependency rates increase consumption requirements at the expense of saving, and they have been a centerpiece in the economic-demographic literature for two decades. It has also long been believed that savings rates are (and were) lower in the countryside and higher in the city. The dependency hypothesis would suggest that some portion of the difference can be explained by migrant selectivity – young adults selecting the cities and shunning the countryside.

Are the rural-urban differences in dependency rates large enough in early nineteenth-century England to have mattered? I think so. Take the issue of saving and accumulation. How big a difference in dependency rates would be required to get a big impact on saving rate differentials? To answer this question directly would require rural and urban household saving data for early nineteenth-century England, data which appear to be nonexistent. But some indirect evidence can shed light on the question. For example, Frank Lewis (1983) successfully applied the hypothesis that the decline in the dependency rate in America between 1830 and 1900 could have accounted for a large share of the marked rise in the aggregate saving rate across the nineteenth century, a rise of which so much has been made by economic historians (Gallman, 1966; David, 1977; Williamson, 1979; Ransom and Sutch, 1983). The American dependency rate fell by about 9 percentage points over the period, not too much bigger than the 6.7 percentage point difference between England's cities and countryside in 1821, implying, *ceteris paribus*, that rural saving rates would have been below urban saving rates during the First Industrial Revolution. A second example takes us even further. Nathaniel Leff (1969) found that the dependency rate accounted for a large share of the difference in saving rates for a cross-section of seventy-four countries in the 1960s, and the variance in the dependency rate for his data was not too much greater than the rural-urban differentials reported here for 1821.[9] Leff's results suggested that the elasticity of the saving rate with respect to the dependency rate was about −1.5. Using Leff's elasticity, and assuming the saving rate to have been around 10 percent in rural England, then it follows that the urban saving rate would have been 13 percent, a fairly big difference and due solely to dependency rate differentials.

This dependency rate effect may have been manifested by a direct influence on household saving behavior, but I doubt it. The influence of dependency rates was more likely to have its impact indirectly, first on poor relief, then on the local tax burden, and thus finally on disposable incomes of potential savers. In any case, the inference seems to be that the young-adult bias must have favored saving and accumulation in England's cities most when the immigration rates were highest, which was during the late eighteenth and early nineteenth centuries.

These favorable demographic features of England's cities must also have served to ease interregional factor-market disequilibria induced by the industrial revolution. One key problem of development is to transfer resources from lagging agriculture to booming industry. Labor and capital markets are hard pressed to make the transfer, and, as a result, they reflect the disequilibria by wage gaps – labor scarcity in the cities and labor surplus in the countryside, and rate of return differentials – capital scarcity in the cities and capital surplus in the countryside. The fact that the cities were full of young adults served to diminish the need for rural-urban factor transfers because, as we have argued, urban populations were equipped with an age structure that served to make them better able to satisfy their investment and labor requirements than would have been the case had they had the age structure of the countryside. In addition, rural emigration of young adults implied a human capital transfer to the cities because the latter needed to invest less in rearing children to adult ages. As we shall see in Chapter 3, that human capital transfer was very large during the First Industrial Revolution.

But perhaps the most interesting implication of the young-adult bias is that cities must have found it increasingly easy to satisfy their growing labor-force requirements by natural increase, thus diminishing their de-

9 The dependency rate in Leff's data (1969, p. 889) was 7 to 11 percentage points higher in the underdeveloped countries than in the advanced countries. Leff's thesis has attracted considered critical attention over the past two decades. I should point out that the newer research has been far less favorable to the thesis.

Table 2.10. *Actual and counterfactual city birth and death rates: The importance of the age/sex distribution in mid nineteenth-century cities*

Item	Rate
Actual crude death rate	24.90 per thousand
"1856" age/sex specific city death rates applied to 1861 census population weights for English cities	
Counterfactual crude death rate	26.32 per thousand
"1856" age/sex specific city death rates applied to 1861 census population weights for England and Wales	
Actual crude birth rate	36.02 per thousand
"1856" fertility rate (= number of births divided by females age 20–45) in the cities times the 1861 census share of females age 20–45 in the population for English cities	
Counterfactual crude birth rate	32.14 per thousand
"1856" fertility rate (= number of births divided by females age 20–45) in the cities times the 1861 census share of females age 20–45 in the population for England and Wales	
Crude rates of natural increase in the cities (= crude birth rates minus crude death rates):	
Actual	11.12 per thousand
Counterfactual	5.82 per thousand
Difference	5.30 per thousand

Sources and notes: See text.

mand for immigrants as time wore on. The explanation is simple enough. Mortality rates were lowest and fertility rates highest among young adults. As city immigration tended to select young adults, crude mortality rates fell and crude birth rates rose. As the natural rate of population, and eventually labor force, growth increased, the need for future immigration declined.

How important were these effects? Table 2.10 reports an initial assessment (a prelude to Section 2.8) using the Registrar General's 1856 age/sex specific death rates, the Registrar General's 1856 fertility rates (births per female aged fifteen to forty-five), and 1861 census population weights. The actual city crude birth and death rates use the age and sex distributions that actually prevailed in English cities. The counterfactual city crude birth and death rates use the age and sex distributions that prevailed in England as a whole. By comparing the two, we can assess the importance of the cities' young-adult bias. It turns out that city death rates would have been about 6 percent higher and city birth rates would have been about 11 percent lower had the cities had the same age/sex distribution as did England as a whole. These differences imply that crude rates of natural increase in the cities would have been cut in half (from 11.12 to 5.82 per thousand) had the cities had the same age/sex distribution as did England as a whole. Immigration rates would have had to increase by more than 40 percent to maintain the same rate of city growth, and the share of the urban population increase due to immigration would have risen from about 44 percent to about 62 percent (Williamson, 1985b, Table 13).

The moral of the tale is clear: Cities offered a built-in demographic mechanism, whereby present-day immigration served to diminish the need for future immigration, and shifting age/sex distributions were doing all the work. It follows that city immigration rates would have declined inevitably from the high levels achieved early in the First Industrial Revolution as long as the economic forces driving city labor demand and employment growth remained relatively stable, as apparently they did.

2.7   How the cities got to be young: The migrant-selectivity bias

Migrants incur costs when they move and these were sufficiently large in nineteenth-century Britain that significant returns over a number of years must have been necessary to motivate even short-distance moves. Older people with shorter expected productive lifetimes and bigger accumulated rural commitments must have found the migration costs too high and the returns too low. Thus, migration must have selected young adults, those who had the greatest chance for immediate employment and who could recoup their migration costs over a long lifetime. If true, it follows that the greater the influence of urban job pull, the greater should have been the selectivity bias. The greater the influence of rural push, the more likely should migration have been a family affair, and the more likely would migrants replicate age/sex distributions like those of the sending region. All of this is based on hypothesis so far, but since we have already seen that England's cities tended to have a relatively large proportion of young adults, it seems likely that the migrants would reveal the same.

The young-adult-selectivity-bias hypothesis can be tested in two ways. We should see it in the stock of city immigrants enumerated in any given census, and we should see it in the flow of city immigrants reconstructed from other demographic information. Consider the stock estimates first.

The 1851 census conveniently published for each city the place of origin of its residents (including whether or not the resident was born in the city), as well as their age. Thus, the published data make it possible to compare city-born with Irish, English, and other city immigrants. The non-Irish city immigrants were mainly those British who had left rural areas or other cities and towns, in that foreigners were a very small share of all non-Irish city immigrants. Table 2.11 summarizes the 1851 census data, in which age is reported as a discrete variable, age twenty distinguishing adults from children. For Britain's cities as a whole, about 41 percent of the nonimmigrants were adults, and the figures for the Irish and non-Irish immigrants were almost twice that figure, about 74 and 77 percent. The adult-selectivity bias mattered a lot in the cities. Had Britain's cities had the same age distribution as their nonimmigrants, adults would have accounted for about 41 percent of their population in 1851, not the 57 percent actually observed.

The reconstruction of city immigrant flows by age and sex is far more difficult. First, we identify the age- and sex-specific population count by location for all intermediate years between, say, 1851 and 1861, by assuming exponential growth rates over the decade. Second, we use data from the Registrar General to calculate crude death rates by age, sex, and location. Third, we calculate the fertility rate by location (the annual number of births per female aged fifteen to forty-five). Given the female population at risk (females aged fifteen to forty-five), we then calculate births each year by location. Finally, we add births, survive the population and age it to generate annual populations by age and sex which would have been enumerated had there been no migration. The difference between the actual census population count and the no-immigration counterfactual population count yields annual city immigration by age and sex.

Table 2.12 summarizes the results of this exercise when applied to the 1840s, 1850s, and 1860s. The age distribution of city immigrants is certainly consistent with the fact that urban England was full of young adults. Indeed, with the exception of the 1840s, there was a net outflow from England's cities of those aged thirty and above. This net emigration was not very large, but the evidence clearly supports the view that the cities did not hold much attraction to those in their thirties and older. In contrast, almost 63 percent of the immigrants were aged fifteen to twenty-nine in the 1850s, although only a little more than a quarter of the national population fell into that age group (Table 2.6). The migration rates for children mirror those for the young adults. That is, a relatively

Table 2.11. *Population distribution by age, immigrants and nonimmigrants, 1851 (in %)*

Region and group	Less Than 20	Greater Than or Equal to 20
SCOTLAND		
Cities		
Irish immigrants	29.5	70.5
Other immigrants	25.6	74.4
Nonimmigrants	62.0	38.0
Total	43.7	56.3
Rural		
Irish immigrants	28.9	71.1
Other	47.8	52.2
Total	46.8	53.2
ENGLAND AND WALES		
Cities		
Irish immigrants	24.6	75.4
Other immigrants	22.7	77.3
Nonimmigrants	58.6	41.4
Total	42.7	57.3
Rural		
Irish immigrants	28.0	72.0
Other	46.7	53.3
Total	46.5	53.5
BRITAIN		
Cities		
Irish immigrants	25.6	74.4
Other immigrants	23.0	77.0
Nonimmigrants	58.9	41.1
Total	42.8	57.2
Rural		
Irish immigrants	28.3	71.7
Other	46.9	53.1
Total	46.5	53.5

Sources and notes: Taken from Williamson, (1985b, Table 14), and calculated from the 1851 Census (*Parliamentary Papers* 1852–1853, v. 88, pt. 1) where "cities" are the aggregate of 61 principal towns in England and Wales (including London) and 9 in Scotland, and "rural" is the residual. "Nonimmigrants" are those born elsewhere. While the 1851 census reports age distribution data for Irish and non-Irish city immigrants, the 1861 census reports it only for those born abroad (including, of course, the Irish), while those born in England and Wales have the data reported by county of birth. The latter does not distinguish between city immigrants and city-born, both of which would be listed as born in the county of which the city is a part. Thus we do not report the 1861 figures here.

Table 2.12. *The age distribution of city immigrants: The 1840s, 1850s, and 1860s*

Age (years)	1840s Number (000)	%	1850s Number (000)	%	1860s Number (000)	%
< 5	95	11.0	102	15.4	281	16.2
5–9	141	16.3	122	18.4	270	20.1
10–14	105	12.1	72	10.9	103	7.7
15–19	117	13.5	101	15.3	193	14.4
20–24	204	23.6	203	30.6	418	31.1
25–29	140	16.2	112	16.9	277	20.6
30–34	28	3.2	−15	−2.2	−48	−3.6
35–39	−36	−4.2	−41	−6.2	−89	−6.6
40–44	15	1.7	6	0.9	−7	−0.5
45–49	−8	−0.9	−7	−1.0	1	0.1
> 50	65	7.5	7	1.0	7	0.5
Total	865	100.0	663	100.0	1,343	100.0

Source: Williamson (1985b), Appendix E. Totals may not add up due to rounding.

high proportion of the immigrants were children less than ten years of age: Almost 34 percent of the city immigrants were children of this age in the 1850s, although only 25 percent of England's population was in that age group.

These findings do not appear to confirm Ravenstein's (1885, 1889) seventh law of migration; namely, that "most migrants are adults: families rarely migrate," because about 45 percent of the migrants are under the age of fourteen. However, Table 2.12 does confirm those modern demographic studies which have shown migration to be young-adult biased (Rogers, 1984, p. 5), as well as those historical studies of nineteenth-century international migrations, which have shown the same (for example, Hvidt, 1975, p. 73, for Danish emigrants; Wrigley and Schofield, 1981, p. 201, for Swedish emigrants; Mokyr and Ó Grada, 1984, p. 487, for Irish emigrants). How do the English migrant age distributions in Table 2.12 compare with a "standard migration schedule" based on modern regional migrations (Rogers, 1984, pp. 46 and 83)? Figure 2.2 offers that comparison, where the migration rates are computed as the ratio of the annual migration flows in Table 2.12 to the 1861 rural populations of England and Wales, and where each of these migration rates is expressed relative to those aged 0–5. It is apparent that the young-adult-selectivity bias in England's cities was unusually powerful. Furthermore, the magni-

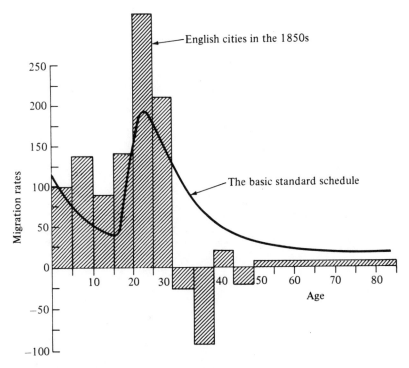

Figure 2.2   Migrant age-selectivity: English cities in the 1850s and the "standard" schedule compared (out-migration rates, where age 0–5 = 100, and where English rural age-specific population is taken as a base).

tude of the young-adult-selectivity bias strongly supports the view that the pull of urban labor market conditions was the dominant force driving city immigration over the decade of the 1850s.

Were the 1850s atypical? Certainly not when compared with the 1860s, because the latter decade appears to reflect an even stronger young-adult bias; the share of the city immigrants fifteen to twenty-nine was more than 66 percent in the 1860s and, as we have seen, it was less than 63 percent in the 1850s. The interesting comparison, however, is with the Hungry Forties. Irish immigration to England's cities was at its peak during the 1840s, and because the conventional wisdom has it that these Irish immigrations were largely pushed by rural famine, we would expect to see those push forces reflected in the migrant age distributions, a larger share of dependents accompanying young adults. Table 2.12 and Figure 2.3 confirm the prediction. There was a significant in-migration of older

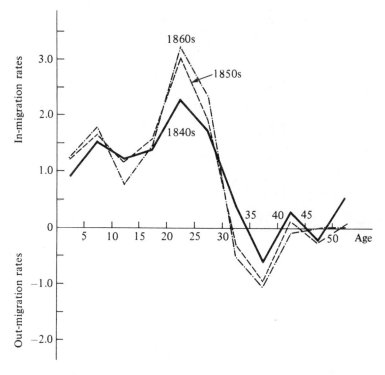

Figure 2.3 The standardized age-specific immigration rate: All cities – the 1840s, 1850s, and 1860s

adults (aged thirty and above) in the 1840s, while net out-migration was true of the subsequent two decades. Furthermore, the share of those aged fifteen to twenty-nine was far smaller in the 1840s. Younger children also entered the cities in smaller numbers. Those less than ten years old accounted for 27.3 percent in the 1840s, rather than the much larger 33.8 percent in the 1850s and 36.3 percent in the 1860s. It appears that the more numerous older adult migrants brought far fewer young dependents in the 1840s.

Do these urban aggregations hide some patterns that were peculiar to London or other large cities? Figures 2.4 and 2.5 break the young-adult-selectivity bias down into North and South, as well as into large and small cities. Three conclusions emerge from those figures. First, the young-adult-selectivity bias prevailed everywhere in urban England. Second, it was more pronounced in the South of England. Indeed, Birmingham,

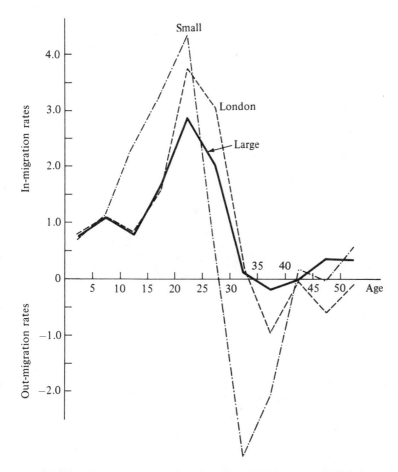

Figure 2.4   The standardized age-specific immigration rate: Southern cities in the 1850s

Manchester, Liverpool, and other large cities up North reveal a far more modest peak in the fifteen to twenty-nine age group and a far more dramatic peak among children less than ten. It appears that immigrants entered those large northern cities with many more young dependents than was true on average. Third, small cities throughout England had a far more pronounced young-adult bias than did large cities. The only explanation I can offer for this result is that immigration to large cities entailed longer distance moves and thus encouraged the migration of whole family units. In any case, the observation is certainly consistent with

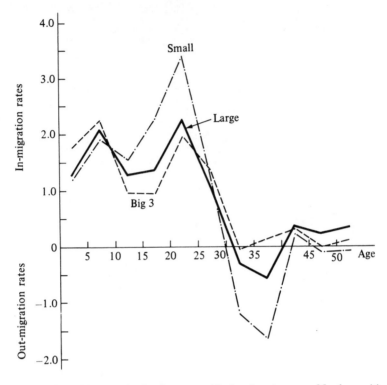

Figure 2.5   The standardized age-specific immigration rate: Northern cities in the 1850s

the fact that smaller cities were much better able to fulfill their population (and labor force) growth requirements with natural increase.

Finally, was there a gender bias to these city immigration patterns? The answer is mixed. True, in every decade female immigrants exceeded male immigrants in London. For all cities as a group, however, the ratio of female to male immigrants was .985 in the 1840s, 1.275 in the 1850s, and .946 in the 1860s, for an average of 1.055 for the three decades as a whole. Thus, the female bias was inconsistent, centering on the 1850s and on London. More to the point of this chapter, however, the young-adult bias differed by gender. As Figure 2.6 illustrates for the 1840s, the young-adult bias tended to be even more pronounced for females than for males, a finding that is fully consistent with the view of labor markets in city and countryside discussed in Chapter 3.

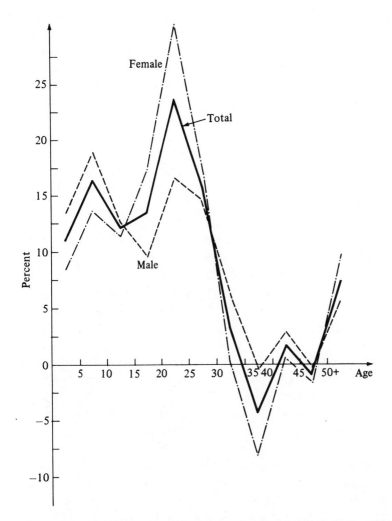

Figure 2.6   Age distribution of the migrants into Britain's cities in the 1840s: By sex

2.8   Counterfactual analysis of the migrant-selectivity bias

We have argued that the young-adult migrant bias may have had important implications for the operation of factor markets linking the booming
cities with the lagging countryside. The argument implied that the

migrant-selectivity bias served to take the pressure off interregional and intersectoral factor markets by reducing the size of the resource transfers from countryside to city necessary to satisfy the labor and capital requirements of the industrial revolution. When applied to labor markets, the argument developed along the following lines: Mortality rates were lowest and fertility rates highest among young adults. Because migration revealed a strong selectivity bias, the cities became crowded with young adults and, as a result, crude mortality rates fell and crude birth rates rose. As the natural rate of city population growth increased, the need for future immigration must have declined. In short, heavy city immigration early in the industrial revolution seems to have implied a slowdown in excess labor-demand growth and immigration rates over time. City immigration rates declined after 1776, and because the decline is explained by a rise in the crude rates of natural increase in the cities, could it be that a large share of these trends over the urban transition is accounted for by the migrant-selectivity bias?

A simulation experiment over the period 1776 to 1871 supplies the answer. The mechanics can be briefly summarized as follows: Given the age and sex distribution of the city population in 1776, and given parameters describing fertility and survival rates, it is a simple matter to generate total births and to survive the population to 1777. The estimated total population thus derived is that which would have been enumerated in the absence of immigration, and the difference between the documented and estimated population in 1777 gives as a residual total immigration over the year 1776–7. The next step is to distribute those immigrants by age and sex. Denote that distribution by the parameter m_{ij}. By applying that parameter to the total immigration already estimated, we can distribute those migrants by age and sex. Now add those migrants to the resident population and we emerge with the age and sex distribution of the cities' population in 1777, including the new arrivals. We then continue the exercise for each year up to 1871.

Two simulations are reported here. The first is called the actual simulation: It assumes that the m_{ij} parameter, which has been estimated for the 1860s, prevailed over the full century. The migrant-selectivity bias for the 1860s is preferred because it appears to have been a decade in which the cities' job pull was strongest and the age-selectivity bias greatest. In contrast, the 1840s seem to reflect atypical rural push forces (driven especially by the Irish fleeing the famine), although the 1850s seem to have generated an atypical female bias. The choice of the 1860s m_{ij} is moti-

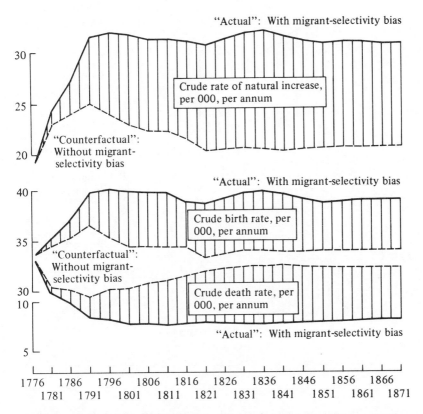

Figure 2.7A   Simulating England's urban demographic change: With and without the migrant-selectivity bias, 1776–1871

vated by the view that migrant selectivity during that decade was more likely to have been typical of the epoch 1776 to 1871 as a whole. (The simulation was also performed using the 1870s m_{ij}'s. Although the impact is not quite as great as for the 1860s m_{ij}'s, the basic results are exactly the same.) The second simulation is a counterfactual. It replicates the first in all dimensions except one: m_{ij} is assumed instead to reproduce the actual age/sex distribution of the cities, that is, it explores the cities' demographic performance in the absence of the migrant-selectivity bias. Throughout, we assume that 1841 fertility and survival rates prevail. Although I certainly do not believe that these rates were constant over the century, the assumption is innocuous for the purpose at hand.

Figure 2.7A summarizes these actual and counterfactual simulations.

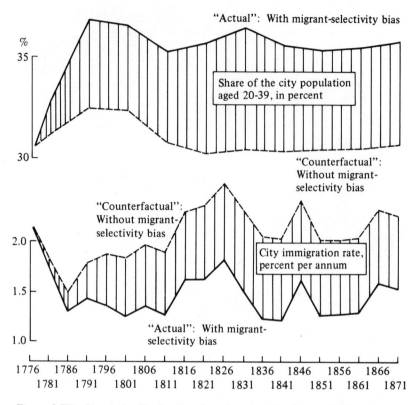

Figure 2.7B   Simulating England's urban demographic change: With and without the migrant-selectivity bias, 1776–1871

Consider city age distributions first. Figure 2.7B reports the gap between the two simulations for the share of the city population aged twenty to thirty-nine. The impact of the migrant-selectivity bias was quick and pronounced. By 1791, only fifteen years after the cities are "shocked" with this glut of young-adult immigrants, the share of the population aged twenty to thirty-nine is already about 4.4 percentage points higher in the cities with the young-adult migrant bias (36.83 versus 32.45 percent). The gap continues to rise to a peak of about 6 percentage points in 1831, after which it falls off to about 5 percentage points in 1861. Not only does the simulation reveal the marked impact of the selectivity bias on urban age distributions, but the gap between the actual and the counterfactual simulations is remarkably close to the census figures reported in Table

2.9, in which the urban-rural gap rises from 5.4 to 6.2 percentage points between 1821 and 1841, falling to 4.8 percentage points in 1861.

Figure 2.7A summarizes the impact of this drift in the cities' age/sex structure on crude birth rates and crude death rates. Once again, the gap between the actual and counterfactual simulations rises sharply early in the century, the migrant-selectivity bias serving to raise the crude birth rate and to lower the crude death rate. These two influences have an additive impact on crude rates of natural increase. Figure 2.7A shows the crude rate of natural increase gap rising sharply up to 1791, when the differential is about 5.4 percentage points. It continues to climb thereafter, reaching about 11.4 percentage points by 1831. The contrast between the two simulations is especially striking between 1791 and 1831. Although crude rates of natural increase decline significantly in the counterfactual simulation (from 26.05 to 20.62 per thousand), they rise modestly in the actual simulation (from 31.46 to 32 per thousand). Table 2.5 shows crude rates of natural increase in the cities rose from the 1770s to the 1820s. The simulations in Figure 2.7A suggest that much, if not all, of that rise was due to changing age/sex distributions induced by the migrant-selectivity bias.

Finally, Figure 2.7B reports the impact of the migrant-selectivity bias on city immigration rates over time. The gap between the two simulations is enormous. In the absence of the selectivity bias, city immigration rates reach a peak of 2.58 percent per annum in 1826. In the presence of the migrant-selectivity bias, it is only 1.81 percent per annum in that year. Indeed, immigration rates tend to rise over time in the counterfactual simulation; in contrast, they tend to fall over time in the actual simulation, as they in fact did.

These results offer strong confirmation of the hypothesis: Due to the young-adult-selectivity bias, heavy city immigration early in the First Industrial Revolution implied an inevitable decline in city immigration over time.

2.9   What have we learned?

How do labor markets cope with the shock of industrialization when the excess demand for labor is urban based? Economists typically try to endogenize the rural-urban migration response, decomposing the labor-market disequilibrium into its rural push and urban pull components, ignoring demographic influences along the way. Demographers typically focus on the demographic response, taking those migrations as exogenous. What we need, of course, is a marriage of the two approaches. This book hopes to emerge with a partial integration of the two so that the interdependence between the industrial revolution, the demographic transition, and the urban transition is better understood. The tentative reconstruction of England's urban transition between 1776 and 1871 is the first step toward that goal.

The English case is especially interesting given the sharp contrasts it appears to offer with the Third World and given that so many of our stylized facts about the urban transition are based on Third World experience. Rural crude birth rates exceed urban crude birth rates in the Third World; the opposite was true in England. Rural crude death rates exceed urban crude death rates in the Third World; the opposite was true in England. Rural rates of natural increase never exceed urban rates by much of the Third World; they exceeded urban rates by a lot in England. Nor does the list of contrasts stop there.

England's urbanization experience during the First Industrial Revolution seems to have been more gradualist than that suggested by Third World stylized urban transitions. Although there is some evidence of a quickening of city growth rates in the first half of the nineteenth century, it is the relative stability in city growth rates that is most surprising. Was this city growth accommodated by natural increase or by immigration? Between 1776 and 1871, the two sources were, on average, of about equal importance, but immigration's contribution was far greater early than late, with the "crossover point" occurring around the 1810s and 1820s. Most of the diminished importance of immigration to city growth can be attributed to the rise in the cities' rates of natural increase. Furthermore, and in contrast with Wrigley and Schofield's findings for England as a whole, declining crude death rates explain most of the rise in cities' rates of natural increase.

Immigration was a more important source of city growth in England. True, the rates of city immigration, ranging from 1.1 to 1.9 percent per annum, were similar to those documented for the Third World, 1.8 percent per annum. But although immigration accounted for less than 40 percent of Third World city growth in the 1960s and 1970s, the figure was close to 60 percent for England between 1776 and 1811.

It is also not true that rural Englishmen were more attached to the land and more reluctant to emigrate when compared with the Third World.

Indeed, the rate of rural emigration doubled in England between 1776 and 1871, reaching rates between 1816 and 1871 ranging between 0.9 and 2.10 percent per annum. The rates for the Third World are no greater, ranging between 1.0 and 1.2 percent per annum.

What role did the age distribution of the cities play over the urban transition? England's cities were full of young adults, and the fact appears to have been central to the urban transition. Dependency rates were far lower in the cities than in the countryside, and labor participation rates were higher. So much so, that this young-adult bias served to diminish the requirements for factor transfers between lagging agriculture and booming industry. It served to augment the ability of the cities to save and accumulate while lowering their relief burdens. It also served to augment the ability of the cities to satisfy their growing labor-force requirements by natural increase, thus diminishing their need for more immigrants.

How did the cities get to be full of young adults? Most of the answer lies with the age-selectivity bias of the city immigrants. While the age-selectivity bias has been appreciated by economists and demographers for some time, perhaps the magnitude of the bias has not. Indeed, almost 63 percent of the immigrants into England's cities in the 1850s were aged fifteen to twenty-nine while less than 27 percent fell into that age range for England as a whole. Furthermore, the bias appears to support the view that city immigration was typically dominated by job-pull forces, rather than rural push induced by enclosure, labor-displacing technological events, and famine.

Although immigration played a bigger role in England's urban transition than in the contemporary Third World, it would have been even greater had it not been for the migrant age-selectivity bias. Given the initial technological shock in England's cities associated with the industrial revolution, the derived demand for labor boomed there. Excess demand for urban labor triggered a rural-urban migration response. Given that the cities had high mortality rates, immigration had to be all the higher to fill those new job vacancies. But the migrants self-selected and young adults dominated the new entrants. This young-adult bias quickly served to change the age distribution of the cities, shifting their populations toward the center of the age distribution, thus raising crude fertility rates and lowering crude mortality rates. As a result, the cities found it easier and easier to fill the new job vacancies with native-born, and immigration slacked off as a result.

Appendix 2.1. Words of caution about the data

The reconstruction of the urban transition reported in this chapter must be treated with caution. The edifice is built on five fragile pillars: (1) the economy-wide crude birth rates, crude death rates, and population totals reported by Wrigley and Schofield; (2) the rural-urban population allocation reported by Law; (3) the crude birth and death rates for rural and urban areas documented in the Registrar General Reports; (4) the adjustment to (3) by Wrigley and Schofield's undercount ratios; and (5), the assumption that rural to urban crude birth and death rate ratios maintained their 1841 levels from 1776 to 1841.

Consider item (4) first. Scholars have long appreciated the fact that births, and to a lesser extent deaths, were undercounted prior to 1874, when the Registration Act was passed to deal with what was thought still to be a problem (Farr, 1885; Glass, 1951, 1973; Teitelbaum, 1974, 1984). In Appendix 8 (pp. 631-7) of Wrigley and Schofield's *Population History of England*, the authors offer a new estimate of the undercount. While, like Wrigley and Schofield, we have applied their undercount ratios uniformly throughout urban and rural England, in fact they varied from region to region. In fact, Teitelbaum has estimated the fertility undercount ratio by county for 1841, and, fortunately for us, there seems to be no correlation between urbanization and the undercount. Indeed, "the adjustment factor in London [for the 1840s] is very close to that of England and Wales as a whole. The same is the case for 1851-1860" (Teitelbaum, 1984, p. 63). Nonetheless, birth and death undercounts remain a potential flaw to the reconstruction offered in this chapter.

To the extent that Wrigley and Schofield's work has survived almost a decade of scrutiny since it was published in 1981, item (1) should trouble us less: This chapter's demography is at least consistent with the best aggregates currently available for England.

Furthermore, although it would be a major advance to replace assumption (5) with some concrete evidence on the pre-1841 period, we do not yet have anything but a few scattered local studies. One alternative might be to rely on those few city CDRs which have been constructed for the 1770s to the 1840s (W. A. Armstrong, 1981, pp. 99-102 on Carlisle; G. T. Griffith, 1926, p. 186 on Leeds, Manchester, Birmingham, Bristol, and Liverpool; A. Armstrong, 1974, p. 110 on York; M. Flinn, 1977, pp. 377, 379, and 383 on Glasgow and Edinburgh). These city CDR trends are plotted in Figure A2.1. Using the city size weights reported in Law (1967, p. 127), the limited evidence in Figure A2.1 was then used to construct aggregate city CDRs up to 1841. However, the calculation implied a rise in aggregate city death rates after 1800 which were sufficiently spectacular that the rural death rate would have had to have fallen very sharply to be consistent with the Wrigley/Schofield nationwide CDR series. Because there is no evidence to support rural mortality trends of that sort, this alternative was rejected. For this and other reasons (like the problem of large eighteenth- and early nineteenth-century undercounts), it seemed least arbitrary to assume that the rural-urban relatives were stable from 1776 to 1841 at the rates implied by the Registrar General Reports for 1838-44 (after adjustment for the Wrigley and Schofield

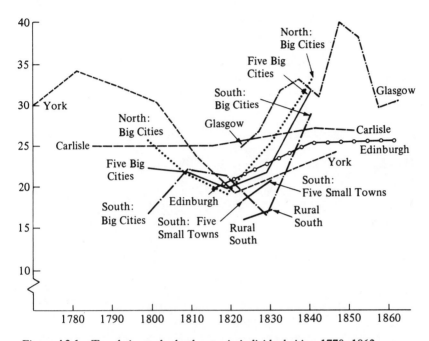

Figure A2.1   Trends in crude death rates in individual cities, 1770–1862

undercount ratios). Although the assumption was unlikely to have held in the short run, our interest here is in decadal changes and even the longer run.

Finally, there is item (2) and C. M. Law's (1967, 1972) urban population estimates. When it was in manuscript, one reader of this book noted that Law and the Registrar General differ in their account of city growth: Law's data imply a growth rate of 2.32 percent per annum across the 1860s, up from 2.07 percent in the 1850s; the Registrar General's data imply a growth rate of 1.45 percent per annum, down from 1.96 percent in the 1850s. The difference is hardly surprising since Law (and others) have shown that the official 1851 and 1861 urban population figures are underestimates, the latter more than the former. The Registrar General's estimates of urban population are flawed for all the boundary and suburb reasons that always plague empirical studies of city growth. In particular, suburbs beyond the existing city boundaries were not included in urban totals and Parliamentary Boroughs were of doubtful urban character. Law is an urban geographer and his urban-rural distributions are consistent and careful, they deal with boundary problems, and they are clearly superior to the published Registrar General's data. For the pre-1841 period, they are without peer. This is not to say that Law's urban population shares could not be improved, but rather to say only that they are an enormous improvement over the alternatives.

One way to test the quality of our reconstruction of the urban transition is to compare the external migration predictions implied by the exercise with other estimates. That is, the difference between the rural emigration and the urban immigration estimated in Table 2.5 yields net emigration to the rest of the world, including Scotland and Ireland. Unfortunately, we do not have independent evidence of quality on these migration streams. However, Wrigley and Schofield supply two such estimates in their book, one using "back projection" (their Table A3.1) and one using corrected census and vital events (their Table A6.8). In thousands:

Decade	England and Wales: Williamson	England (less Monmouth): Wrigley/Schofield	
		Census & vital events	Back projection
	Table 2.5	Table A6.8	Table A3.1
1776–86	53	–	44
1786–96	53	–	45
**			
1801–11	−58	73	62
1811–21	−16	74	91
1821–31	246	125	141
1831–41	215	64	192
1841–51	391	87	239
1851–61	479	364	231
1861–71	333	244	219

These net emigration estimates suggest that our Table 2.5 reconstruction is consistent with the trends underlying the Wrigley and Schofield back projection for every decade but 1801–21. Of course, our net emigration estimates include Welsh emigrants to the rest of the world while theirs treats the Welsh moving to England as net immigration from the rest of the world, but on the whole the first column tracks the last column reasonably well.

All in all, although these five pillars may have their flaws, the tentative reconstruction of the urban transition offered in this chapter seems to survive this critical assessment without crippling damage.

Appendix Table 2.2. *The Cairncross and Williamson urban registration districts compared*

Urban registration districts in common (N = 49):

Ashton-under-Lyme	Dover	Norwich
Bath	Exeter	Nottingham
Bedford	Gloucester	Oldham
Birmingham	Halifax	Oxford
Bolton	Huddersfield	Preston
Bradford	Hull	Plymouth
Brighton	Ipswich	Reading
Bristol	Leeds	Salisbury
Bury	Leicester	Sheffield
Cambridge	Lincoln	Southampton
Canterbury	Liverpool	Stockport
Carlisle	London	Wolverhampton
Chester	Macclesfield	Worcester
Colchester	Maidstone	Yarmouth
Coventry	Manchester (plus Salford)	York
Derby	Northampton	Portsmouth

Urban registration districts in Williamson, excluded from Cairncross? (N = 17):

Boston	Lancaster	Sunderland
Cardiff	Merthyr Tydfil	Swansea
Dorchester	Newcastle-upon-Tyne	Truro
Dudley	Newport	Tynemouth
Durham	Shrewsbury	Winchester
Gateshead	South Shields	

"Urban" registration districts in Cairncross, excluded from Williamson (N = 62):

Northern textile towns		Northern industrial towns	
Blackburn	Kidderminster	Barrow	Potteries
Burnley	Leek	Burton	Rotherham
Dewsbury	Rochdale	Cockermouth	Rugby
Glossop	Saddleworth	Crewe	Stafford
Haslingden	Todmorden	Doncaster	Walsall
Keighley	Wharfedale	Middlesborough	Whitehaven
		Millam	

Southern industrial towns		Northern residential towns	
Falmouth	Penzance	Blackpool	Morecambe
Grimsby	Redruth	Harrogate	Rhyl
Helston	Swindon	Leamington	Scarborough
Kettering	Tilbury	Llandudno	Southport
Luton	Wellingborough	Malvern	

Appendix Table 2.2. *(cont.)*

Old towns	Southern residential towns	
Wakefield	Bournemouth	Poole
King's Lynn	Brentwood	Reigate
	Cheltenham	Southend
	Clacton	Staines
	Cromer	Thanet
	Eastbourne	Torquay
	Easthampstead	Tunbridge
	Guildford	Watford
	Hastings	Weston-Super-Mare
	Herne Bay	Worthing
	Isle of Wight	Uxbridge
	Maidenhead	

Military towns	
Aldershot	Godstone
Chatham	Sheerness
Deal	St. Germans
Farnham	Weymouth
Folkestone	Windsor

3. Migrant selectivity, brain drain, and human capital transfers

3.1   Introduction

Although some cities grow without industry and some industries grow outside of cities, modern industrialization tends to be city-based. As a result, industrial revolutionary events tend to augment the demand for labor and capital in the city far more rapidly than in the countryside. Labor and capital supplies, on the other hand, tend to be abundant in rural areas, a result of centuries of gradual agrarian-based preindustrial development. One of the fundamental problems created by industrial revolutions is, therefore, to reconcile excess factor demands in the cities with excess factor supplies in the countryside. How do labor and capital markets cope with the disequilibrium?

This question is as old as the British industrial revolution itself. Indeed, the previous chapter was motivated by the same question in which we identified the size of the population transfers that took place between countryside and city from the 1780s to well into the mid-Victorian era. City immigration rates turn out to have been high even by the standards of the contemporary Third World. The same was true of rural emigration. We also identified a selectivity bias in those migrations, young adults favoring the cities, leaving children and elderly dependents behind.

Those young-adult migrations implied a human capital transfer because, as a consequence, the cities needed to invest less in rearing children to adulthood. As Melvin Reder pointed out some time ago, "it is cheaper to import workers than to grow them" (Reder, 1963, p. 224), because, after all, the costs of child rearing are borne by the area of origin. But in spite of the potential importance of the resource transfer, we have no quantitative notions as to its size during industrial revolutionary episodes, when city immigration rates reach their peak. That is not to say that there have been no studies assessing the benefits of immigration to receiving regions. Rudolph Blitz (1977) made the assessment for West German "guest workers" in the post-World War II period, Larry Neal and Paul Uselding (1972) did

59

the same for American immigration up to World War I, and Joel Mokyr and Cormac Ó Grada (1982) performed a similar exercise for nineteenth-century Irish emigration. Their findings suggest that international migrations can imply very significant capital transfers. Would we find the same for British cities during the First Industrial Revolution?

This chapter estimates the size of the human capital transfer implied by the rural emigration to Britain's cities. Section 3.2 sets the stage for this calculation by developing estimates of the commodity costs of children, their earnings, and thus their net rearing costs. With these in hand, Section 3.3 capitalizes those rearing costs for 1850. It turns out that the human capital transfers embodied in the city immigrants were very large.

3.2   The resource content of the migrants: Setting the stage

Making a hard problem simpler

A comprehensive assessment of the human capital content of the immigrants flowing into Britain's cities would, of course, include net rearing, education and other skill-formation costs, but we need not cast our net that wide in assessing the human capital content of what was primarily unskilled, young labor with limited formal schooling. Like Neal and Uselding, we shall in fact focus on rearing costs alone in what follows.

Peter Lindert's research on the American fertility transition (Lindert, 1978; see also Lindert, 1980) has established a standard for estimating the rearing cost of children. Lindert developed a relative cost concept that included a number of refinements, among them explicit attention to child-survival probabilities and the time cost of all family member inputs to rearing. Although we shall lean heavily on Lindert's accounting concepts in what follows, child-rearing costs will be limited to commodity costs only. Although this simplification makes the estimation of the value of children in early nineteenth-century England far easier, we should remember that it only serves to place a lower bound on the value of these human assets as they migrated to cities. The true value of the human capital transfer must have been somewhat higher than what is estimated here.

The commodity costs of children

The first step in estimating the net rearing costs of children is to construct adult male consumption equivalents (AMCE) for children by age and

Table 3.1. *Two estimates of adult-male consumption equivalences, by age and sex*

Age (years)	Prais & Houthakker		Sydenstricker & King	
	Male	Female	Male	Female
< 1	.350	.350	.220	.220
1	.520	.520	.241	.241
2	.520	.520	.281	.281
3	.520	.520	.306	.306
4	.520	.520	.332	.332
5	.570	.570	.352	.352
6	.570	.570	.375	.375
7	.570	.570	.397	.396
8	.570	.570	.419	.412
9	.570	.570	.442	.429
10	.790	.630	.470	.451
11	.790	.630	.499	.481
12	.790	.630	.537	.514
13	.790	.630	.590	.553
14	.810	.650	.657	.596
15	.810	.650	.736	.648
16	.810	.650	.812	.705
17	.810	.650	.876	.739
18	1.000	.880	.928	.760
19	1.000	.880	.960	.776
20	1.000	.880	1.000	.800

Sources: With some adjustments, from Prais and Houthakker (1955), Table 29, p. 141, based on "all food" and Sydenstricker and King (1921), Table III, p. 854, based on "combined expenditures."

sex.[1] The best-known example of this work in America is that of W. O. Atwater and A. P. Bryant (1899), although Seebohm Rowntree (1901) did the same for York shortly thereafter. The technique was sharpened by Edgar Sydenstricker and Willford King (1921), and their work will motivate one set of child commodity cost estimates here. An alternative approach to the AMCE estimation problem was pursued by S. J. Prais and Hendrick Houthakker (1955, chp. 9), who derived them from Engel Curves. The results of these two studies are summarized in Table 3.1. The two AMCE schedules reveal the same overall patterns, but they differ enough to matter to the rearing cost calculations. The consumption rate of

1 An excellent and exhaustive summary of early studies of this sort can be found in Williams and Zimmerman (1935), but most readers will find Lindert's summary more helpful (Lindert, 1978, pp. 102–110).

youngsters is quite a bit higher in the Prais and Houthakker AMCE schedule than in the Sydenstricker and King schedule. Thus, for any twenty-year-old migrating into English cities in 1850, the Prais and Houthakker schedule will give the higher present value figures because their estimated rearing costs are larger earlier in the child's life cycle. In all subsequent calculations, therefore, the Prais and Houthakker AMCE schedule will give an upper bound to the rearing cost content of the immigrants and the Sydenstricker and King AMCE will give a lower bound.

The second step in estimating the human capital content of the immigrants is to use these AMCE schedules to construct child commodity consumption costs for urban and rural areas in our benchmark year, 1851. To do so, we need estimates of adult-male consumption for the working-class groups who dominated the rural-urban migrations. We have used W. A. McKenzie's (1921, pp. 227 and 229) "hypothetical" budgets for farm laborers (rural) and unskilled wage laborers (urban) for this purpose.[2] The results are reported in Table 3.2.

Child earnings and net rearing costs

Participants in the standard-of-living debate have always questioned the roles of work and earnings of women and children in households headed by adult males. The pessimists have alleged that working-class families became more dependent on the earnings of children and, furthermore, that the employment of teenage and young-adult offspring shifted the authority of fathers to capitalists. The alleged increased participation rate of offspring in market work is thought to have undermined traditional family roles and fathers' self-esteem (Smelser, 1959, chps. IX–XI; Thompson, 1968, chp. 10). The out-migration of teenage and young-adult offspring from rural households to urban employment may have had an even more significant impact on the economic value of children and attitudes toward family size, an issue I have confronted at length elsewhere (Williamson, 1986a).

2 MacKenzie's "hypothetical" household budgets are for 1860. By applying the AMCEs in Table 3.1, MacKenzie's typical family can be converted into adult-male equivalents, and thus average household consumption can be converted into adult-male consumption levels. Child commodity costs are then derived by applying the AMCEs to these adult-male consumption levels. These are then converted to 1851 prices by applying the cost-of-living indices in Williamson (1985a, Appendix Table A.8, p. 220). To reconstruct child-rearing costs for earlier years, we rely on trends in real earnings in Lindert and Williamson (1983, p. 13), where rural child costs are taken to follow their "farm laborers" series and urban child costs are taken to follow their "middle group" series.

Table 3.2. *The commodity costs of children in 1851, urban and rural: Two estimates (in £s)*

Age (years)	Prais & Houthakker				Sydenstricker & King			
	Urban male	Urban female	Rural male	Rural female	Urban male	Urban female	Rural male	Rural female
< 1	4.095	4.095	2.597	2.597	2.574	2.574	1.632	1.632
1	6.084	6.084	3.858	3.858	2.820	2.820	1.788	1.788
2	6.084	6.084	3.858	3.858	3.288	3.288	2.085	2.085
3	6.084	6.084	3.858	3.858	3.580	3.580	2.271	2.271
4	6.084	6.084	3.858	3.858	3.884	3.884	2.463	2.463
5	6.669	6.669	4.229	4.229	4.118	4.118	2.612	2.612
6	6.669	6.669	4.229	4.229	4.388	4.388	2.783	2.783
7	6.669	6.669	4.229	4.229	4.645	4.633	2.946	2.938
8	6.669	6.669	4.229	4.229	4.902	4.820	3.109	3.057
9	6.669	6.669	4.229	4.229	5.171	5.019	3.280	3.183
10	9.243	7.371	5.862	4.675	5.499	5.277	3.487	3.346
11	9.243	7.371	5.862	4.675	5.838	5.628	3.703	3.569
12	9.243	7.371	5.862	4.675	6.283	6.014	3.985	3.814
13	9.243	7.371	5.862	4.675	6.903	6.470	4.378	4.103
14	9.477	7.605	6.010	4.823	7.687	6.973	4.875	4.422
15	9.477	7.605	6.010	4.823	8.611	7.582	5.461	4.808
16	9.477	7.605	6.010	4.823	9.500	8.249	6.025	5.231
17	9.477	7.605	6.010	4.823	10.249	8.646	6.500	5.483
18	11.700	10.296	7.420	6.530	10.858	8.892	6.886	5.639
19	11.700	10.296	7.420	6.530	11.232	9.079	7.123	5.758
20	11.700	10.296	7.420	6.530	11.700	10.296	7.420	6.530

Source: See text.

The truth of the matter, however, is that we know very little about trends in children's work and earnings across the industrial revolution. Peter Lindert and I (1980, pp. 24–32) thought we saw some evidence for a decline in child labor participation rates in England over the century following the 1790s, but their relative earnings when fully employed rose,[3] so that their average earnings relative to adult males actually increased from 1790 to 1889–90. We thought that most of this rise was due to the greater value of child market work in the city compared with the countryside.

With the appearance of better data for the late nineteenth century, it is clear that child earnings were a significant share of household income and their earnings rate relative to the male head of the household was significant

---

3 Goldin and Sokoloff (1982) found the same for American manufacturing in the antebellum period. They also documented a rise in the earnings of employed children compared to adult males.

Table 3.3. *The relative earnings of children in rural England, 1787 to 1877 (adult-male earnings = 1.0)*

Age (years)	1790	1787–1896	1797	1843	1861	1867	1877
Males							
8	.037	.033		.111			
9	.037	.033					
10	.128	.090					
11	.128	.090		.111			.126
12	.128	.090		.222			
13	.173	.172			.315	.261	
14	.173	.172			.315		.281
15	.276	.206			.315		
16	.276	.206				.435	
17	.276	.206				.348	
Females							
7			.031				
8							
9							
10							
11							
12			.171				
13						.065	
14							
15							
16							.124
17							

Sources: 1790: Lindert and Williamson (1980), Table 7, p. 28, based on Corfe Castle parish inhabitants. 1787–1796: *ibid.*, based on David Davies and Sir Frederick Morton Eden. 1797: Eden (1797), Appendix No. XII, household budgets from Berkshire, Norfolk and Suffolk. 1843: Burnett (1969), p. 262. 1861: Purdy (1861), p. 358. 1867: Royal Commission on Labour, *Paliamentary Papers* (1893–1894), Appendix D, pp. 52–4. 1877: Little (1878), pp. 508–9.

as well. We see it in Massachusetts working-class households in 1875, in New York working-class households in 1889–90, and in Georgia working-class households in 1901 (Lindert, 1978, p. 122). We can also see it in late nineteenth-century European urban working-class households (Haines, 1985). But what about England in the 1840s or before? Here the evidence is less abundant, but it appears to be good enough to estimate, roughly at least, the relative earnings of children in urban and rural areas.

Our interest is in the relative earnings of children in rural and urban England. The rural data are scattered and sketchy, and they cover the

Table 3.4. *The relative earnings of Sunday School children in Manchester and Stockport, 1833 (adult-male earnings = 1.0)*

Age (years)	Males			Females		
	Factory	Other	Total	Factory	Other	Total
9	.097	.126	.099	.111	.087	.107
10	.122	.137	.123	.134	.085	.129
11	.154	.098	.147	.148	.119	.143
12	.170	.146	.165	.177	.122	.169
13	.208	.156	.196	.222	.166	.213
14	.232	.213	.228	.254	.226	.248
15	.286	.232	.274	.294	.268	.291
16	.312	.368	.318	.316	.295	.314
17	.351	.411	.366	.340	.316	.337
18	.365	.394	.368	.375	.346	.372

Source: Lyons (1979), Tables 2 and 4, pp. 33a and 38a, based on *Parliamentary Papers* (1833), Appendix D.1, p. 88. These children's earnings are computed relative to adult males, where the latter is taken to be spinners in cotton textiles in the Manchester area in 1833.

period from the 1790s to the 1870s. Although it relates to farm laboring families, child earnings include that from cottage industry as well. The most detailed evidence on rural working-class households comes from Corfe Castle parish for 1790 and from the famous Eden and Davies farm family samples of the 1790s, but we have additional evidence from the mid nineteenth-century Royal Commissions as well. Some of this information is collected in Table 3.3 and it suggests that the relative earnings of children were remarkably stable between the 1790s and the 1870s. When time dummy variables are introduced in relative earnings regressions, there appears to be no evidence of drift in the relative earnings structure by age in rural England over the century.

The urban child earnings data in Table 3.4 are far more detailed, but they appear to be based on a truncated sample. Although the 1,331 Sunday School children surveyed in 1833 Manchester and Stockport (496 males and 835 females) were all likely to have been employed, the same was unlikely to have been true for all working-class children in 1833 Manchester, but it may have been close. That is, the 1833 Factory Report documents that in the Leeds area, 87 percent of the children aged ten to fifteen were employed (*Parliamentary Papers*, 1833, Appendix C.2, pp. 47 and 59). In addition, although the 1833 report primarily sampled working children in a booming urban labor market in which the demand for child labor was strong, the sample was not restricted to factory jobs (about 15 percent had jobs other than factory work).

Whatever their flaws, the 1833 urban data appear to be the best available for this period, and the bias is in the right direction. That is, the 1833 child earnings data imply a much flatter age-earnings curve than that implied by the United States Commissioner of Labor survey of 857 industrial working-class families in England and Wales in 1889–90 (Lindert and Williamson, 1980, Table 7, p. 28).[4] It is unclear how much of this

4 For both sexes, and taking the earnings of 17-year-olds equal to 1.0, these two samples reveal the following:

Age	Children in working-class families in England & Wales 1889–90	Sunday School children in Manchester & Stockport 1833
7 years & younger	0	0
8	0	0
9	.007	.293
10	.007	.358
11	.046	.412
12	.046	.474
13	.311	.582
14	.311	.676
15	.311	.804
16	1.000	.898
17	1.000	1.000

As the text points out, the 1833 earnings data exhibit a much flatter age-earnings curve. Are the 1833 Sunday School data therefore of doubtful quality? I suspect not, because the 1833 Factory Report confirms the Manchester Sunday School earnings data. The Factory Report also published earnings by age and sex, although the data was collected only from cotton mills in Manchester. The sample is large, however, based as it was on forty-three responses to surveys sent to the cotton mills. The following wage data is based on 17,255 employed workers, 66 percent of whom were aged twenty or less (*Parliamentary Papers*, 1833, Appendix D.2, p. 107), and where adult males = 1.0:

Age	Males		Females	
	Number	Earnings	Number	Earnings
9 years	498	.125	290	.132
10 & 11	819	.163	538	.169
12 & 13	1021	.223	761	.217
14 & 15	853	.287	797	.285
16 & 17	708	.365	1068	.358
18, 19 & 20	758	.460	1582	.397

These age-earnings schedules follow quite closely those in Table 3.4.

difference in the age-earnings curve for urban children is attributable to changes over time in age-specific labor-demand forces, to child labor laws and schooling laws, to family attitudes toward their children's labor participation, and to the 1833 sample's truncation. If it is the latter, our use of the 1833 data will serve to overstate the earnings of urban children through their middle teens, and thus understate net rearing costs in the cities. Because we hope to show that human capital transfers in England's cities were large in the mid-nineteenth century, the bias is in the right direction, namely downward.

Relative earnings functions were estimated on both the rural and urban data, in which males and females were pooled and dummy variables were added for gender ($D_F = 1$ if female). The gender dummies were allowed to affect both intercept and slope in these earnings-by-age regressions. Among the functional forms explored, the semilogarithmic function seemed to summarize the data best (t-statistics in parentheses):

Urban

$$\text{RELATIVE EARNINGS} = \underset{(11.269)}{-.846} + \underset{(.444)}{.047 \ D_F} + \underset{(14.364)}{.417 \ \ln\text{AGE}} - \underset{(.409)}{.017 \ D_F \ \ln\text{AGE}}$$

(3.1)

$$\bar{R}^2 = .954$$

Rural

$$\text{RELATIVE EARNINGS} = \underset{(6.060)}{-.737} + \underset{(2.066)}{.567 \ D_F} + \underset{(7.620)}{.367 \ \ln\text{AGE}} - \underset{(2.316)}{.257 \ D_F \ \ln\text{Age}}$$

(3.2)

$$\bar{R}^2 = .652$$

These regressions were then used to generate the predicted relative earnings of children reported in Table 3.5. We shall assume that these relative earnings schedules by gender and location remained stable over the first half of the nineteenth century.

The next step is to convert these relative earnings schedules into actual children's earnings (by age and gender) for 1851. All we need for this purpose are estimates of adult-male earnings. Here we use the Lindert and Williamson (1983, p. 7) estimates for farm laborers and for their "middle group," estimates which correspond to unskilled rural and urban

Table 3.5. *Children's earnings in 1851, urban and rural*

Age (years)	Earnings relative to full-time male				Earnings in 1851 £			
	Urban male	Urban female	Rural male	Rural female	Urban male	Urban female	Rural male	Rural female
<8	0	0	0	0	0	0	0	0
8	.020	.033	.025	.058	1.072	1.723	.726	1.682
9	.069	.080	.069	.071	3.670	4.216	2.004	2.057
10	.113	.122	.107	.082	5.994	6.447	3.107	2.394
11	.153	.160	.142	.093	8.097	8.464	4.124	2.698
12	.189	.195	.174	.102	10.016	10.307	5.053	2.975
13	.223	.227	.204	.111	11.782	12.001	5.924	3.231
14	.253	.256	.231	.119	13.417	13.570	6.708	3.467
15	.282	.284	.256	.127	14.939	15.030	7.434	3.687
16	.309	.310	.280	.134	16.362	16.397	8.131	3.893
17	.334	.334	.302	.141	17.700	17.680	8.770	4.087
18	.358	.357	.323	.147	18.960	18.890	9.380	4.269

Source: The relative earnings figures are predicted from regression equations (3.1) and (3.2) in the text. The 1851 nominal earnings figures are derived by multiplying the relative earnings figures by adult male (full-time) annual earnings, where urban = £52.95 and rural = £29.04. The adult-male earnings estimates are from Lindert and Williamson (1983), p. 7 and where rural=farm laborers and urban=middle group.

adult-male workers. Estimated child earnings for 1851 are also reported in Table 3.5.[5]

The final step is to subtract child commodity costs from earnings to get net rearing costs. The results are presented in Figures 3.1 and 3.2. As we anticipated, the commodity cost estimates based on Prais and Houthakker exceed those based on Sydenstricker and King by enough so that net rearing costs between them differ significantly. As a result, we shall continue to view Prais and Houthakker as an upper bound and Sydenstricker and King as a lower bound in our human capital calculations.

There are some clear morals that emerge from these two figures, and they play a role in subsequent arguments. First, rural areas clearly were cheap places to raise children. They were cheap, not because they were fed less, clothed more poorly, or educated less; rather, they were cheap primarily because of low child mortality (rearing investment was less likely to be wasted by a child's subsequent death) and because of low housing

5 To reconstruct child earnings for earlier years, we rely on trends in real earnings of these two adult-male groups (Lindert and Williamson, 1983, p. 13, using interpolation where necessary).

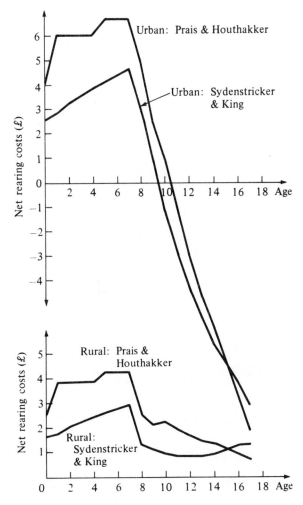

Figure 3.1   Net rearing costs for females, 1851, urban and rural: Two variants

rents. Cities, of course, would always prefer to have the countryside bear
the burden of rearing the future urban labor force. But even from the
nation's point of view, it would have made good economic sense to raise
that future labor force in the countryside. Second, while male children
switched from net marginal economic burdens to net marginal economic
benefits between ages ten and fifteen in both urban and rural areas,
females did not. Indeed, while urban females switched from marginal

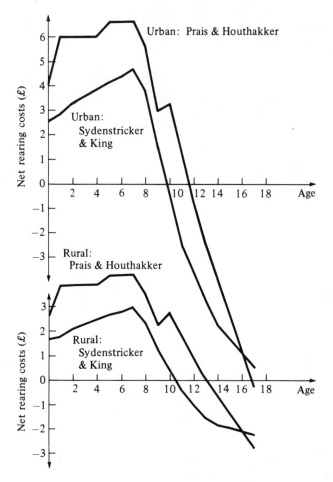

Figure 3.2   Net rearing costs for males, 1851, urban and rural: Two variants

burdens to marginal benefits between ages nine and eleven, they never switched to economic benefits in the countryside, at least in terms of market work. These rough estimates offer empirical support for the standard view that there was little market demand for female labor in the countryside after the demise of cottage industry, especially in the South, where grain production was more male-intensive. Third, if efficient financial institutions had linked urban and rural areas, and thus if financial remittances to parents in the countryside had been easy, parental income would have been maximized if female and male offspring were allowed to leave for higher wages in the city as soon after age ten as possible. However, financial institutions were far from efficient, and remittances to the countryside must have been difficult. Under such conditions, parental income would have been maximized by encouraging female offspring to leave for the city as soon as possible, while male offspring should have been kept at home for as long as possible. All of this follows if economic calculus played an important role in family decision making regarding the timing of offsprings' migration from countryside to city, and the sex-specific migration flows underlying the evidence presented in Chapter 2 seem to be roughly consistent with that calculus. Females in their teens and early twenties were much more likely to emigrate from rural England than males (especially in the South), although this was far less true of those in their late twenties, and not true at all of those above that age.[6]

What do we know about remittances?

Did migrant children remit a significant part of their urban wages back to their parents in the English countryside?

The answer to this question is obviously central to any assessment of the net transfer embodied in the migrations, or, for that matter, to any assessment of the rural demand for children and the potential fertility response to the rising rate of rural emigration across the First Industrial Revolution. Even if emigrant children contributed a far smaller share of

6 The figures for the 1840s reported in Table 2.12 can be broken down by sex, yielding:

	Estimated age/sex distribution of city immigrants 1841–51					
	London		Urban non-London		All urban	
Age Class	Males	Females	Males	Females	Males	Females
10–14	14,835	12,518	30,434	27,600	45,270	40,119
15–19	10,559	23,114	23,472	37,811	34,032	60,925
20–24	26,235	49,756	32,673	57,421	58,908	107,177
25–29	26,243	34,678	26,044	27,201	52,288	61,879
30–39	10,485	−8,588	9,838	−18,308	20,324	−26,896
40–49	1,925	−5,754	7,199	2,220	9,125	−3,555

Thus, the ratio of female-to-male immigrants aged 15–29 was higher in London than in the rest of England's cities, and the ratio of female-to-male immigrants declines sharply between ages 15 and 49 everywhere (e.g., in London the ratio falls from 2.19 age 15–19, to 1.32 age 25–29, becoming negative thereafter).

their earnings to their distant parents than they would have had they stayed at home, working children earned more in the city, and thus they may still have added more to their rural parents' total income. While Oded Stark (Stark, 1981; Stark and Katz, 1985) believes that city employment opportunities for young adults raise (through remittances) the value of rural children in the Third World, English archival evidence is, as far as I can tell, completely mute on the issue. There is absolutely no mention of children's remittances in any of the English rural household surveys from the Eden and Davies studies in the 1790s to the Royal Commission inquiries of the 1870s and 1880s. If future research confirms it, the absence of child remittances to parents in rural England would be consistent with nineteenth-century Poor Laws. David Thomson (1984) has shown public support of the elderly to have been very generous, at least up to the 1870s and the reform crusade, and generous public support of the elderly would hardly have encouraged emigrant children to remit back to parents. This need not have been true of other agrarian societies that had far less generous state relief of the elderly, like Ireland. Nor would it necessarily have been true of other agrarian societies, like Ireland, which had much higher emigration rates and thus bigger remittance flows to help finance subsequent migrations of siblings.

That children present in the household added significantly to family income is not the issue. We have already seen that they did so in mid nineteenth-century England. Michael Anderson (1971) found the same for nineteenth-century Lancashire, as did Michael Haines (1981, 1985) for late nineteenth-century urban working-class households. Indeed, the standard view is that while "the added burden of young children early in the life cycle created hardships . . . , the children . . . [contributed] at least some of their earnings to the family later on" (Haines, 1985, p. 46). Based on an 1889–90 survey of industrial families in Europe, Haines (1985, Table 3.1) estimates that for families headed by a parent in his or her forties, children's income accounted for 31.8 percent of total family income. However, almost all of these estimates are for urban, not rural, families. Furthermore, such evidence relates only to the incomes of children present in the household. In short, these studies tell us very little about the remittance of children's urban wages back to rural villages whence they migrated.

What about the contemporary Third World literature that makes so much of urban remittances to rural areas? Henry Remple and Richard Lobdell (1978) undertook a comprehensive survey of this literature more than a decade ago. Based on some fifty studies, Remple and Lobdell concluded the following: (1) urban-rural remittances are very large in Africa, ranging from 10 to 13 percent of urban incomes; (2) although there is some limited evidence of a like sort for Asia, there is almost none for Latin America; and (3) remittances tend to be far higher for international than for internal migrations. As Remple and Lobdell point out, however, none of these studies control for emigrant funds carried by the migrants, especially for those youths going to urban areas for additional education. When these emigrant funds are subtracted from immigrant remittances, net remittances turn out to be quite small, even for Africa.[7] Furthermore, there is some evidence that these net remittances "become insurance premiums paid to protect the migrant against problems which could arise if current urban employment is lost because of lay-offs, disability and illness. The possibility of such insurance policies exists only in those societies where some viable rural alternative is still available to the migrant" (Remple and Lobdell, 1978, p. 336). It now seems easier to reconcile the contemporary African evidence documenting significant rural-urban remittances with the absence of any such evidence for England up to 1851. No viable rural alternative existed for those who had emigrated from the English countryside; financial institutions did not exist to make it possible for the urban working class to remit easily to the English countryside in the early nineteenth century; and transport costs linking urban and rural England were sufficiently high in the prerailroad age to make it very expensive for children to carry back remittances themselves.

Although we do know quite a bit about international remittances during the nineteenth century, these remittances must be treated with caution because they tended to be higher for international than for internal migrations and because international remittances tended to be passage money for kin. Nonetheless, the evidence is informative. Douglass North (1960, pp. 616–18) estimated that the average per migrant remittance to England and Ireland from America (1848–60) was $28.43, or about 7.8 percent of average annual earnings of nonfarm employees.[8] Although this remittance rate appears high, immigrant funds brought in by the average migrant were even higher (6.9 percent of average annual earnings for the Irish and 20.7 percent for the English), implying that net remittances were small or even negative. Indeed, North concluded that "remittances dur-

7 This conclusion has been disputed by Stark (1980). See also Stark and Lucas (1985).

8 The underlying earnings figure is from Lebergott (1964), Table A-19, p. 528.

ing the [ante bellum period] went mostly for passage money and *not for continuous support of people remaining in the old country*" (North, 1960, p. 616, italics added). Matthew Simon (1960) believed the same was true for late nineteenth-century immigrants in America.[9]

Readers with knowledge of Irish history might view with skepticism the proposition that child remittances to parents in rural England were modest at best in the early nineteenth century. There is reason to believe, however, that English experience was very different from Irish experience. For example, after a review of the evidence documenting large remittances from North America to the United Kingdom, Dudley Baines (1985, p. 85) tells us that "It is thought that the majority of the remittances to the U.K. went to Ireland." In any case, no one denies the role of remittances in financing the migration of kin. Emigrant remittances in the 1830s may "have defrayed the expense of about one-sixth of the Irish sailing from Liverpool" to America (Adams, 1932, p. 181), and in 1838 they may have "paid for more than half" (p. 226). The issue is not remittances for passage, however, but rather remittances to augment the resources of those who stayed behind. Even here, Ireland appears to have been different from England because postfamine emigrant remittances to Ireland became "a regular part of the the the income of thousands of farmers" (Adams, 1932, p. 393). The emphasis on postfamine is important: first, because the famine itself elicited a remittance response; and second, because "Prior to mid-century, channels for sending home money or prepaid passage tickets had been varied but often troublesome and uncertain" (Miller, 1985, p. 357).

We have offered a number of reasons why postfamine Irish experience with remittances would have differed sharply with English experience up to 1851. First, the Irish emigrations were international, and such migrations seem to generate far higher remittance rates even today. Second, financial institutions were far better equipped to handle remittances in the postfamine period than in the decade prior to mid-century. Third, England had generous public relief of the elderly and Ireland did not. And,

---

9 The *Report of the Commissioners Appointed to Take the Census of Ireland for the Year 1841* guessed that the average Irishman returning from Britain "brought back five pounds with him" (*Parliamentary Papers*, 1843, p. xxvi). If this figure can be extrapolated to all Irish immigrants to Britain's cities, then it might have amounted to as much as 10 percent of their annual earnings (based on unskilled city earnings reported in Lindert and Williamson, 1983, p. 13). However, it seems unlikely to have applied to the Irish immigrants who stayed in Britain's cities.

fourth, Ireland suffered a subsistence crisis during the famine and English agriculture did not.

Although we certainly need some better evidence on the issue, what we do have does not suggest that English children remitted funds back to their rural parents after emigrating to cities in the early and mid nineteenth century. They certainly may have done so in Ireland, Italy, and other agrarian countries undergoing international emigration later in the century, but there is no reason to expect the same for England up to 1851.

3.3   The human capital transfer embodied in the migrants

How to estimate the transfer

How shall we estimate the size of the human capital transfer embodied in those city immigrants whose rearing costs were incurred elsewhere?

Chapter 2 offered decadal estimates of immigration into Britain's cities, by age and sex. The total migrations over the 1840s can easily be converted into an average annual flow. The annual flow over the 1840s will be labeled here as 1850 city immigration. Although we shall focus on the results for 1850 in what follows, similar estimates will also be constructed for 1860 and 1870.

The next step is to assign those 1850 immigrants a date of birth, a twenty-year-old female immigrant having been born in 1830, twenty-five-year-old male immigrant having been born in 1825, and so on. Having done so, we then apply our age/sex-specific child costs to each of these individuals as they age through time up to the point of migration in 1850. This entails the application of the 1851 net rearing cost schedules underlying Figures 3.1 and 3.2, but with a twist. That is, the 1851 net rearing cost schedules are allowed to shift upward over time so as to reflect the standard-of-living trends that took place from the late eighteenth century to 1851.[10] The estimated rearing costs are then capitalized to get their present value in 1850.

Only positive net rearing costs are considered throughout. It made little difference to the city that a twenty-year-old male immigrant had been a net economic benefit to his rural parish since age twelve. What mattered

10 These are based on the trends reported in Lindert and Williamson (1983). See footnotes 2 and 5 above.

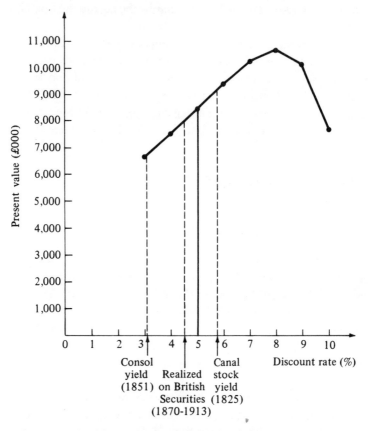

Figure 3.3   Children's rearing costs embodied in the 1850 immigrants to Britain's cities under various discount rates

to the city was that a previous rearing investment was made in this young male, which the city itself did not have to incur. Furthermore, to simplify the calculations, all migrants aged sixty and above are treated as aged sixty.

The sensitivity of the human capital transfer estimate to various assumptions can and should be assessed. These include the choice between the Prais-Houthakker and the Sydenstricker-King AMCE schedules, the choice between urban and rural rearing costs, and the choice between various discount rates. Consider the role of the discount rate first. Figure 3.3 plots the human capital transfer under a range of discount rates from 3 to 10 percent. This range seems to capture all plausible rates relevant to the city economy in mid-century.[11] Because the rearing costs embedded in the city immigrants were incurred somewhere in the past, why don't these 1850 present values continue to rise with higher discount rates? Why do they reach a peak at 8 percent and fall thereafter? The answer is simple enough: net city immigration was negative for those in their late thirties and late forties, and the higher the discount rate, the greater the weight attached to their net rearing costs. At some high discount rate, therefore, these middle-aged emigrants begin to dominate, lowering the human capital transfer estimated. In any case, we shall assume a discount rate of 5 percent in what follows, a figure that appears to fall within the range of plausible rates bounded by the consol yield in 1851 and canal-stock yields in 1825.[12]

The size of the transfer

Table 3.6 confirms that the size of the human capital transfer in 1850 was substantial. The resources embodied in the city immigrants in that year ranged between £4,254,000 and £7,383,000, for an average of £5,819,000. Based on Charles Feinstein's (1978, p. 40) gross domestic fixed capital formation estimates, this human capital import was about 15.6 percent of actual urban investment in 1850.[13] Table 3.7 poses a somewhat different question, one motivated by Neal and Uselding's (1972) assessment of the contribution of American nineteenth-century immigration: What would it have cost the cities to have replaced the immigrants with native-born? Because the cities had high child-mortality rates, the total investment in rearing costs to replace those immigrants would have been even higher than the costs embodied in the immigrants themselves. Calculated in this way,

11 Some might argue that low-income households may have faced somewhat higher discount rates, but Gregory King thought that labor earnings should be capitalized at 6.75 to 10 percent per annum based on even poorer late seventeenth-century households (Lindert, 1985, p. 57).

12 The canal stock yield figure is from Clapham (1930, p. 81), the realized rate on British securities is from Edelstein (1982, chps. 5 and 6), and the consol rate is from Mitchell and Deane (1962, p. 455).

13 To give the reader a better appreciation for the magnitude of the human capital transfers, here and below we take these transfers as a share of urban or rural gross domestic fixed capital formation. Obviously, the share would be lower if the transfers were taken as a share of *total* investment, human and nonhuman. Since this chapter was completed, Feinstein has published (1988, Appendix Table IX, p. 444) revised estimates of gross domestic fixed capital formation. Although the revisions are significant, they do not appear large enough to change any of the conclusions in the text.

Table 3.6. *The human capital transfer embodied in city immigrants and rural emigrants in 1850 (1851 prices)*

Assumptions	I_H Present value of net rearing costs (r = 5%) (£000)	Share of I_H in	
		Urban investment (%)	Rural investment (%)
City immigrants valued at urban rearing costs			
Prais-Houthakker	7,383	19.7	
Sydenstricker-King	4,254	11.4	
Average	5,819	15.6	
Rural emigrants valued at rural rearing costs			
Prais-Houthakker	8,454		70.5
Sydenstricker-King	4,904		40.9
Average	6,679		55.7

Source: See text for the construction of the present value of net rearing costs. The underlying urban and rural investment figures are 37.445 and 11.985 million £. They refer to gross domestic fixed-capital formation, in 1851–1860 prices, and are an average for the decade 1841–1850. The figures are derived by splitting Feinstein's (1978, p. 40) national investment totals into rural and urban parts. The allocation rules were: the urban share of residential investment was derived by the ratio of urban-population increase to total population increase across the 1840s; investment in public building, industrial building and machinery, mining, gas and water were all allocated to urban: and the urban share of investment in railways, roads, bridges, carriages, canals, docks, and ships was taken to be the same as the ratio of investment in industry and "other urban" (public buildings, mining, gas, and water) to investment in industry, "other urban," and agriculture.

Table 3.7 suggests that the human capital investment would have been some 17.8 percent of actual urban investment in 1850.

England's rural emigrants left for the New World as well as for England's cities, and England's city immigrants included Irish, Scots, and foreigners. As a consequence, the size and composition of England's rural emigrant flows differed from that of her urban immigrant flows. It follows that the human capital export from the countryside need not have been the same as the human capital import into the cities. Furthermore, annual investment levels were far smaller in rural than in urban England, so that the shares of human capital transfers in annual urban and rural investment need not have been the same either. Indeed, the human capital embodied in the rural emigrants in 1850 was about £6,679,000, or 55.7 percent of rural investment in that year. This enormous capital export is

Table 3.7. *What if city immigrants and rural emigrants had to be replaced with native-born in 1850? A second human capital transfer calculation (1851 prices)*

Assumptions	I_H Present Value of net rearing cost (r = 5%) (£000)	Share of I_H in	
		Urban investment (%)	Rural investment (%)
City immigrants valued at urban rearing costs			
Prais-Houthakker	8,446	22.6	
Sydenstricker-King	4,865	13.0	
Average	6,656	17.8	
Rural emigrants valued at rural rearing costs			
Prais-Houthakker	11,593		96.7
Sydenstricker-King	6,726		56.1
Average	9,160		76.4

Source: This calculation repeats that of Table 3.6, except here we include the mortality experience of children. The age/sex-specific mortality rates are based on the Registrar General, 1838–1844, adjusted for the undercount ratio. See Williamson (1985b), Appendix Table E.1, p. 80.

even higher when we consider the cost of replacing those emigrants: Table 3.7 suggests a figure of 76.4 percent of rural investment.

These human capital flows were certainly substantial, and it appears that they may have been higher in 1850 than later in the nineteenth century. Based on a replication of the calculations in Table 3.6, we find the following for 1860 and 1870 (where the figures are in 1851 prices, and in £000):

	Urban	Rural
1850	5,819	6,679
1860	3,410	5,043
1870	3,546	5,376

That human capital transfers to English cities were highest in 1850 is no surprise. Indeed, had we the necessary data, the human capital transfer embodied in city immigrants as a share in urban investment was probably even higher in the 1770s and 1780s, when the rate of city immigration was also at its peak. The big surprise, however, is that human capital transfers

from the English countryside were highest in 1850. The extensive literature on rural depopulation in the late nineteenth century (Graham, 1892;
Saville, 1957) implies that the human capital export from the English
countryside would have been lower in 1850 than it was to become a few
decades later. Apparently, that was not the case.

3.4   Tying some demo-economic knots

City immigration rates were very high during the First Industrial Revolution. This result is quite surprising when viewed in terms of conventional labor histories which tend to describe late eighteenth- and early
nineteenth-century England in terms of "poorly integrated" and "regionally segmented" labor markets. The result is less surprising, however,
when these immigration rates are compared with more recent experience
in the Third World. In the Third World, these rates have been so dramatic that an enormous literature has developed on the immigrant absorption problem. Yet England experienced city immigrant rates no lower than
the Third World, between the 1770s and the 1810s averaging about 1.3
percent per annum. Furthermore, as we pointed out in Chapter 2, these
rates of population immigration understate rates of labor immigration,
and the latter may have been as high as 1.7 percent per annum. In short,
city immigration during the First Industrial Revolution seems to have
responded vigorously to accommodate excess labor demands in the cities.

As we shall see in Chapter 7, however, these high rates of city immigration were apparently not enough to clear labor markets, at least when
judged by the evidence that wage gaps between city and countryside persisted. Obviously, excess labor demands in the cities placed great stress on
interregional labor markets. Yet, relatively elastic long-run labor supplies
within the cities themselves served to take the pressure off interregional
labor markets. Chapter 2 argued that a major source of that elastic local
labor supply was a long-run demographic response of the following sort:
Rapid city immigration early in the industrial revolution fostered a dramatic
shift in city age distributions. Because the migrations were characterized by
a very strong selectivity bias, the cities became full of young adults. This
immigration-induced shift in favor of young adults served to lower the
crude mortality rate and to raise the crude birth rate, all of which augmented future rates of resident city labor-force growth, crowding out potential new immigrants, thus causing the rate of city immigration to decline
over time. Furthermore, the size of the demographically induced local

labor supply response would have been greater the larger had been the initial excess labor demand and initial city immigration. The size of the cities' local labor-supply response was, therefore, intimately related to the size of the initial labor demand "shock" and the immigrant response. This demo-economic interaction was an important ingredient, it seems, to the operation of labor markets during the First Industrial Revolution.

The investment requirements associated with the industrial revolution created excess demand for capital in the cities too. So much so, that an important literature has developed that serves to assess the operation of conventional capital markets in facilitating the transfer of the rural "surplus" to the city. By restricting their attention of the transfer of the rural surplus to the city through conventional channels, development economists have found the transfer to have been large only in the case of Taiwan (Lee, 1971). Indeed, it was small even during USSR's First Five-Year Plan, when agriculture was squeezed by Stalinist policies (Ellman, 1975). Recently, in fact, development economists have challenged the Marxian thesis that the burden of providing surplus funds for industrial capital formation in early stages of development must fall upon agriculture. The new view stresses heavy investment requirements in agriculture and that agriculture needs to retain its surplus for accumulation if food production is to keep up with population growth (Ishikawa, 1967; Georgescu-Roegen, 1969; Hayami and Ruttan, 1971). British economic historians generally seem to support this view and find that industry relied on self-finance during the First Industrial Revolution (Postan, 1935; Crouzet, 1965, 1972). Evidence of modest transfers from the countryside has encouraged the inference that the cities must have relied primarily on internally generated funds, and, further, that financial capital markets linking city with countryside failed.

This and the previous chapter suggest that this assessment may be too narrowly drawn. First, the young-adult-migrant bias must have served to augment city savings (while suppressing rural savings) through life-cycle and dependency rate effects. Second, the immigration to city from countryside implied a very large human capital transfer. On both counts, Britain's cities must have found it possible to devote a larger share of their current income to the accumulation of adult human capital, social overhead, dwellings, and plant and equipment (although Chapter 10 will show that even this larger share was not enough).

It may turn out that interregional capital markets did fail, but they certainly worked in far more subtle ways than conventional financial histories have led us to believe.

4. The demand for labor and immigrant absorption off the farm

4.1 Internal migration between farm and nonfarm employment

The previous two chapters have focused on migration between city and countryside. What about migration off the farm? After all, the countryside offered nonfarm employment opportunities, and these were quite significant in most parts of England. Under such conditions, rural emigration and off-farm emigration need not have been the same.

Not too long ago, Sidney Pollard (1978) offered estimates of emigration from British agriculture over the century following 1751, concluding that "only about one-fifth of the additional working force in nonagrarian occupations was derived from the direct transfer out of agriculture," and by comparison natural population increase was of "immense importance" (Pollard, 1978, Table 34 and p. 141). Pollard's conclusion would appear to be at variance with Chapter 2, in which we found that immigration contributed to about half of city growth (Table 2.5). However, Pollard made his calculations based on simplifications that matter to his conclusions. First, he ignored external migrations in his calculations, the Irish in particular. In effect, he treated the Irish as part of the nonagricultural natural increase. Second, Pollard assumed that the rate of natural increase was the same everywhere. I am sure that Pollard would be the first to agree that the natural rates were quite different in agriculture and nonagriculture. As we have seen in Chapter 2, the rate of natural increase was much higher in the countryside. The natural rate differentials were, in fact, much higher than in the contemporary Third World, making the problem of matching excess urban labor demand with excess rural labor supply all the more difficult. The greater were those differentials, the more has Pollard understated the rate of natural increase in the agricultural labor force and thus the more has he understated emigration from agriculture.

Table 4.1 repairs Pollard's calculations. It is true that the nonagri-

Table 4.1. *Emigration from agriculture and immigration into nonagriculture, 1781 to 1861*

Period	Average employment (000)			Total increase in nonagriculture	Increase in nonagriculture due to		
	Total	Agriculture	Nonagriculture		Immigrants from agriculture	Immigrants from Ireland	Natural increase
1781–1801	4,400	1,625	2,775	650	268	26	356
1801–1811	5,150	1,750	3,400	600	218	34	348
1811–1821	5,850	1,800	4,050	700	295	42	363
1821–1831	6,700	1,800	4,900	1,000	375	77	548
1831–1841	7,800	1,850	5,950	1,100	303	77	720
1841–1851	9,050	2,000	7,050	1,100	149	235	716
1851–1861	10,250	2,050	8,200	1,200	423	73	704

Period	Annual emigration rate from agriculture (%)	Annual immigration rate into nonagriculture from			Rate of natural increase in nonagriculture (%)	Total rate of increase in nonagriculture (%)	Nonagriculture increase due to immigration (%)
		Agriculture (%)	Ireland (%)	Both sources (%)			
1781–1801	.82	.48	.05	.53	.64	1.17	45
1801–1811	1.25	.64	.10	.74	1.02	1.76	42
1811–1821	1.64	.73	.10	.83	.90	1.73	48
1821–1831	2.08	.77	.16	.93	1.12	2.05	45
1831–1841	1.64	.51	.13	.64	1.21	1.85	35
1841–1851	.75	.21	.33	.54	1.02	1.56	35
1851–1861	2.06	.52	.09	.61	.86	1.47	41

Sources and notes: The employment figures are midpoint averages for the period stated, and the annual observations are taken from Deane and Cole, 1962, Table 31, p. 143, and Pollard, 1978, Table 34, p. 141. I assume that the vast majority of (permanent as opposed to seasonal) Irish labor had nonagricultural employments. I also assume higher rates of natural increase in agriculture, reflecting rural/urban fertility and mortality differentials. The details of the calculations underlying this table can be found in Appendix 4.1.

83

cultural immigration rate was somewhat lower than the city immigration rate estimated in Chapter 2. It appears that the most rapid annual immigration rate from British agriculture was during the 1820s, .77 percent, and even this figure falls below the average for the contemporary Third World. However, the total immigration rate (including the Irish) was considerably higher in the 1820s, .93 percent, and this is not very far below the estimate for the city immigration rate offered in Chapter 2 (1.07 percent: Table 2.5). Furthermore, during the decade of the 1820s immigration accounted for more than 45 percent of the increase in nonagricultural employment, more than double the "one-fifth" estimated by Pollard.

The big difference between the city and the nonagricultural immigration rates appears during the French wars, when the former was about double the latter, a result that turns out to be quite consistent with Peter Lindert's new estimates of employment growth (Lindert, 1980). Lindert's estimates will be discussed below, but we note here that manufacturing and service employment did not undergo impressive growth during the French wars, suggesting that rapid city growth was led more by a shift of nonagricultural activities away from rural locations and toward the towns, and less by economy-wide industrial and service employment growth. The replacement of rural-based handicrafts with urban-based factories was the most important manifestation of that effect.

Note, however, that the drift in those immigration rates in Table 4.1 imply the operation of Irish crowding-out. When the Irish immigration rate reaches its peak in the 1840s, the rate of immigration from British agriculture reaches its trough, an enormous fall from .51 percent per year in the 1830s to .21 percent per year in the 1840s. Furthermore, when Irish immigration picks up after the 1810s, the rate of immigration from British agriculture falls off with a decade lag. In both the short run and the long run, there appears to be some suggestion of Irish crowding-out. This theme will be discussed at length in Chapter 6.

4.2   Where were the nonfarm jobs?

Where were the jobs that absorbed the farm exodus? Was it rapid job creation in manufacturing that pulled the farm emigrant to the city, or was it the threat of agricultural unemployment that pushed the farm emigrant into low-productivity jobs in the city service sector? These are very old

Table 4.2. *The sources of civilian employment growth in nonagriculture, 1755 to 1861*

Period	Manufacturing	Mining	Services	Nonagriculture
A. Percentage per annum:				
1755–1811	0.70	4.31	0.79	0.92
1821–1861	na	na	na	1.56
1841–1861	1.45	4.69	1.88	1.82
B. Percentage of nonagricultural employment increase due to:				
1755–1811	23.8	22.4	53.8	
1841–1861	34.6	11.5	53.8	

Sources: The figures for 1755–1811 are taken from Lindert (1980, Table 3, pp. 702–3). Excludes men in the army, titled, paupers, and pensioners. Also laborers are allocated between building trades, manufacturing, and agriculture, those sectors in which Lindert tells us laborers are "excluded"). Lindert's figure for all nonagriculture is a bit below that offered by Pollard (1978, Table 34, p. 141), 1.07 percent per year, the latter based on Deane and Cole. The figures for 1821–1861 are from Deane and Cole (1962, Table 31, p. 143).

questions that concerned Marx and Mayhew then just as much as they concern the International Labor Organization and the World Bank now.

Sources of employment growth, 1755–1861

Table 4.2 disaggregates nonagricultural employment growth into three sectors. Based on Lindert's estimates, Panel A makes it clear that manufacturing was hardly the leading sector driving nonagricultural employment growth during the French wars. On the contrary, employment growth in manufacturing was a bit below that of services and far below that of mining. Of course, rapid employment growth in a small sector may not create very many jobs, so Panel B offers a more relevant calculation, namely, the share of the nonagricultural employment increase which was attributable to each sector. Panel B shows that between 1755 and 1811, manufacturing and mining job creation were of about equal importance, and services were more than twice that of both. It appears that the service sector was the main source of new urban jobs up to 1811, not manufacturing. These results are quite consistent with the fact that the wars choked off trade and therefore made it difficult for British producers to vent their manufacturers on to foreign markets. Manufacturing employment growth suffered as a consequence. Conditions changed somewhat after the wars because new jobs in manufacturing increased as a share in total new nonagricultural jobs. However, at least between 1841 and 1861, the service sector maintained its position as the main source of new urban jobs.

The point of this exercise is that booming nonagricultural labor demand across the British industrial revolution cannot be understood by looking at manufacturing alone. Mining and the heterogeneous service sector were equally or even more important.

Did urbanization outrun industrialization?

The rapid expansion of employment in the service sector documented in Table 4.2 might catch the eye of those development economists who have stressed "disappointing" manufacturing employment performance in Third World cities since 1950. Indeed, many development economists have argued that employment growth in urban services is simply a residual supporting the cities' reserve army, the latter the result of rural push, not urban pull.

Writing in the 1950s, Bert Hoselitz (1955, 1957) argued that the rate of urbanization was "too fast" in the Third World, Asia in particular. Hoselitz's assessment was based largely on one statistic: The ratio of the population urbanized to the labor force employed in industry was far bigger in the Third World than in nineteenth-century Europe. His thesis encouraged the view that the pull of industrial employment in nineteenth-century cities was far stronger than it is now in the Third World, and that in the past rural push played a more modest role. Hoselitz thinks that Malthusian pressures and institutional changes on the land must be pushing labor into Third World cities at a far faster rate than in the past, and that problems of labor absorption must be swelling the size of the urban service sector. As we shall see later in this book, Michael Todaro (1969) picked up on this theme, arguing that city immigrants are attracted to the city by the expectation of getting the good industrial jobs, thus glutting the low-wage service sector while waiting for those jobs. Compared with past industrial revolutions, Hoselitz and Todaro think urbanization has outrun industrialization in the contemporary Third World.

The overurbanization debate has become more sophisticated since the 1950s, but Hoselitz was the first to reduce it to an explicit test: Did industrial employment support a larger share of city populations in England and the rest of nineteenth-century Europe than in Asia in the 1950s? Hoselitz found that it did, and there the debate appeared to rest. It was recently reopened, however, with the appearance of new evidence that augmented the data base to include all developing countries over a longer period (Preston, 1979; UN, 1980, pp. 17–19).

It seems to me that Hoselitz posed the wrong question. The evolution of technologies, public commitment to social overhead, and the structure of demand all guarantee that in the past developing cities had different employment patterns than they have now. Furthermore, because labor participation rates in English cities were higher (compared with the countryside) than they are now in contemporary Third World cities (Section 2.5), the ratio of the employment share industrial to the population share urban should have been higher in England on that score too. In any case, the relevant question is whether industry was a more effective engine of city employment growth in the nineteenth century. This issue cannot be resolved by comparing Hoselitz's statistic for 1850 England with 1950 India. However, it can be resolved by comparing changes in the Hoselitz statistic between 1850 and 1870 in England and between 1950 and 1970 in India. Does the Hoselitz statistic typically rise over time, thus implying a tendency toward overurbanization during industrial revolutions? Does English experience conform to the contemporary stylized facts, or was the First Industrial Revolution an outlier?[1]

Table 4.3 confirms Hoselitz's original finding that nineteenth-century European and contemporary Third World cities differed. His statistic is 2.01 in 1950 and only 1.00 in the mid nineteenth century. However, the table also shows that the drift in his statistic over time is remarkably similar for late nineteenth-century Europe, for England between 1750 and 1911, and for the Third World between 1950 and 1970. Each exhibits a modest rise over time in the ratio of the population urban to the labor force employed in industry, too modest to have caused alarm, and too similar to suggest support for Hoselitz's inference that rural push forces are more powerful today than they were in eighteenth- and nineteenth-century Europe. If there is a tendency for urbanization to outrun industrialization, it seems likely that it can be explained quite adequately by the demise of rural cottage and small-scale industries in response to urban-based factory competition in early stages of the industrial revolution, and by the rise of essential urban services in later stages. With regard to the

---

1 This discussion is marred by the difficulty of identifying rural-industrial workers, and in dealing with multiple occupations and part-time work. However, because the same data problems are inherent in 1850–70 Britain and 1950–70 India, one can only hope that there is no systematic bias that would interfere with the comparative assessment reported in the text.

Table 4.3. *Ratio of percentage urban to percentage of labor force in industry: The Third World, late nineteenth-century Europe, and England 1750 to 1911 compared*

A. Third World	1950	1970	1970/1950
Africa			
East Africa	1.50	1.69	1.13
Middle Africa	2.48	2.64	1.06
Northern Africa	2.35	2.32	0.99
Southern Africa	1.52	1.66	1.09
Western Africa	1.66	1.53	0.92
Latin America			
Caribbean	1.99	2.14	1.08
Middle America	2.48	2.52	1.02
Temperate South America	2.09	2.50	1.20
Tropical South America	2.24	2.86	1.28
Asia			
East Asia	2.15	1.87	0.87
East South Asia	2.07	1.99	0.96
Middle South Asia	1.91	1.49	0.78
West South Asia	1.74	2.42	1.39
Unweighted average	2.01	2.13	1.06

B. Late 19th Century Europe	Beginning year (B)	End year (E)	E/B (standardized to two decades)
France, 1856/60–1910/11	1.05	1.32	1.10
Sweden, 1870–1910	1.24	0.82	0.83
Denmark, 1870–1910	0.99	1.48	1.20
Italy, 1871–1911	1.01	1.18	1.08
Prussia, 1880/82–1905/7	1.09	1.21	1.09
U.S., 1840–1910	0.68	1.34	1.28
Netherlands, 1850–1910	1.24	1.35	1.03
Austria-Hungary, 1880–1910	0.75	1.09	1.30
Norway, 1880–1910	0.87	0.90	1.02
Belgium, 1850–1910	1.03	1.14	1.04
Unweighted average	1.00	1.18	1.18

C. England			
1750–1811	1.01	1.21	1.06
1811–1851	1.21	1.26	1.02
1851–1911	1.26	1.70	1.12

Sources: Panel A: UN, 1980, Table 9, p 18. Panel B: The industrial employment shares are computed from Mitchell, 1978, pp. 51–63; the urbanization figures are from Bairoch and Goertz, 1986, Table 3, p. 288; Berry and Horton, 1970, p. 75; del Panta, 1979, p. 231; Matzerath, 1981, p. 174; U.S. Department of Commerce, 1975, Series A 57–72, pp. 11–12 and Series D 167–81, p. 139. Panel C: Table 4.4.

Table 4.4. *Percentage population urban and percentage employment industrial: England, 1750 to 1911*

Year	(1) Percentage population urban	(2) Percentage employment industrial	(3) (1)/(2)
1750	24.1	23.8	1.01
1801	33.8	29.7	1.14
1811	36.6	30.2	1.21
1821	40.0	38.4	1.04
1831	44.3	40.8	1.09
1841	48.3	40.5	1.19
1851	54.0	42.9	1.26
1861	58.7	43.6	1.35
1871	65.2	43.1	1.51
1881	70.0	43.5	1.61
1891	74.5	43.9	1.70
1901	78.0	46.3	1.68
1911	78.9	46.4	1.70

Source: Col. (1): England: 1750 from Law, 1972, Table 1, p. 18; 1801–1911 from Law, 1967, Table XI, p. 141. Col. (2): 1750, England and Wales, from Lindert and Williamson, 1982, Table 3, pp. 396–7 (manufacturing, building, and mining); 1801–1911, Britain, from Deane and Cole, 1962, Table 30, p. 142 (manufacturing, mining, and industry).

former, because the replacement of rural industry by urban factories obviously fosters urbanization, the same is not necessarily true of industrialization, so Hoselitz's statistic is likely to rise on those grounds. And there is certainly a long historical tradition which stresses that replacement. In Alec Cairncross's words: "the competitive power of large-scale, urban enterprise . . . brought about the displacement of rural crafts and small country industries . . . The displaced labour in the countryside, ousted by urban or American competition, found a cure for unemployment by moving to the towns and to America" (Cairncross, 1949, p. 76).

The evidence does not support the thesis that urbanization outruns industrialization in any dramatic way, and the First Industrial Revolution tightly conforms to that general finding. Although the summary in Table 4.3 (Panel C) shows that quite clearly for England 1750–1851, Table 4.4 offers more detail. During the impressive growth spurt after Waterloo, industrialization was clearly the force driving urbanization: Hoselitz's statistic actually falls from 1811 to 1841, implying that industrial employment shares were rising faster than urban shares. There is certainly no evidence of overurbanization here. Table 4.4 also shows that the sources of urbanization varied over time. Between 1750 and 1811, "industry" was not the most important source of city employment growth, because English manufactures were excluded from European markets for a good portion of the period. And as P. J. Cain and A. G. Hopkins (1987) have recently reminded us, in the late nineteenth century urban services were booming while British manufacturing was struggling with retardation. Table 4.4 confirms this view: from 1841 to 1891, Hoselitz's statistic rises as England enters a new regime of urbanization in which city growth is now being driven by the rapid expansion in the derived demand for labor in urban services.

4.3   The sources of nonfarm labor demand

A simple model for the epoch 1821–61

Figure 4.1A and 4.1B offer a simple characterization of the nonagricultural labor market, which will help organize our discussion for the remainder of the chapter. In both cases, total nonagricultural employment (manufacturing, services, and mining) appears on the horizontal axis, and according to Deane and Cole (1962, Table 31, p. 143) it grew at 1.75 percent per year between 1821 and 1861. The real wage facing nonagricultural firms (not to be confused with workers' living standards) is on the vertical axis, and it grew at .91 percent per year over roughly the same period.[2]

The two figures offer two different views of migration. Figure 4.1A supposes that all immigration into nonagriculture was attributable to the pull of wages and employment conditions there. Thus, the labor supply curves are taken to be very elastic, reflecting a powerful response of potential immigrants to rising wages in nonagriculture. Labor supply shifts rightward in response to the natural increase forces underlying

2 Between 1819 and 1861, the nominal wage for the urban unskilled grew very slowly, .14 percent per year (Williamson, 1985a, Tables 2.4 and 2.11, pp. 12, 29, "nonfarm common labor"). The price of nonagricultural output, however, declined at the rate of .77 percent per year, a weighted average of manufacturing, mining, and services (prices taken from Williamson, 1985a, Table 9.2, pp. 130–33 and Appendix Table E.1, p. 247; output weights taken from Williamson, 1985a, Tables D.2 and D.5, pp. 240 and 244, an average of 1821 and 1861). Thus, the real wage facing nonagricultural firms grew at $[.14 - (-.77)] = .91$.

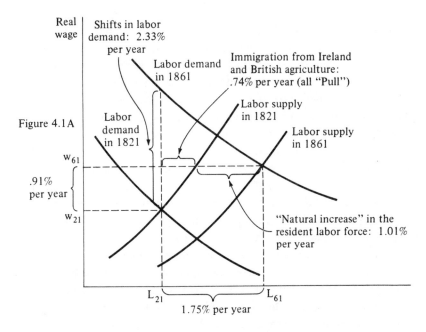

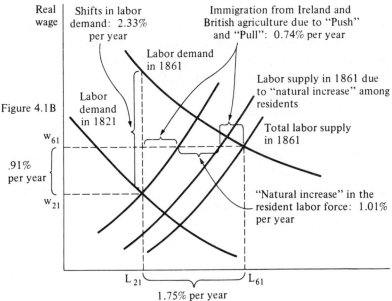

Figure 4.1 The nonagricultural labor market, 1821–61

demographic behavior of the resident labor force. In equilibrium, the incremental labor supply matching the observed employment growth comes from two sources, the natural increase in the resident non-agricultural labor force and immigration which is pulled into nonagri-culture by booming labor demand conditions. Table 4.1 suggests that the former contributed 1.01 percent per year to the annual employment growth and immigration contributed .74 percent per year (.53 percent per year due to immigration from British agriculture and .21 percent per year due to immigration from Ireland).

Figure 4.1B supposes instead that immigration into nonagriculture was attributed to the combined effects of the pull of nonagricultural wages and the push of conditions in Ireland and British agriculture. Here, that .74 percent per year due to immigration has two sources, push and pull. Otherwise, the story is much like Figure 4.1A.

These two figures make it clear that there were four forces at work that influenced immigrant absorption and wages in this labor market. These were: (1) the shift in labor supplies generated by the combined effects of demographic forces in the nonagricultural sector and all push forces in Ireland and in British agriculture; (2) the elasticity of labor supply condi-tioned primarily by potential migrants' response to employment condi-tions in nonagriculture; (3) the elasticity of nonagricultural labor demand; and (4) shifts in nonagricultural labor demand over time. The latter two forces are familiar to development economists who worry about the immi-grant labor absorption potential of Third World cities.

Immigrant labor-absorption problems: The elasticity of labor demand

Development economists have always stressed a technological asymmetry between modern and traditional sectors. They view the modern sector (usually manufacturing) as capital-intensive where the elasticity of substi-tution between capital and labor is low. In contrast, they view the tradi-tional sector (usually agriculture) as labor-intensive where the elasticity of substitution is high.[3] These conditions imply that the elasticity of demand

---

3 One of the earliest statements of the problem in two sectors can be found in the classic article by Eckaus (1955), but these factor-intensity and substitution elastic-ity characterizations are now standard in both development theory and empirical analysis.

for labor in the modern sector is low, conditions that make the absorption of immigrant labor difficult because it takes a big drop in wages to encourage firms to expand employment by very much. The elasticity of labor demand will be even lower if the price elasticity of product demand is low, a condition typical of many Third World economies that, by hiding behind protective policies, are relatively close to trade.

The Third World evidence appears to support this view of limited substitution, low price elasticities of output demand, high capital intensity, and thus of inelastic labor demand (Chenery and Raduchel, 1971; Kelley and Williamson, 1984, chp. 2). The same does not seem to have been true of England in the first half of the nineteenth century. England was open to trade in manufactures, and the volume of that trade was large and expanding, especially after Peel's 1842 Act and Repeal in 1846. Thus, elasticities of output demand for most nonagricultural products were fairly high. Furthermore, capital-labor choices were not constrained in the same way that the transfer of capital-intensive technologies from industrialized countries often constrains labor-intensive choices in the Third World. In short, there is reason to believe that the elasticity of demand for labor in Britain was quite a bit higher off the farm than in the contemporary Third World.

But can we be more precise? How elastic was the nonagricultural demand for immigrant labor in Britain around 1841? The historical data are not adequate, of course, to supply exact estimates, but it might help to examine the elasticities implied by the general equilibrium model in Chapters 6 and 7. These rough estimates should at least be adequate to test the hypothesis that labor demand off the farm was relatively elastic in 1841.

Table 4.5 (column 1) reports the full general equilibrium impact on the real wage from a 1 percent change in the nonagricultural labor force.[4] Clearly, the more pronounced the decline in the real wage in the face of an immigrant-augmented labor force, the greater the immigrant-absorption problem in nonagriculture. A small decline in the real wage implies that the nonagricultural economy was better able to absorb the emigrants leaving British agriculture and Ireland. Table 4.5 also reports the elasticity of labor demand in response to a real wage change (column 2): according to these

4 Fuller details of the calculation can be found in Williamson, 1986b, pp. 713–14. However, the results reported in Table 7 of that paper differ slightly from those reported here in Table 4.5. The reason is that here we focus on nonagriculture and there we considered the British economy as a whole.

Table 4.5. *The elasticity of labor demand in nonagriculture*

Observation	(1) Elasticity of the real wage with respect to labor force growth	(2) Elasticity of labor demand with respect to the real wage
A. British nonagriculture, c1841	−0.64	−1.57
B. Manufacturing in industrial economies, 1960s and 1970s	−0.39 to −5.56	−0.18 to −2.59
C. United States, 1970	−0.22	−4.55

Sources and notes: See text and Williamson, 1986b, pp. 712–14 for the British estimates in row A. These refer to unskilled labor. Row B is taken from a survey by Hammermesh and Grant (1979) while row C is taken from an assessment of contemporary U.S. immigrant absorption in Grossman (1982). These refer to total labor (skilled and unskilled).

estimates, that demand elasticity was quite high in Britain around 1841, about 1.6. Although this must be viewed as a long-run elasticity – the economy is given all the time it needs to rearrange resources within sectors and between them, it may still seem high. After all, Cormac Ó Grada (1984) finds an elasticity of about .6 for British cotton textiles between 1835 and 1856. Indeed, even under the optimistic assumption of Cobb-Douglas technologies – in which the scope for substitution between capital and labor is quite large – the elasticity of demand for labor cannot exceed unity within any sector. That statement certainly holds for one sector, like agriculture, but it need not hold for a nonagricultural economy with many sectors. In the latter case, the demand for labor can be affected indirectly by the substitution between various outputs. Cheap labor will encourage the expansion of labor-intensive sectors, thus increasing the ability of the nonagricultural economy as a whole to absorb an immigrant-augmented labor force. So it was in Britain during the industrial revolution, and so it is in our model. In any case, these elasticities are hardly unusual even by the standards of industrial economies in the mid twentieth century. Jean Grossman (1982) has found the real wage impact of immigrant labor supply to be even smaller for contemporary America (about −.2) than we estimate for early nineteenth-century Britain (about −.6). The survey by Daniel Hammermesh and James Grant (1979) reports a range of own-wage elasticities which brackets the estimate for Britain reported in Table 4.5. Indeed, the mid-point in their range of estimates is −1.39, not very different than our British estimate of −1.57.

*Immigrant labor-absorption problems: Measuring shifts in
labor demand*

The relative rise in nonagricultural employment is driven primarily by
lagging employment demand growth in agriculture. I say "primarily" because if emigration from agriculture is sluggish, wage gaps between city
and countryside will widen, and city employment will be choked off by
increased labor scarcity, a topic explored at length in Chapter 7. If we
ignore that possibility for the present, then it follows that the relative rise
in nonagricultural employment is determined solely by the degree to
which nonagricultural employment demand growth outpaces that of agriculture.

Suppose we write the demand for nonagricultural (U) and agricultural
(R) labor as

$$D_u = A_u w_u^{\epsilon u}$$

$$D_R = A_R w_R^{\epsilon R}$$

where w is the real wage. Because our interest is in employment growth
over time, it will prove useful to convert these two labor demand functions
into rates of change:

$$\overset{*}{D}_u = \overset{*}{A}_u + \epsilon_u \overset{*}{w}_u = \overset{*}{L}_u$$

$$\overset{*}{D}_R = \overset{*}{A}_R + \epsilon_R \overset{*}{w}_R = \overset{*}{L}_R$$

where the $\overset{*}{A}_j$ capture shifts in labor demand. Deane and Cole (1962, p.
143) document employment growth in agriculture and nonagriculture
1821 to 1861 to have been .26 and 1.75 percent per year, the latter
exceeding the former by 1.49 percent. Over the same period, real wages
that employers had to pay for nonfarm work grew much faster than they
did on the farm, .91 versus .21 percent per year. Given estimates of the
elasticity of labor demand in the two sectors, the shifts in labor demand
between 1821 and 1861 can be identified, that is $\overset{*}{A}_j = \overset{*}{L}_j - \epsilon_{j\overset{*}{w}j}$.

Table 4.6 reports a range of sectoral labor-demand estimates, from one
based on a low elasticity, $-.4$, to a higher one that we favor, -1.6. It
appears that nonagricultural employment demand shifted to the right at
something like 1.5 or 2.9 percent per year faster than did agricultural

Table 4.6. *Measuring unbalanced labor-demand growth, 1821 to 1861: Nonagriculture less agriculture (percentage per annum)*

Assumed elastic-ity of demand in nonagriculture: ϵ_U	Assumed elasticity of demand in agriculture: ϵ_R				
	-0.4	-0.8	-1.0	-1.2	-1.6
-0.4	1.77	1.69	1.64	1.60	1.52
-0.8	2.13	2.05	2.01	1.97	1.82
-1.0	2.32	2.23	2.19	2.15	2.06
-1.2	2.50	2.41	2.37	2.33	2.25
-1.6	2.86	2.78	2.74	2.69	2.61

Sources: See text and footnote 1 in this chapter. The table is calculated from the expression
$$\overset{*}{A}_R = \overset{*}{L}_R - \epsilon_R \overset{*}{w}_R \text{ and } \overset{*}{A}_U = \overset{*}{L}_U - \epsilon_U \overset{*}{w}_U$$
where the $\overset{*}{A}_i$ measure per annum rates of labor demand growth in agriculture (R) and non-agriculture (U). The table reports the matrix for various $[\overset{*}{A}_U - \overset{*}{A}_R]$ estimates conditional on ϵ_i. As the text indicates: $\overset{*}{L}_R = 0.26$ and $\overset{*}{L}_U = 1.75$ between 1821 and 1861; and $\overset{*}{w}_R = 0.21$ and $\overset{*}{w}_U = 0.91$ between 1819/1821 and 1861. The underlying $\overset{*}{A}_i$ estimates are:

$\hat{\epsilon}_i$	$\overset{*}{A}_R$	$\overset{*}{A}_U$
-0.4	.344	2.114
-0.8	.428	2.478
-1.0	.470	2.660
-1.2	.512	2.842
-1.6	.596	3.206

employment demand, an impressive differential indeed. Furthermore, because agricultural labor demand grew so slowly over the three decades (see Sources to Table 4.6), the vast majority of this unbalanced growth in labor demand was attributable to growth in nonagriculture itself.

Immigrant labor-absorption problems: Sources of shifts in labor demand

Shifts in labor demand over time are driven by four forces. In discussing these, I will invoke poetic license and talk in terms of manufacturing, although it should be clear by now that mining and services both played an important role in driving nonagricultural employment growth during the First Industrial Revolution.

First, there are output prices (that is, output demand) and input prices to consider. If world market conditions tend to raise the relative price of manufactures or lower the relative price of intermediate inputs, manufacturing will boom, the derived demand for labor will shift outward to the right, and immigrants will be absorbed by this rapid rate of job creation. Between 1821 and 1861, however, just the opposite took place. Instead, the terms of trade moved against manufacturing. In cotton textiles, for example, the terms of trade fell by more than 30 percent over the three decades following 1821.[5] It has long been argued by economic historians that a good share of that fall in the terms of trade was due to rapid technological advance in British textiles. A plausible argument can be made, however, that other world market conditions were also helping drive down the relative price of British manufactures after the French wars (Williamson, 1987, p. 279). First, there is the rapid expansion of competitive foreign supplies to consider. Between 1820 and 1860, Britain's share in world trade among France, Germany, Italy, the United States, and Britain declined from 27 to 25 percent, and Britain's share in industrial production also declined, from 24 to 21 percent (Capie, 1983, pp. 5–6). This extraordinary expansion of industrial production among Britain's competitors served to glut world markets and drive down the relative price of manufactures. Second, the rise in European protectionism on the Continent must also have weakened Britain's terms of trade. Thus, to the extent that some of those price trends were attributable to world market conditions exogenous to Britain, then they must have choked off the demand for labor and held back rightward shifts in labor demand.

Second, there is capital accumulation to consider. Capital accumulation in manufacturing, *ceteris paribus*, clearly served to augment capacity, create jobs and shift labor demand to the right. Although the rate of capital deepening (an increase in capital per worker) was very slow in the British economy during the industrial revolution, the rate of capital widening (an increase in employment at fixed capital per worker) was much more impressive. According to Charles Feinstein's new estimates (1988, Appendix Table XI, p. 448, gross fixed reproducible capital in constant prices), the nonagricultural capital stock grew at 2.65 percent per year between 1830 and 1860.

Third, total factor-productivity growth in manufacturing should have augmented labor demand there. For an open economy like Britain, where output demands were fairly price elastic and where manufactures could

5 The gray cloth export price index is taken from Sanberg (1968, pp. 8 and 10) and the cotton price index is taken from Mitchell and Deane (1962, p. 491). The ratio of the former to the latter declines from 100 in 1821 to 69.6 in 1851.

be vented on to foreign markets, rapid total factor productivity growth surely played an important role in fostering the expansion of that sector, thus causing the demand for labor to shift out to the right. Productivity advance (and acreage expansion) in agriculture had the opposite effect.

Marx made the claim in Chapter XXV of *Capital* that capitalist development is uneven across sectors, and that unbalanced technological advance tends to breed an increasing concentration of production and employment in the nonagricultural sectors. What limited evidence we have on sectoral rates of total factor-productivity growth seems to confirm the premise of unbalanced rates of total factor-productivity growth favoring modern nonagricultural sectors during industrial revolutions. It is certainly consistent with nineteenth-century United States evidence (Williamson and Lindert, 1980, chp. 7), and it seems to be consistent with Third World data as well (Kelley and Williamson, 1984, App. C; Chenery, Robinson, and Syrquin, 1986, chp. 8). Donald McCloskey (1981, Table 6.2, p. 114) has argued that the evidence, such as it is, supports the view for Britain between 1780 and 1860, in which productivity growth rates are estimated to have been 1.8 percent per year in industry and transport, much higher than in agriculture, .45 percent per year. I agree with McCloskey's characterization (Williamson, 1985a, p. 247), although lack of hard evidence has certainly kept the debate alive.[6]

Fourth, there is the possibility of labor-saving to consider. Ever since Marx started us thinking about labor displacement and the reserve army, labor-saving has become entrenched in the lexicon of growth theorists, economic historians, and development economists. Yet, surprisingly little has been done by economic historians to isolate its impact on the derived demand for labor during the British industrial revolution. Certainly there have been many anecdotal accounts of how certain craftsmen were displaced by modern technology (e.g. the handloom weavers), but a comprehensive assessment of the impact of these disequilibrating technological forces has yet to be made. True, Ephraim Asher (1972) found evidence of labor-saving in cotton textiles from 1820 to 1880, but others have met with less success (Phillips, 1982, p. 102). Indeed, G. N. von Tunzlemann (1981, p. 158) finds no evidence to support the labor-saving hypothesis: "Labour-intensive technical changes must have been about as powerful as labour-saving ones in their effects, so that up to about 1830 the direction

6. N. F. R. Crafts disagrees. See the exchange between the two of us (Crafts, 1987; Williamson, 1987). Joel Mokyr (1987) has argued that the evidence is simply inadequate to support either view.

Table 4.7. *Estimating the sources of shifts in unskilled nonagricultural labor demand, 1821 to 1861*

Source	Per annum shift in labor demand (%)
Total shift	+2.33
Shift due to:	
Productivity change in nonagriculture	+2.24
Change world market conditions	−1.78
Economy-wide capital accumulation	+1.08
Economy-wide skills accumulation	+1.04
Productivity and acreage changes in agriculture	−0.29
Other	+0.04

Sources and notes: See text and the discussion in Williamson, 1986b, pp. 712–14.

of technical change was neutral." If this characterization were supported by future research, Britain would contrast sharply with America after 1820 (David, 1975, chp. 1; Williamson and Lindert, 1980, chp. 7) and certainly with the Third World where labor saving is generally agreed to have been pronounced (Morawetz, 1974; Cline, 1975; Kelley and Williamson, 1984, chps. 4–6). The jury is still out on labor-saving during the First Industrial Revolution.

Table 4.7 uses the model underlying Chapters 6 and 7 to estimate the total shift in the demand for nonagricultural unskilled labor from 1821 to 1861. It also decomposes the total shift into the component parts discussed above. The reader should be warned that these calculations are crude approximations only. Furthermore, Tables 4.6 and 4.7 are not quite comparable because Table 4.7 deals with unskilled labor and Table 4.6 deals with all labor. However, Table 4.7's estimates of labor-demand shifts, 2.33 percent per year, does fall about in the middle of the range of estimates offered in Table 4.6, about 1.5 to 2.9 percent per year.

The message emerging from Table 4.7 is certainly worth stressing. The demand for unskilled nonagricultural labor was shifting rightward over these four decades at about 2.3 percent per year. This buoyant labor-demand growth was driven in large part by unbalanced productivity change favoring nonagriculture at agriculture's expense (2.24 − .29 = 1.95). Although capital and skills accumulation mattered about as much (1.08 + 1.04 = 2.12), deteriorating world market conditions served as an important offset (−1.78).

4.4   The bottom line

While Britain was burdened with an unbalanced labor supply, high natural rates of labor-force growth in the countryside and low rates in the cities, demand in the cities was favorable enough so that excess supply in the countryside could have been absorbed fairly easily, at least in the long run. That is, the long-run elasticity of demand for nonagricultural labor appears to have been high and the demand for nonagricultural labor was shifting to the right at a fast clip. Stating that Britain's cities could absorb those rural labor surpluses fairly easily in the long run is quite different from stating that her cities absorbed those labor surpluses in the short run without a hitch.

So, two questions remain. Were those excess labor supplies in the British and Irish countryside so big that even the favorable city labor demands were overwhelmed in the short run? Did nonagricultural labor markets accommodate the influx of immigrants only slowly, causing serious problems of absorption in the short run and medium term?

Appendix 4.1. Estimating emigration from agriculture and immigration into nonagriculture, 1781–1861

Table 4.1 in the text repairs Pollard's (1978) estimates of emigration from British agriculture following 1781. Pollard assumed that natural rates of increase were the same in agriculture and nonagriculture. Chapter 2 used the Registrar General's *Annual Reports* to construct crude birth rates, crude death rates, and crude rates of natural increase for urban and rural England around 1841. We repair Pollard's calculations by assuming instead that these natural increase differentials in the late 1830s and early 1840s applied to the eight decades 1781–1861.

Define the following terms:

$$T = \text{total labor force}$$
$$A = \text{agricultural labor force}$$
$$NA = \text{nonagricultural labor force}$$
$$M^I = \text{change in the Irish workforce ("migrants"), all urban}$$
$$a = A/T = \text{share of the labor force in agriculture}$$

then the per annum rate of growth in the total labor force can be decomposed into the following parts:

$$\overset{*}{T}_t = z_t(.00624) (1 - a_t) + z_t(.01012) (a_t) + M^I_t/T_t$$

which is simply a weighted average of natural rates of population increase (the smaller figure for England's "principal cities and towns" and the larger figure for rural England: *Parliamentary Papers*, 1847–8 (25) and 1849 (21) adjusted by Wrigley and Schofield's (1981, p. 636) undercount ratio), adjusted by a factor z_t which reflects any drift in the labor-participation rate over time, to which is added the impact of the Irish. Because we know $\overset{*}{T}_t$ and a_t (Deane and Cole, 1962, p. 143; Pollard, 1978, p. 141), and because we know M^I_t/T_t (Table 6.6), we can solve for the z_t as

$$z_t = [\overset{*}{T}_t - M^I_t/T_t]/[(.00624) + (.00388)a_t].$$

With these estimates of z_t in hand, it is a simple matter to compute estimates of the natural rates of labor force growth as

$$z_t(.00624) = \text{natural rate of labor-force growth in nonagriculture}$$
$$z_t(.01012) = \text{natural rate of labor-force growth in agriculture}$$

These rates can then be used to compute counterfactual rates of labor-force growth in both sectors (that is, in the absence of migration), which, when compared with the reported labor-force figures, yields migration as a residual.

5. Absorbing the city immigrants

5.1 How did city labor markets work? The Todaro model

Debate over Third World urbanization generates the same gloomy pessimism that characterized Britain in the early nineteenth century. Even the rhetoric is the same, Victorian and modern critics both citing urban underemployment, primitive housing, inadequate public services, poverty, and inequality (Williamson, 1988). As we have seen, many modern analysts view the Third World as "overurbanized," a position shared by many Victorian reformers in nineteenth-century England. According to this view, the cities are too large and too many, and they got that way somehow through perverse migration behavior. Pushed off the land by technological events in agriculture, by famine, and by Malthusian pressure, rural emigrants flood the cities in far greater numbers than modern-sector jobs can be created for them. Attracted by an irrational optimism that they will be selected for those scarce high-wage city jobs, the rural emigrants keep coming. Lacking high-wage jobs in the growing modern sectors, the glut of rural immigrants spills over into low-wage service sectors, unemployment, and pauperism, while their families crowd into inadequate housing blighting an otherwise dynamic city economy. The cities find it difficult to cope with the immigrant influx, and authorities look for ways to close the cities to new immigrants.

By focusing on expected rather than current earnings differentials, Michael Todaro (1969) developed a framework that could account for the apparent irrationality of rural immigrants rushing to the city even in the face of unemployment and underemployment. The Todaro framework and its extensions (Harris and Todaro, 1970; Stiglitz, 1974; Corden and Findlay, 1975; Cole and Sanders, 1985; Hatton and Williamson, 1989) has enjoyed considerable popularity over the past decade or so.

The hypothesis is simple and elegant. Although similar statements can be found sprinkled through the development literature, the most effective illustration can be found in Max Corden and Ronald Findlay (1975),

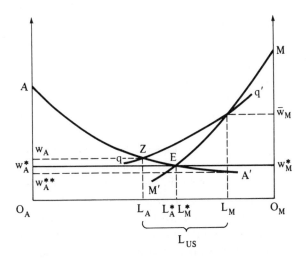

Figure 5.1   The Todaro-Corden-Findlay model

reproduced in Figure 5.1. There are only two sectors analyzed in Figure 5.1, but they are sufficient to illustrate the point. Under the extreme assumption of wage equalization through migration, and in the absence of wage rigidities, equilibrium is achieved at E (the point of intersection of the two labor-demand curves, AA' and MM'). Here wages are equalized at $w_A^* = w_M^*$, the urbanization level is $O_M L_M^*/L$ (the share of the total labor force, L, employed in urban jobs, $O_M L_M^*$), where M denotes urban manufacturing and A denotes agriculture. Because wages were never equalized in nineteenth-century Britain, and because they are not equalized in the contemporary Third World either, the Todaro model incorporates the widely held belief that the wage rate in manufacturing is pegged at artificially high levels by unions, by minimum wage legislation, by private-sector emulation of inflated public-sector wage rates, or by employers' efforts to minimize turnover, say at $\bar{w}_M$. If, for the moment, we assume away unemployment, then all those who fail to secure the favored jobs in manufacturing would be forced to accept low-wage jobs in agriculture at w_A^{**}. Although this exposition of the model has yet to accommodate Todaro's emphasis on urban unemployment, this incomplete version at least allows for a wage gap between the two sectors, a gap of which so much has been made in both British economic history and the Third World (Chapter 7).

Under the assumptions made thus far, Figure 5.1 makes it clear that the level of employment in the urban sector would be choked off by the high wage in manufacturing, but would city immigration also be forestalled? As Chapter 2 pointed out, rates of city growth have been dramatic in the Third World. Furthermore, there has been an expansion in what have been called informal urban services in which, it is alleged, low-wage underemployment prevails. Todaro explains this apparent conflict (that is, immigration in the face of urban unemployment or underemployment at very low wages) by developing an expectations hypothesis which, in its simplest form, states that the favored jobs are allocated by lottery, that the potential migrant calculates the expected value of that lottery ticket, and compares it with the certain employment in the rural sector. Migration then takes place until the urban expected wage is equated to the rural wage. Given $\bar{w}_M$, and a wage in traditional urban services so low that it can be ignored, at what rural wage would the migrant be indifferent between city and countryside? If the probability of getting the favored job is simply the ratio of manufacturing employment to the total urban labor force, then the expression

$$w_A = (L_M/L_U)\bar{w}_M$$

indicates the agricultural wage at which the potential migrant is indifferent to employment locations. This is in fact the qq' curve in Figure 5.1. The equilibrium agricultural wage is now given by w_A, and those underemployed or unemployed in the city (e.g., the size of the informal service sector plus those without any work at all) is thus given by L_{US}.[1]

The new equilibrium at Z in Figure 5.1 seems to offer an attractive explanation for the stylized facts of Third World labor markets. It yields a wage gap, $\bar{w}_M - w_A$, and urban low-wage employment or unemployment, L_{US}. Moreover, when the dynamic implications of the model are explored, it turns out that an increase in the rate of manufacturing job creation need not cause any diminution in the size of the low-wage informal service sector. Indeed, in Todaro's words (1969, p. 147) "as long as the urban-rural [wage gap] continues to rise sufficiently fast to offset any sustained increase in the rate of job creation, then . . . the lure of relatively high

---

1 The qq' curve is a rectangular hyperbola with unitary elasticity. The elasticity of the labor demand curve MM' is assumed to be less than unity in Figure 5.1. Although this assumption is commonly invoked by development economists, Chapter 4 has argued that it was considerably more elastic in Britain in the first half of the nineteenth century.

permanent incomes will continue to attract a steady stream of rural migrants into the ever more congested urban slums."

As we shall see in Chapter 7, a rise in the wage gap can be documented in many parts of the Third World and it was an attribute of British industrialization after the French wars.

The model makes some bold assertions about how urban labor markets operate and how immigrants are absorbed into those markets. First, it asserts that immigrants earn lower incomes than nonimmigrants, the latter having first claim on the favored jobs. That is, migrants should tend to cluster in low-wage informal service sectors and have higher unemployment rates. Second, it asserts that immigrants earn less in the cities when they first arrive, suffering high underemployment and unemployment rates, than they earned in the rural areas they left. Third, it implies that those immigrants who stay in the city and do not return discouraged to rural areas exhibit far steeper age-earnings curves than the nonmigrants. After all, they are initially unemployed or enter the low-wage urban service sector before getting absorbed by the high-wage modern sectors. Central to the model, therefore, are assertions about migrant experience with unemployment and underemployment.

5.2   Absorbing city immigrants in nineteenth-century Britain

It may seem odd to have begun a chapter on immigrant absorption problems in British cities during the First Industrial Revolution by turning first to the Third World literature, but there are three good reasons for doing so. First, there appear to be striking similarities between the two cases. Second, the Third World debate may help give a sharper focus to any study of the operation of urban labor markets in earlier epochs in which the evidence is weaker and the issues are less well defined. Third, because there have been few efforts to assess the immigrant absorptive capacity of British cities during the First Industrial Revolution, the Todaro model might be a useful way to organize that assessment.[2] Indeed,

---

2 There is no shortage of local studies and social histories of city migrant experience during the First Industrial Revolution. Apart from the classic accounts by Mayhew, Rowntree and Booth, there are excellent recent monographs like Lees' *Exiles of Erin* (1979) and Anderson's *Family Structure in Nineteenth Century Lancashire* (1971).

Sidney Pollard (1981, pp. 902–3) has already used the Todaro model to characterize British nineteenth-century urban labor markets:

> numerous studies have shown that people move, not so much for better-paid jobs, but for jobs . . . Indeed, many migrants did not even come for jobs, but for the expected opportunity of finding jobs . . . the millions of migrants keep flocking in although . . . the chance of a job is small. Once the workers settled, the costs of moving again and the ignorance of conditions elsewhere inhibited . . . further . . . adjustment.

The testable hypotheses embedded in Pollard's statement are numerous, and many of them reappear in the development literature cited above. First, people moved in response to job vacancies, not simply to a higher-wage environment. Thus, city unemployment rates and the length of the job queue must have been a critical determinant of migration behavior. Second, migrants were motivated by expected earnings. Because expectations mattered at least as much as actual job availabilities, a significant share of the city immigrants must have suffered long unemployment spells, pauperism, and low earnings before those high-wage employment expectations were fulfilled. Third, migrants flocked to Britain's cities even though the chances of finding a good job were often slim. It follows that they must have left behind jobs with greater short-run earnings potential. Fourth, once settled, rural-urban migrants found it difficult to move on to other cities where employment opportunities may have appeared much better. Thus, urban-to-urban migration must have been a small share of total migration, implying that urban labor markets in Britain were poorly linked.

Pollard (1981, p. 902) goes on to stress these poor regional labor market linkages, an aspect of British labor markets which has long been a tradition in the literature from Ravenstein (1885, 1889), to Redford (1926), and to Hunt (1973):

> Labor markets in the 1840s . . . were regional; between regions wage levels in given occupations varied randomly, according to industrial demand, the power of trade unions, traditions, and many other factors . . . Workers from the southern half of Britain, if they wanted to move, did not move to the industrial towns at all, . . . but went to London or the colonies. In the north, they tended to go to the nearest town, as Redford showed long ago for England as a whole . . . They therefore did not choose the best bargain but the town that was accessible . . .

Thus, we can add another hypothesis to our list; namely, that urban labor markets were regional and only weakly linked at best. Rather, wages were

set independently by local demand forces. Migration was simply insufficient to force any city to respond to the discipline of national labor markets. The costs of migration and ignorance of employment opportunities
tended to create regionally segmented labor markets.

Pollard is not alone in adopting language that would sound familiar to
the development economist. In their massive volume *British Economic
Growth 1856–1973*, R. C. O. Matthews, Charles Feinstein, and J. C.
Odling-Smee offer views about the operation of urban labor markets in
nineteenth-century Britain, which stress what development economists
have come to call informal urban service-sector employment, but what
British historians call low-wage casual labor:

> There is fairly abundant qualitative evidence that . . . there was a
> chronic surplus of unskilled labor . . . The chronic labor surplus was not
> of the Keynesian type. It more resembled that found in underdeveloped
> countries . . . The classic examples of unemployment and underemploy-
> ment associated with casual working were in the docks and in the build-
> ing trades . . . The surplus labor crowded into occupations where there
> was a chance of *some* employment . . . and the urban surplus continued
> to be replenished by the immigration of rural surplus labor. (Matthews,
> et al., 1982, pp. 82–3)

Certainly Mayhew (1861) made much of London's informal services, and
low-wage casual labor, sweatshops and street vending all have played an
important part in nineteenth-century labor histories since (for example,
Jones, 1971; Green, 1982). But while Todaro stresses the role of the
urban service sector as a holding area for the reserve army of immigrants
who have been pulled into the city in anticipation of getting those high-
wage modern sector jobs, Mayhew's London street people seem instead
to have been pushed into those low-wage jobs (the residuum: Dendy,
1983):

> According to Mayhew [1861, vol. 1, pp. 320–3; vol. 2, p. 5], three
> groups of people became street traders: those who were bred to the
> streets; those who took to them for love of the wandering life; and those
> who were driven there . . . it was this latter group which provided the
> recruits for an "extraordinary increase" in the late 1840s of street trad-
> ers in London. (Green, 1982, p. 133)

Whether one supports Todaro's pull view or Mayhew's push view of city
immigration, both predict an additional hypothesis, perhaps the most
important: City immigrants must have had lower earnings than nonimmigrants. Furthermore, because successful immigrants eventually moved up

the occupational ladder from low-paying jobs (low relative to city natives) into the higher paying jobs, city immigrants must have had steeper age-earnings profiles than nonimmigrants, especially if discouraged and unsuccessful immigrants tended to return to their rural parishes. Thus, these views seem to predict that urban labor markets were selective, favoring nonimmigrants, but that as time wore on, and as the new immigrants gained more experience, city immigrants who stayed "caught up" with the nonimmigrants.[3]

Finally, the literature has made much of the fact that rural labor markets were regionally segmented. To quote Pollard again (1978, pp. 103–4):

> It is well known that there was nothing like a single national labor market at the beginning [of the British industrial revolution].
>
> Labour mobility . . . far from wiping out . . . economic differentials – as it ought to have done in a proper labour market – tended still further to confirm them.

This view has important implications for the earnings experience of city immigrants by source. The Irish may have gone into low-wage jobs partly because their reservation wage back in Ireland was so low. The English rural immigrant into Britain's cities may, in contrast, have had a higher reservation wage since they could fall back on generous poor relief in their rural parish, an option unavailable to the Irish. The English urban-to-urban migrant, on the other hand, might have had an even higher reservation wage given his greater familiarity with labor market conditions elsewhere.

This chapter attempts to test these hypotheses using admittedly very imperfect data drawn from the 1851 census. Section 5.3 will discuss how

---

3 The ability of new immigrants to "catch up" and to overcome their initial economic disadvantage has generated an extensive and long debate in America. One recent assessment of American immigrant experience can be found in Barry Chiswick (1979, p. 358): "When immigrants first arrive they have a lower earnings than the native born with similar demographic characteristics because of the less than perfect transferability of skills . . . With the passage of time, however, immigrants acquire knowledge . . . and adjust their skills and credentials to the new environment. They also acquire skills that are relevant only in the particular workplace in which they are employed." In short, Chiswick finds evidence of "catching up" among immigrants in contemporary America. More recent research by Borjas (1984) and others has found the "catching up" to be more modest than originally thought, but see Chiswick's recent rebuttal (Chiswick, 1986).

occupation, employment, earnings and migrant status can be exploited from that source. Section 5.4 contains some hypothesis-testing. Section 5.5 illustrates how this empirical analysis augments our understanding of how urban labor markets worked during the First Industrial Revolution.

5.3   Urban workers in 1851: Earnings and unemployment

The 1851 *Census of Great Britain* asked a number of questions that might be useful to explore the employment and wage experience of migrants who had been pouring into Britain's cities since the end of the French wars. Beside recording current residence, the census enumerators also asked where the respondent was born, so that individuals can be identified by migrant status. I have classified people according to the following five migrant categories: nonmigrants (born in the city of residence), migrants from rural areas in Britain, migrants from other urban areas in Britain, migrants from Ireland, and migrants from foreign countries. (Unfortunately, the enumerators did not ask how long the immigrants had been resident at the current location, so we cannot relate earnings experience to length of time in the city's labor market.) The allocation of places along urban and rural lines follows the appendixes to the 1851 census where towns and boroughs are listed, lists that have been used by historians interested in urbanization since the census was taken. They are also consistent with the urban-rural allocation used in Chapters 2 and 3.

In addition to age, sex, and family relationships, the enumerators also asked employment questions. While the quality of their answers might well be challenged, they do make it possible to infer both employment status and main occupation when working, although those working may not have been employed in their main occupation at the time of the enumeration. As Table 5.1 indicates, the responses can be classified into one of five categories: not working (retired, sick, unemployed, pauper, resident of workhouse, student, etc.), working, landed proprietor, family member assisting (relatives assisting the household head on the farm and elsewhere), and those missing data. For those working, an enormous amount of occupational detail is supplied. This detail can be aggregated into the twenty-nine occupational categories listed in Table 5.1. The aggregation is essential if this occupational data is to be matched up with what we know about full-time annual earnings.

The critical step in the exercise involves converting the occupational

Table 5.1. *Employment and occupation data included in the 1851 Census enumeration*

A. *Employment Status*		
Not working	Retired, sick, unemployed, pauper, etc. ⎫	Included
Working	Principal operation or other work ⎭	in analysis
Landed proprietor ⎫		Excluded
Family member assisting ⎬		from
Missing data ⎭		analysis
B. *Occupation*		
1. Farm laborers	Agricultural laborer, shepherd, woodman, gardener, nurseryman, groom, horsekeeper, fisherman	29.04£
2. General nonagricultural laborers	Coal heaver, chimney sweep, brickmaker, road laborer, railway laborer, laborer	44.83
3. Messengers and porters	Warehousing, storage, conveyance on roads, but excludes government employed	88.88
4. Government low-wage	Watchmen, guards, porters, messengers, Post Office letter carriers, janitors and other low-wage government employed	66.45
5. Police and guards	Includes both public and private sector	53.62
6. Miners	Miners, quarriers and marble masons	55.44
7. Government high-wage	Clerks, Post Office sorters, warehousemen, tax collectors, tax surveyors, solicitors, architects and other high-wage government employed	234.87
8. Skilled in shipbuilding	Shipwrights, ship builders, boat and barge builders	64.12
9. Skilled in engineering	Engineers, fitters, turners, iron moulders, those involved in watch making, machine making	84.05
10. Skilled in building trades	Bricklayers, masons, carpenters, plasterers	66.35
11. Skilled in textiles	Weavers, spinners, those engaged in wool, silk, flax, cotton, hemp, paper, straw, feathers, quills	58.64
12. Skilled in printing trades	Compositors, engravers	74.72
13. Clergy	Clergymen and ministers	267.09
14. Solicitors	Solicitors, barristers, lawyers, judges, law court officers	1837.50
15. Clerks	Clerks, accountants, auctioneers	235.81
16. Doctors	Surgeons, doctors, chemists, veterinarians	200.92
17. Teachers	School masters in elementary school, authors, professors, teachers, persons of science	81.11
18. Engineers	Engineers, surveyors, architects, pattern designers, draughtsman	479.00
19. Military	Professional military officers	150.66
20. Domestic servants	Servants, nurses, housekeepers	21.99
21. Unskilled textiles	Piecers, warpers, reelers, factory worker	29.32
22. Skilled craftsmen	Blacksmiths, basket maker, coach maker, journeyman	69.58

Table 5.1. *(cont.)*

23. Apprentices	Apprentices	34.79
24. Helpers	Helpers, assistants, boys, errand boys	14.66
25. Merchants	Salesman, broker, dealer, merchant	57.21
26. Proprietors	Baker, grocer, butcher, shopkeeper, tailor, brewer, innkeeper, victualler, barber	36.94
27. Factory managers	Overlooker, manager, superintendant	234.87
28. Miscellaneous	Artists, poets	21.99
29. Missing data	Excluded from analysis	

Source. See text.

detail into crude estimates of current earnings. Occupation is only one of many variables that can influence an individual's earnings. In addition, earnings potential is influenced by age, sex, experience, intelligence, health, discrimination, occupation of father, schooling, family resources devoted to the individual during rearing, and luck. Apart from age and sex, the 1851 Census doesn't supply such information. Unfortunately, the census doesn't supply actual individual earnings figures either. As a result, we have no other option but to reconstruct estimates of potential earnings based solely on occupation and employment status. Obviously, such data must be treated with care. It will only inform us about very general patterns. It will also limit any inferences we can make about the operation of city labor markets across regions. Although the data will inform us about intercity variance in occupation mix, it will not reveal the extent to which earnings varied across cities within occupations. That is, it will not capture wage gaps across regions. Nevertheless, although the earnings estimates are crude, there is no reason to expect a systematic bias by migrant status.

The long trek from the enumerators' manuscripts to our reconstructed machine-readable urban subsample has involved many scholars, but two have been instrumental to what follows. Michael Anderson was awarded a Social Science Research Council (SSRC) grant in 1972 to construct a magnetic tape based on a sample drawn from the enumerators' books of the 1851 *Census of Great Britain.* The national sample entailed a stratified two percent systematic cluster sample from the enumerators' books. The sampling procedure is described in detail in Anderson's final report to the SSRC (Anderson, Collins, and Stott, 1980). Carolyn Tuttle then secured a subsample of the main tape, requesting those eighteen counties that were among the most urban in mid nineteenth-century Britain.[4] In addition, Tuttle coded occupations by the twenty-nine categories listed in Table 5.1 (actually thirty, when "landed proprietors" are included), and then assigned each with an average earnings estimate.[5] Although Tuttle has constructed this data for another purpose, they appear to be relevant to the issues raised in this chapter. These male occupations certainly cover the full spectrum of urban jobs – high-wage service-sector jobs (clerks, warehousemen, solicitors, accountants, chemists), favored jobs in industry and the building trades (shipwrights, boat builders, fitters, turners, bricklayers, masons, carpenters, factory spinners, factory weavers, compositors, blacksmiths, coach makers), and low-wage casual labor in the service sector (watchmen, guards, porters, janitors, tailors, barbers, coal heavers, chimney sweeps, day laborers, street traders).

The final step was to restrict Tuttle's subsample to urban populations, because our interest here is in employment and earnings experience of city immigrants. The urban subsample includes 20,893 individuals, and they are broken down by age, sex, and migrant status in Table 5.2. One feature of Table 5.2 ought to be stressed immediately because it confirms the findings of Chapter 2: Migrants reflect a young-adult-selectivity bias. That is, the share of the migrants aged fifteen to forty-nine was 58.6 percent, and the figure for nonmigrants was only 42.2 percent.[6] Obviously, any attempt to assess differences in earnings experience between

4 The counties included in the 1851 subsample are: South of England – Middlesex, Hampshire, Hertfordshire, Northamptonshire, Essex, Suffolk, Norfolk, Wiltshire, Dorsetshire, Devonshire; North of England – Lancashire, Northumberland, West Riding, East Riding; and Scotland – Lanarkshire, Perthshire, Forfarshire, Renfrewshire. Among big cities, only Birmingham, Bristol, and Edinburgh are excluded from the subsample.

5 Tuttle's assignment of earnings with occupation is summarized in Table 5.1. Her sources are the following: Lindert and Williamson (1980, Tables 3 and 4); *Parliamentary Papers*, 1842, Vol. 6; *Parliamentary Papers*, 1887, Vol. 89; *Parliamentary Papers*, 1898, Vol. 83, Part II; and Bowley (1900). A detailed documentation can be found in Tuttle (1985, chp. 4), but she relies on fairly standard sources used extensively by historians interested in nineteenth-century wages and earnings, and sources I have used at length elsewhere (Williamson, 1985a).

6 Table 2.12 estimated the share of city immigrants aged fifteen to forty-nine to have been 54.3 percent in the 1850s. Although this figure is close to the 58.6 percent census sample figure reported in the text, they need not be precisely the same. The census sample figure refers to the stock of all city residents who had migrated into Britain's cities at any point prior to 1851, while the Table 2.12 estimate refers to the flow of city immigrants in the 1850s. In short, one refers to stocks and the other to flows, one refers to a sample and the other to the population, and one refers to 1851 and the other to the 1850s.

Table 5.2. *Number of urban workers in the 1851 subsample analysis*

Age	Nonmigrants			Migrants			Total		
	Male	Female	Total	Male	Female	Total	Male	Female	Total
0–9	1,155	1,126	2,281	1,331	1,270	2,601	2,486	2,396	4,882
10–14	360	395	755	641	654	1,295	1,001	1,049	2,050
15–19	300	347	647	576	724	1,300	876	1,071	1,947
20–29	448	561	1,009	1,381	1,683	3,064	1,829	2,244	4,073
30–39	267	288	555	1,181	1,297	2,478	1,448	1,585	3,033
40–49	189	223	412	835	918	1,753	1,024	1,141	2,165
50–59	131	156	287	523	606	1,129	654	762	1,416
60+	112	158	270	444	607	1,051	556	765	1,321
Missing	0	1	1	4	1	5	4	2	6
Total	2,962	3,255	6,217	6,916	7,760	14,676	9,878	11,015	20,893

Notes: These totals exclude all those with the following employment status reported by the census enumerators: "landed proprietors," "family members assisting," and "missing data." These individuals accounted for only 250 of the total urban subsample, 21,143, or 1.2 percent. The figure would have been far higher, of course, if the subsample included those employed in rural areas where "landed proprietors" and "family members assisting" were much more common. All ambiguities on place of birth were resolved, so no individuals were excluded on this score.

migrants and nonmigrants must control for age given the size of the young-adult-selectivity bias.

5.4   Testing competing views of urban labor-market absorption

Ravenstein (1885, 1889) noted that migration during the industrial revolution tended to be limited to short-distance moves, the close rural and small-town market serving as the labor supply for growing demands in the cities. Pollard (1981, p. 903) invokes Ravenstein's finding when he suggests: "Once the workers settled, the costs of moving again and the ignorance of conditions elsewhere inhibited . . . further adjustment." Because the 1851 census reported place of birth only, we have no way of learning the extent to which migrants were multiple movers, so Pollard's proposition cannot be tested. Yet, the implication of Pollard's thesis is that once having moved into a given city lack of further mobility tended to weaken links between city labor markets. It suggests that city immigration was limited to pairwise migration from specific rural to specific urban

Table 5.3. *Adults (15+) in the urban subsample by region and migrant status*

| Migrant status | Current location | | | |
	South	North	Scotland	Total
Urban migrant	1,518	732	193	2,443
Rural migrant	5,038	1,257	405	6,700
Irish	144	582	371	1,097
Other foreign	318	157	60	535
All migrants	7,018	2,728	1,029	10,775
Nonmigrants	1,761	834	585	3,180
Total	8,779	3,562	1,614	13,955

locations with little interurban migration. The evidence presented in Table 5.3 suggests a sound rejection of that inference because almost a quarter of the migrants in Britain's cities were in fact from other cities. Although the evidence of extensive urban-to-urban migration is consistent with Ravenstein's step-by-step migration, it does not offer an effective test of his proposition. It does imply, however, that city labor markets must have been fairly well integrated. The numbers of urban-to-urban migrants are just too big to expect otherwise.

Although the Irish were an additional tenth of all city immigrants in 1851, the vast majority were, nonetheless, immigrants from rural Britain (62.2 percent). Indeed, according to our 1851 urban subsample almost half of Britain's city population was born in rural Britain (48 percent). The figure varies significantly across regions, of course, as the Irish seem to have crowded out potential rural emigrants in Scotland and the North of England, but not in the South of England.

The Todaro model implies that the earnings of young, new immigrants (with high incidence of unemployment and underemployment) were likely to have been less than they could have received at home. Although the 1851 census enumerators did not identify when an immigrant arrived in the current location, the data they collected certainly seem to reject the view that young, rural emigrants earned less in the city than they might have earned in the parishes from whence they came. Fully employed farm laborers in England earned £29 or less in 1851 (Lindert and Williamson, 1983, Table 2, p. 4, assuming an implausibly high employment rate of fifty-two weeks per year), and rural migrants in their twenties earned

Table 5.4. *1851 earnings estimates: Adults from the urban subsample (£s)*

Age (years)	Non-migrants	Migrants, from				
		Rural	Urban	Irish	Other foreign	Total
Males						
15–19	53.49	55.46	47.19	43.04	23.04	50.15
20–29	68.22	69.89	74.52	53.90	62.09	68.58
30–39	73.06	70.46	69.43	58.76	72.47	69.07
40–49	80.74	68.43	75.79	51.76	100.51	70.88
50–59	62.91	77.91	69.24	73.59	69.84	75.26
60+	81.15	50.04	94.95	29.23	203.15	63.81
Average	68.22	67.09	70.19	53.17	82.23	67.22
Females						
15–19	29.46	25.62	28.00	34.59	20.67	27.02
20–29	29.62	24.20	27.90	27.63	22.85	25.39
30–39	25.91	16.69	18.88	15.38	19.11	17.19
40–49	19.77	13.83	19.55	12.22	16.60	15.06
50–59	18.51	15.90	14.97	14.20	14.85	15.56
60+	20.41	16.35	30.58	13.43	7.67	18.44
Average	25.86	19.24	23.64	21.10	19.06	20.40

almost £70 in the cities even after adjusting for unemployment experience (Table 5.4; aged twenty to twenty-nine, rural male migrants). Even teenage rural immigrants earned far more in the cities than their fathers did in English agriculture (Table 5.4: aged fifteen to nineteen, rural male migrants). Although young Irish males earned somewhat less (Table 5.4: aged twenty to twenty-nine, Irish males) than migrants from rural Britain, they certainly earned far more than they could have in Ireland (about £8 in 1840 according to Mokyr, 1985a, Table 2.6, p. 26). Although these comparisons fail to adjust for higher living costs and the greater disamenities of the cities, it seems to me unlikely that such urban-rural nominal earnings differentials could be largely explained by such factors. Chapter 7 will confirm that hunch.

Nor does the data in Table 5.4 support the view that male immigrants earned significantly less than nonimmigrants. The average earnings of male nonmigrants was about £68, but migrants earned only one pound less, £67. Although the Irish earned quite a bit less, £53, immigrants in British cities did about as well on average as the nonmigrants.

These comparisons already include the impact of unemployment, but because the Todaro model stresses city unemployment experience we

Table 5.5. *1851 estimates of percentage not working: Adults from the urban subsample (in %)*

Age (years)	Nonmigrants	Migrants, from				
		Rural	Urban	Irish	Other foreign	Total
Males						
15–19	11.0	15.1	22.0	6.5	60.9	17.7
20–29	2.5	2.7	1.6	1.2	7.1	2.5
30–39	1.5	1.6	1.5	6.9	5.7	2.5
40–49	3.2	3.8	3.0	2.7	5.5	3.6
50–59	2.3	4.8	5.6	1.9	10.7	5.0
60+	16.1	19.4	21.9	51.2	22.2	23.0
Average	5.2	5.9	6.3	7.6	12.1	6.6
Females						
15–19	32.0	33.9	40.8	20.3	54.5	34.7
20–29	38.3	46.9	46.1	34.5	55.1	45.8
30–39	44.1	67.2	64.6	68.3	68.6	66.8
40–49	55.6	69.2	63.9	74.7	64.5	68.4
50–59	54.5	62.1	66.9	62.5	69.2	63.2
60+	55.7	61.9	64.2	75.0	77.8	63.8
Average	43.3	56.7	55.7	52.2	62.9	56.3

ought to isolate that variable by itself. Table 5.5 reports the percentage of adults not working. There is some evidence that confirms the Todaro job-search model because the unemployment rate[7] for nonmigrant males, 5.2 percent, was a bit below that of migrant males, 6.6 percent. However,

7 I use the terms "unemployment" and "not working" interchangeably, although the latter is clearly more accurate. To repeat, adult males not working include unemployed, sick, retired, paupers, and so on. It is not clear just how long one had to be without work to get the unemployed label, but it appears to refer to employment status at the time of enumeration only. In any case, those unemployed would be without any kind of work, not simply without work in their principal occupation.

The average male unemployment rate reported in Table 5.5 is 6.6 percent, quite a bit higher than the rate recorded for the urban skilled in engineering, metal, and shipbuilding unions, 3.9 percent (Mitchell and Deane, 1962, p. 64). It is apparent, however, that 1851 was a better year than the 1840s as a whole (4.4 percent: Lindert and Williamson, 1983, p. 15) or the 1850s as a whole (5.1 percent: Mitchell and Deane, 1962, p. 64). The fact that urban unemployment rates were relatively low in 1851 may help explain why the variance in unemployment accounts for such a small share (only 28 percent) of total earnings variance among males in our sample. Nevertheless, it was variance in male occupation that drove variance in total male earnings in 1851, not variance in unemployment experience.

there is no evidence to support the view that the young (presumably "new") male immigrants to the cities had significantly higher unemployment rates than nonmigrants of the same age: The unemployment rates for males in their twenties was exactly the same for migrants and nonmigrants, 2.5 percent. Furthermore, Irish males in their twenties had lower unemployment rates than nonmigrants. Female migrants, however, had much higher "unemployment rates" (and lower earnings) than nonmigrants, a result attributable, I assume, to their higher fertility rates.

In short, the evidence in Tables 5.4 and 5.5 does not support the hypothesis that young male migrants had significantly lower earnings and higher unemployment rates than young male nonmigrants. Nor does it support the view that "new" city immigrants earned less than they would have at their source of emigration. At first glance, the evidence does not appear to offer support for the Todaro model or for Pollard's view of the operation of urban labor markets. It seems more consistent with the view that migrant absorption in Britain's urban labor markets was very fast and that migrants responded to actual wages and current job opportunities, rather than to expectations of future employment in high-wage jobs.

We can, of course, squeeze far more information out of this data if we exploit regression analysis. But before we do, some concessions must be made to data limitations. Our earnings estimates are unlikely to tell us very much about the true earnings received by any of the 13,955 adults in our urban subsample. They are simply too crude to be used for that purpose. As a result, we will aggregate the individual data to groups whose estimated earnings are more likely to approximate their true earnings. We shall use ninety group observations in what follows (e.g., 3 regions × 5 migrant classes × 6 age groups), and the regressions will weight each observation by the number in each group. The analysis is restricted to males. Finally, although the regressions reported in Tables 5.6 and 5.7 introduce regional dummies, I do not discuss those results in the text. Although the underlying earnings estimates do not capture wage gaps across regions, it seems inappropriate to give the impression that these regressions have much to say about regional earnings variation. On the contrary, they tell us only about occupational and unemployment variation across regions.

The first regression is reported in Table 5.6. Two questions are explored in that table. First, did migrants as a group earn less than nonmigrants? The dummy variable MIGR makes it possible to see if migrants really did earn less than nonmigrants after controlling for other

Table 5.6. *Determinants of earnings (Y) in 1851, British cities: Adult-male immigrants vs. nonimmigrants*

Variable j	$\hat{\beta}_j$	t-statistic
Constant	51.972	6.001**
MIGR	−2.574	.247
NORTH	−.875	.204
SCOTLAND	9.013	1.524
NONMIGXAGE20	14.855	1.360
NONMIGXAGE30	20.088	1.630
NONMIGXAGE40	27.217	2.001*
NONMIGXAGE50	9.702	.632
NONMIGXAGE60	28.531	1.757*
MIGRXAGE20	18.452	2.540**
MIGRXAGE30	19.036	2.557**
MIGRXAGE40	20.889	2.632**
MIGRXAGE50	25.334	2.862**
MIGRXAGE60	13.658	1.475
$\overline{Y}(\pounds s)$	67.443	
STANDARD ERROR	17.383	
$\overline{R}^2$	.062	
F(13,76)	1.454	
N	90	

Notes: See notes to Table 5.7.

influences. Second, did migrants as a group trace out different age-earnings paths than nonmigrants? To get an answer here, we introduce interaction terms between the migrant status dummies (MIGR and NONMIG) and age (in which the age class fifteen to nineteen is taken as the norm). The purpose of this exercise is to shed further light on migrant absorption experience. If the Todaro model is correct, "new" immigrants should have lower earnings than nonimmigrants, but the immigrants should "catch up" to the nonmigrants the longer they stay in the city. If the Todaro hypothesis holds true, the age-earnings paths for migrants should be steeper than for nonmigrants.[8]

The results suggest that (1) migrants did not earn significantly less than nonmigrants, and (2) age-earnings paths look pretty much alike for migrants and nonmigrants. The statement that age-earnings paths "look

8 This inference should be strengthened by the presence of a selectivity bias. Discouraged migrants may have returned home as years wore on, leaving successful migrants behind.

Table 5.7. *Determinants of earnings (Y) in 1851, British cities: Adult-male immigrants by source vs. nonimmigrants*

Variable j	$\hat{\beta}_j$	t-statistic
Constant	50.390	7.720**
URBMIG	−5.119	.479
RURMIG	3.720	.417
IRISH	−12.295	.870
OTHERFOR	−29.374	1.234
NORTH	1.736	.516
SCOTLAND	13.207	2.849**
NONMIGXAGE20	14.980	1.825*
NONMIGXAGE30	20.356	2.199*
NONMIGXAGE40	27.343	2.676**
NONMIGXAGE50	10.225	.887
NONMIGXAGE60	29.272	2.399*
URBMIGXAGE20	27.621	2.608**
URBMIGXAGE30	22.827	2.099*
URBMIGXAGE40	29.290	2.535**
URBMIGXAGE50	22.276	1.634
URBMIGXAGE60	47.626	2.937**
RURMIGXAGE20	14.416	1.969*
RURMIGXAGE30	15.175	2.022*
RURMIGXAGE40	13.067	1.649
RURMIGXAGE50	22.801	2.634**
RURMIGXAGE60	−4.858	.551
IRISHXAGE20	10.735	.705
IRISHXAGE30	15.545	.984
IRISHXAGE40	8.549	.476
IRISHXAGE50	30.933	1.566
IRISHXAGE60	−16.652	.794
OTHERFORXAGE20	39.444	1.526
OTHERFORXAGE30	49.056	1.902*
OTHERFORXAGE40	77.770	2.847**
OTHERFORXAGE50	47.572	1.537
OTHERFORXAGE60	180.216	5.774**
$\overline{Y}(\pounds s)$	67.443	
STANDARD ERROR	13.057	
$\overline{R}^2$	.471	
$F(31,58)$	3.555	
N	90	

Notes: The regression is based on 90 weighted observations. The observations are based on mean earnings in 90 = 3 regions × 6 age classes × 5 migrant statuses where

Regions	Ages	City migrant status
North of England (NORTH)	15–19 (AGE 15)	Nonmigrant (NONMIG)
South of England (SOUTH)	20–29 (AGE 20)	Urban immigrant (URBMIG)

Notes to Table 5.7. *(cont.)*

Regions	Ages	City migrant status
Scotland (SCOTLAND)	30–39 (AGE 30)	Rural immigrant (RURMIG)
	40–49 (AGE 40)	Irish immigrant (IRISH)
	50–59 (AGE 50)	Other foreign immigrant (OTHERFOR)

Cell "norm" in the regressions is teenagers (aged 15–19), located in the South of England, who were born in the city of location (nonmigrants).

The dependent variable is constructed by: those not working get an earnings figure of zero, and those working get an earnings figure based on occupation (see Table 5.1). There are 13,955 individuals underlying the 90 group means (see Table 5.3). "Landed proprietors," "family members assisting," and those missing occupation data are all excluded.

On the t-statistics: * denotes 5% and ** denotes 1%.

pretty much alike" is likely to be a bit too vague for some readers (we shall be more precise below), but the predicted paths are plotted in Figure 5.2, where the similarity between migrants and nonmigrants is clearer, especially from their teenage years through their thirties.

A second regression is reported in Table 5.7, where we now distinguish between all four city migrant types: urban migrants (URBMIG), rural migrants (RURMIG), the Irish (IRISH), and other foreigners (OTHERFOR). Most of the findings in Table 5.6 are repeated in Table 5.7. Although the coefficients on IRISH and OTHERFOR are large and negative, and although the coefficient on RURMIG is positive, the t-statistics are small enough to warrant the tentative conclusion that none of the migrant groups had different earnings from nonmigrants in 1851, after controlling for age and location.

The regression reported in Table 5.7 does not allow for a really robust test of many of the hypotheses listed in Section 5.2. To test those hypotheses properly, we should allow migrant status to influence earnings by region as well as allow age-earnings paths by migrant status to vary by region. Unfortunately, the addition of the necessary interaction terms would quickly exhaust our degrees of freedom (recall N = 90). Instead, Appendix 5.1 offers extensive hypothesis testing where we exploit various maintained hypotheses. The appendix reports the constraint tested (the null hypothesis) in terms of variables already defined, the maintained hypothesis (the form of the regression and restrictions on variable coefficients), the relevant *t* and F tests, and our conclusions.

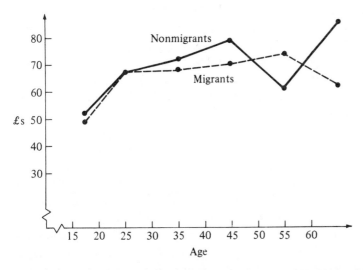

Figure 5.2   Predicted earnings of urban males from the 1851 Census: Migrants and nonmigrants (Source: Derived from Table 5.6)

Table 5.8. *Absorbing male immigrants in Britain's cities: Summary of hypothesis testing*

Question	Answer
1. Did migrants have different earnings than nonmigrants?	No
2. Did migrants have different age-earnings paths than nonmigrants?	No
3. Did native-born migrants have different earnings than nonmigrants?	No
4. Did native-born migrants have different age-earnings paths than nonmigrants?	No
5. Did migrants have different earnings by source of origin?	Yes
6. Did migrants have different age-earnings paths by source of origin?	Yes
7. Did Irish and other foreigners have different earnings than native-born migrants?	Yes
8. Did Irish and other foreigners have different age-earnings paths than native-born migrants?	Yes
9. Did age-earnings paths vary by region?	No

Note: Results taken from Appendix 5.1.

An overall summary of Appendix 5.1 is offered in Table 5.8, where the hypotheses are posed as questions. It appears that migrants as a group did not have different earnings than nonmigrants, nor did they have different age-earnings paths. Furthermore, native-born migrants (the dominant migrant group) did not have different earnings from nonmigrants, nor did they have different earning paths. This seems to be the critical finding: City immigrants from rural and urban Britain exhibited the same earnings experience as nonimmigrants in 1851. Whatever were the labor-market adjustments the native-born migrant had to make, they were not reflected in unemployment or occupational experience. Although they were predominantly unskilled, the native-born migrants did not suffer any significant disadvantage relative to the nonmigrants born in the city. City assimilation and absorption of the native-born migrant seem to have taken place relatively smoothly, and the absorption experience of the migrants seems to have been pretty much the same everywhere in Britain's cities.

However, the Irish and other foreign immigrants did enter urban labor markets at an earnings disadvantage. They did have lower earnings than nonmigrants and native-born migrants. However, among the Irish lower earnings were not due to higher unemployment, because unemployment rates were, as we have seen, actually lower among young Irish males (aged fifteen to twenty-nine, Table 5.5). Rather, it was due to their greater frequency in lower-wage occupations. The Irish also had different age-earnings paths. Although the Todaro model predicts that the disadvantaged Irish should have "caught up" as they were absorbed into city labor markets over time, it turns out that the Irish age-earnings paths were flatter, not steeper. This can be seen most clearly from predictions generated by the regressions in Table 5.7. For urban males in the South of England:

Age	Earnings			
	Irish	Nonmigrants	Difference	% Difference
15–19	38.10£	50.39£	−12.29£	24.4
20–29	48.83	65.37	−16.54	25.3
30–39	53.65	70.75	−17.10	25.2
40–49	46.65	77.73	−31.08	40.0
50+	45.24	70.14	−25.90	35.5

5.5   Implications and qualifications

Unemployment, poverty, and inequality blighted Britain's cities in the mid nineteenth century, but the same was true of the countryside. As a result, there is nothing inconsistent between the well-known finding of poverty in

Britain's cities during the First Industrial Revolution and a relatively efficient city labor market that absorbed the migrants quickly into the labor force.

The imperfect 1851 Census data analyzed here seems to support the view that Britain's cities absorbed the flood of migrants with considerable ease. With the significant exception of the Irish, male immigrants into Britain's cities did not exhibit lower earnings than nonimmigrants. Nor did they exhibit higher unemployment rates. They also exhibited the same age-earnings experience. Although the evidence is imperfect, what we do have seems to be inconsistent with the view that migrants entered the city in response to expected future high earnings, suffering unemployment or underemployment in the traditional low-wage service sectors while they waited for the better jobs. Rather, they appear to have been motivated by current job prospects, and those prospects appear to have been confirmed. This is not to say that migrants were never unemployed or that they could not be found in the low-wage service sectors in large numbers. Nor have I argued that Todaro's emphasis on urban unemployment and expected earnings differentials does not play a role in more modern economies (indeed, see Hatton and Williamson, 1989, in which the Todaro model is supported by American experience in the interwar period). The evidence from the 1851 Census simply suggests that immigrants in Britain's nineteenth-century cities had the same experience as nonmigrants.

These findings are, of course, conditional on the quality of the evidence, and the 1851 Census certainly has its limitations. The enumerators never asked how long a migrant had been resident in the city, so we cannot properly explore their earnings experience immediately following immigration. Todaro may find this shortcoming in the data a critical flaw because his model was designed to explore the behavior of current, not past, immigrants. In addition, although the enumerators recorded occupation and employment status, they did not report income or earnings. As a result, we have found it necessary to reconstruct their earnings from independent evidence on average full-time earnings associated with their reported occupations, and their reported employment status. Although this reconstruction appears to be the best option available, Todaro might argue that it is not good enough.

My guess is that some unknown bias in the data is unlikely to account for the main findings reported here. That view is encouraged by similar findings that have emerged from a decade of research on city-labor markets in the Third World (Mazumdar, 1976; Yap, 1977; Merrick, 1978;

Mohan, 1980; Kelley and Williamson, 1984; Williamson, 1988). The maintained hypothesis emerging from this chapter therefore seems to be that Britain's mid nineteenth-century cities absorbed the migrants fairly quickly, that current, not expected, employment prospects dominated migrant decisions, and that "overoptimistic irrationality" was never an attribute of those migrations. Of course, it is quite possible that the Todaro model would have far better success when applied to industrial earnings in the twentieth century when urban unemployment and city unemployment relief both became more pronounced (Hatton and Williamson, 1989), but it does not have much success when applied to Britain during her industrial revolution.

Appendix 5.1. *Hypothesis testing: City adult males in Britain, 1851*

Conclusions	Constraint tested (Null hypothesis)	Maintained hypothesis	Statistic	Significance level
1. Earnings of migrants as a group are not significantly different from nonmigrants	Coefficient on MIGR equals zero	Earnings constrained to be the same for all migrants, and age-earnings paths constrained to be the same for everyone	$t(81) = -.526$	* Constraint cannot be rejected
2. The age-earnings path for migrants as a group is not significantly different from that of nonmigrants	Coefficients on interaction terms of the form MIGXAGE all equal zero	(a) Earnings the same for all migrants	$F(5,76) = .523$	*
		(b) Earnings allowed to differ across migrants by source of origin	$F(5,73) = .594$	* Constraint cannot be rejected
3. Earnings of native-born migrants as a group are not significantly different from nonmigrants	Coefficients on URBMIG and RURMIG equal zero	(a) Earnings of Irish and other foreign allowed to differ, but age-earnings paths are the same		
		(i) No regional differences in earnings allowed	$F(2,80) = .378$	*
		II Regional differences in earnings allowed	$F(2,78) = .362$	*
		(b) Age-earnings paths of Irish and other foreign also allowed to differ		
		(i) No regional differences in earnings allowed	$F(2,70) = .489$	*
		(ii) Regional differences in earnings allowed, but same age-earnings paths by region	$F(2,68) = .325$	*
		(iii) Regional variations in age-earnings paths allowed as well	$F(2,58) = .393$	* Constraint cannot be rejected

Appendix 5.1. (cont.)

Conclusions	Constraint tested (Null hypothesis)	Maintained hypothesis	Statistic	Significance level
4. Age-earnings paths of native-born migrants as a group are not significantly different from that of nonmigrants	Coefficients on all interaction terms of the form URBMIGXAGE and RURMIGXAGE equal zero	Age-earnings paths allowed to differ for Irish and other foreign. Urban migrants and rural migrants assumed to differ by the shift terms URBMIG and RURMIG		
		(a) No regional difference in earnings allowed	$F(10,60) = 1.526$	*
		(b) Regional differences in earnings allowed, but same age-earnings path by region	$F(10,58) = 1.679$	*
		(c) Regional variation in age-earnings paths are allowed	$F(10,48) = 1.874$	10% Constraint cannot be rejected
5. Migrants have different earnings according to source of origin	Coefficients on URBMIG, RURMIG, IRISH, OTHERFOR, and MIGR are equal	Regional differences in earnings allowed.		
		(a) Migrants constrained to have the same age-earnings paths as nonmigrants	$F(3,68) = 3.781$	2.5%
		(b) Migrants allowed to have different age-earnings paths than nonmigrants	$F(3,73) = 3.708$	2.5% Constraint rejected

Appendix 5.1. (cont.)

Conclusions	Constraint tested (Null hypothesis)	Maintained hypothesis	Statistic	Significance level
6. Migrants have different age-earnings paths according to source of origin	Coefficients on URBMIGXAGE, RURMIGXAGE, IRISHXAGE, and OTHERFORAGE are equal	Regional differences in earnings allowed. The various categories of migrants are allowed to have different earnings. The age-earnings path for nonmigrants differs from that of all migrant types	$F(15,58) = 3.926$	5% Constraint rejected
7. Irish and other foreigners have different earnings from native-born migrants	Coefficients on IRISH and OTHERFOR are zero.	All native-born constrained to have same earnings. Everyone has the same age-earnings path, except for Irish and other foreigners, who are allowed to have different age-earnings paths		
		(a) No regional differences in earnings allowed	$F(2,82) = 4.287$	2.5%
		(b) Regional differences in earnings allowed	$F(2,80) = 5.661$	2.5% Constraint rejected
8. Irish and other foreigners have different age-earnings paths from native-born migrants	Coefficients on interaction terms of the form IRISHXAGE and OTHERFORXAGE equal zero	All native-born constrained to have the same earnings behavior.		
		(a) No regional differences in earnings allowed	$F(10,70) = 4.356$	.5%
		(b) Regional differences in earnings allowed	$F(10,68) = 4.261$	.5% Constraint rejected

Appendix 5.1. (cont.)

Conclusions	Constraint tested (Null hypothesis)	Maintained hypothesis	Statistic	Significance level
9. Earnings vary across regions	Coefficient on NORTH and SCOTLAND equal zero	(a) Only Irish and other foreigners allowed to have different earnings	$F_{(2,80)} = 2.755$	10%
		(b) All migrants allowed to have different earnings by source of migrant	$F_{(2,78)} = 2.539$	10%
		(c) In addition, Irish and other foreigners allowed to have different age-earnings paths, but		
		(i) All native-born are alike	$F_{(2,70)} = 4.026$	2.5%
		(ii) Native-born migrants are allowed to differ from nonmigrants	$F_{(2,68)} = 3.745$	5.0%
		(iii) In addition, native-born urban and rural migrants are allowed to have different age-earnings paths	$F_{(2,58)} = 4.097$	2.5% Constraint rejected
10. Age-earnings paths do not vary significantly across regions	Coefficients on interaction terms of the form NORTHXAGE and SCOT-LANDXAGE equal zero	Same as 9(c) above		
		(i) ibid.	$F_{(10,60)} = 1.019$	*
		(ii) ibid.	$F_{(10,58)} = 1.012$	*
		(iii) ibid.	$F_{(10,48)} = 1.279$	* Constraint cannot be rejected

* denotes that test does not pass the 10% level of significance.

6. The impact of the Irish on British labor markets

6.1 Irish immigration and the labor-surplus model: Three questions

To add to all the other social problems that Britain's cities had to face during the First Industrial Revolution, they also had to absorb the Irish. Rapid growth after the French wars made the absorption easier, but the Irish immigrants still serve to complicate any assessment of Britain's economic performance up to the 1850s. Would the cities have been able to cope with growth far more easily in their absence? Would common labor's living standards in the city have risen much more rapidly? Was rural out-migration strongly suppressed by Irish competition in Britain's cities? Was migration from the agrarian South deflected from northern cities by a glut of Irish labor? Did British industrialization receive a powerful boost by an elastic supply of cheap Irish labor?

Did the Irish depress the standard of living of British labor?

Qualitative accounts suggest that Irish immigration into Britain did not really become important until after the French wars, the 1820s often being offered as the benchmark decade. It is also true that unskilled labor's real-wage gains lagged far behind during the otherwise impressive secular boom up to the 1850s (Lindert and Williamson, 1983). Inequality was also on the rise (Williamson, 1985a), suggesting that the Irish glut at the bottom of the distribution may have played an important role.

The gross correlation is seductive, lagging living standards and rising inequality coinciding with Irish immigration, but a clear assessment has always been clouded by the difficulty of controlling for everything else. What about labor-saving technical change? What about rural labor pushed off the land by enclosures? What about the demographic transition among the English themselves, an event that served to glut the labor market with more young workers at about the same time that the Irish arrived in great numbers?

129

That immigration lowers wages of comparably skilled native-born, *ceteris paribus*, is obvious. What is not so obvious, however, is whether the Irish had a significant quantitative impact on real wages in Britain, especially if *ceteris paribus* did not hold.

Certainly historians writing about the British industrial revolution sixty years ago thought the Irish mattered. Arthur Redford (1926, p. 159), for example, thought "the main social significance of the Irish influx lay with its tendency to lower the wages and standard of living of the English wage-earning classes." And although Redford thought this tendency was obvious during the famine of the late 1840s, "the disastrous social effect of the Irish influx was, however, already apparent in the 'thirties." Clapham (1930, pp. 57–66) agreed. The roots of this conventional wisdom seem to lie primarily with the opinions of contemporary observers who had strong views on real wages and the Irish absorption problem, even as early as the 1820s. Fear of an Irish glut was already apparent in the 1825 *Select Committee on Disturbances in Ireland* as well as the 1827 *Select Committee on Emigration:* both committees relied heavily on witnesses like Malthus, McCulloch, and cotton manufacturers from Lancashire.[1]

Although Sidney Pollard (1978, p. 103) sees a "unanimity about the historical facts" in this literature, no one has yet tested the proposition that the Irish had a significant impact on real wages from the early 1820s to the 1850s. So said E. H. Hunt (1973, p. 299) more than a decade ago: "We are left with a substantial body of literary evidence which suggests that immigration reduced wage rates . . . but no quantitative assessment of these influences has been possible." And although Hunt implies that the assessment is impossible, Cormac Ó Grada (1977, p. 65) feels instead that nobody has tried: "the importance of Irish immigration as an ingredient in the famous 'standard-of-living' debate has never been properly considered."

Did the Irish crowd out potential emigrants from Britain's countryside?

If the Irish had an impact on real wages by their immigration into Britain's cities, surely they must have discouraged potential native-born migration to the booming cities. There are three places to look for the discouraged native-born would-be migrant: low migration rates from the poor South

1 All of these witnesses have their comments reproduced in the "Report on the State of the Irish Poor in Great Britain," (*PP*, 1836, vol. 34, pp. xxxiii and 59–66).

to the booming industrial North, low out-migration rates from British agriculture to urban employment, and rising rates of native-born emigration to the New World. Consider the internal migration patterns.

The relatively modest migration from England's poor agrarian South to the industrializing North has always drawn comment, and the 1836 *Report on the State of the Irish Poor in Great Britain* (p. xxvi) makes it plain that it was Irish crowding-out that accounted for it:

> It might be thought that the Irish who have settled in England have displaced an equal number of native labourers. To a certain extent, this is doubtless the case; and if there had been no unemployed population in Ireland, unquestionably the demand for labour in the manufacturing districts of the North of England would, in part, have been satisfied by a migration from the South.

In the *First Annual Report of the Poor Law Commission,* James Phillips Kay projected those crowding-out effects into the late 1830s.[2] Kay expected new Irish immigrants to crowd out the potential native-born migrant from the South, and it appears he may have been correct. Even the efforts by the Poor Law Commission, led by Edwin Chadwick, failed to encourage the migration of southern paupers to the North.

Could Irish crowding-out also explain why the rate of out-migration from English agriculture seems relatively modest at some critical points in time? Chapter 4 offered some evidence to support this view. Recall what Table 4.1 showed: When the Irish immigration rate reached its peak in the 1840s, the rate of immigration from British agriculture reached its trough. Furthermore, when Irish immigration picked up after the 1810s, the rate of immigration from British agriculture fell off with a lag. There does indeed seem to be some suggestion of Irish crowding-out in these figures.

Did Irish labor supplies foster industrialization?

No doubt cheap labor can give a temporary industrial location advantage to any town. Thus, the *Report on the State of the Irish Poor in Great Britain* (p. xxxvi) felt that a crucial ingredient to urban growth up North was "an unlimited supply of Irish laborers." But what about the impact of unlimited supplies of Irish labor on industrialization at the national level? Pollard (1978, pp. 102, 115) summarizes the view of the majority: "cheap and elastic labour supply itself played an instrumental part in the progress of industrialization . . . Ireland functioned predominantly as a labour reser-

2 "First Annual Report of the Poor Law Commission" (*PP,* 1835, vol. 35, p. 188).

voir . . . disguised unemployment on Irish soil corresponds to the agricultural sector in the Lewis [labor surplus] model, and Irish labour became an integral part of British industrialization."

Certainly the thesis seems plausible: Disguised unemployment in Irish agriculture would have ensured an elastic labor supply for Britain, the elastic labor supply would have held wages down, which, in turn, would have favored the expansion of labor-intensive sectors (like textiles). In addition, elastic labor supplies would have redistributed income away from labor and toward capital; that is, making more investment and accumulation possible. So far, however, the thesis has not been confronted with any quantitative evidence.

This chapter will offer a tentative assessment of all three of these important questions – real wages, crowding-out, and industrialization. As Ó Grada (1977, p. 65) suggested some time ago, the assessment requires two bits of information: the size of the Irish immigrations and the nature of labor demand in Britain. Most of this chapter is devoted to a reconstruction of these two ingredients. Once we have them in hand, we can then get some answers to the questions involving Irish labor absorption during the British industrial revolution.

6.2   Who were the Irish and where did they go in Britain?

The Irish were unskilled

Since Adam Smith noted that the Irish accounted for most of the porters, coalheavers, and prostitutes in eighteenth-century London, conventional wisdom has had it that the Irish in Britain were overwhelmingly unskilled.[3] Certainly expert witnesses whose accounts appeared in the 1836 *Report on the State of the Irish Poor in Great Britain* viewed the Irish that way, and the 1851 census confirmed it with hard data. Agricultural seasonal laborers aside, that the vast majority of the Irish laborers were in unskilled employment in 1851 can be readily documented for Liverpool, Leeds, and Bradford.[4] Detailed analysis of London's 1851 Census enumerations suggests the same (Lees, 1979, pp. 92–101 and 1969, Table 2,

---

3 The literature is voluminous. See, for example, Clapham, 1933; Redford, 1926, chp. 9; Thompson, 1963, pp. 433–4; Hammond and Hammond, 1947, p. 38; Freeman, 1957; Hunt, 1973, p. 286; Ó Tuathaigh, 1981; Fitzpatrick, 1984.
4 Excellent town studies can be found in: Lawton, 1959, pp. 50–2; Dillon, 1973, p. 6; and Richardson, 1968, p. 52.

p. 371). Furthermore, it has been suggested that the Irish "arrived in England with a high rate of illiteracy, approaching twice that of the English" (Steele, 1976, p. 224). If true, it could have been due partly to the costs of migration, since the poorer Irish could only afford transportation to Britain rather than America (Lees, 1979, p. 43).

In short, it seems reasonable to view the Irish immigrant in Britain as unskilled (as in America: Mokyr and Ó Grada, 1982), thus swelling labor supplies in low-wage occupations. It follows that they would have had only a trivial impact on the skilled labor supply. It also seems reasonable to treat the Irish as entering a competitive unskilled urban labor market in which wage discrimination was infrequent. Nonetheless, the Irish may well have been slow to acquire skills and thus to move out of low-wage occupations. Their slow rate of upward mobility may have been due to occupational discrimination (as argued persuasively by Nicholas and Shergold, 1987) or to the fact that being poor they could ill afford the investment in acquiring skills either for themselves or their children (a position I favor).

The Irish were urban

When the British census first asked "where were you born?" in 1841, the answers confirmed what observers believed they already knew: The Irish immigrants concentrated in urban areas. Furthermore, the main ports of entry on the passage across the Irish Sea were Liverpool, London, Glasgow, and Bristol, so it is hardly surprising that the heaviest concentrations of the Irish-born tended to be in those cities very early in the nineteenth century (Lees, 1979, p. 44; Collins, 1981, p. 197; Ó Tuathaig, 1981, p. 52). In short, the Irish exodus was "part of a much wider pattern of rural-to-urban migration within a developing Atlantic economy" (Lees, 1979, p. 42).

Where did the Irish go in Britain? Table 6.1 offers a summary by reference to two statistics: the percent of Britain's Irish-born in various parts of Britain, CELTSHARE; and the percent of a given area's population that was Irish-born, PERCELT. While PERCELT offers a measure of density independent of the size of the urban labor market of which the Irish were a part, CELTSHARE may be dominated by the sheer size of that labor market. PERCELT tells us more about the labor-market attractions of a given area than does CELTSHARE, and the two measures often behave quite differently. For example, although London absorbed the largest share of Britain's Irish, it did not have a very high Irish density. Indeed, had London had the same Irish-born density as did the next six

Table 6.1. *Where did the Irish go in Britain? The percentage distribution of the Irish-born, 1841 to 1861: Major areas in Britain (in %)*

City or Region	CELTSHARE			PERCELT		
	1841	1851	1861	1841	1851	1861
Seven biggest cities						
London	17.6	14.9	13.3	3.9	4.6	3.8
Liverpool	11.9	11.5	10.4	17.3	22.3	18.9
Glasgow	10.7	8.2	7.7	16.2	18.2	15.7
Manchester	8.3	7.2	6.5	11.6	13.1	11.3
Edinburgh	1.3	1.7	1.8	4.0	6.5	5.2
Birmingham	1.1	1.3	1.4	2.6	4.0	3.8
Leeds	1.2	1.2	1.3	3.3	4.9	5.0
Seven biggest cities	52.1	46.0	42.4	6.8	8.2	7.2
"All" cities	(a)	(a)	(a)	5.5	6.9	6.0
Lancashire	25.5	26.1	27.0	6.4	9.3	8.9
All Britain	100.0	100.0	100.0	2.3	3.5	3.5
Addendum: Share in total British population of the seven biggest cities	17.9	19.5	20.6			

(a) The number of cities underlying the calculations for these three census years varies; thus, "all" cities under CELTSHARE are not comparable.

Sources and Notes: Census data, where CELTSHARE equals percent of Britain's Irish-born residing in that area, and PERCELT equals percent of that area's population Irish-born.

biggest cities in Britain, her share of Britain's Irish-born in 1841 might have been more like a third rather than 17.6 percent. The same was true of Edinburgh, Birmingham, and Leeds, all of which had a large share of the Irish, but only because they were big cities, not because the Irish favored them for any other reason. In any case, Table 6.1 certainly confirms that the Irish were urban: In 1841, 52.1 percent of them were in Britain's seven biggest cities at a time when those cities had only 17.9 percent of Britain's population.

Table 6.1 also suggests a drift of the Irish away from big-city locations to smaller, rapid-growing industrial city locations, especially those up North. The seven biggest cities found their share of the Irish-born declining sharply over the two decades 1841–61 even though most of them experienced a rise in the Irish density or PERCELT. Their share (CELTSHARE) dropped from 52.1 percent in 1841, to 46 percent in 1851, and to 42.4 percent in 1861. This drift away from Britain's big cities is all the more striking given that these seven cities increased their share of total population from 17.9 to 20.6 percent over the same period.

Why did the Irish choose to locate with greater density in some cities while avoiding others? Did they really favor large cities, or did large cities simply have other attractive attributes that served to pull the Irish to them in disproportionately large numbers? Did the previous decade's growth of the city serve to pull in the Irish who responded to the rate of job creation? Did the cost of migration, and thus a city's distance from the main ports of entry, matter? And when all else is considered, did the Irish still favor the North of England over the South of England?

Table 6.2 offers some answers by exploring the determinants of PERCELT for all three census dates. The number of cities included in the analysis varies from date to date according to the availability of data, but the findings appear to be consistent. First, city size never plays a statistically significant positive role. Large cities never had a stronger attraction than small cities for the Irish immigrant. Second, the city's growth rate in the previous decade was a very strong attraction for the Irish. I interpret the causation here to run from rapid city job creation to Irish pull. Skeptics may wish to argue that other forces pushed the Irish to those cities, that the cheap labor thus generated tended to favor industrial location there, and thus that jobs were eventually created to employ the Irish. It seems to me that the Irish could hardly afford to wait for such jobs to be created, and thus would have moved on to other cities offering more immediate employment. Third, the Irish avoided the South of England, favoring instead the North of England and Scotland about equally, suggesting that the higher cost of passage to London and Bristol mattered.

These regressions seem to do surprisingly well in accounting for the variance in Irish density across British cities. It appears that job pull and the cost of migration played the key roles.

The Irish were adults

Chapter 2 showed that migrants in Britain's cities tended to be dominated by young adults. Table 6.4 should serve to dispel the notion that the Irish obeyed different laws of migration, at least with regard to age selectivity. Although 74.4 percent of the Irish immigrants in Britain's cities were adults at the time of the 1851 census enumeration, 77 percent of the non-Irish immigrants were adults.

The gap between the Irish immigrant and the total British age distribu-

Table 6.2. *Why did the Irish go where they did? Explaining the Irish-born population share in British cities (PERCELT) in 1841, 1851, and 1861*

Independent variable	1841	1851		1861		
	N = 39	N = 39	N = 52	N = 39	N = 52	N = 70
CONSTANT	6.393(3.79)	8.672(4.70)	8.549(5.55)	9.041(6.98)	8.840(7.91)	8.746(9.60)
CITYSIZE	$10^{-7} \times$ 9.672(0.60)	$-10^{-6} \times$ 2.003(1.37)	$-10^{-6} \times$ 1.330(0.93)	$-10^{-6} \times$ 2.067(1.95)	$-10^{-6} \times$ 1.696(1.62)	$10^{-7} \times$ 3.368(0.34)
CITYGROWTH	.820(2.14)	1.499(2.40)	1.023(2.37)	1.368(2.89)	.995(2.30)	.678(2.73)
DISTANCE	-.036(2.50)	-.049(3.05)	-.048(3.48)	-.051(3.69)	-.050(4.03)	-.047(4.86)
SOUTH	-4.042(3.81)	-6.131(5.30)	-5.242(5.50)	-5.812(6.08)	-5.037(6.36)	-4.853(6.83)
SCOTLAND	3.248(1.50)	2.660(1.12)	.701(0.36)	1.469(0.74)	.582(0.35)	.573(0.54)
S	2.672	2.934	3.007	2.462	2.549	2.636
$\bar{R}^2$	.520	.609	.509	.609	.511	.546

Source and notes: The dependent variable is PERCELT, the percentage a given city's population was Irish-born. The independent variables are: CITYSIZE, total population in city; CITYGROWTH, per annum population growth in city over previous decades; DISTANCE, city's distance in miles from Glasgow, Liverpool, Bristol, or London, whichever is closest; and regional dummy variables, SOUTH, SCOTLAND and NORTH (= the north of England) includes the counties of Cheshire, Lancashire, the Ridings, Durham, Northumberland, Cumberland, and Westmorland. These data rely on the censuses. The smallest N = 39 sample of cities includes London, Glasgow, Edinburgh, Liverpool, Manchester, Leeds, Birmingham, Bristol, and 31 smaller cities in England and Wales. Ten of the cities are in the North, 27 in the South, and 2 in Scotland. The N = 52 sample adds Perth, Merthyr-Tydill, and 11 English towns to the original N = 39 sample. The N = 70 sample includes 61 cities and towns in England and Wales, plus 9 in Scotland. t-statistics in parentheses.

Table 6.3. *The share of the British population Irish-born, 1851 and 1861*

	Percent Share of	
Year and region	Irish in total	Irish ≥ Age 20 in total ≥ age 20
1851:		
All Scotland	7.2	9.4
Scotland's cities	12.6	15.8
All England & Wales	2.9	3.9
England & Wales cities	6.1	8.0
All Britain	3.5	4.7
Britain's cities	6.9	8.9
1861:		
All Scotland	6.7	10.2
Scotland's cities	10.6	15.7
All England & Wales	3.0	4.5
England & Wales cities	5.2	7.8
All Britain	3.5	5.3
Britain's cities	6.0	8.8

Sources and notes: See notes to Table 6.4.

tions was really quite enormous. For example, 83.4 percent of the Irish in Britain's cities were adults in 1861 (greater than or equal to twenty) and the figure for the non-Irish in Britain's cities was much lower, 54.7 percent. Rural areas reveal the same gap, 81.2 versus 53.1 percent. Furthermore, the data in Table 6.4 confirm the traditional view that the famine served to lower the selectivity bias: 74.4 percent of the Irish-born in Britain's cities were adults in 1851, a figure somewhat lower than for 1861.[5]

The age selectivity of the Irish immigrants is likely to matter to any assessment of the impact of the Irish on British labor markets. This can be seen quite clearly in Table 6.3. Although the Irish-born in Britain were

5 Certainly the age selectivity of Irish emigrants has long been appreciated. For example, Irish emigrants under age fifteen accounted for only 14.8 percent of total Irish emigrants in the 1860s while they accounted for 32.8 percent of the Irish population itself (Mokyr, 1983, p. 234). The same was true of Irish emigrants to America in the 1830s (Erickson, 1981, pp. 183–4; Mokyr and Ó Grada, 1982; Ó Grada, 1983). And what was true of the early nineteenth century was even more true of the late nineteenth century (Ó Grada, 1975, p. 146).

Table 6.4. *Population distribution by age; immigrants and nonimmigrants, 1851 and 1861 (in %)*

	1851		1861	
Region & group	Less than 20	Greater than or equal to 20	Less than 20	Greater than or equal to 20
Scotland				
Cities				
Irish immigrants	29.5	70.5	17.6	82.4
Other immigrants	25.6	74.4 ⎫		
		⎬	47.4	52.6
Nonimmigrants	62.0	38.0 ⎭		
Total	43.7	56.3	44.3	55.7
Rural				
Irish immigrants	28.9	71.1	17.9	82.1
Other	47.8	52.2	48.4	51.6
Total	46.8	53.2	47.0	53.0
England & Wales				
Cities				
Irish immigrants	24.6	75.4	16.2	83.8
Other immigrants	22.7	77.3 ⎫		
		⎬	45.0	55.0
Nonimmigrants	58.6	41.4 ⎭		
Total	42.7	57.3	43.5	56.5
Rural				
Irish immigrants	28.0	72.0	19.1	80.9
Other	46.7	53.3	46.7	53.3
Total	46.5	53.5	46.2	53.8
Britain				
Cities				
Irish immigrants	25.6	74.4	16.6	83.4
Other immigrants	23.0	77.0 ⎫		54.7
		⎬	45.3	
Nonimmigrants	58.9	41.1 ⎭		
Total	42.8	57.2	43.6	56.4
Rural				
Irish immigrants	28.3	71.7	18.8	81.2
Other	46.9	53.1	46.9	53.1
Total	46.5	53.5	46.3	53.7

Sources and notes: For 1851: The 1851 Census where "cities" are the aggregate of 61 principal towns in England and Wales (including London) and 9 in Scotland. For 1861: The 1861 Census where "cities" are the aggregate of 61 principal towns in England and Wales (including London) and 20 in Scotland. In both cases, "nonimmigrants" are those born in the city, and "immigrants" are those born elsewhere. The 1861 Census does not distinguish between city immigrants and city-born for those born in England and Wales, but rather only county of birth (of which the city may be a part).

only 3.5 percent of the total population in 1851, the Irish-born twenty years of age or older were 4.7 percent of the British population age 20 or older, a good deal bigger share. Indeed, Irish-born adults were 8.9 percent of all adults in British cities at the time of the 1851 census, a figure two and a half times their population share in Britain as a whole. Similar results emerge when Scotland, England, and Wales are examined independently. Age selectivity can also play a role in interpreting trends. While the share of the Irish-born in the British population remained unchanged between the 1851 and 1861 censuses (3.5 percent), Irish-born adults increased their share from 4.7 to 5.3 percent.

6.3   How big was the Irish inflow?

The debate over magnitudes

Most of the debates surrounding the impact of the Irish on the British economy during the First Industrial Revolution hinge on the size of the migrations. Unfortunately, "there are no reliable estimates of even total emigration during the years between Waterloo and the Famine" (Ó Grada, 1977, p. 65). The Emigration Commissioner's figures for the 1820s and 1830s are nothing more than informed guesses, and the British census enumerators did not ask "where were you born?" until 1841. But some effort must be made to estimate the Irish in Britain prior to the Great Famine. After all, without those estimates how are we to assess the impact of Irish labor supplies on the British standard of living, on the crowding-out of native-born labor, on the deflection of discouraged native-born from Britain's cities, and on industrialization with cheap labor? Furthermore, there is reason to believe that the Irish migrations were quantitatively important even prior to the Great Famine. Indeed, in the *Report on the State of the Irish Poor in Great Britain* Cornewall Lewis argued that the Irish migrations of the 1820s and 1830s were "nearly unparalleled in the history of the world" (*PP*, 1836, vol. 34, p. 429).

Before moving on to the new estimates offered in this section, some quantitative underbrush must be cleared away. First, it should be made clear that the annual immigration of the Irish into Britain is of limited interest to us here. Instead, it is the stock of Irish in Britain who survived that matters to any assessment of the labor-market impact, and mortality rates were high in the very cities in which the Irish tended to settle.

Second, the immediate descendants of the Irish-born must be included in the accounting. After all, in the absence of the Irish immigrants, the British labor force would have been diminished still further because the children of the immigrants would never have made their entrance into the labor market fifteen to twenty years later. Because the Irish-born tended to be young adults, they would also have tended to produce more offspring after arrival than would a comparable-sized native-born population. The age selectivity of the immigrants would, therefore, have served to augment future labor-force growth rates through this influence (and, of course, it would have served to lower future labor-force growth rates in Ireland). Third, it is not the Irish population in Britain that concerns us here but rather the Irish labor force. We have already seen that the immigrants tended to be young adults, and thus they should have had higher labor participation rates than the native-born. The critical issue, however, is whether they were sufficiently higher to really matter. Fourth, this chapter's focus will be the Irish impact on the total British labor force, of which the cities were a part. When confronted with the evidence that "only" 3.5 percent of the British population was Irish in 1851, the literature typically points out that the share was far higher in the cities (6.9 percent) and in the northern cities in particular. In addition, the literature also points out that the Irish were a far higher proportion of some notable occupations. Thus, for example, the Irish are viewed by Pollard (1978) as "shock troops" in Manchester's textile industry, even though they might appear less important to the overall British economy. Qualifications like Pollard's are important only if one believes that the British labor market was highly segmented, and that wages were not linked between various city and industry labor markets. If, on the contrary, they were closely linked, then the fact that the Irish were a very high share of the total employed in some cities and industries is unimportant in assessing the impact of the Irish. Only the aggregate British labor-force impact would matter. Although this chapter will raise this issue again, I do not believe that British labor markets were regionally segmented anything like the degree necessary to make the economy-wide assessment inappropriate. What follows, therefore, are estimates of the impact of the Irish on British labor markets in the aggregate.

Estimating the Irish in Britain, 1787–1871

Estimating the stock of Irish in Britain faces two main problems: reconstructing the Irish-born in Britain prior to the 1841 Census and converting the Irish-born into what Clapham called the "effective Irish." The details of the estimation can be found in Appendix 6.1; Table 6.5 (col. 2) reports a summary.

These estimates of the Irish in Britain, 1787–1871, are certainly consistent with the traditional view that the Irish immigrants were extensive prior to the Great Famine (O'Brien, 1921, pp. 207–21; Redford, 1926, pp. 132–70; Adams, 1932). The yearly rates of growth of the Irish in Britain implied by these estimates are as follows:

1787–1821	6.7%	1831–41	3.7%	1851–61	1.0%
1821–31	4.7	1841–51	5.4	1861–71	−.4

The big surprise is that the growth of the Irish in Britain was as high between the 1780s and the late 1820s as it was during the famine conditions of the Hungry Forties. It could be argued, of course, that the base is so small in 1787 to make the 6.7 percent yearly growth up to 1821 in some sense irrelevant. In any case, the estimates gain further credibility by the fact that the decadal growth rates appear to be consistent with qualitative accounts of the Irish migrations. The estimates capture the migration boom of the 1820s, the slump of the 1830s, the famine-fed migration boom of the 1840s, and the cessation of the flows thereafter.

The impact of the Irish on the British labor force

We have already seen that the Irish immigrants were disproportionately young adults, but we need far more information to infer their likely labor force impact. The details of this tentative calculation are reported in Appendix 6.2, in which activity rates by age and sex for the contemporary Third World are applied to the age-sex distributions reported for the Irish in the British censuses. This is hardly the first application of Third World activity rates to British demographic history; Wrigley and Schofield did the same in *The Population History of England* to isolate the likely impact of changes in the age distribution on dependency rates from 1541 to 1871 (1981, pp. 443–50).

According to these illustrative calculations, the Irish-born had higher labor participation rates than did British residents in general, and the gap was very large. The following figures summarize the details:

Census year	Irish-born	British	Difference
1831	.569	.443	.126
1841	.569	.452	.117
1851	.555	.455	.100
1861	.611	.456	.155

These estimates gain additional credibility from the fact that the British rates almost exactly correspond to Feinstein's for 1831 (.443 versus .441) and 1861 (.456 versus .467).[6] The "dip" in 1851 also faithfully reflects the fact that the famine in the 1840s generated Irish migrations that were more a family affair, involving more dependents. In short, there is reason to believe that the activity rates underlying our labor-force estimates are close to the mark.

When the Irish-born labor participation rates are applied to the Irish, we get the estimates of the Irish laborers in Britain in Table 6.5 (col. 3). As a share of the British labor force, the Irish rise from 3.4 to 8.8 percent over the four decades following 1821. The biggest jump, of course, is registered during the Hungry Forties, when almost one-quarter of the increase in the British labor force was Irish. Furthermore, the timing of the increase is suggestive: The period when the Irish impact on the British labor force was most significant (1821–61) coincides with an episode of rapid industrialization and rising inequality (Williamson, 1985a).

Table 6.6 offers an explicit counterfactual: How fast would the British labor force have grown in the absence of the Irish? For the four decades as a whole following 1821, the answer seems to be that the British labor force would have grown by .15 percent per year less, while during the Hungry Forties it would have grown by .26 percent per year less. Are these differences big enough to have mattered? In some sense they seem small, but in a relatively slow-growing economy like this one, "small" numbers can be deceiving. In any case, a lower growth rate in the un-skilled labor force in a Britain without the Irish may have had a very profound impact upon those with whom the Irish directly competed.

6.4   How the British labor market absorbed the Irish

Immigrant absorption in partial equilibrium

Any economic model predicts that immigration tends to make labor cheap in the recipient country, at least in the short run. In Britain between the 1820s and the 1850s, this would have been manifested, other things constant, by high pauper and poor-relief incidence among the immigrant Irish and the unskilled native-born with whom they competed for jobs. It

6 Feinstein, 1978, p. 85.

Table 6.5. *The Irish in British labor markets, 1787 to 1871*

Year	(1) Irish-born in Britain (000)	(2) Irish in Britain (000)	(3) Irish laborers in Britain (000)	(4) British labor force (000)	(5) Percentage British labor force Irish (%)	(6) Percentage of increase in British labor force Irish (%)	(7) British labor force without the Irish (000)
1787	20.0	40.0	22.8	3,930	.58		3,907.2
1821	182.0	365.0	207.7	6,200	3.35	8.15	5,992.3
1831	290.0	580.0	330.0	7,200	4.58	12.23	6,870.0
1841	415.7	831.5	473.1	8,400	5.63	11.93	7,926.9
1851	727.3	1,403.7	779.1	9,700	8.03	23.54	8,920.9
1861	805.7	1,555.0	950.1	10,800	8.80	15.55	9,849.9
1871	774.3	1,494.4	913.1	12,000	7.61	-3.08	11,086.9

Sources and notes: Cols. (1) and (2) are taken from Appendix 6.1. Col. (3): Labor-participation rates are taken from Appendix 6.2, where the labor-participation rates are 1781 = .569, 1821 = .569, 1831 = .569, 1841 = .569, 1851 = .555, 1861 = .611, and 1871 = .611. Col. (4): The 1787 figure is taken from Floud and McCloskey, 1981, p. 126. The remaining figures are taken from Deane and Cole, 1962, p. 143. Col. (5) = col. (3) ÷ col. (4). Col. (6): Increase in col. (3) ÷ increase in col. (4). Col. (7) = col. (4) minus col. (3).

Table 6.6. *British labor-force growth with and without the Irish, 1787 to 1861 (percentages per annum)*

Period	(1) Actual: With the Irish	(2) Counterfactual: Without the Irish	(3) Difference
1787–1821	1.35	1.27	.08
1821–1831	1.51	1.38	.13
1831–1841	1.55	1.44	.11
1841–1851	1.45	1.19	.26
1851–1861	1.08	1.00	.08
1787–1821	1.35	1.27	.08
1821–1841	1.53	1.41	.12
1841–1861	1.26	1.09	.17
1821–1861	1.40	1.25	.15

Sources and notes: Col. (1) calculated from Table 6.5, col. (4). Col. (2) calculated from Table 6.5, col. (7).

should also have been manifested as a high incidence of the immigrants among low-wage occupations, pushed into marginal service employment by the labor glut. Such employment would include Mayhew's street traders and what in the Third World literature is now called the "unorganized" service sector. In the short run, the impact should have been most pronounced in the northern cities, the main points of Irish entry. In the longer run, the Irish should have tended to lower real earnings of the unskilled everywhere as local labor gluts spread, through internal migration, to all parts of Britain. The real issue, however, is not whether the Irish tended to lower real wages in Britain, but rather the extent to which growth in real wages and living standards was suppressed.

Simple partial equilibrium analyses should help motivate these issues. As we shall see, two critical parameters are required to evaluate Britain's absorptive capacity: the elasticity of demand for (unskilled) labor and the elasticity of supply of the British native-born. Suppose the domestic labor supply is augmented by an exogenous influx of Irish ("pushed" by the Malthusian devil, the potato famine, or the demise of cottage industry), and the domestic labor market is given sufficient time to surmount downward wage rigidity. What real wage decline is required to induce British firms to hire the Irish-augmented labor force? If we view Figure 6.1 as a description of urban labor markets, high native-born labor-supply elas-

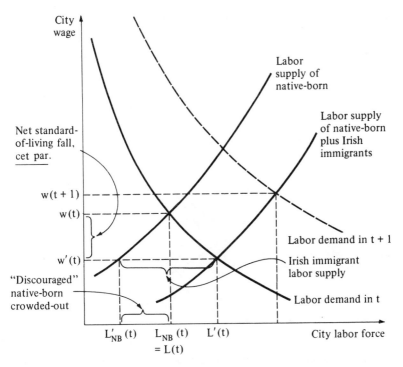

Figure 6.1   Labor absorption in British cities with immigrants pushed from Ireland: Partial equilibrium

ticities make sense because they would reflect the presence of a large rural
sector which serves as alternative employment for the potential British city
immigrant. Thus, the high native-born labor-supply elasticity implies "discouraged" native-born crowded out of city labor markets by "unfair" Irish
competition, and large changes in the ethnic composition of the urban
labor force are implied as well. The more the British are responsive to the
crowding-out, the less will a real wage decline be necessary to accommodate the Irish. High-demand elasticities for unskilled labor would imply
high absorption rates on the demand side, therefore inducing only modest
crowding-out of the native-born and implying equally modest real wage
declines to accommodate the new immigrants.

Figure 6.1 is drawn under the assumption that the Irish immigration is
exogenous, so that the Irish-augmented labor supply shifts to the right by
equal amounts at every wage level. In other words, push forces in Ireland

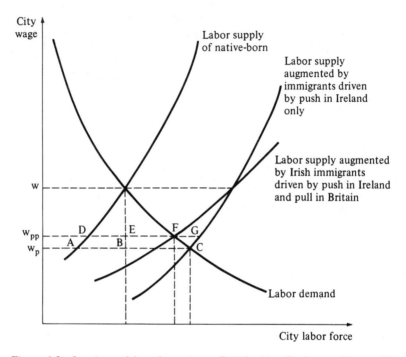

Figure 6.2   Immigrant labor absorption in British cities: Push vs. pull in partial equilibrium

are assumed to do all the work, while the pull of labor-market conditions in Britain's cities is ignored. The assumption is extreme, and it conflicts with the findings of Section 6.2, in which pull forces were stressed. It also implies an asymmetric treatment of native-born and Irish immigrants to Britain's cities. Suppose instead that the Irish also respond to employment conditions in Britain, higher wages attracting them and lower wages discouraging them. How would Figure 6.1 be revised? The aggregate labor-supply curve would be more elastic so that the same exogenous push forces in Ireland would serve to crowd out some of the Irish themselves, and a portion of the Irish would return home discouraged. These two cases, one with push only and one with both push and pull, are described in Figure 6.2. Here, we see that when the migrants are in addition responsive to employment conditions in Britain's cities, fewer native-born are crowded out and the real-wage declines by less (w_p versus w_{pp}). The contrast can be summarized by using the notation in Figure 6.2:

	Push Only		Push and Pull Combined
Labor-force expansion	BC	>	EF
Size of the push	AC	=	DG
Irish immigration	AC	>	DF
Irish crowded out	0	<	FG
Native-born crowded out	AB	>	DE
Wage decline	$(w - w_p)$	>	$(w - w_{pp})$

To the extent, therefore, that we continue to take the Irish immigrations as exogenous, we overstate their impact on the real wage and internal migration in Britain.

Figure 6.1 also employs simple comparative statistics: "labor demand in t" is drawn under the conventional assumption of fixed endowments and constant technologies. This characterization is obviously inappropriate for Britain between 1821 and 1861. Britain absorbed the Irish while undergoing capital accumulation, skill growth, and technical progress. These buoyant growth conditions, stressed at length in Chapter 4, are characterized by "labor demand in $t+1$" in Figure 6.1. Assuming no change in the wage elasticities underlying the labor demand and supply functions, the impact of the Irish influx on employment and the real wage is exactly the same along "labor demand in t." What is different about this more relevant case, of course, is that the real wage increases despite the immigration. To fully understand the Irish absorption problem, we need to know more than the elasticity of labor demand. We also need to know by how much the demand for labor shifted to the right over the period.

Immigrant absorption in general equilibrium

The qualitative narrative underlying Figures 6.1 and 6.2 is simple enough. Its quantitative application to the nineteenth-century British economy is a bit more complex. The application makes use of a four-sector general equilibrium model which has been developed, estimated, and applied to another set of problems (Williamson, 1984, 1985a). Appendix 6.3 repeats the model for those who wish the formal details. Although this section will stress only some key attributes of the model, readers who are prepared to take it on faith can skip ahead to Section 6.5. Even those readers who choose to skip ahead will wish to learn that the model has been estimated with data drawn from the early 1820s. It was also asked to predict British economic trends between 1821 and 1861. It did extremely well (Williamson, 1985a, chp. 9). Thus encouraged, we can use the model to assess the issue of Irish absorption with some confidence.

To begin with, unemployment is not a feature of the model and wages are assumed to clear sectoral and regional labor markets. Although the assumption of full employment and flexible wages seems appropriate for a period as long as four decades, what shall we assume about class mobility and wage gaps between city and countryside? Regarding the former, I am persuaded by the sociologists, the Marxists, and the unorthodox economists. Regarding the latter, I am persuaded that wage gaps are not crucial to the problem of Irish absorption. Consider each in turn.

Labor historians have long maintained that labor markets were stratified by occupation in nineteenth-century Britain. Mobility across occupations of different skills was extremely limited, implying that labor supplies by skill were highly wage-inelastic. Although pay may have been determined within a given market by conventional market forces, the absence of interoccupational mobility made it possible for large pay gaps between skills to persist. Since John Stuart Mill (1852) and J. E. Cairnes (1874, pp. 64–8), "unorthodox" economists have coined terms to deal with class immobility of this sort – noncompeting groups and labor-market segmentation. While this paradigm has often been invoked in analysis of nineteenth-century Britain, it is also a popular view of Third World labor markets, most recently of Brazil (Morley, 1982).

The more were British labor markets segmented by occupation, the more would the absorption of the Irish fall on the unskilled themselves, and the less would the adjustment shift onto the higher skilled occupations. Indeed, while an Irish-augmented unskilled labor force certainly served to raise British capitalists' profits and landlords' rents, it may also have served to raise the wages of skilled labor as well. The greater the labor-market segmentation across skills, the more were Irish unskilled, and the lower the substitution between skilled and unskilled labor, the more would the Irish immigrations have raised the skilled wage of the native-born, thus increasing earnings inequality in Britain. Section 6.2 has already confirmed that the Irish were unskilled, and there is a very large literature that confirms that the Irish moved only very slowly out of unskilled jobs (Redford, 1926, pp. 159–64; Clapham, 1933, p. 597; Hunt, 1973, p. 298; Werly, 1973; Steele, 1976; Pollard, 1978, pp. 103–5 and 112–14; Lees, 1979, chp. 4). As a consequence, I assume immobility between skill classes in what follows.

On the other hand, the Irish appear to have been spatially mobile. Indeed, as we pointed out earlier in this chapter, Sidney Pollard (1978, p. 113) has called them the mobile shock troops in industrializing Britain. It is certainly true that wages were not equalized across regions, and nowhere is that more apparent than for wage gaps between city and countryside, an issue that will receive detailed attention in the next chapter. However, as long as wage gaps were relatively stable over these four decades (and they were between the late 1820s and the 1850s),[7] the assumption of regional labor mobility is innocuous. I assume as much in this chapter.

So far, I have focused on labor markets in the model. Let us now flesh out the rest of the economy in which those labor markets are embedded. The model contains six factors of production: farmland, capital, unskilled labor, skills, home-produced intermediate resource inputs (for example, coal), and imported raw-material inputs (for example, cotton). Although the intermediates and imported raw materials are determined in each period by demand and supply, the remaining factor inputs are taken as given endowments, which, of course, are allowed to grow over time.

These six factors of production are used to produce four outputs: agriculture, manufacturing (including the building trades), services, and mining. Capital and unskilled labor are assumed to move freely among all four sectors; skilled labor is mobile between the industrial and service sectors to which its use is restricted; land is used only in agriculture; the imported raw-material input is used only in manufacturing; and the home-produced intermediate resource input is used in both manufacturing and services.

The economy is open to trade in all final consumption and investment goods, except services, a nontradable. The model also conforms to the reality that Britain was a net importer of agricultural goods and raw materials while a net exporter of manufactures. The prices of all these tradables are determined by commercial policy and world-market conditions.

The remaining six prices are determined endogenously: rent earned on an acre of cleared farmland under crop or pasturage, returns to capital, unskilled labor's wage, the wage for skills, the price of services, and the price of home-produced products of the mines. The first four of these

7 In Table 7.1, an index of nominal-wage gaps between city and countryside takes on an average value of 130 between 1851 and 1861, while it is 132 in 1827. Although the wage gap rises sharply after the Napoleonic Wars, it remains at high and fairly stable levels from the late 1820s to the 1850s.

prices are factor rents, central to understanding Irish absorption, inequality, and the standard of living. Each of these can be converted into real or relative prices. For example, the standard-of-living debate can be confronted by deflating nominal wages of the unskilled by the cost-of-living index, the latter constructed by a weighted average of the various prices in the model, the weights taken to be the budget shares implied by the demand system embedded in the model.

Final demands are endogenous, and they are a function of relative prices, real income per capita, and population. The trade account is assumed to be in balance.

This exposition is sketchy, but it illustrates the character of the model, and it may also motivate some reluctant readers to look at Appendix 6.3 for the details. However, a word of caution should be added, which shall be repeated in Chapter 7: The purpose of this modeling exercise is *not* to supply precise estimates of the impact of the Irish on British labor markets. Rather, it serves only to give us some feel for the likely magnitudes. Indeed, in Section 6.7 I will argue that the model overstates the case in favor of a big Irish impact. The actual impact is likely to have been even smaller.

6.5   Britain's immigrant absorptive capacity

How elastic was the demand for immigrant unskilled labor in nineteenth-century Britain? We asked a similar question in Chapter 4, but there the focus was on nonfarm labor demand. Although the procedure is very much the same, here it is the economy-wide unskilled labor demand at issue.

Table 6.7 reports the full general equilibrium impact on the real unskilled wage from a 1 percent change in the unskilled labor force and in the population of which the unskilled households were a part. The smaller the decline in the real wage the better is the economy able to absorb the immigrants. Table 6.7 also reports the elasticity of labor demand in response to a real-wage change. According to the model, that long-run, economy-wide demand elasticity lay between 1.3 and 1.4, a bit less than that for nonfarm labor (estimated at 1.6 in Table 4.5), but high nonetheless.

Not only was the demand for unskilled labor fairly elastic during the period of Irish immigrations, but the demand for unskilled labor was shifting to the right at a rapid rate. The model estimates that the unskilled labor demand function was growing at about 2 percent per year between 1821 and 1861. Although this rate of demand shift was somewhat less

Table 6.7. *Immigrant absorptive capacity in Britain, given resource endowments, technology, and world-market conditions*

	Elasticities	
	---	---
	Impact of $\overset{*}{L}$ and $\overset{*}{POP}$ on the real unskilled wage	Impact of the real unskilled wage on labor demand
Year	(1)	(2)
1821	−0.767	−1.304
1861	−0.705	−1.418
1891	−0.729	−1.372

Sources and notes: See text for a description of col. (1). It estimates the joint impact of an unskilled labor-supply increase, $\overset{*}{L}$ (and of the population of which that unskilled labor supply was a part, $\overset{*}{POP}$) on the real unskilled wage. Col. 2 inverts column (1) and measures the impact of a 1 percent rise in the unskilled real wage on the demands for unskilled labor.

than that for nonfarm labor alone (2.3 percent per year: Table 4.4), it was large enough to exceed unskilled labor-supply growth (1.4 percent per year) by quite a bit, thus creating increased unskilled labor scarcity and a rise in the real wage.

Britain must have found it relatively easy to absorb the Irish. The elasticity of demand for unskilled immigrant labor was probably quite high, and the demand for unskilled labor seems to have shifted to the right at a fairly fast rate. Given those favorable demand conditions, the only thing that would have created absorption problems in British labor markets would have been a very large supply of new Irish immigrants. As we shall see, the Irish migrations were simply not large enough to overwhelm those favorable demand conditions.

6.6   Counterfactual: A British industrial revolution without the Irish?

What was the impact of the Irish immigrants? To help get an answer, this section will pose three alternative counterfactuals.

First, we shall explore the impact of the Irish over the four decades as a whole had the famine never taken place. This "no Irish famine influx" counterfactual supposes that the Irish in Britain grew at the same rate in the 1840s as they did in the previous two decades. Because it turns out that the Irish immigrated to Britain at a very high rate even before the famine decade, the British labor force would have been only marginally affected, the labor force growth rate declining from 1.4 percent per year in fact to 1.38 percent per year in the "no Irish famine influx" counterfactual world. This is certainly a relevant counterfactual if our purpose were simply to assess the impact of the Irish famine on British labor markets. Second, we shall explore the impact on Britain had no more Irish arrived after 1821, and had the Irish in 1821 maintained their numbers with death rates just offsetting birth rates. This "no more Irish after 1821" counterfactual poses a much greater impact on the British labor force over the four decades as a whole than does the "no Irish famine influx" counterfactual. Although it is hard to imagine such a counterfactual world, because it implies the passage of immigrant restrictions in 1821 – a political event that was never seriously debated – it is precisely the counterfactual that is most relevant for assessing the Irish impact on British labor markets after 1821. Finally, we shall explore the impact of the Irish on the Hungry Forties alone. Although this "no more Irish after 1841" counterfactual implies the passage of immigrant restrictions during a decade of Irish economic distress – an event that was never a viable political issue – it still serves to offer an estimate of the impact of the Irish during a decade that has attracted much comment and debate.

To avoid any confusion, I should emphasize one counterfactual that is not explored in this chapter. Nowhere do I try to assess the impact on British labor markets had the Irish in Britain suddenly returned home. No doubt their departure would have created serious labor scarcity, but I don't think this has ever been an issue in the literature. Rather, the issue has always come down to the impact of new Irish immigrants.

Table 6.8 assesses the first two counterfactuals over the full four decades. The key message emerging from the table is that Irish immigration mattered little to British development over these four decades. The impact is always of predictable sign, but the magnitudes are almost always very small. Suppose we focus on the most meaningful counterfactual, "no more Irish after 1821." The counterfactual labor-force growth would have declined by more than the population growth rate since, as we have already seen, the Irish had far higher labor participation rates. The counterfactual decline in the unskilled labor force, from 1.4 to 1.22 percent per year, is not trivial. Who would have gained? British common labor would have gained, of course, since the unskilled real wage would have grown at 1.06 rather than .92 percent per year. Part of the relatively slow rise in

Table 6.8. *The British industrial revolution without the Irish, 1821 to 1861*

| Per annum growth in: | Model's predictions 1821–1861 | | |
| | | Counterfactuals | |
	Actual with the Irish	No Irish famine influx	No more Irish after 1821
Labor force	1.40%	1.38%	1.22%
Population	1.23	1.21	1.10
Unskilled real wage	0.92	0.94	1.06
Land rents, deflated	1.82	1.81	1.68
Returns to capital, deflated	−0.47	−0.48	−0.57
Skilled real wage	1.71	1.70	1.61
Real income	2.35	2.35	2.28
Real income per capita	1.12	1.14	1.18
Real income, non-Irish	2.32	2.32	2.30
Real income per capita, non-Irish	1.20	1.20	1.18
Manufacturing output, deflated	3.17	3.16	3.13
Agricultural output, deflated	1.37	1.35	1.21
Manufacturing less agricultural output	1.80	1.81	1.92
Agricultural employment	0.93	0.90	0.65
Nonagricultural employment	1.58	1.57	1.44
Emigration rate from agriculture	−0.84	−0.87	−1.12

Source: See text.

income at the bottom of the distribution in Britain was due to an Irish glut from below. But the magnitudes are hardly large enough to persuade me that a major role should be assigned to the Irish accounting for lagging real-wage gains during the First Industrial Revolution. The Irish are simply not crucial to the British standard-of-living debate. Who would have lost? All other British, of course. British landlords would have enjoyed less dramatic increases in rents for conventional Ricardian reasons. British capitalists would have faced even greater declines in their returns to capital for conventional diminishing-returns reasons. And skilled British workers – Hobsbawm's "labor aristocracy" – would have found their increased scarcity a little less noticeable, as one of the complementary inputs, unskilled labor, would have been a little more scarce.

Once again, however, the key message is that British incomes were little affected by the Irish immigrations. Furthermore, the effects on British incomes were offsetting across social class. The British unskilled suffered a bit from Irish competition, while all other classes gained, landlords and capitalists in particular. The net effect was small. This can be seen most clearly in the middle of Table 6.8, where the impact on real income per capita is reported. Yes, per capita real incomes would have been higher had there been no more Irish after 1821. Yes, per capita real incomes of the non-Irish would have been lower had there been no more Irish after 1821, but the fall in per capita real income gains from 1.20 to 1.18 percent per year would surely have gone unnoticed. In short, while the non-Irish enjoyed real-income gains by the presence of Irish unskilled after 1821, those gains were tiny.

What about industrialization? Because the labor force would have grown at a slower rate without the Irish, output would have grown slower too, including manufacturing. But which sectors would have been hardest hit? The answer is obvious: those sectors that were most unskilled-labor-intensive. Because agriculture was more unskilled-labor-intensive than industry, output would have shifted toward industry in the absence of the Irish. To repeat, Table 6.8 rejects the hypothesis that the Irish fostered industrialization. Had there been no Irish in Britain, agriculture would have suffered far more than industry. Only if we are concerned with industrial employment and output in isolation – as those witnesses from Manchester before the parliamentary committees in the 1830s were – can we conclude that the Irish fostered industrialization in Britain. Even here, the impact on manufacturing output growth would have been tiny, from 3.17 percent per annum with the additional Irish immigrants after 1821, to 3.13 percent per annum without them. And if instead we focus on industry's relative share of total output and employment, it then appears that the Irish inhibited industrialization in Britain.

The finding that Irish immigration tended to favor the expansion of agriculture more than manufacturing may seem odd to readers who are well aware that the Irish were never employed in agriculture with the same frequency as in industry (except, perhaps, seasonally). The resolution of the apparent anomaly is close at hand: in the absence of the Irish (whose point of entry was the urban labor market), British farm labor would have been encouraged to emigrate from agriculture at a more rapid rate. This can be seen at the bottom of Table 6.8. Had there been no more Irish after 1821, agricultural employment growth would have declined (from .93 to .65 percent per year), in part because of a decline in agricultural

Table 6.9. *The Hungry Forties without the Irish*

Per annum growth in:	Model's predictions 1841–1851	
	Actual: With the Irish (%)	Counterfactual: No more Irish after 1841 (%)
Labor force	1.45	1.12
Population	1.19	0.91
Unskilled real wage	0.88	1.14
Land rents, deflated	1.87	1.61
Returns to capital, deflated	−0.44	−0.62
Skilled real wage	1.73	1.57
Real income	2.37	2.25
Real income per capita	1.18	1.34
Real income, non-Irish	2.29	2.27
Real income per capita, non-Irish	1.34	1.32
Manufacturing output, deflated	3.16	3.10
Agricultural output, deflated	1.41	1.13
Manufacturing less agricultural output	1.75	1.97
Agricultural employment	1.01	0.50
Nonagricultural employment	1.62	1.36
Emigration rate from agriculture	−0.69	−1.20

Sources and notes: See text. The "Actual: With the Irish" experiment repeats that of Table 6.8 except that the labor-force and population-growth rates of the 1840s replace those of the four decades, 1821–1861, as a whole.

output growth and in part because of the rise in labor scarcity encouraging farmers to use less unskilled labor. And with the decline in agricultural employment growth, the rate of emigration from agriculture would have risen from −.84 to −1.12 percent per year. It appears that the Irish had a far bigger impact on rural-urban migration in Britain than they did on overall labor scarcity. One important explanation for the relatively low rates of emigration from British agriculture during the First Industrial Revolution is the crowding-out effect of the Irish.

Now let us turn our attention to the Hungry Forties. Table 6.9 reports the counterfactual impact had there been "no more Irish after 1841" (more accurately, had the Irish in 1841 just maintained their numbers across the 1840s). That may seem a bit extreme – there would have been

Irish immigration during the 1840s, even in the absence of the famine –
but perhaps not so extreme when we recall that growth of the Irish-born
in Britain slowed down dramatically in the 1850s, and in fact total Irish-
born actually declined in the 1860s. In any case, the counterfactual places
an upper bound on the impact of the Irish during this critical decade.

For the Hungry Forties, most of the effects reported for the four decades
as a whole are heightened. Unskilled real-wage improvements were suppressed far more during the famine decade: real wages of the unskilled
would have grown at 1.14 percent per year in the absence of more Irish,
rather than 0.88 percent. Furthermore, the emigration rate from agriculture
would have been almost double what it was had there been no more Irish after 1841, a finding that appears to account for the unusually low rates of out-
migration observed for the 1840s (Table 4.1). Note, however, that Table 6.9
repeats a finding that emerged from Table 6.8: it appears that total non-
Irish real income per capita was not greatly affected by the Irish presence.

6.7   Assessing the elastic labor-supply model

The classical labor-surplus model

Writing in the first half of the nineteenth century, post-Smithian economists developed their dynamic models to deal with economic and demographic events they thought they saw going on around them after the
1780s. The evidence that underlay those models was mostly anecdotal. It
has taken historians more than a century to establish something approximating a hard data base for the First Industrial Revolution. But based on
street-level observations, expert witnesses before parliamentary committees, foreign-trade data, incomplete tax returns, and scraps of demographic information, the classical economists thought they saw the dimensions of the First Industrial Revolution clearly. The phenomenon that
struck them as most notable was stable real wages. How was it possible for
rapid industrialization to occur while at the same time the standards of
living of the working classes changed but little?

Marx tried to explain these events by appealing to technological forces.
Labor-saving technological change in industry and enclosures pushing
labor off the land in agriculture both served to augment the reserve army,
keeping the lid on common labor's real wage. Thus, Marx's model offered
a derived labor-demand explanation, technologically driven. Although

Malthus appears to have been unaware that an industrial revolution was taking place around him, his model could explain these events by appealing to a demographic response. Any improvement in real wages in the short run served to foster early marriage, greater fertility within marriages, as well as an elastic Irish immigration response. Malthus's elegant demographic-economic model implied a labor-supply explanation, an elastic labor supply ensuring a long-run subsistence wage floor, and no standard-of-living improvement for common labor. Others appealed to conditions in agriculture. For them, "disguised unemployment" in the Irish and English countryside ensured an elastic labor supply to the rapidly growing industrial sector, and, as a result, no standard-of-living improvement for common labor. In these classical labor-surplus models of stable real wages, rapid capital accumulation goes hand in hand with an absence of capital deepening, because any increase in the capital stock induces an equal increase in employment along an elastic labor-supply function.

In contrast, Ricardo seems to have appealed to capital scarcity and slow industrialization to get stable real wages and labor surplus. In the Ricardian model, the causation seems to go from slow capital-deepening to labor surplus, not vice versa. Given the inelastic supply of land, rents increase their share in national income, a savings shortfall results from landlords' lack of thrift, and accumulation slows down. As capital-deepening comes to a halt, labor's marginal product stabilizes at subsistence wages.

As the British economy passed through a "turning point" (the term used by John Fei and Gustav Ranis, 1964, chp. 6) in the middle of the nineteenth century, and real wages began to rise markedly, British economists lost interest in these classical growth paradigms. Instead they adopted the more optimistic neoclassical paradigm, which became the dominant interpretation of economic growth for almost a century. But as Third World development attracted economists' attention in the 1950s, W. Arthur Lewis (1954) asked us to take another look at those discarded classical models, the "non-Ricardian" paradigms in particular. The implication was that the Third World in the 1950s closely resembled Britain in the late eighteenth and early nineteenth century, and thus if the classical models worked well then, they should work well for the Third World too. Lewis's celebrated "labor surplus" model emerged as a result.

Lewis's model underwent extensive refinement and elaboration after it first appeared in 1954. In the early 1960s, Fei and Ranis (1964) formally extended the model and applied it to Japan and South Asia. In 1966, A. K. Sen showed us exactly what assumptions were required to make the labor-surplus model operational, and shortly thereafter Avinash Dixit (1973) placed it within the mainstream of growth theory. It remained for Lance Taylor (see, for example, Taylor et al., 1980) to embed the fixed-real-wage paradigm into large-scale macro models of Third World economies. Furthermore, there has been at least one serious empirical application of this tradition to European economic history. In his *Industrialization in the Low Countries,* Joel Mokyr applied a creative "pseudo" labor-surplus model to the Lowlands between 1795 and 1850 (Mokyr, 1976, especially chapters 5 and 6), a useful effort that broke new ground.

The point of this recitation is simply to remind us that the labor-surplus model has its roots with the classical (non-Ricardian) economists, and that the classical economists developed their paradigms to account for British economic experience during the first decades of the industrial revolution. They thought that elastic labor supplies were an important part of the process, and that Irish immigrations were an important part of the elastic labor supplies.

The role of the Irish

The evidence in this chapter contradicts the elastic labor supply hypothesis, or at least the role that the Irish are said to have played in it. Although the Irish immigrations into Britain during the First Industrial Revolution did tend to inhibit rural out-migration of the native-born, they did not play a significant role in accounting for common labor's lagging living standards, nor did they foster industrialization.

These are revisionist findings. Could it be that they are simply the result of an irrelevant model, one which applies inappropriate assumptions with blind, cliometric zeal? The issue is not whether or not to model the Irish absorption problem. Model we must, for the issue is much too important to be left any longer to assertion, anecdotal evidence, and persuasive rhetoric. Nor, in my opinion, should future debate dwell on whether a neoclassical model is the appropriate way to attack the problem. I doubt very much that a model with rigid wages, unemployment, and pauperism would yield a significantly different assessment than that contained in Section 6.6.

Throughout this chapter I have suggested that the estimate of the Irish impact on the British economy is an upper bound, and the true impact was somewhat smaller. I certainly believe that to be the case for all the counterfactuals where we have altered Irish labor supplies, especially since we have taken Irish immigration to be driven by exogenous "push." Section

6.4 argued that proper attention to immigrant "pull" would reduce the impact of the Irish. But what about my assumptions regarding labor absorption? Have I overdrawn the ease with which the British economy absorbed the Irish? In a sense I have.

For example, I have assumed throughout that Irish and non-Irish common labor were perfect substitutes, the Irish crowding the native-born out of unskilled urban jobs and lowering native-born unskilled earnings. If in fact they were less than perfect substitutes (unskilled labor markets segmented along ethnic lines), then the Irish themselves would have borne an even larger share of the absorption burden, and the crowding-out effect on the unskilled native-born would have been less than I have estimated here. The evidence does appear to support the view that Irish and non-Irish unskilled were perfect substitutes within Paisley mills, Liverpool docks, railroad-construction sites in the South of England, and Mayhew's East London labor markets. But were they perfect substitutes between those places? In the very short run they were not, so that labor markets at the point of Irish entry were hardest hit, past and present Irish migrants absorbing much of the labor-market adjustment through unemployment and lowered wages. In the long run, however, I believe interregional migration of common labor served to distribute the incidence of labor absorption more evenly across the British economy as a whole. The model adopts the long-run view. If the reader prefers the short-run view, then he should lower our estimate of the impact of the Irish on living standards and rural out-migration among the non-Irish.

There is another even more compelling reason why these revisionist findings should be viewed as an understatement. Nowhere in the comparative static exercise in Section 6.6 have I considered the potential dynamic response to the Irish immigrations, and each of these would have made the long-run absorption of the Irish even easier. First, the non-Irish labor supply must have been smaller than it would have been in the absence of the Irish. After all, by competing for city jobs the Irish immigrants encouraged more native-born to emigrate to the New World and discouraged more foreign potential immigrants from coming to Britain. Perhaps in the very long run the Irish even encouraged the native-born to marry a bit later and have fewer children than they would have had in the absence of the Irish, reducing the native-born labor supply still further. In short, in the absence of the Irish, native-born and other foreign labor-supply sources would have partially filled the gap, minimizing the impact of the Irish absence. Second, although abundant Irish common labor served to increase the relative scarcity of native-born skills, some portion of the expansion of skills between 1821 and 1861 was surely induced by that scarcity. It seems likely, therefore, that the Irish immigration encouraged a more rapid accumulation of skills among the non-Irish than would have taken place in the absence of the Irish. Third, there are many sound economic arguments that would favor the view that capital accumulation must have been more rapid in the presence of the Irish than would have taken place in their absence. The rate of return to capital would have been higher with the Irish (given a lower capital-labor ratio in the short run), encouraging more saving and accumulation in response. Furthermore, because wages were lower and profits were higher in the presence of the Irish than they were in their absence, it follows that the Irish immigrations should have generated an accumulation response by raising the share of income accruing to potential savers, an argument that has always been central to the classical growth model. Each of these three potential dynamic responses would have made the migrant absorptive capacity of the British economy even higher. In that the empirical assessment in Section 6.6 ignored these responses, we have exaggerated the impact of the Irish, an impact already estimated to be small.

The elastic labor-supply model does not appear to be well supported by evidence drawn from the historical episode for which it was initially designed. In contrast, a model with elastic labor demand seems to be better supported by the evidence. Irish immigration cannot account for much of the slow rise in workers' living standards between the 1820s and 1850s. Irish immigration was simply too small to matter much given the impressive absorptive capacity of the British economy during the First Industrial Revolution.[8]

8 What about the impact of the Irish on industrialization? More caution is warranted at this point. It is true that the counterfactuals reported in Tables 6.8 and 6.9 fail to support the notion that Irish immigration fostered British industrialization in any significant way, but those results are based on a model that assumes complete labor mobility between regions and sectors. Suppose the assumption was seriously violated? If regional and industrial labor markets were highly segmented, the Irish immigrations would have had a bigger impact on industrialization than is estimated here. After all, Irish immigrants entered British labor markets through urban gates, and the locations where their relative numbers were largest were the northern industrial towns. To the extent that labor markets in those industrial towns were partially isolated from the rest of Britain, labor supplies would have increased by more there, wages would have suffered more, profits would have gained more, and industrialization would have been more pronounced. As I stated earlier in this chapter, I do not believe that labor-market segmentation was sufficiently pronounced to alter seriously the impact of migration on industrialization estimated here, especially over a period as long as four decades.

Appendix 6.1. Estimating the Irish in Britain, 1787–1871

As the text indicates, there are two steps involved in estimating the stock of Irish in Britain over the late eighteenth and nineteenth centuries: first, to reconstruct those figures for the pre-1841 period before the census enumerators asked "where were you born;" and second, to inflate the Irish-born to what Clapham called the "effective Irish." Throughout, our interest is solely in the stock of Irish resident in Britain at various benchmark dates rather than the flow of Irish immigrants in any given year. The focus on Irish stocks is explained by two factors: the stocks of Irish-born in Britain are far easier to estimate than the annual flows of immigrants; and, more importantly, we are interested only in the impact of the survivors and their immediate descendants on the British labor market in the long run.

The reconstruction of the Irish-born in Britain for the pre-1841 period is guided by estimates for major recipient areas prior to the 1841 Census. For example, expert opinion offered estimates of the share of the Irish in Manchester in 1787, and again for Lancaster County in 1835, the latter based on the 1836 Poor Inquiry reporting *The State of the Irish Poor in Great Britain* and the *First Annual Report of the Poor Law Commission* (1835). Given the 1841–71 Census estimates of Manchester's and Lancaster County's share of the Irish-born, and given documentation of the "drift" of the Irish away from large cities, like Manchester, over time (see Section 6.2), we can estimate the Irish in Britain in 1787 and 1835. Similarly, James Cleland's private census of Glasgow enumerated the Irish in 1821 and 1831. Again, given Glasgow's share of the Irish-born during 1841–71, and given the drift of the Irish away from the large cities, like Glasgow, over time, we can estimate the Irish in Britain in 1821 and 1831. If Manchester, Lancaster County, and Glasgow had contained only small concentrations of Irish, this interpolation of the past might be questionable. As Appendix Table 6.2 documents, however, these were always especially important Irish migrant destinations.

Appendix Table 6.1 summarizes the estimating procedure in some detail. It should be stressed that these estimates of the stock of Irish-born in Britain appear to be consistent with the qualitative accounts of the annual immigrant flows in the literature. Thus, the period 1787–1821 is seen as one of modest immigration and relatively slow growth in the stock of Irish-born in Britain (1836 *Report on the State of the Irish Poor in Great Britain*, pp. iv–v; Handley, 1947, p. 86; MacDonald, 1937, p. 79; Redford, 1926, pp. 133–4). There is some evidence of an acceleration in Irish immigration into Britain during the 1816–19 period of agricultural distress, when in fact Irish vagrants appear to be searching for generous local welfare in England (Redford, 1926, p. 138). The pace of migration continued at this relative fast rate throughout most of the 1820s in part due to Irish famine, in part due to the continued crowding-out of the cottage textile industry in Ireland, in part due to the impressive decline in fares for passage across the Irish Sea, and in part due to the urban boom in Britain's cities (Clapham, 1930, v. 1, p. 61; Clapham, 1933, p. 601; 1871 *Census of Scotland*, v. I, p. xix; Redford, 1926, pp. 132–170; 1836 *Report on the State of the Irish Poor in Great Britain*, p. 429). Most accounts agree that the rate of immigration slowed down during the 1830s as good crops and

Appendix Table 6.1. *Estimating the Irish in Britain, 1787–1871*

	Scotland		England & Wales		Great Britain		
Year	Effectively Irish	Irish-born	Effectively Irish	Irish-born	Effectively Irish	Irish-born	Sources and notes
1787	15,000	7,500	25,000	12,500	40,000	20,000	A. Redford (1926, p. 135) states that by 1787 "Manchester was said to have an Irish population of more than 5,000." In 1841, the census shows that 8.3% of the British Irish-born were in Manchester, a figure that falls continually to 1861 as the Irish disperse to small towns. By interpolation, Manchester's share of Britain's Irish is estimated at about 13%, assuming the "dispersion" to have occurred at a fairly stable rate. Similarly, Manchester's share in England's Irish-born is estimated to have been about 20%. Scotland is derived as a residual. The ratio of "effectively Irish" to Irish-born (the former including the children of immigrants) is taken to be 2, based on Thomas Parker in the 1836 Poor Inquiry (*PP.* 1836, 34, p. 42). This ratio of 2 is repeated by experts well into the 1870s, as we shall see below.
1821	126,000	63,000	239,000	119,000	365,000	182,000	According to James Cleland (1820, 1832, 1840; see also Clapham, 1930, vol. I, p. 61), who took the Glasgow census in 1821 and 1831, there were 25,000 Irish-born in Glasgow in 1821. The 1841 British census shows that 10.7% of the British Irish-born and 35.1% of the Scottish Irish-born were in Glasgow, figures that fall continuously to 1861. By the same argument and interpolation as with the 1787 estimates, Glasgow's share in Britain's Irish-born is taken to have been 13.7% and in Scotland's Irish-born, 39.8%. England and Wales derived as a residual. The ratio of effectively Irish to Irish-born is taken as 2, as above in the 1787 estimate.

Year							Notes
1831	190,000	95,000	390,000	195,000	580,000	290,000	According to James Cleland (see 1821 above), there were 35,556 Irish-born in Glasgow in 1831. By the same argument and interpolation as with the above estimates, Glasgow's share in Britain's Irish-born is taken to have been 12.2%, and in Scotland's Irish-born, 37.5%. England and Wales is derived as a residual. The ratio of effectively Irish to Irish-born is taken as 2, as above in the 1787 estimate.
1835	180,000 (117,000)	90,000 (58,000)	410,000 (273,000)	205,000 (137,000)	590,000 (390,000)	295,000 (195,000)	According to George Lewis in the 1836 Poor Inquiry (*PP.* 1836, 34, pp. vi–viii), there were almost 100,000 Irish in Lancaster County in 1833. The lower number in parentheses is based on Lewis's low estimate. James P. Kay (First Annual Report of the Poor Law Commission PP. 1835, 35, p. 185) disagreed, and set the figure at 150,000. The upper number is based on Kay's high estimate, figures that I favor. Lewis and Kay both included "immediate descendants" and thus were estimating the effectively Irish. In the 1841 census, Lancaster's share of Britain's Irish-born was 25.5% and 36.6% of the English Irish-born. These rates are applied without adjustment to 1833. Scotland is derived as a residual. The Irish-born is taken to be .5 of the effective Irish, as above in the 1787 estimate.
1841	252,642	126,321	578,808	289,404	831,450	415,725	The Irish-born figure is taken directly from the 1841 census. The ratio of the effective Irish to the Irish-born is again taken to be 2, this time based on the *Census of Scotland* for 1871 (*PP,* 1873, 73, p. xxxiv), where both are reported and 400,000/207,770 = 1.93, a figure that differs very little from Thomas Parker's 1821 estimate (see 1821 above).
1851	400,218	207,367	1,003,521	519,959	1,403,739	727,326	The Irish-born figure is taken directly from the 1861 census. The ratio of the effective Irish to the Irish-born is taken to be 1.93 and the "islands of the British Seas" are excluded (see 1841 above).

Appendix Table 6.1. (cont.)

Year	Scotland		England & Wales		Great Britain		Sources and notes
	Effectively Irish	Irish-born	Effectively Irish	Irish-born	Effectively Irish	Irish-born	
1861	393,880	204,083	1,161,154	601,634	1,555,034	805,717	The Irish-born figure is taken directly from the 1861 census. The ratio of the effective Irish to the Irish-born is taken to be 1.93 and the "islands of the British Seas" are excluded (see 1851 above).
1865	318,500	205,558	1,268,700	587,595	1,587,200	793,154	J. H. Clapham (1933, p. 603) estimated that 5 to 7% of the English population was effectively Irish in 1865, and that the figure for Scotland was 10%. Given the 1865 populations (Mitchell and Deane, 1962, p. 9) and 6% as the effective Irish share in England and Wales, the effective Irish estimates follow. The 1855 Irish-born estimates are linear interpolations between 1861 and 1871. Clapham appears to have understated the Irish in Scotland, while overstating the Irish in England and Wales. Since the latter dominates the British totals, his estimate for Britain's Irish appears to be too high as well.
1871	400,000	207,770	1,094,418	566,540	1,494,418	774,310	The Irish-born figure is taken directly from the 1871 census. The ratio of the effective Irish to the Irish-born is taken to be 1.93 and the "islands of the British Seas" are excluded (see 1851 above).

Appendix Table 6.2. *Distribution of the Irish in Britain, 1821–1861*

Area	Estimated 1821 (%)	Share in Britain's Irish-born in		
		Actual 1841 (%)	Actual 1851 (%)	Actual 1861 (%)
Four major cities				
Glasgow	c13.7	10.7	8.2	7.7
Liverpool	c13.4	11.9	11.5	10.4
London	c21.8	17.6	14.9	13.3
Manchester	c10.2	8.3	7.2	6.5
Other towns & rural	c40.9	51.5	58.2	62.1
Lancaster County	c24.2	25.5	26.3	27.0
England & Wales	c64.5	69.6	71.5	74.7
Scotland	c35.5	30.4	28.5	25.3

Sources and notes: Various censuses. The estimated 1821 figures are derived by linear extrapolation.

rapid growth came to both Ireland and Britain (Clapham, 1933, pp. 600–1; Redford, 1926, p. 151). The 1840s were, of course, a different story and here we have documentation as we enter the 1841–71 census period.

Estimating the Irish-born is only the first step. The second step involves the addition of the children of the Irish-born to inflate the Irish-born to "effectively Irish." This is discussed in the notes to Appendix Table 6.1. We note here that the ratio of the "effective" Irish to Irish-born was remarkably stable from the 1830s to the 1870s, when such estimates of the ratio were frequently offered by experts.

The resulting estimates of the "effectively Irish" in Britain are utilized in Section 6.3, where the impact of the Irish immigrations on the growth of the British labor force is discussed in detail.

Appendix 6.2. British and Irish-born labor-participation rates, 1821–61

Because our purpose is to assess the impact of Irish immigrations on British labor markets during the First Industrial Revolution, estimates of the Irish-born in Britain must somehow be translated into labor-supply figures. This appendix does so by applying activity rates from contemporary low-income industrializing societies to British experience in the early nineteenth century.

The censuses report population by age and sex for Britain as a whole throughout the period 1821–61, and, with a little effort, similar estimates can be constructed for the Irish-born 1841–61. If we had information on activity rates by age and sex, it would be a simple matter to infer aggregate Irish-born and British labor-participation rates for each census date 1821–61. There are at least two excellent activity-rate schedules available in the literature. The first was published by Eva Mueller (1976), whose interest was to asssess the economic value of children in peasant agriculture. Although Mueller's activity-rate schedule has already been used by Wrigley and Schofield (1981, pp. 443–50) to reconstruct the dependency ratio in England 1541–1871, and by Peter Lindert (1983, p. 154) to assess the causes of English demographic change over the same period, the schedule is of limited use here. First, it describes peasant agriculture only, while Britain in the 1820s is already quite removed from the agrarian status quo. Second, Mueller is not reporting activity rates, but rather "work contribution rates" that are the product of activity rates and productivity, the latter based on direct productivity observation from Korean agriculture in 1930 as well as indirect evidence offered by age-sex wage surveys from places like rural Egypt in 1964–5 (Mueller, 1976, pp. 115–20). I shall report below the implications of the application of Mueller's schedule to early nineteenth-century Britain; however, I favor the application of another schedule constructed by John Durand (1975). Durand has made comparable and pooled census evidence from eighty-five countries drawn from the period 1946–66, offering mean activity rates by age and sex at five levels of development (Durand, 1975, Tables 5.2 and 6.5, pp. 95–133). His Level I seems to approximate best Britain in the early nineteenth century.

Appendix Table 6.4 reports the Durand Level I schedule activity rates for sixteen age classes. The table also reports the age and sex distribution of the population in 1861 England and Wales. When these population weights are applied to the Durand Level I age-sex activity rates, an English labor-participation rate of .455 is implied. This figure is quite close to Charles Feinstein's independent 1861 estimate for Britain, .467 (Feinstein, 1978, p. 85, based on the labor-force estimates of Deane and Cole, 1962, Table 321, p. 143).

Appendix Table 6.3 aggregates those sixteen age classes for easy comparison with Mueller's schedule. Appendix Table 6.3 further aggregates these age clases into the two which are also reported for the Irish-born in the published censuses 1841–61.

Suppose the Durand Level I schedule is applied to the British age-sex distributions at the census dates 1821–61: What would the aggregate British labor-participation rate look like? Appendix Table 6.5 supplies the estimates. First, note

Appendix Table 6.3. *Activity rates by age and sex (ℓ_{ij}) applied to early nineteenth-century Britain*

Age Class	Mueller schedule			Durand Level I schedule		
	Male	Female	Total	Male	Female	Total
0–4	0	0	0	0	0	0
5–9	0	0	0	0	0	0
10–14	.150	.090	.120	.150	.090	.120
15–19	.750	.280	.515	.755	.506	.629
20–54	1.000	.300	.650	.959	.531	.735
55–59	.600	.130	.365	.938	.436	.680
60–64	.600	.130	.365	.867	.334	.588
65+	.350	.050	.200	.655	.201	.407
< 20	.193	.081	.137	.194	.129	.161
≧20	.904	.260	.567	.929	.487	.698

Sources and notes: The Mueller activity rates are taken from Wrigley and Schofield (1981, Table 10.5, p. 445), which in turn were based on Mueller (1976, p. 118). The Durand Level I activity rates are taken from Durand (1975, Tables 5.2 and 6.5, pp. 95 and 133) for ages greater than or equal to 15 and from Mueller for ages less than 15. Durand supplies far more age class detail than is shown above, and those reported here use 1861 census weights from England and Wales (*PP.* 1863, 53, pt. 1, pp. x–xi) to perform the aggregation. Durand offers five age-sex activity rate schedules by level of development, and Level I corresponds best with independent estimates of the 1861 aggregate British labor-participation rate offered by Feinstein (1978). See text.

that the Durand Level I estimate for 1831 almost exactly replicates the Feinstein estimate for that year, .443 versus .441, which certainly reinforces our confidence in the estimating procedure. Second, the aggregate British labor-participation rates drift upward over time, reflecting a decline in the child-dependency rate as Britain passes beyond her peak rates of fertility and population growth early in the period. This modest upward drift in the aggregate labor-participation rate is repeated in the Mueller estimates. Another source of the rise in the British labor-participation rate is, of course, the rise in the share of adult Irish immigrants in the British population.

The main purpose of this exercise, however, is to infer labor-participation rates among the Irish-born in Britain. Appendix Table 6.5 reports the application of the Durand Level I activity schedules to the Irish-born in Britain. For 1861, the Irish-born estimates use four activity rates, two sexes and two age classes (less than twenty years of age, and greater than or equal to twenty years of age), because the published Irish-born population distributions are limited to that breakdown. The 1841 and 1851 Irish-born population distributions are even more limited. As Boyle and Ó Grada (1984, p. 20) have recently reminded us, there is no published information on the ages of Irish-born in Britain in the 1841 Census, and there is no published information on the sexes of Irish-born in Britain in the 1851 Census.

Appendix Table 6.4. *Activity rates by age and sex (ℓ_{ij}) based on Durand Level I schedule, and 1861 census populations for England and Wales*

Age Class	Male		Female	
	Population	Activity rate	Population	Activity rate
0–4	1,354,907	0	1,345,875	0
5–9	1,172,960	0	1,171,106	
10–14	1,059,889	.150	1,045,287	.090
15–19	957,930	.755	974,712	.506
20–24	860,210	.915	969,283	.526
25–29	734,287	.965	834,877	.526
30–34	661,690	.973	725,088	.535
35–39	590,280	.977	634,262	.541
40–44	551,058	.975	583,069	.546
45–49	453,310	.973	477,530	.535
50–54	392,196	.960	414,367	.505
55–59	299,000	.938	315,004	.436
60–64	265,536	.867	290,704	.334
65–69	175,538	.786	201,034	.266
70–74	128,428	.642	152,917	.195
75+	119,040	.475	154,850	.124
All	9,776,259		10,289,965	.455

Sources and notes: The Durand Level I activity rates are taken from Durand (1975, Tables 5.2 and 6.5, pp. 95 and 133) for ages greater than or equal to fifteen and from Mueller (1976, p. 118) for ages less than fifteen. The population distributions are based on 1861 census figures for England and Wales (*PP.* 1863, 53, pt. 1, pp. x–xi).

If, however, we are willing to assume that the 1851 Irish-born age distribution applies to 1841 and that the 1841 sex distribution applies to 1851, then we can reconstruct the age-sex Irish-born distributions for both census years. Appendix Table 6.5 reports the results of this exercise for 1841 and 1851. Because there are no census counts of the Irish-born for 1821 and 1831, I have assumed that the 1841 rates prevailed for these earlier years as well.

Appendix Table 6.5 appears to confirm conventional qualitative wisdom. First, the selective character of migration is quite apparent. Irish immigrants tended to be young adults, and this effect was sufficiently dominant to make the labor-participation rates of the Irish-born far higher than the average British labor force at every census date. The differences are quite large: Irish-born labor-participation rates were 10 percentage points higher than the average for Britain in 1851, 13.1 percentage points higher in 1821 and 15.5 percentage points higher in 1861. Furthermore, the Irish-born labor participation rate underwent trends consistent with conventional qualitative wisdom. It has long been argued that the famine influx in the late 1840s and early 1850s was more a family-push affair than in the

Appendix Table 6.5. *British and Irish-born labor-participation rates: Various estimates for 1821–1861*

Census Year	Irish-born		All British		
	Mueller	Durand Level I	Mueller	Durand Level I	Feinstein
1821	(.473)	(.569)	.360	.438	na
1831	(.473)	(.569)	.364	.443	.441
1841	.473	.569	.370	.452	na
1851	.452	.555	.372	.455	na
1861	.502	.611	.371	.456	.467

	Excess Irish-born over British:	
	Mueller	Durand Level I
1821	.113	.131
1831	.109	.126
1841	.103	.117
1851	.080	.100
1861	.131	.155

Sources and notes: The Feinstein estimates are taken from Feinstein (1978, p.85), who uses the labor-force estimates in Deane and Cole (1962, Table 31, p. 143). The Mueller and Durand Level I estimates use the schedules in Appendix Table 6.3 (less than 20 and greater than or equal to 20). The population weights are taken from the various censuses. See text for a description in the 1841 and 1851 Irish-born population weights. The figures in parentheses for 1821 and 1831 simply assume the 1841 Irish-born figures to hold for the earlier census years.

prefamine and postfamine periods, when the migrations were more job-pull related and thus biased toward young adults (Hunt, 1973, p. 287; Lees, 1979, p. 43; Clapham, 1933; Handley, 1947; Adams, 1932; Redford, 1926). The Irish-born labor-participation rates in Appendix Table 6.5 reflect this influence by declining across the 1840s and then rising sharply across the 1850s.

Appendix 6.3. A formal statement of the long-run model[1]

The long-run model of the British economy after Waterloo is characterized by five "domestic" factors of production, four of which are primary inputs and one of which is an intermediate input (i = J, K, L, S, B):

farmland (J), excluding improvements other than initial clearing for cultivation or pasture;
capital (K), consisting of all nonhuman asset services in the business and government sector, other than farmlands, and excluding dwellings;
unskilled labor (L), or total manhours, compensated at the unskilled wage rate, including "own labor time" utilized in owner-occupied farms and in nonfarm proprietorships;
skills (S), or all attributes of labor inputs generating earnings in excess of the unskilled wage; and
intermediate resource inputs (B), used directly in the manufacturing sector or indirectly in the urban sectors "facilitating" manufacturing production.

In addition, there is one imported intermediate input:

imported raw material inputs (F), processed by manufacturing and unavailable at home.

It should be emphasized that the first four primary-factor stocks listed above are "givens" in that model: that is, we invoke the traditional assumption of comparative static analysis – factor endowments are determined exogenously. The flow of both intermediate inputs (F and B), however, will be determined endogenously in response to domestic demand and supply as well as to foreign trade.

These factor inputs are used in the production of four sectoral outputs (j = A, M, C, B):

agriculture (A), or all national income originating in agriculture, forestry, and fisheries;
manufacturing (M), or all national income originating in manufacturing, building, and construction;
the tertiary sector (C), or all national income originating in finance, trade, gas, electricity and water, private services, local and national government, transport and communications; and
intermediate resources (B), or all national income originating in mining and quarrying.

The empirical counterparts to the model's sectors have been listed above with a pragmatic eye on the existing national accounts.

We assume that the economy is open to trade in all final consumption and investment goods, except the tertiary sector, which produces nontradable "home" services. The home-produced intermediate good B cannot be traded internation-

---

1 A more complete exposition of this model can be found in Williamson (1985a, chp. 8).

ally (for example, coal) while the foreign-produced intermediate good F cannot be produced at home (for example, cotton). Furthermore, the model conforms to the reality that Britain was a net importer of the agricultural good, while a net exporter of the manufactured good. We shall also invoke the "small country" assumption and allow prices of all tradables to be determined exogenously by the combined influences of British commercial policy, world market conditions, and international transport costs. That is, we assume that demands for exportables and supplies of importables are both highly price elastic in nineteenth-century Britain.

Production relationships can be summarized as:

$$A = A(L, K, J),$$
$$M = M(L, K, S, B, F),$$
$$C = C(L, K, S, B),$$
$$B = B(L, K).$$

Capital and unskilled labor are assumed to move freely among all sectors, skilled labor is mobile between the industrial and tertiary sectors to which its use is restricted, land is specific to agricultural production, the imported intermediate resource is an input to manufacturing only, while the home-produced intermediate resource (coal) is used in manufacturing and the service sector (primarily in transportation and public utilities). Skill inputs are ignored in the resource sector (for example, coal mining) partly for empirical reasons – we have been unable to document the skill labor content of mining activity in nineteenth-century Britain – and partly in the belief that coal mining and other extractive activities were extremely unskilled and labor intensive.

The assumption of complete mobility of unskilled labor across regions and sectors may appear to violate a tradition among wage historians that nineteenth-century British labor markets were segmented, that regional wage differentials were commonplace, and that "wage gaps" between farm and city employment persisted well into the twentieth century. The assumption of complete mobility need not be inconsistent with that tradition, however, since our specification would also be consistent with roughly constant percentage wage differentials over time. This assumption of relatively stable wage differentials between unskilled farm and urban common labor is, in fact, confirmed with the British wage evidence from the late 1820s to the 1850s (see Table 7.1 and footnote 7 in Chapter 7).

The assumption of complete capital mobility across sectors implies, of course, that average net rates of return were everywhere the same (or at least that they moved alike over time). Although they surely were not everywhere the same (Chapter 7), all that matters here is that sectoral rates of return moved alike over time. Even this assumption was likely to have been violated in the short run, but over long epochs the assumption has far more to recommend it. For analysis of short-run problems (like an assessment of the Irish influx during the famine years of the late 1840s), the long-run model can and should be constrained so that capital is immobile between sectors. This exercise has been performed. Since the results are very similar to those forthcoming with the long-run model, we do not report the former here.

Given six inputs and four produced outputs, there are nine prices (and/or rents) in the model since one of the produced outputs is also an input. By invoking the small-country assumption, P_A, P_M, and P_F are taken as exogenous. The remaining six prices will be determined endogenously:

d =   rent earned on an acre of cleared farmland under crop or pasturage;

r =   rent (or rate of return) earned on reproducible nonhuman capital (and the return on equity $i = r/P_K$, where P_K = price of capital);

w =   the wage rate (or annual earnings) for unskilled labor;

q =   the wage premuim for skilled labor;

P_C =   the price of tertiary services; and

P_B =   the price of home-produced products.

The first four of these prices are the factor rents that are so central to the inequality debates in British history. For example, the total wages share in our model is simply the ratio of $(wL + qS)$ to national income. Pay ratios are measured by q/w, and the distribution of earnings is approximated by unskilled labor's share, $wL/(wL + qS)$. Furthermore, the distribution of income among property income recipients can also be explored, at least in part, by the behavior of rents (dJ) and profits (rK), offsetting and competing factor shares whose owners were in abrasive public debate throughout the century (especially over the Corn Laws: see Williamson, 1986c). And, of course, given estimates of the Irish in the British labor force, and given that the Irish were overwhelmingly unskilled, it is a simple matter to confront British income distribution issues along ethnic lines. Finally, while all six endogenous prices are nominal values, it is a trivial matter to convert any of them into real or relative prices. For example, the standard-of-living debate can be confronted simply by deflating the nominal wage of common labor by some cost-of-living index, the latter constructed by taking a weighted average of the model's P_j where the weights are supplied by the budget shares implied by the demand system elaborated below.

In addition to the six endogenous prices, the model will also predict the historical behavior of the following seven quantities:

A =   the quantity of the agricultural good that is home-produced;

M =   the quantity of the manufactured good that is home-produced;

C =   the quantity of tertiary services that are home-produced and consumed;

B =   the quantity of the home-produced resource that is extracted;

A_M =   the quantity of the agricultural good that is imported;

M_X =   the quantity of the manufactured good that is imported;

F =   the quantity of the foreign-produced intermediate good that is imported.

With these seven quantities determined, two remaining quantities can be derived residually:

A_D = home demand for the agricultural good; and
M_D = home demand for the manufactured good.

Note that industrial output mix is determined endogenously in the model. For example, the relative demise of agriculture is measured by the endogenous behavior of $P_A A$ as a share in national income, while industrialization is measured by the behavior of $P_M M$ as a share in national income. We have, then, a model of industrialization where world market conditions, domestic productivity, and "elastic" Irish labor supplies can all play a critical role as "engines of growth."

Under competitive assumptions, the equality of price and average costs yields four cost equations:

$$P_A = a_{jA}d + a_{KA}r + a_{LA}w \tag{1}$$
$$P_M = a_{KM}r + a_{LM}w + a_{SM}q + a_{BM}P_B + a_{FM}P_F \tag{2}$$
$$P_C = a_{KC}r + a_{LC}w + a_{SC}q + a_{BC}P_B \tag{3}$$
$$P_B = a_{KB}r + a_{LB}w \tag{4}$$

where the a_{ij}'s are physical input-output ratios. Each of these a_{ij}'s is an endogenous variable, and their determinants will be discussed at greater length below. These cost equations take on an extremely convenient form when they are converted into rate-of-change equations involving sectoral factor cost shares, θ_{ij}, for the ith factor in the jth sector. These factor shares add up to unity in each sector, because costs are assumed to exhaust the value of product. To explore linear approximations involving rates of change, we use the asterisk notation for rates of change per annum: $\overset{*}{X} = (dX/dt)/X$. Differentiating the cost equations and converting them into rates of change yields:

$$\overset{*}{P}_A = \overset{*}{d}\theta_{jA} + \overset{*}{r}\theta_{KA} + \overset{*}{w}\theta_{LA} \qquad\qquad + \sum_i \overset{*}{a}_{iA}\theta_{iA} \tag{5}$$
$$\overset{*}{P}_M = \overset{*}{r}\theta_{KM} + \overset{*}{w}\theta_{LM} + \overset{*}{q}\theta_{SM} + \overset{*}{P}_B\theta_{BM} + \overset{*}{P}_F\theta_{FM} + \sum_i \overset{*}{a}_{iM}\theta_{iM} \tag{6}$$
$$\overset{*}{P}_C = \overset{*}{r}\theta_{KC} + \overset{*}{w}\theta_{LC} + \overset{*}{q}\theta_{SC} + \overset{*}{P}_B\theta_{BC} + \sum_i \overset{*}{a}_{iC}\theta_{iC} \tag{7}$$
$$\overset{*}{P}_B = \overset{*}{r}\theta_{KB} + \overset{*}{w}\theta_{LB} \qquad\qquad + \sum_i \overset{*}{a}_{iB}\theta_{iB} \tag{8}$$

The $\sum_i \overset{*}{a}_{ij}\theta_{ij}$ terms are weighted sums of increases in physical input-output ratios. These may look more familiar if they are rewritten as *minus* the weighted sum of increases of output-input ratios, where the input cost shares serve as weights. In other words, each of these expressions is simply the negative value of the rate of exogenous total factor productivity growth ($\overset{*}{T}_j$) measured in nominal prices. Regrouping so as to put all terms involving endogenous variables on the right-hand side and exogenous on the left, the cost equations simply become "price dual" expressions for sectoral total factor productivity growth:

$$\overset{*}{P}_A + \overset{*}{T}_A = \overset{*}{d}\theta_{jA} + \overset{*}{r}\theta_{KA} + \overset{*}{w}\theta_{LA} \tag{9}$$
$$\overset{*}{P}_M - \overset{*}{P}_F\theta_{FM} + \overset{*}{T}_M = \overset{*}{r}\theta_{KM} + \overset{*}{w}\theta_{LM} + \overset{*}{q}\theta_{SM} + \overset{*}{P}_B\theta_{BM} \tag{10}$$

$$\overset{*}{T}_C = \overset{*}{r}\theta_{KC} + \overset{*}{w}\theta_{LC} + \overset{*}{q}\theta_{SC} + \overset{*}{P}_B\theta_{BC} \quad - \overset{*}{P}_C \quad (11)$$

$$\overset{*}{T}_B = \overset{*}{r}\theta_{KB} + \overset{*}{w}\theta_{LB} \quad\quad\quad\quad\quad - \overset{*}{P}_B \quad (12)$$

The next six equations describe full-employment equilibrium conditions in each factor market, where factor prices are assumed to clear each market so that excess supplies are zero. Total aggregate demand for each factor is the sum over all sector uses, and these are equated to exogenous factor supplies (with the exception of B and F, which are endogenously determined):

$$J = a_{JA}A \quad (13)$$
$$K = a_{KA}A + a_{KM}M + a_{KC}C + a_{KB}B \quad (14)$$
$$L = a_{LA}A + a_{LM}M + a_{LC}C + a_{LB}B \quad (15)$$
$$S = \quad\quad\quad a_{SM}M + a_{SC}C \quad (16)$$
$$B = \quad\quad\quad a_{BM}M + a_{BC}C \quad (17)$$
$$F = \quad\quad\quad a_{FM}M \quad (18)$$

As we have already pointed out, the stock of land, capital, unskilled labor, and skills are exogenously given, while the home production and the quantity imported of the resource goods are both determined endogenously. Equations (13) through (18) can be converted into rate-of-change form by introducing λ_{ij}'s (the share of the ith factor used in the jth sector). Again putting endogenous variables on the right-hand side and exogenous on the left, differentiation yields:

$$\overset{*}{J} = \overset{*}{A} + \overset{*}{a}_{JA} \quad (19)$$
$$\overset{*}{K} = \lambda_{KA}(\overset{*}{A} + \overset{*}{a}_{KA}) + \lambda_{KM}(\overset{*}{M} + \overset{*}{a}_{KM}) + \lambda_{KC}(\overset{*}{C} + \overset{*}{a}_{KC}) + \lambda_{KB}(\overset{*}{B} + \overset{*}{a}_{KB}) \quad (20)$$
$$\overset{*}{L} = \lambda_{LA}(\overset{*}{A} + \overset{*}{a}_{LA}) + \lambda_{LM}(\overset{*}{M} + \overset{*}{a}_{LM}) + \lambda_{LC}(\overset{*}{C} + \overset{*}{a}_{LC}) + \lambda_{LB}(\overset{*}{B} + \overset{*}{a}_{LB}) \quad (21)$$
$$\overset{*}{S} = \lambda_{SM}(\overset{*}{M} + \overset{*}{a}_{SM}) + \lambda_{SC}(\overset{*}{C} + \overset{*}{a}_{SC}) \quad (22)$$
$$0 = \lambda_{BM}(\overset{*}{M} + \overset{*}{a}_{BM}) + \lambda_{BC}(\overset{*}{C} + \overset{*}{a}_{BC}) - \overset{*}{B} \quad (23)$$
$$0 = (\overset{*}{M} + \overset{*}{a}_{FM}) - \overset{*}{F} \quad (24)$$

Each rate of change in input-output ratios ($\overset{*}{a}_{ij}$) consists of two parts, one of which is endogenous ($\overset{*}{b}_{ij}$) while the other is an endogenous response to factor prices ($\overset{*}{c}_{ij}$): e.g., $\overset{*}{a}_{ij} = \overset{*}{b}_{ij} + \overset{*}{c}_{ij}$. In what follows, we shall pull the $\overset{*}{b}_{ij}$ terms together into summary measures of the factor saving resulting from exogenous productivity change. These factor-saving measures, $\pi_i = -\Sigma\lambda_{ij}\overset{*}{b}_{ij}$, quantify the economy-wide savings on the use of each ith factor. The exceptions involve B and F, as we assume that the intermediate resource is used in fixed proportions in manufacturing and services. This implies that $\overset{*}{a}_{FM} = \pi_F$ and that $\pi_B = \lambda_{BM}\overset{*}{a}_{BM} + \lambda_{BC}\overset{*}{a}_{BC}$, and that all other $\overset{*}{a}_{ij}$ will not be affected by substitution between that factor and B or F.

The induced part of each change in an input-output ratio is determined by firm optimizing behavior (with the exception of $\overset{*}{c}_{BM} = \overset{*}{c}_{BC} = \overset{*}{c}_{FM} = 0$, which obey Leontief fixed-coefficient assumptions). Thus $\overset{*}{c}_{ij}$ is defined in terms of elasticities of factor substitution and factor price movements ($\overset{*}{V}_j$):

$$\overset{*}{c}_{ij} = \sum_k \Theta_{kj}\sigma^j_{ik}(\overset{*}{V}_k - \overset{*}{V}_i).$$

Final product demands are endogenous. The budget constraint serves to eliminate the demand equation for tertiary services, and the remaining two final demand equations take the form:

$$A + A_M = D_A(y/P)^{\eta A}(P_A/P)^{\epsilon A}(P_M/P)^{\epsilon AM}(P_C/P)^{\epsilon AC}Pop \tag{25}$$
$$M - M_X = D_M(y/P)^{\eta M}(P_A/P)^{\epsilon AM}(P_M/P)^{\epsilon M}(P_C/P)^{\epsilon MC}Pop \tag{26}$$

where we have imposed in addition the market clearing condition that sectoral supplies equal final aggregate demand. D_j is an exogenous shift term, y is nominal gross national product per capita, P is a general price (or cost-of-living) index, Pop is total population, η_j is the income elasticity of demand for j, and ϵ_j and ϵ_{jk} are own-price and cross-price elasticities of demand for j. Nominal income is defined as:

$$Y = P_A A + P_M M + P_C C + D$$

where resource output, $P_B B$, is excluded since it is an intermediate good, and D is the net trade deficit in nominal terms. Differentiating the nominal income expression yields:

$$\overset{*}{Y} = \o_A(\overset{*}{P}_A + \overset{*}{A}) + \o_M(\overset{*}{P}_M + \overset{*}{M}) + \o_C(\overset{*}{P}_C + \overset{*}{C}) + \o_D\overset{*}{D} \tag{27}$$

where the $\o_j$'s are the shares of total nominal income attributable to each component of income. Using (27), we can differentiate the demand equations, putting exogenous variables of the left-hand side:

$$\overset{*}{D}_A + \overset{*}{P}_A \epsilon_A + \eta_A\o_A + \overset{*}{P}_M(\epsilon_{AM} + \eta_A\o_M) + (1 - \eta_A)P\overset{*}{O}P + \eta_A\o_D\overset{*}{D}$$
$$= (\alpha_A - \eta_A\o_A)\overset{*}{A} + \alpha_{AM}\overset{*}{A}_M - \eta_A\o_M\overset{*}{M} - \eta_A\o_C\overset{*}{C} - \overset{*}{P}_C(\epsilon_{AC} + \o_C\eta_A) \tag{28}$$
$$\overset{*}{D}_M + \overset{*}{P}_A \epsilon_{AM} + \eta_M\o_A + \overset{*}{P}_M(\epsilon_M + \eta_M\o_M) + (1 - \eta_M)P\overset{*}{O}P + \eta_M\o_D\overset{*}{D}$$
$$= (\alpha_M - \eta_M\o_M)\overset{*}{M} - \alpha_{MX}\overset{*}{M}_X - \eta_M(\o_A\overset{*}{A} + \o_C\overset{*}{C}) - \overset{*}{P}_C(\epsilon_{MC} + \o_C\eta_M) \tag{29}$$

where α_A and α_{AM} represent the shares in the final demand for agricultural goods home produced and imported respectively, α_M represents the ratio of home-produced manufactured goods to home final demand for manufactured goods, and α_{MX} represents the ratio of exports of the manufactured good to home final demand for the manufactured good.

A final equation ensures that the trade account is in balance:

$$P_A A_M + P_F F = P_M M_X + D \tag{30}$$

Putting this equation in rate-of-change form yields:

$$\overset{*}{P}_A z_A + \overset{*}{P}_F z_F - \overset{*}{P}_M z_M - \overset{*}{D} z_D = \overset{*}{M}_X z_M - \overset{*}{A}_M z_A - \overset{*}{F} z_F \tag{31}$$

where z_A and z_F represent the share of the agricultural and the resource good in the nominal value of total imports, and z_M and z_D represent the share of the manufactured good exports and the nominal trade deficit in the nominal value of total imports.

The complete system is summarized by thirteen rate-of-change equations. The thirteen endogenous variables include four factor price changes – $\overset{*}{d}$, $\overset{*}{w}$, $\overset{*}{q}$, and $\overset{*}{r}$; two product price changes – $\overset{*}{P}_C$ and $\overset{*}{P}_B$; and seven output or trade volume changes: $\overset{*}{A}$, $\overset{*}{M}$, $\overset{*}{C}$, $\overset{*}{B}$, $\overset{*}{A}_M$, $\overset{*}{M}_X$, and $\overset{*}{F}$. The exogenous variables are the sectoral rates of total factor productivity growth ($\overset{*}{T}_j$), the rates of factor-saving produced by technological change (π_1), three prices in rates of change ($\overset{*}{P}_A$, $\overset{*}{P}_M$, $\overset{*}{P}_F$), the factor-supply growth rates ($\overset{*}{J}$, $\overset{*}{K}$, $\overset{*}{L}$, $\overset{*}{S}$), the population growth rate ($\overset{*}{POP}$), and the demand and trade balance shift terms ($\overset{*}{D}_j$, $\overset{*}{D}$).

Appendix 6.4. Applying the long-run model to the period 1821–61: Actuals, counterfactuals, and history

Given estimates of the exogenous variables in the model developed in Appendix 6.3, it is a simple matter to predict how the British economy should have grown between 1821 and 1861. For the four decades as a whole, these exogenous variables have been estimated to have grown at the following rates (Williamson, 1985a, chp. 9 and Appendix E):

$$\overset{*}{P}_A = -0.36 \qquad \overset{*}{L} = 1.40 \qquad \overset{*}{T}_A = 0.30$$
$$\overset{*}{P}_M = -1.43 \qquad \overset{*}{K} = 2.50 \qquad \overset{*}{T}_C = 0.37$$
$$\overset{*}{P}_F = -0.54 \qquad \overset{*}{S} = 1.46 \qquad \overset{*}{T}_B = 0.50$$
$$\overset{*}{D} = 4.46 \qquad \overset{*}{J} = 0.03 \qquad \overset{*}{T}_M = 1.0475$$
$$\overset{*}{POP} = 1.23$$

I call the model's predictions using these exogenous variables "Actual: With the Irish." If the model is a good one, it should replicate history fairly well. Elsewhere (Williamson, 1985a, chp. 9) I have shown that it does.

The "Actual: With the Irish" predictions are reported in text Tables 6.8 and 6.9. The counterfactual predictions in those two tables only vary the growth rates in the unskilled labor force ($\overset{*}{L}$) and in the population ($\overset{*}{POP}$). Each of these counterfactual $\overset{*}{L}$ and $\overset{*}{POP}$ figures is derived from the Irish and Irish labor-force estimates summarized in text Table 6.5.

7. Did British labor markets fail during the industrial revolution?

7.1 Two competing views

Did factor markets fail during the British industrial revolution? Did distortions in capital markets serve to starve industrial firms for finance and suppress accumulation there? Did urban-rural wage gaps, inelastic city-labor supplies and lack of integrated labor markets serve to drive up the cost of labor in the cities, thus choking off the rate of industrialization? With regards to labor-market failure, the literature is of two minds.

Labor markets did fail

An extensive traditional literature takes the view that migrants were reluctant to move, wage gaps were large, and regional labor markets were fragmented.

A century ago, Earnst Ravenstein (1885, 1889) published his classic work on internal migration, subsequently augmented by Arthur Redford (1926) and Alex Cairncross (1949, 1953). Ravenstein asked how many migrated, when they migrated, who migrated, where they migrated from, and where they migrated to. The same questions dominate modern migration studies. Thus, for example, the literature has been busy substantiating Ravenstein's and Redford's observation that the majority of migrants went only a short distance, and often by steps. Such observations have encouraged the belief that workers failed to move to the highest wage areas and thus that the perfect labor-market thesis must fail.

There is an equally long tradition among British labor historians that there was a multiplicity of labor markets between 1750 and 1850, that regional labor markets were very poorly integrated, and that local autonomy reigned (Pollard, 1978). The labor-markets-failed view also leans heavily on the evidence that wage gaps were pronounced during the industrial revolution. Indeed, E. H. Hunt (1973) reported an enormous amount of regional wage variation well into the late nineteenth century.

178

Labor markets did not fail

Nick Crafts has recently argued that British labor was released from agriculture early and fast, implying that this factor reallocation contributed to significant economy-wide productivity gains. This labor release by British agriculture at an early stage of development (Crafts, 1985, p. 2) implies economy-wide productivity gains to the extent that labor had higher marginal productivity in industry. Indeed, this kind of reasoning is central to such development economists as Simon Kuznets (1971) and Hollis Chenery and Moshe Syrquin (1975), as well as to the growth accounting of Edward Denison (1967, 1974). Crafts feels that by 1840 labor markets were fairly well integrated (Crafts, 1985, pp. 3 and 7), although wage gaps between agriculture and industry were still pronounced (Crafts, 1985, p. 68). Comparisons with other early developers have persuaded Crafts that Britain's relative factor-market integration and early labor release was important to her early success.

Consistent with Crafts' early-release-of-labor thesis, Chapter 2 has documented that emigration rates from the English countryside rose dramatically after the French wars, reaching very high levels by the 1840s. Indeed, the rates of rural emigration were even higher than in the Third World, where so much has been made of rapid urbanization.

Others have shown that British migrants were responsive to labor-market signals (Nicholas and Shergold, 1985a, 1985b), and that the elasticity of migration to earnings differentials were no smaller than those found in other economies, past and present (Greenwood and Thomas, 1973; Vedder and Cooper, 1974).

In short, this revisionist literature suggests that British labor markets linking city and countryside were well integrated and at least as successful in transferring labor to the dynamic urban sectors as those in developing countries that have followed Britain's example.

Making an assessment

Ravenstein-like documentation of migrant flows or Hunt-like documentation of nominal-wage gaps is not nearly enough to test the labor-markets-failed hypothesis. Although costs of migration in the pre-railway age may have generated wage gaps between surplus and deficit regional labor markets, stability in those gaps over time would imply a well-integrated national labor market. And even if wage gaps rose over time, such evidence could not be viewed as unambiguous support for the view that imperfect labor markets were succumbing to the disequilibrating shocks of unbalanced growth across the industrial revolution. After all, rising nominal wage gaps, especially between town and countryside, may simply have reflected the relative rise in the cost of city life, including the disamenities associated with crowding and high density. Furthermore, short distance moves need not shed any light at all on the labor-market-failure hypothesis. Workers need only move at the margin, and the statement holds for the marginal worker as well as for the marginal move.

Even if labor markets were in disequilibrium during the First Industrial Revolution, did it matter in any important quantitative sense? If so, how did it matter? What was the impact of the alleged labor-market failure on British growth, accumulation, and industrialization? Neither of the two competing views has posed these questions. Rather, the debate has focused on the less interesting question: Were labor markets perfect? Because labor markets are not even perfect today, the more interesting question, it seems to me, is whether the nineteenth-century imperfections were large enough to matter, and, if so, how they mattered.

This chapter will offer an answer to this question by focusing on wage gaps between city and countryside. It will also assess the impact of capital-market distortions. Section 7.2 will review the evidence on rising nominal-wage gaps and the rural emigration response across the First Industrial Revolution, the magnitudes placed in comparative perspective. Section 7.3 constructs the nominal-wage gaps for the 1830s, and they turn out to be large even by the standards of the contemporary Third World. The nominal-wage gaps are converted to real wage gaps in Section 7.4, where attention is paid to cost-of-living differentials, urban disamenities, and poor relief. The real-wage gaps are much smaller, but they hardly disappear. Section 7.5 makes a simple comparative static assessment of the quantitative importance of these wage gaps by computing the deadweight loss associated with the labor-market failure. The figures turn out to be fairly small.

Why, then, has the fuss over labor-market failure persisted for so long? I think the answer lies with the employment, distribution, and accumulation effects associated with the labor-market failure. Section 7.6 introduces these issues in partial equilibrium. Section 7.7 then uses general equilibrium to compare the quantitative impact of labor-market failure with capital-market failure. The results are striking: it appears that the traditional literature is correct, labor markets did fail, but capital-market failure was even more pronounced. Both served to constrain British industrialization during the First Industrial Revolution to less than optimal rates. We confront one final puzzle in Section 7.8: Why didn't manufacturing capital migrate to the countryside to exploit rural labor surplus in the South of England?

7.2. Labor-market disequilibrium and migration response: The evidence for failure

Rising nominal-wage gaps

Table 7.1 shows that an index of the gap between the average nominal earnings of unskilled nonfarm and farm laborers rose sharply across the first half of the nineteenth century. The table suggests that the nominal wage gap did not begin to rise during the British industrial revolution until well after the French wars. Indeed, the index implies that wartime conditions served to erode the wage gap. Because the conflict caused a contraction in foreign trade and a rise in the relative price of grains, agriculture was favored. Under such conditions, it is hardly surprising that the wage gap would tend to collapse as labor demands were relatively strong in the countryside. With the end of the wars, however, the pace of British industrialization accelerated and agriculture resumed its long-run relative demise. Thus, the derived demand for labor shifted dramatically toward urban sectors (Chapter 4) during an episode when the natural rates of increase in the labor force favored the countryside (Chapter 2). If labor-market disequilibrium was ever to appear in Britain, the times were certainly ripe for it after 1820. Trends in the wage-gap index would appear to reflect those disequilibrating forces because it rises sharply to a peak in 1851. The gap never reaches its mid-nineteenth-century peak again.[1] Thus, if we are looking for evidence of labor-market failure, the 1830s, 1840s, and 1850s are clearly the place to start.

1 Based on somewhat different data, Bellerby (1956, Table 45, p. 33; 1953, p. 135) has also documented similar trends. Comparing nominal agricultural wages with average industrial wages, he finds a peak wage gap in the 1850s, declining for the remainder of the century followed by a rise again between the 1880s and the 1900s. Based on Brassey and Gilboy, Colin Clark (1957, p. 530) also finds a peak in 1851, but he believes the late eighteenth-century gaps to have been even higher.

Table 7.1. *Trends in the nominal-wage gap, 1797 to 1911 (1797 = 100)*

Year	Index
1797	100
1805	86.6
1810	96.7
1815	105.1
1819	99.7
1827	132.4
1835	134.7
1851	148.3
1861	111.5
1871	102.0
1881	104.2
1891	135.8
1901	140.7
1911	129.4

Source: Williamson (1985a), Table 3.8, p. 49. The gap is calculated as the difference between the weighted average of nonfarm unskilled earnings (e.g., common laborers, porters, police, guards, watchmen, coal miners) and the farm-earnings rate, divided by the farm-earnings rate. Thus, it is the percentage differential by which nonfarm unskilled wages exceeded farm wages, the common measure used in the development literature.

How big was the rural-urban wage gap during these three decades when the index reaches its peak? Hunt and Crafts both contend that the wage gap is best captured with the available evidence by comparing agricultural wages with unskilled wages in the building trades (Hunt, 1973, p. 5; Crafts, 1982, p. 64). We can construct the gaps for the North and South of England separately, and because many have argued that the English labor market was regionally segmented (Pollard, 1978, pp. 103–4; 1981, p. 902), it might be wise to do so. Table 7.2 estimates these nominal-wage gaps for the 1830s. In the South of England, the wage gap was very large indeed. Annual unskilled wages in the London building trades exceeded those of farm laborers in the southern counties by an enormous factor, 106.2 percent. These nominal gaps include the influence of seasonal unemployment in both city and countryside, but they exclude poor relief and in-kind payments. As we shall see below, the addition of rural poor relief and in-kind payments to the labor earnings of able-bodied farm laborers would serve to diminish the size of the gap in the South, but not by much. For the North of England, the wage gap was much smaller. Annual unskilled wages in the five towns of Coventry,

Table 7.2. *Nominal-wage gaps in the 1830s*

Region	Annual wages (£)	Description and source
London 1831	48.07	Laborers in the building trades (for bricklayers, plasterers, and masons), 21.75sh./week. Assumes 44.2 weeks worked per year. Mayhew estimated that 30 percent of London's workers in the building trades were unemployed during slack seasons. If the slack season is taken as 6 months, then weeks worked per year is 26 + (.7)26 = 44.2. See G. Jones (1971), p. 41 and Boyer (1986). The weekly wages are from Bowley (1900a) p. 83.
Northern towns 1838–40	36.38	Laborers in the building trades, average summer weekly wages, weighted average of Coventry, Huddersfield, Newcastle, Macclesfield, and Manchester, where weights are 1841 population (*Parliamentary Papers* 1843, vol. 22, p. 10). Also assumes 44.2 weeks worked per year. The weekly wages are from Bowley (1900b), pp. 300–310.
Rural south 1833	23.31	Agricultural laborers, average weekly wage (excluding poor relief payments) across 21 shires, where we assume 44.2 weeks worked per year in grain-growing counties of the Southeast, and 48 weeks worked per year in Southwest. The counties are: Middlesex, Surrey, Kent, Sussex, Hants, Berks, Oxford, Herts, Bucks, Northampton, Hunts, Beds, Cambs, Essex, Suffolk, Norfolk, Wilts, Dorset, Devon, Cornwall, and Somerset. The weekly wages range from 8.50 to 13.08sh., and they are taken from Bowley (1900a), end table, col. 8.
Rural north 1837	26.70	Agricultural laborers, average weekly wage (excluding poor relief payments) across 18 shires, where we assume 48 weeks worked per year. The counties are: Glou, Heref., Salop, Staffs, Worc., Warwick, Leic., Lincs, Notts, Derby, Cheshire, the three Yorks, Durham, Northumb., Cumb., Westmore. The weekly wages are from Bowley (1900a), end table, col. 11.
Southern wage gap:	106.2%	
Northern wage gap:	36.3%	
Average (weighted) wage gap:	73.2%	

Sources: The average wage gap is computed from a weighted average of the North and South wages, where the weights are 1841 county populations (Mitchell and Deane, 1962, p. 20), London and 41 northern towns (*Parliamentary Papers* 1843, vol. 22, Preface, p. 10).

The wage gap is computed as the difference between urban and rural relative to the rural wage.

Huddersfield, Newcastle, Macclesfield, and Manchester exceeded those of farm laborers in the northern counties by 36.3 percent.

Table 7.2 also implies that those big wage gaps in the South of England were less a function of lower rural wages in the South compared to the North, and more a function of the high urban wages in London compared with northern towns. Indeed, Section 7.4 will present some evidence which suggests that the gap between northern and southern farm wages can be explained largely by more generous agricultural poor relief and in-kind payments down South.

For the moment, however, it should suffice simply to note that a weighted average of the two regions yields an all-England nominal gap of 73.2 percent.

Migration response

As we have seen in Chapter 2, rural emigration appears to have responded to the labor-market disequilibrium produced by the unbalanced growth associated with the industrialization spurt after about 1820. In contrast with the conventional wisdom that English rural labor was reluctant to move and thus failed to respond vigorously to the wage gaps (Redford, 1926, pp. 84 and 94; Pollard, 1978, pp. 103–15), the rates of emigration from the English countryside rose dramatically after the French wars and reached what appear to be very high levels by the 1840s.

With the exception of the war-induced good times for English agriculture between 1801 and 1806, Table 2.5 documented that rural emigration took place at every point across the century 1776–1871. After the French wars, the rates of rural emigration were high by almost any standard. Although they ranged between .87 and 2.10 percent per annum after 1816, they ranged between .97 and 1.21 percent per annum in the Third World in the 1960s and 1970s (Kelley and Williamson, 1984, Table 3-13, p. 93). More important to the issues at hand, however, the rate of rural migration rose sharply over the period, especially after the French wars. The average emigration rate between 1776 and 1816 was only .63 percent per annum. Furthermore, there was considerable instability in the rate over these four decades of modest industrialization and stop-go during wartime, and there is no evidence of significant upward trend. The same was true of wage gaps. After 1816, the emigration rates surged upward, as did wage gaps. By the 1840s, the emigration rate was 1.65 percent per annum, or about two and a half times the pre-1816 rate. By the 1860s, the rate was 2.08 percent per annum, or more than three times the pre-1816 rate.

The 1830s seem, therefore, to lie in the middle of a dramatic epoch of high and rising emigration from the countryside at precisely the time when wage gaps were also high and rising, thus offering a strong inducement to potential migrants.

7.3   Nominal-wage gaps: A comparative assessment

Were these wage gaps large? Because all industrializing countries find it difficult to cope with the economic and demographic shocks associated with industrial revolutions, wage gaps are a manifestation of factor-market disequilibrium that both economic historians and development economists have come to expect during such episodes of dramatic growth and transformation. Thus, did British labor markets fail by the standards of other industrial revolutions?

Table 7.3 offers a partial answer. Here we compare British experience with that of nineteen Third World economies in the 1960s and 1970s, and with that of seven nineteenth-century developing economies. The British wage gaps are crudely adjusted for seasonal unemployment while the others are not, but in most other dimensions the underlying calculations are similar. Each of these estimates attempts to focus on homogeneous labor, unskilled male labor's wages being used throughout.[2] Indeed, unskilled wages in the building trades are used in all of the Third World

2 There is no shortage of studies in both the historical and development literature that appeals to various, and inappropriate, proxies of labor market disequilibrium. The most famous is by Simon Kuznets (1966), who uses average labor productivities to infer the resource allocative gains from the demise of agriculture. Of course, it is marginal labor productivities that matter, and average productivities are likely to be a very poor proxy for the marginal productivities given the far higher human and physical capital intensities that prevail outside agriculture. Additional examples are offered by those who compare average industrial wages with agricultural wages. Because industry averages include skilled labor which embody human capital, such wage gaps exaggerate the size of the labor-market disequilibrium. Let me simply cite two examples of historical studies that use this approach. One is offered by Bellerby's otherwise excellent work on the British farm sector (Bellerby, 1953, p. 135; 1956, pp. 233–4), which figures importantly in Eric Jones' impressive survey of the agricultural labor market in England (E. Jones, 1964, p. 328). The second is illustrated by Mazumdar's (1973, p. 495) classic study of the Bombay textile industry.

Table 7.3. *Nominal-wage gaps for unskilled labor: Some comparative data*

Observation	Wage gap (%)	Description and source
South of England 1830s	106.2	Table 7.2
North of England 1830s	36.3	Ibid.
All England 1830s	73.2	Ibid.
Third World 1960s–1970s	41.4	Squire (1981), Table 30, p. 102. As with the English data, these are also based on unskilled in urban construction and agriculture. They also exclude payments in kind and wage supplements. There are 19 countries underlying this average (excluding four cases of negative gaps): Guatemala, Chile, Pakistan, Ivory Coast, Morocco, Mexico, Cameroon, Uruguay, Argentina, Panama, Sri Lanka, Kenya, Tunisia, Malawi, Trinidad and Tobago, Venezuela, Costa Rica, Tanzania, and Malaysia.
Nineteenth-century developing nations	51.2	Clark (1957), Table II, pp. 526–31. Agricultural wages include payments in kind, while unskilled urban wages seem to be for general laborers. The countries included are: Argentina 1872; Australia 1887; Denmark 1872; France 1892, 1801; Hungary 1865; Japan 1887; and US 1890, 1820–1829. Clark also reports figures for the UK where the average 1843–1869 = 37.3%, well below our estimate for the 1830s.

Notes: Throughout, the percentage unskilled wage gap is computed as the difference between urban and rural relative to rural wage.

estimates, and they also seem to have been used in most of the nineteenth-century estimates as well. Furthermore, wage supplements and poor relief are excluded everywhere in the table, although more will be said about these issues later on.

Based on Table 7.3, it appears that wage gaps in the North of England were a little smaller than those typical of the Third World and the rest of the developing nineteenth-century world economy. The wage gaps in the South of England, however, far exceeded those typical of developing countries. If we are looking for relative failure in labor markets, the South of England is where we are most likely to find it. And the South of England was sufficiently important to the total labor market that on average British wage gaps were indeed comparatively large.

7.4   Were wage gaps illusory?

Cost-of-living differentials

These nominal wage gaps must be deflated before the efficiency of the British labor market in the early nineteenth century can be assessed. Indeed, we know that living costs were considerably higher in the large cities and, as Chapter 9 will suggest, a good part of the explanation is likely to lie with dwelling rents.

Rents were higher in the cities primarily due to land scarcity, forgone dwelling investment during the French wars, and unanticipated accelerating demand in the 1820s through 1840s, although construction costs may also have been higher given higher nominal city wages. Furthermore, as urbanization took place across the industrial revolution, urban land got even scarcer and labor-intensive products like dwellings rose in relative costs (especially in the absence of significant productivity advance in the building trades), thus increasing the relative cost of new urban housing. There is reason to believe, therefore, that some portion of the rise in the nominal-wage gap between the 1790s and the 1850s was driven by rising city rents and thus by the rising relative cost of living in the city.

Some evidence in support of this view will be offered in Chapter 9, where a strong upward drift in city rents is documented. Based on three city rent series, it appears that nominal rents increased by about 2.5 percent per annum in the English cities, almost 30 percent in each decade. As long as rural rents lagged behind, rising city rents should have served to increase the nominal wage gap even if the real wage gap remained stable over the half century prior to the 1830s and 1840s. And it does appear that rural rents lagged behind. This was true of rural Dorset, Essex, Kent, and Suffolk, where rents increased by about 1.1 percent per annum from the 1770s to the 1840s (Richardson, 1977, pp. 129–30, 193–4, 247–8, and 379–80), although they increased more rapidly after the 1790s, 1.5 percent per annum. Caird thought rural rents increased by about .9 percent per annum after 1770 (Caird, 1967 ed, p. 474), and his estimates were based on sixteen rural counties. According to these figures, something like half of the rise in the nominal wage gap between city and countryside between 1797 and 1851 might have been explained by the relatively rapid rise in city rents.[3]

---

3 The nominal-wage gap in Table 7.1 rises by .73 percent per annum between 1797 and 1851. If we take the rental share in budgets to have been something like

The high cost of city rents in the 1830s and 1840s is confirmed by the evidence offered in Chapter 9. City rents for the working class were about two and a half times those prevailing in rural England. Furthermore, the evidence presented in Chapter 9 suggests that it was city land scarcity and nominal wage costs facing city building trades that contributed to the wide variance in dwelling rents across England.

We need more comprehensive cost-of-living estimates than simply rents if these nominal wage gaps are to be deflated. A paper by Crafts (1982) offered the first serious attempt to construct spatial cost-of-living deflators for this period. In the early 1840s, the Poor Law Unions were required to report the prices they paid for provisions, and one such return was published in the *Parliamentary Papers* for 1842–3 (1843, vol. 45, pp. 2–33). These provisions were generally of the same quality as those purchased by employed laborers, and the prices were sensitive to local market conditions. Although it is true that by buying in bulk the workhouses obtained provisions at something like 20 percent below shop prices, it seems reasonable to assume that this volume discount was everywhere roughly the same.

Crafts constructs cost-of-living deflators for two urban areas (London and what he calls Northern Industrial)[4] and for eight rural areas (North Midlands, North, Northwest, East, West, Home Counties, Southeast, and South Midlands). As it turns out, some of Crafts' rural areas include workhouses in localities which the census authorities in 1841 included in the top seventy-four cities and towns of England (*PP*, 1843, vol. 22). As a result, if city living costs were higher than those in the countryside, Crafts' figures may understate the difference. Nevertheless, we shall accept Crafts' Poor Law provision prices in what follows.

Crafts shows that cities did have high living costs and that real-wage gaps were less than nominal-wage gaps. However, there are two aspects of Crafts' calculations that might be improved by revision. First, Crafts guesses at rents, taking them to be three times those of rural areas

---

20 percent in the city and 10 percent in the countryside, it follows that the rural cost of living would have risen by .14 percent per annum due to rent inflation alone (1.4 percent per annum times .1), while the city cost of living would have risen by .5 percent per annum (2.5 percent per annum times .2), the difference being .36 percent per annum, or about half the rise in the nominal gap.

4 Crafts' Northern Industrial includes Stoke on Trent, Walsall, West Bromwich, Wolstanton, Wolverhampton, Blackburn, Burnley, Chorlton, Leigh, Prescot, Salford, West Derby, Bradford, Dewsbury, Ecclesall Bierlow, Halifax, Sheffield, Wakefield, and Stockport.

Table 7.4. *Regional cost-of-living differentials in the 1840s (London = 100)*

Region	(1)	(2)	(3)	(4)
			Williamson's geo-metric weights	
	Crafts' economiser			
	Rural rent weights	Urban rent weights	London weights	Northern town weights
London	100.0	100.0	100.0	100.0
Northern towns	94.7	95.4	91.3	91.3
North Midlands rural	90.2	83.0	82.6	82.1
North rural	90.1	82.9	82.2	82.1
Northwest rural	87.4	80.6	81.4	80.6
East rural	93.7	86.1	86.6	84.6
West rural	95.9	87.9	87.0	84.7
Home Counties rural	96.5	88.5	87.3	85.2
Southwest rural	93.4	85.7	89.9	87.9
South Midlands rural	90.7	83.6	84.0	81.8
Northern rural	na	na	82.1	81.7
Southern rural	na	na	86.8	84.6
Urban-rural differential:				
North	na	na	9.2	9.6
South	na	na	13.2	15.4
All England	na	na	10.9	12.4

Source: Cols. (1) and (2) are from Crafts (1982), Table 6, p. 62, where his rural and urban budget weights for rents are .065 and .15, respectively. Cols. (3) and (4): the prices of provisions are from *ibid.*, Table 2, p. 55, the same prices used by Crafts to construct his Economiser; rents are taken from Table 9.2; and the budget weights are from Williamson, (1985a), Appendix Table A.1, p. 210, where northern rural rent weights are .083, southern rural rent weights .085, and urban rent weights .191.

1841 population weights used to construct northern and southern rural. See Table 7.2 for sources.

(Crafts, 1982, pp. 61–2) and assumes them to be everywhere the same between all rural areas and between all urban areas. We have already seen that these assumptions appear to be wide of the mark. Second, Crafts uses budget weights that are likely to understate the importance of dwelling expenditures.

Table 7.4 offers regional cost-of-living differentials by adding our new rent estimates to Crafts' provision prices, and by applying what I view to be more appropriate budget weights. Although the difference between Crafts' "Economiser" indices and my geometric weight indices is not

Table 7.5. *Cost-of-living differentials: Some comparative data*

Country	Date	Ratio of urban to rural cost of living	Source
North of England	1840s	1.12	Table 7.4, urban weights, col. 4.
South of England	1840s	1.15	Table 7.4, urban weights, col. 3.
All of England	1840s	1.13	Table 7.4, urban weights.
United Kingdom	1937–1938	1.05	Bellerby (1956), p. 250, rural weights.
United Kingdom	1904	1.09–1.14	Bellerby (1956), p. 251, urban and rural weights, respectively.
Ireland	1940	1.06	Bellerby (1956), p. 252, rural weights.
Canada	1949	1.10	Bellerby (1956), p. 255, rural weights.
Sweden	1934	1.13	Bellerby (1956), p. 256, rural weights.
United States	1941	1.14–1.30	Koffsky (1949), pp. 151–178, urban and rural weights, respectively.
Peru	1971	1.27	Thomas (1980), p. 89, based on Peru's "coastal" region.
Ghana	1961–1962	1.04–1.12	Knight (1972), p. 209, urban and rural weights, respectively.

great, the new figures do suggest somewhat larger rural-urban cost-of-living differentials. In short, the cost of living for unskilled workers was 13.2 percent lower in the rural South than in London, while it was 10.5 percent lower in the rural North than in the northern towns. For England as a whole, it was 12.3 percent lower (the average of columns 3 and 4).

Because these cost-of-living differentials are too small to account for anything but a modest share of the nominal wage gaps observed, it might be wise to ask whether they are small by the standards of other countries. Based on the limited survey in Table 7.5, it would appear that England in the 1840s fit well within the bounds of cost-of-living differentials experienced by other industrializing economies. It also suggests that we need to look elsewhere for explanations of those big nominal wage gaps in England during the First Industrial Revolution.

Urban disamenity premia

What about the poor quality of urban life? We shall see in Chapter 9 that urban employers had to pay a premium to attract potential rural emigrants to locations of poorer environmental quality. There we assess the value of those ghastly urban disamenities by estimating hedonic earnings equations on the parish wages reported in the 1834 Poor Law Inquiry. The exercise is successful, making it possible to place a value on disamenities incurred when migrating from a relatively pleasant village environment (e.g., Sweet Auburn) to a very unpleasant big-city environment (e.g., Sheffield). According to these estimates, it required a wage premium of 12 to 30 percent to compensate workers for the inferior urban environmental standards in the North of England, while a smaller compensation of 8 to 20 percent was required in the South.

In short, city employers had to pay a higher nominal wage for two reasons – they were expensive places to live and they were environmentally unpleasant places to live. It appears that environmental forces were at least as important an influence as high living costs in contributing to the nominal-wage gap.

Poor-relief adjustments

One final adjustment remains. As Karl Polanyi (1944), Arthur Redford (1926) and so many others have pointed out, prior to 1834 and the passage of the new poor laws, poor relief served to augment the wage income of agricultural laborers, especially in the grain-producing South of England. Because able-bodied farm laborers were being supported during slack season, and because those payments are not included in the nominal wage earnings estimates reported in Table 7.2, they must somehow be added. If we fail to do so, the true wage gap will be overstated, especially in the South of England, where, as we have seen, market-wage gaps were the greatest and rural poor relief most generous.

Fortunately, George Boyer (1985) has recently constructed some estimates that seem to fit our needs nicely. Boyer had to face two problems in constructing estimates of the extent to which farm laborers' incomes were augmented by relief payments. First, he had to estimate the share of a parish's relief expenditures that actually went to agricultural laborers and their families (in contrast with the non-able-bodied poor). Boyer believes that a share ranging between 33 and 50 percent is most plausible. To err on the conservative side, and given that not all rural laborers received relief, we have used Boyer's 33 percent estimate in what follows. Second, poor-relief expenditures were correlated with grain specialization. Thus, parishes in the East, Southeast, and Home County regions were the heart of the more generous Speenhamland system, while those in the West and South Midlands had much less generous relief, and those to the North had little relief (of able-bodied) at all. We shall, as a result, assume no agricultural relief (of able-bodied) in the rural North, and take the levels in the West and in the South Midlands to have been only about one quarter of the main Speenhamland counties.

Based on Boyer's data, it appears that poor-relief payments increased the incomes of unskilled rural labor by about 10.5 percent over their wage earnings in the Speenhamland counties, by about 7.1 percent in the South of England as a whole, and by about 4.4 percent in England overall (Appendix 7.1).

Addendum: What about in-kind payments?

Measured wage gaps between farm and city ought to include in-kind payments. Although the existence of in-kind payments in nineteenth-century Britain is well known, evidence documenting their contribution to the average farm laborer's total earnings is surprisingly scarce; that is, we know very little about how many workers received such payments and the value of the payments when they were recieved. Lee Alston and T. J. Hatton (1988) have found in-kind payments to have been very large on American farms around 1925, but evidence relating to Britain a century earlier is limited to the rural queries taken in the summer of 1832 (*Parliamentary Papers*, 1834, vols. 30–4) and the scraps of information surveyed by Ivy Pinchbeck (1981). In-kind payments appear to have been far more typical of southern farming than northern farming, and they primarily took three forms: gleaning rights, small land allotments for subsistence crops, and subsidized cottage rents. Based on private correspondence, George Boyer guesses that these in-kind payments in the South in the 1830s might have been something like the following (at least for those receiving such payments): the value of gleaning perhaps 1.5–2£; the value of commodity output from land allotments perhaps 1–2£; and the rental value of subsidized cottages perhaps 2£. Boyer views these to be the

Table 7.6. *Decomposing the nominal-wage gap*

Item	The wage gap (in %)		
	South	North	All England
(1) Nominal wages	106.2	36.3	73.2
(2) Adjusted by cost of living	79.0	21.9	52.1
(3) Also adjusted by rural poor relief of able-bodied	67.1	21.9	46.1
(4) Also adjusted by disamenities premium for city life			
(4a) Premium 1	54.7	8.7	33.2
(4b) Premium 2	39.5	−6.2	17.9

Source: Row (1) is taken from Table 7.2, Row (2) is derived by applying the cost-of-living deflators in Table 7.4 to the nominal wages in Table 7.2. Row (3) is based on Boyer (1985), Table 1 and discussed in the text, where poor-relief payments to rural laborers is added on to real wages. Row (4) is derived by inflating these rural real wages by the disamenity premium estimates discussed in the text and Chapter 9.

maximum in-kind payments likely to have been made to those who received them, and not everyone, of course, received them. For example, perhaps only 15 percent of farm laborers in the South actually received land allotments, so the average farm laborer may have gained only .2–0.3£ from that source. If roughly the same share applied for subsidized cottages, then the average laborer may have received only .3£ from that source. Adding all of these guesses up suggests in-kind payments to the average farm laborer in the South were around 2–2.6£, or from 9 to 11 percent of their wage income (23.31£: Table 7.2). These are crude guesses only, but if they are close to the mark they would not alter by much the results presented in the lower left-hand corner of Table 7.6. In any case, they are too crude to include in the discussion that follows.

Bottom line: Were wage gaps illusory?

Table 7.6 offers a final accounting of the wage gap in the 1830s. After adjusting for the fact that cities were expensive, that cities were environmentally unattractive and required some compensation for the "bads" prevailing there, and that poor relief was used to augment workers' incomes in the countryside during slack season, much of the wage gap disappears. This is especially true of the South of England, where city living costs were so high (London rents in particular) and where rural relief was more significant. Thus, although the nominal-wage gap between London and the rural South was an enormous 106.2 percent, the true real-income gap ranged between 39.5 and 54.7 percent. That is, the gap down South is cut by more than a half when an effort is made to measure it properly. In the North of England, the wage gap tends to evaporate entirely when proper adjustments are applied. Here, the nominal gap was 36.3 percent, although the true real-income gap is estimated to have been 8.7 percent or less. The wage-gap and labor-market failure appear to have been solely a southern problem. For England as a whole, the nominal-wage gap was 73.2 percent, although the true real-income gap is estimated to have been far less, ranging between 17.9 and 33.2 percent.

Much of the wage gap was illusory, but it fails to disappear entirely. Spatial labor-market disequilibrium was an attribute of the First Industrial Revolution. Yet, the labor-market disequilibrium in England in the 1830s no longer looks unique. That is, when all of these necessary adjustments to the nominal-wage gap are made, the true English wage gap begins to look very much like the experience of other nineteenth-century developing countries, and even like that of the contemporary Third World.

7.5   The quantitative importance of labor-market failure: Deadweight losses

The issues

How badly did labor markets fail during the First Industrial Revolution? Economic historians typically attack this question in one of two ways. First, they seek evidence of open unemployment, of disguised unemployment, or of wage gaps between workers of comparable skill, because (most) theory suggests that such evidence offers clear symptoms of market failure. Second, they seek evidence of institutional or government intervention which (most) theory tells us will generate evidence of market failure, such as labor unions and monopsony power. Since every economy exhibits such evidence, one is never sure how to interpret such descriptive histories. How would we recognize significant labor-market failure when presented with such evidence?

Lurking behind each of these histories is an explicit counterfactual: If there had been an optimal allocation of labor in England in the 1830s, by how much would national income have been raised? Would industrialization have taken place much more rapidly? And who would have gained the most by the elimination of the labor-market failure?

Because the efficiency of unfettered markets is an article of faith to so many neoclassical economists, and because the pervasiveness of imperfections and their contribution to market failure is an equally strong article of faith to their critics, we must proceed with caution. I propose to adopt the null hypothesis of the Chicago School, namely no appreciable increment in aggregate economic welfare could have been achieved had wage gaps disappeared and had the distribution of labor been optimal in England in the 1830s.[5]

The Chicago School null hypothesis strikes me as a harsh test of the efficient operation of English labor makets. After all, we are assuming, like most development economists, that the real-wage gaps documented in Table 7.6 reflect disequilibrium. They may not. First, they may reflect the real (as opposed to psychic) costs of moving. Second, they may reflect our inability to fully control for differences in the quality of labor (even among young, unskilled males), immigration to the city having selected individuals with attributes that had real economic value to city employers. Third, they may reflect urban employers' attempts to minimize turnover, in which case the cost of an efficiency unit of labor may in fact have been equalized between sectors even though measured wage gaps persisted. Fourth, higher urban wages may simply reflect lower life expectancies in the cities, the higher "spot" wage necessary to generate similar discounted earnings over lifetimes. Fifth, the higher male adult wage may simply compensate for more limited earnings opportunities for other family members. Although I may be shown wrong by future research, my guess is that none of these factors were important because the city workers being considered were largely young, unmarried, and unskilled day laborers in the building trades.

Finally, higher wages in urban employment may reflect greater job uncertainty or the cost of job search. As Chapter 5 stressed, this latter view is the essential contribution of the Todaro model (Todaro, 1969; Harris and Todaro, 1970), applied so extensively to Third World labor

---

5 Berry and Sabot (1978), pp. 1200 and 1230. I have found their stimulating survey of labor-market performance in developing countries very useful in organizing my own thoughts about England in the 1830s.

markets and thought by Pollard (1978, pp. 902–3) to be applicable to nineteenth-century England as well. "Good" city jobs are defined here as high paying and with a relatively high degree of employment certainty. Thus, Todaro stresses the role of "casual" employment in the urban service sector as a holding area for the reserve army of immigrants who have come to the city in the anticipation of getting the more attractive jobs. Certainly Mayhew (1861) made much of London's traditional urban service sector and unskilled casual labor has played an important part in nineteenth-century labor histories since. The key here, of course, is that there may have been higher uncertainty attached to unskilled casual work in the city (like the building trades), and that the measured wage gaps reflect some compensation for such uncertainty.[6] The limited evidence marshaled in Chapter 5 did not support this view, but if it were true then we would have another argument for the view that the measured wage gaps in Table 7.6 may not reflect labor-market disequilibrium at all.

Thus, the Chicago School null hypothesis is a harsh standard by which to judge the efficiency of English labor markets in the 1830s.

"Partial" general equilibrium analysis

How can the Chicago School null hypothesis be tested? I propose first to implement empirically the analysis in Figure 7.1. This familiar diagram shows employment distribution between agriculture and nonagriculture in the presence of wage gaps. Given wages in the two sectors, and given the two derived labor-demand functions, then the deadweight loss associated with labor-market failure is the shaded area in the diagram. In the presence of the failure, national income is simply the sum of the areas under each of those two derived demand curves, up to employment at ℓ. If the wage gaps are eliminated, migrants will have left agriculture for nonagricultural employment, and employment will be optimally distributed at ℓ^*. National income has now been increased by the shaded area, or by the elimination of the deadweight loss.[7] Because we have already constructed the real-wage estimates for the two sectors (e.g., the wage gaps in Table 7.6), and because Deane and Cole (1962, Tables 31 and 37, pp. 143 and 166) supply rough but adequate estimates for labor-force distribution and

6 The issue here is not predictable seasonal unemployment. Such factors are already embedded in the wage earnings estimates in Tables 7.2 and 7.6.

7 Donald McCloskey performed a similar experiment to assess the impact of improved capital markets between 1780 and 1860. However, he did not focus on the issue of optimal resource allocation. See McCloskey (1981, pp. 118–19).

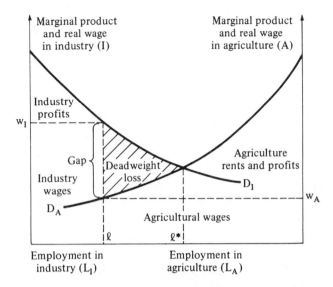

Figure 7.1   "Partial" general equilibrium analysis of wage gaps in two sectors

national income for 1831, all that remains is to guess at alternative values
of the labor-demand elasticities in the two sectors. We shall consider a
range of estimates. Assuming a Cobb-Douglas production function in
agriculture, and given the price elasticity of demand for agricultural
goods, then Marshall's formula yields the elasticity of demand for labor in
agriculture.[8] If one views the English economy as relatively closed to
trade, then the elasticity is about .7. If instead one views the English
economy as relatively open to trade, then the elasticity is more like 1.1. I
find the latter assumption more attractive, but both will be utilized so that
we can place bounds on our results. For nonagriculture, Table 4.5 already
offered an estimate for c1841 of about 1.6, a figure that lies midway in a

8 Given a Cobb-Douglas production function in agriculture, and assuming the
   economy to be closed to trade, the elasticity of demand for agricultural labor is
   written $(1 - \theta_{LA}) + \theta_{LA}(\epsilon_A) = \eta_{LA}$ where θ_{LA} is labor's share and ϵ_A is the price
   elasticity of demand for agricultural goods. Estimates for these two parameters
   for 1821 can be found in Williamson (1985a, Appendix D). I should emphasize
   that the typical "partial" general equilibrium analysis of distortions ignores the
   interaction between factor markets and product markets. Thus, if the removal of
   a distortion causes labor emigration from agriculture, agricultural output should
   contract and agricultural prices should tend to rise, unless the small country case
   is invoked. The opposite is the case, of course, in industry. The analysis in this
   chapter includes these interactions between factor and product markets.

wide range of contemporary estimates from twentieth-century America –
.25 to 3.0.[9] Table 7.7 exploits this range so that we can be assured that
our results are robust. However, the discussion that follows will rely on
the elasticity of .75, a figure on the conservative side of the 1.6 estimate
reported in Table 4.5.

Table 7.7 summarizes the results of the experiment. Three initial wage
gaps are postulated. If the reader feels uneasy with my estimates of urban
disamenities, but accepts the rural-urban price deflators, then he will
favor the wage gap of 52.1 percent. I favor the conservative estimate of the
size of the urban disamenity premium, so a wage gap of 33.2 percent
seems more relevant to me. No doubt the Chicago School among my
readers will favor the larger urban disamenity premium estimate and
therefore the lower wage gap of 17.9 percent. I have bracketed in Table
7.7 the case that I think is the "best guess," but most of the findings are
robust across all cases.

What do we find? In no case does the deadweight loss exceed 1.5
percent of 1831 national income, although the best guess estimate is more
like .5 percent, a tiny number.[10] It hardly seems possible to develop a case
for English labor-market failure on the basis of such estimates. Nor is it
possible to argue that labor-market failure of this sort played a significant
role in constraining British growth during the industrial revolution. A
corollary is that any improvement in labor-market efficiency after 1831
cannot have contributed much to growth performance over the remainder
of the nineteenth century, Edward Denison, Simon Kuznets, and development economists notwithstanding.[11] Nor is this evidence very kind to a
similar thesis offered by Nick Crafts. In his recent book, Crafts (1985, p.
2) argued that British agricultural labor was released early and fast, and

9 Estimates of the elasticity of demand for labor in manufacturing can be found in
the survey by Hammermesh and Grant (1979, Table 2, pp. 526–8).

10 Small deadweight losses are typical in the applied public finance and labor
economics literature, so these results for English wage gaps in 1831 should come
as no surprise. Thirty years ago, Leibenstein (1957) was able to report seven
studies in which such deadweight loss calculations were performed, and in no
case did any of them exceed 1 percent of national income. Similar findings were
reported in the early 1970s by Dougherty and Selowsky (1973). More recently,
Shoven and Whalley (1984) have shown the same.

11 In a series of publications on the "sources of growth," Denison has argued that
the reallocation of labor from low to high productivity sectors contributed in large
measure to rapid growth in post-World War II Japan (Denison and Chung, 1976,
chp. 5) and in much of post-World War II Europe (Denison, 1967, chps. 18 and
21). He did so by invoking the Kuznets Effect (Kuznets, 1966), a statistical
approach that ignores the economics embedded in Figure 7.1. This tradition is
carried to late nineteenth-century Britain by Matthews et al. (1982, chp. 9).

Table 7.7. Assessing the deadweight loss of labor market disequilibrium in 1831: "Partial" general equilibrium in two sectors, agriculture and nonagriculture

(1) Initial wage gap (%)	(2) Labor demand elasticities η^A	(3) η_{NA}	(4) Emigrants Number (000)	(5) Share of agricultural labor force (%)	(6) Deadweight loss £ (000)	(7) Share of nat'l income (%)	(8) Average wage (£) In disequilibrium	(9) In equilibrium	(10) % change in Agricultural wage	(11) Average wage	(12) % Increase in nonagricultural employment
52.1	.68	.25	262.2	14.6	1857	.55	37.51	34.00	26.1	−9.4	4.9
52.1	.68	.75	368.2	20.5	2722	.80	37.51	37.76	40.0	.7	6.8
52.1	.68	3.00	430.5	24.0	3272	.96	37.51	40.32	49.5	7.5	8.0
52.1	1.10	.25	330.3	18.4	2295	.68	37.51	32.43	20.2	−13.5	6.1
52.1	1.10	.75	516.1	28.7	3762	1.11	37.51	36.67	36.0	−2.2	9.6
52.1	1.10	3.00	642.0	35.7	4850	1.43	37.51	40.28	49.3	7.4	11.9
33.2	.68	.25	180.7	10.0	814	.24	33.69	31.51	16.8	−6.5	3.3
33.2	.68	.75	256.8	14.3	1193	.35	33.69	33.82	25.4	.4	4.8
33.2	.68	3.00	303.1	16.8	1438	.42	33.69	35.37	31.2	5.0	5.6
33.2	1.10	.25	227.2	12.6	1010	.30	33.69	30.49	13.1	−9.5	4.2
[33.2	1.10	.75	360.9	20.1	1662	.49	33.69	33.05	22.6	−1.9	6.7]
33.2	1.10	3.00	456.4	25.4	2164	.64	33.69	35.18	30.5	4.4	8.5
17.9	.68	.25	104.6	5.8	254	.07	30.59	29.45	9.2	−3.7	1.9
17.9	.68	.75	150.4	8.4	372	.11	30.59	30.66	13.7	.3	2.8
17.9	.68	3.00	179.3	10.0	449	.13	30.59	31.47	16.7	2.9	3.3
17.9	1.10	.25	131.2	7.3	316	.09	30.59	28.89	7.1	−5.6	2.4
17.9	1.10	.75	212.0	11.8	521	.15	30.59	30.22	12.1	−1.2	3.9
17.9	1.10	3.00	272.9	15.2	684	.20	30.59	31.32	16.1	2.4	5.1

Sources and notes: The initial (real) wage gaps are taken from Table 7.6, "All England," for three cases: 52.1%, cost of living adjusted only; 33.2% and 17.9%, cost of living adjusted plus poor relief plus two alternative city disamenities premia adjustments. The labor-demand elasticities assumed in the experiments are discussed in the text. The calculations implement Figure 7.1, and we require the following additional initial values for 1831: $L_A = 1.8$ million, $L_{NA} = 5.4$ million (Deane and Cole, 1962, Table 31, p. 143); and national income = £340 million (Deane and Cole, 1962, Table 37, p. 166). I have bracketed what seems to me the "best guess" among all of these experiments.

that this factor reallocation contributed significantly to economy-wide productivity gains. If the labor-market disequilibrium generated by the industrial revolution up to 1831 implied only a tiny deadweight loss, how could the elimination of that loss contribute much to overall growth thereafter or even before?

Table 7.7 deals with two sectors split along agricultural and nonagricultural lines. Because agriculture employed only about a quarter of the labor force in 1831 (1.8 million out of 7.2 million), perhaps it is inevitable that the deadweight loss would be so small. Furthermore, the wage gaps documented in Table 7.6 might be viewed by some to apply to rural versus urban employment, not just agricultural versus nonagricultural employment, and rural employment was a far larger share of total employment, in fact more than half (4 million out of 7.2 million). Yet, when the two sectors are split along rural and urban lines, the largest deadweight loss is still no bigger than 2.5 percent of national income, and the best guess figure is only .6 percent.

So far labor-market failure during the First Industrial Revolution doesn't seem to have cost the average Englishman very much, and an optimal allocation of labor would have added very little to aggregate economic welfare. Why, then, do British economic historians make such a fuss over the lack of a fully integrated national labor market?

7.6   The quantitative importance of labor-market failure: Distribution and accumulation effects

Who lost and who gained?

While the deadweight loss associated with labor-market failure estimated so far seems to be trivial, distributional incidence is another matter entirely. Figure 7.2 tells us exactly who gains and who loses. With the disappearance of wage gaps, and with the emigration of labor from agriculture, wages would have risen in agriculture and fallen in industry. Given no change in capital, land, or technology in either of the two sectors, it follows that rents (plus profits) in agriculture would have diminished and profits in industry would have increased. Profits in industry would have risen by ABHC, an increase in their producers' surplus. Rents (or, more likely, farmers' profits) in agriculture would have fallen by EHGF, a decrease in their producers' surplus. It is not clear, however, how common labor would have fared.

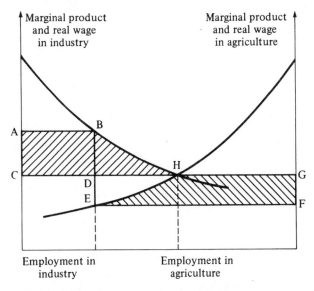

Figure 7.2 "Partial" general equilibrium analysis of wage gaps: Who gains and who loses?

Table 7.8. *Who gained and who lost from labor-market failure? Some estimates for 1831*

Item	Figure 7.2 notation	Gains (+) and losses (−) (millions £)	Share in 1831 national income
	ABDC minus		
Change in wage bill	DGFE	+4.554	+1.3%
Change in industry profits	minus ABHC	−16.066	−4.7
Change in agricultural rents	plus EHGF	+9.850	+2.9
Change in national income	BHE	−1.662	−0.5

Note: This example uses the "best guess" case in Table 7.7, where the wage gap = 33.2%, $\eta_A = 1.1$, and $\eta_{NA} = 0.75$.

Laborers gain in agriculture but lose in industry for an ambiguous net change of DGFE minus ABDC. The net change in the wage bill will be influenced by relative labor-demand elasticities: If they are lower in agriculture, workers gain; if they lower in industry, workers lose.

Table 7.8 offers some estimates of who gained and who lost from labor-market failure based on the best guess case in Table 7.7. The estimates make it quite clear that the offsetting distributive effects of labor-market failure are likely to have been far greater than the overall efficiency losses. Farmers and/or landlords gained much from labor-market failure (9.85 million £) while capitalists lost even more (16.066 million £). Furthermore, these gains and losses appear to have been a significant share of total nonwage incomes: agricultural rents (plus profits) may have been augmented by as much as 34 percent by the labor-market failure while profits in industry may have been reduced by as much as 20 percent.[12]

These big numbers are, of course, only tentative estimates, but they suggest that we need to know far more about the causes of the labor-market failure. They also suggest that the calculation of deadweight losses may be the least interesting means of assessing factor-market failure.

Industrialization and accumulation responses

The example also suggests how misleading comparative static deadweight loss calculations can be when assessing the importance of factor-market failure to growth, accumulation, and industrialization. Although it is true that the elimination of the deadweight loss would have augmented national income only by about .5 percent – about a year's worth of growth in per capita income according to Crafts' growth estimates (Crafts, 1985, Table 2.11, p. 45) – it must have tended to choke off industrial employment by much more. In the absence of the labor-market failure, nonagricultural employment would have been augmented by 6.7 percent – almost four years' worth of employment growth according to Deane and Cole's figures for the 1830s (Deane and Cole, 1962, Table 31, p. 143).

Furthermore, to the extent that the classical saving postulate holds (Marglin, 1984, pp. 324–8), industrial capital accumulation was also choked off by labor-market failure. That is, if the reinvestment rate out of industrial profits was far higher than out of rents (and farmers' profits), then aggregate savings were lower in the presence of labor-market failure, and so too must have been the rate of accumulation economy-wide. Even if the classical saving postulate did not hold, imperfect capital markets

---

12 These calculations rely on Deane and Cole's (1962, Table 37, p. 166) estimates of 1831 value added in agriculture (79.5 million £) and in nonagriculture (260.5 million £). Labor's share in agricultural value added is assumed to be .51, and in industry it is assumed to be .63 (Williamson, 1985a, p. 241). Thus, the calculations take nonlabor income to be about 39 million £ in agriculture and about 96.4 million £ in nonagriculture.

would have ensured that the rate of accumulation in industry would have been lower given the lower profits in the presence of labor-market failure. This, after all, is the central premise of the classical labor-surplus model (for its modern guise, see W. A. Lewis, 1954, and for an historical application to the low countries, see Mokyr's 1976 "pseudo" labor-surplus model).

The finding that labor-market failure significantly augmented agricultural rents at the expense of industrial profits certainly has its attraction. After all, most of us now agree that Britain achieved only modest rates of accumulation during the First Industrial Revolution (Williamson, 1984; 1985a, chp. 11), even when compared with the rest of Europe (Crafts, 1985, p. 64). One of the explanations for this has been that British capital markets failed to innovate those changes that would have made external finance more accessible to industrial firms (Mokyr, 1985, pp. 33–8). Now we have another explanation; namely, that labor-market failure served to choke off industrial profits and thus accumulation.

7.7   Factor-market failure in general equilibrium

Other forces making for too many farmers

There were other forces at work that tended to make English agriculture too big in the 1830s. Imperfect capital markets starved industry for funds, driving a wedge between rates of return in industry and agriculture. Since the industrial capital stock was, therefore, too small, industrial jobs were fewer than they would have been had capital markets been perfect. There were too many workers in agriculture on that score as well.[13] Which of

13 In addition, commercial policy served to encourage more labor (and capital) to stay in agriculture than would have been the case under free trade. Tariffs served to take away incentive for industrial expansion as domestic prices were twisted to favor agriculture and to hurt industry. Because by 1840 there were duties on raw cotton, timber, copper and other raw materials, "the effective rate of protection for factors of production specialised in manufacturing was slightly negative" (McCloskey, 1980, p. 307; and Capie, 1983, pp. 12–18). And, of course, there were the Corn Laws. Susan Fairlee (1969, Table 3, p. 106) estimates that the Corn Laws served to increase grain prices some 20 percent above what they would have been under free trade in the 1830s. Surely this policy by itself meant there were too many farmers in England around 1831. But were the Corn Laws quantitatively more important than factor-market failure? Elsewhere, I offered an answer to this question (Williamson, 1986c).

these two forces had the biggest allocative and distributional impact on the English economy in the 1830s – labor-market failure or capital-market failure?

Capital-market failure has long been a staple in the literature on the British industrial revolution, and it has an equally long tradition in contemporary development economics (McKinnon, 1973). As Postan (1935, p. 71) put it, "the reservoirs of savings were full enough, but conduits to connect them to the wheels of industry were few and meagre." This view was so common even in the early nineteenth century, that the classical economists took it for granted that industrial profits and their reinvestment were the central determinants of accumulation and industrialization. Indeed, this view persists even today in growth paradigms that invoke the Cambridge Savings Equation (Marglin, 1984, pp. 324–8), as well as in the labor-surplus model favored by development economists (Lewis, 1954).

The capital-market-failure thesis is not without its critics. Crouzet, for example, doubts that capital-market failure played a very important role in the First Industrial Revolution, even in the eighteenth century: "the eighteenth century capital market seems, to twentieth century eyes, badly organized, but the creators of modern industry do not seem to have suffered too much from its imperfection . . . English industry . . . seems to have overflowed with capital" (Crouzet, 1965, pp. 187–8).

True, self-finance was the rule in British industry during the industrial revolution, but one wonders to what extent this result was induced by a capital-market failure that made external finance so scarce. As Joel Mokyr has recently put it, "the question should be whether the Industrial Revolution in Britain would have occurred faster and more efficiently if financial constraints had been less stringent" (Mokyr, 1985, p. 38).

The literature on capital-market failure during the First Industrial Revolution seems to suffer the same shortcomings that we have already found in the labor-market-failure literature. Not enough attention has been paid to evidence of capital scarcity that really matters; namely: Was the rate of return to capital far higher in industry than in agriculture? Here, precision is impossible. McCloskey suggests that rates of return on industrial capital may have been as much as three times that of agriculture, 5 percent per annum in the latter and 15 percent in the former (McCloskey, 1981, p. 119), a figure that excludes capital gains. Based on scraps of evidence taken from the mid nineteenth century, the rates in industry appear to be more like two and a half times that of agriculture, still a wide discrepancy.[14] If more perfect capital markets had been able to eliminate these rate of return differentials, would the allocative gains have been significant? McCloskey (1981, pp. 118–19) doesn't think so, although his estimates are much too low because he doesn't allow labor to chase after capital as the latter gets reallocated. Even if McCloskey is right, shouldn't we also explore the implications of capital-market failure for distribution, industrialization, and accumulation? Deadweight loss calculations, as we have seen above, may miss the point.

A general equilibrium assessment

I propose to offer some illustrative answers to these questions by appealing to a simple computable general equilibrium model. A variant of the model has already been used in Chapter 6. As Appendix 7.2 makes clear, the model has been modified to accommodate the purposes of this chapter, but its basic attributes are the same. To repeat, it is a four-sector model composed of agriculture, industry, services, and mining. There are four social classes that supply inputs to the production process (landlords supplying agricultural land, capitalists and farmers supplying capital, common labor supplying unskilled labor, and the labor aristocracy supplying skills). The economy is a net importer of agricultural products and raw materials, and a net exporter of manufactures. The prices of the three tradables – raw materials, agricultural products, and manufactures – are taken to be set by world market conditions and commercial policy, while the nontradables – services and the products of the mines – are determined endogenously by domestic demand and supply. The model was designed to deal with comparative static issues only, but it is ideal for making exactly the kinds of distributional and resource allocative assess-

14 F. M. L. Thompson (1963, p. 251) estimates the rate of return on industrial capital in 1846 to have been 8–9 percent. Paul David (1975, pp. 264–5) uses Thompson's data on estate improvements between 1847 and 1879 to get a rate of return on agricultural capital of 3.6 percent. Thompson himself feels that between 1846 and 1853 there were "no measurable returns" in agriculture (Thompson, 1963, p. 249). David also estimates the rate of return to agricultural mechanization to have been 2–4.5 percent between 1846 and 1853. Taking the rate of return to industrial capital at about 8.5 percent (Thompson's 8–9 percent in 1846), and the rate of return to agricultural capital at about 3.25 percent (David's 2–4.5 percent in 1851), then the ratio was about 2.4, the figure reported in the text and used in subsequent calculations. It might be relevant to note that the United States had very similar rate-of-return differentials between industry and agriculture in 1850 (James and Skinner, 1985, p. 528; Atack and Bateman, 1987, p. 261).

ments posed above. It can be used to assess the impact of factor-market failure on sectoral employment (were there too many farmers?), on national income (how big was the deadweight loss?), on industrialization (was industrial output constrained?), and on distribution (were profits, and thus accumulation, too low?). Those readers who are suspicious of such models may be appeased by the discovery that, where comparisons are relevant, most of the results of the simple partial equilibrium analysis above are reproduced in the more complex general equilibrium exercise below. Magnitudes, however, are bigger. In any case, the purpose of the general equilibrium model is not to supply precise estimates of the impact of factor-market failure, but rather to give us some quantitative feel for likely magnitudes. No more, no less.

Table 7.9 presents the main findings under the assumption that capital is "quasi-mobile" between sectors; that is, imperfect capital markets drive a wedge between rates of return inside and outside agriculture, but capital migrates to the highest returns until that wedge is reestablished (where industrial rates of return are 2.4 times that of agriculture). The assumption of capital "quasi-mobility" implies a long-run assessment of the impact of factor-market failure. I believe this is the appropriate assumption. Otherwise, capital is not allowed to chase after labor, and the impact of the labor-market failure will be understated. Table 7.9 assesses the impact of an elimination of labor-market failure (the 1831 "best guess" real-wage gap is allowed to disappear), and an elimination of capital-market failure (the ratio of industrial to agricultural rates of return is reduced to 1 from the 2.4 figure prevailing in the late 1840s). Table 7.10 presents the findings under the assumption that capital is completely immobile between agriculture and nonagriculture (although mobile within nonagriculture). The table therefore offers a shorter run assessment of the impact of the elimination of wage gaps. I believe this is an inappropriate assumption for the reasons given above. Consider the results reported in Table 7.9 first.

To begin with, the results listed in each column of Table 7.9 should accord with economic intuition. The elimination of the wage gap, for example, tends to create labor scarcity in agriculture, output contracts, and employment contracts even more, since the relative scarcity of labor rises. Symmetrically, output expands in nonagriculture, and employment expands even more, since the relative scarcity of labor falls. The impact on output in the two sectors exceeds that attributable to employment changes alone because capital is allowed to chase after labor and the higher returns. Profits rise in nonagriculture, but by less than output. The explanation is a

Table 7.9. *The impact of factor-market failure, assuming capital mobile*

Impact	(1) Eliminating the wage gap and labor-market failure (%)	(2) Eliminating the rate-of-return gap and capital-market failure (%)	(3) Eliminating both gaps and labor-plus-capital-market failure ($\neq (1) + (2)$) (%)
A. Agriculture			
Percent rise in agriculture output (constant prices)	−20.4	−56.1	−69.6
Emigrants from agriculture as a percent of agricultural labor force	−39.0	−51.4	−57.9
B. Nonagriculture			
Percent rise in nonagricultural output (constant prices)	+13.4	+35.8	+39.8
Percent rise in nonagricultural employment (unskilled labor only)	+15.5	+20.4	+23.0
Percent rise in nonagricultural profits (nominal)	+11.2	+64.6	+78.1
C. Manufacturing			
Percent rise in manufacturing output (constant price)	+24.1	+63.6	+73.4
Percent rise in manufacturing employment (unskilled labor only)	+25.3	+40.6	+47.2
Percent rise in manufacturing profits (nominal)	+23.6	+114.7	+141.8
D. Economy-wide increase in real GNP	+3.3	+8.2	+7.0

Notes: See text. Col. (3) does not add entries in (1) and (2), but reports the impact of the joint change.

bit more subtle. Because the capital-labor ratio tends to fall in non-agriculture as the relative scarcity of labor falls, one would have thought that the rate of return to capital there would rise and thus that profits would rise by even more given that the capital stock has been augmented. But the rise in profits is somewhat less than expected because the prices of the nontradables (services and mining) decline. In any case, profits do rise with the elimination of the wage gaps, a result we found in the partial equilibrium analysis as well. Manufacturing output by itself gets an even bigger boost from the elimination of the wage gaps, primarily because, given the

Table 7.10. *The impact of labor-market failure, assuming capital immobile*

Impact	Eliminating the wage gap and labor-market failure (%)
A. Agriculture	
Percent rise in agricultural output (constant prices)	−10.5
Emigrants from agriculture as a percent of agricultural labor force	−29.5
B. Nonagriculture	
Percent rise in nonagricultural output (constant prices)	+5.5
Percent rise in nonagricultural employment (unskilled labor only)	+11.7
Percent rise in nonagricultural profits (nominal)	+5.5
C. Manufacturing	
Percent rise in manufacturing output (constant prices)	+11.0
Percent rise in manufacturing employment (unskilled labor only)	+16.7
Percent rise in manufacturing profits (nominal)	+10.8
D. Economy-wide increase in real GNP	+0.6

Notes: See text and Table 7.9.

small-country assumption, the price of output remains stable there. Finally, and perhaps least interesting, real GNP increases with the elimination of the deadweight losses associated with labor-market distortions.

Now consider the magnitudes. The deadweight losses reported in Table 7.9 are considerably higher than they were in the partial equilibrium case reported in Table 7.7 (3.3 versus .49 percent of GNP), primarily because capital is allowed to chase after labor in the general equilibrium case. (The deadweight losses are much smaller in the capital immobile case in Table 7.10, 0.6 percent of GNP, almost exactly the partial equilibrium result.) These deadweight losses associated with labor-market failure are hardly trivial, to be sure, but they are considerably smaller than those associated with capital-market failure (8.2 percent). Thus, the impact of capital-market failure on the British economy in the 1830s appears to have been far greater than the impact of labor-market failure.[15]

15 Note that the combined effects of labor-market and capital-market failure in Table 7.9 are *not* additive. Albert Fishlow and Paul David (1961) alerted us to that possibility some time ago. That is, perfect labor markets are a partial remedy for capital-market failure and perfect capital markets are a partial remedy for labor-market failure. However, Table 7.9 also shows that the deadweight losses associated with eliminating both factor-market failures is *less* than that of eliminating capital-market failure alone. That result is impossible in theory, but it has appeared in fact due to difficulties in handling nonlinearities in the solution.

Of course, this is only a simple model of the British economy, and many of the parameters embedded in it are only guesses, so the empirical results reported in Table 7.9 should not be viewed as definitive. Nonetheless, the results are suggestive.

First, nonagricultural employment in general, and manufacturing employment in particular, must have been seriously choked off by factor-market failure up to the 1840s. Although Britain's industrialization performance was certainly impressive after the French wars, it would have been far more impressive in the absence of these domestic factor-market distortions. Indeed, nonagricultural employment would have been 23 percent higher. If that increase is stretched over the two decades 1821–41, it implies that nonagricultural employment growth would have been about 3 percent per annum, not the 2 percent per annum actually achieved (Deane and Cole, 1962, p. 143). Manufacturing output would have been 73.4 percent higher. And if that increase is stretched over the period 1815 to 1841, it implies that manufacturing output growth would have been about 5.2 percent per annum, not the 3.1 percent per annum actually achieved (Harley, 1982, p. 276, "Divisia"). Thus, factor-market distortions seriously inhibited industrialization in Britain after the French wars, although capital-market failure was the more serious constraint.

Second, these distortions had important distributional implications. Profits in nonagriculture would have been much higher (by 78.1 percent), and they would have been increased even more in manufacturing (by 141.8 percent, or more than double the actual profits that accrued to capitalists there). If the reinvestment rate out of nonagricultural profits was relatively high, as most of us believe, then the elimination of factor-market distortions would have resulted in a significant rise in saving and accumulation, especially so in manufacturing. The elimination of the capital-market distortions would also have made accessible to all potential savers the high rates of return in industry, and if saving was responsive to the rate of return, then economy-wide accumulation would have gotten an even bigger boost.

As we pointed out, Table 7.10 assumes capital to be immobile, so only the impact of labor-market failure can be assessed here. The influence of these distortions is much smaller than in Table 7.9, where capital is allowed to chase after labor. I prefer the longer run assessment implied by Table 7.9, where imperfect and distorted capital markets are at least allowed some success in seeking out higher returns. Nonetheless, even under capital immobility assumptions, wage gaps still have a significant influence. Elimination of the wage gap would have raised GNP by 0.6 percent (the deadweight loss), nonagricultural employment by 11.7 percent, and nonagricultural output by 5.5 percent.

7.8   Why didn't manufacturing capital migrate to the countryside to exploit the rural labor surplus in the South?

Those large wage gaps in the South of England certainly pose a puzzle. One can, of course, offer plausible explanations for the inability of rural emigration to eliminate the labor-market disequilibrium between London and the southern countryside. The rate of emigration of the rural workforce was impressive, but Chapter 2 has shown that it was restricted to young adults. For whatever the reason, those in their thirties and above rarely migrated. Even though those in their teens and twenties were very responsive to employment opportunities in London, that age cohort was, after all, a small share of the total rural labor force. Thus, the ability of rural emigration to accommodate the labor-market disequilibrium was limited.

But surely there were no such constraints on the migration of manufacturing capital to the countryside in the South. Why didn't manufacturing capital migrate to the countryside and exploit the rural labor surplus in the South? Why didn't Ipswich, Great Yarmouth, or Southampton become the Prestons, Bradfords, and Huddersfields of the South? Certainly factories migrated to labor-surplus areas up North. And certainly they did so in New England early in America's antebellum development, as they did in Japan early in the Meiji industrialization effort.

Why did the factories fail to migrate to rural surplus areas in the South of England? Was power so much more expensive in the rural South that the advantage of cheap labor was offset? Were transport costs of finished manufactures so much higher? Were the agglomeration economies in key sectors, like textiles, so overwhelming that migration of factories away from the booming North was cost-inefficient even in the face of cheap southern labor? Or, is this another example of factor-market failure?

This chapter does not offer an answer to these questions, but they certainly need attention.[16]

16 Like most of this chapter, Pollard (1978, p. 108) posed the question in terms of rural labor surplus, wage gaps, and insufficient emigration from the agricultural South: "urban manufactures depended on labour from their near neighbour-

7.9 Implications

Factor markets did fail during the First Industrial Revolution, and it had important implications for employment growth in the cities, for the structural transformation of the economy, and perhaps even for accumulation. In a world in which capital and labor were mobile but only imperfectly so, the following tentative implications seem warranted.

Economists almost always find deadweight losses associated with market failure to be modest. Industrial revolutions may be an exception. Labor-market failure around 1831 may have cost Britain about 3 percent of GNP, a significant amount for an economy whose per capita income was growing at only about .5 percent per annum (Crafts, 1985, p. 45). When capital-market failure is added, however, the figure rises to 7 percent. Factor-market failure did matter in an aggregate sense, although the really significant failure was in capital markets.

In spite of high rates of emigration and an "early release" of farm labor in Britain, there were far too many farmers and laborers in agriculture. Wage gaps between city and countryside starved industry for labor and glutted the countryside. As a result, the agricultural labor force in 1831 may have been too big by more than a third. In addition, rate-of-return differentials imply that industry was starved for and agriculture was glutted with capital. Too much capital in agriculture meant too many farmers working with that capital. The combined influence of labor- and capital-market failure may have made the agricultural labor force too big by more than half in 1831. If these tentative estimates are close to the mark, they suggest one explanation for British agriculture's dramatic relative decline across the remainder of the nineteenth century.

Industrial output and employment growth was certainly dramatic after the French wars, but, nonetheless, that growth was seriously constrained by factor-market distortions. Around 1831, nonagricultural employment

hood, even though wages were already . . . relatively [high] . . . They did not, as the Lewis model would have one believe, go for labour from the overpopulated and low-wage agricultural South." In contrast, a recent paper by Gregory Clark (1987, p. 170) does pose the question in terms of a failure of manufacturing capital to migrate to the "overpopulated" rural areas: "One remarkable feature of world industrialization since 1780 has been the extent to which workers have migrated to a few industrial centers, instead of capital and management migrating to the available supplies of cheap labor." I believe Clark exaggerates the pervasiveness of this "remarkable feature": It was far truer of the South of England than in the North, or in New England, or in Meiji Japan.

would have been higher by about a fifth had factor-market distortions been absent. The rate of industrialization was retarded on that score, and labor-market failure contributed a good share to that result.

Recent work suggests that the rate of accumulation was slow in Britain during the French wars and after. One likely explanation among others is that capital markets failed to accommodate adequately investment demands in industry, and that industrial accumulation was, therefore, constrained by profits. The results reported here suggest that labor-market distortions contributed to low profits by making labor too expensive in the cities and towns. Capital markets contributed to low profits, of course, by starving industry for capital. Nonagricultural profits might have been about 78 percent higher in 1831 had these factor-market distortions been absent. In addition, we have that puzzling finding that manufacturing capital was reluctant to move out into the countryside in the South of England so as to exploit surplus labor there. If these findings are even close to the mark, they offer a promising explanation for slow rates of accumulation in Britain.

What remains to be seen, of course, is whether these tentative findings will hold up under more detailed scrutiny. There are two avenues that might be pursued, both of which would serve to deflate, but not destroy, the significance of these findings. First, the assumptions employed here might well be challenged. The most important of these is probably that the prices of tradables – manufactures and agricultural commodities – are taken as exogenous. To the extent that the decline of agriculture and the expansion of manufacturing would have raised agriculture's terms of trade, then the impact of factor-market failure was smaller than estimated. How much smaller hinges on alternative assumptions about price elasticities of foreign supply of agricultural goods and foreign demand for manufactures. Second, the view that wage and rate of return gaps reflect disequilibrium and factor-market distortion may also be challenged. If, for example, the rate-of-return gaps reflect risk, then we have overstated the influence of capital-market failure. If, for example, the wage gaps can be partially explained by moving costs, differences in efficiency embodied in labor, or any of the other forces listed in Section 7.5, then we have overstated the influence of labor-market failure. Indeed, some might wonder how labor- or capital-market disequilibria could persist so long. After all, measured wage and rate-of-return gaps remain an attribute of British factor markets throughout the nineteenth century, although they never seem to get larger than in the middle of the century, where we have made the factor-market failure assessment. We need two ingredients to make the persistence of factor-market disequilibria plausible – unbalanced factor-demand expansion and constraints on mobility. The former has always been an attribute of industrial revolutions. The latter can be explained in a world in which only new capital and young adult labor migrate. In an economy with low rates of accumulation, new capital (current investment) is a small share of total capital in place, making it difficult to eliminate rate-of-return differentials. And even though the rate of rural emigration of young adults was very rapid, those who migrated were almost never in their thirties and above. For one reason or another, older rural laborers simply did not leave. Thus, the labor-market disequilibrium between city and countryside could not be accommodated by even the responsive migration of an age cohort which, after all, was only a small share of the total rural labor force.

What also remains to be seen is whether factor-market failure was more serious in early nineteenth-century Britain than it was in the followers who were about to mimic the First Industrial Revolution. Is it possible that the more rapid growth of the followers can be explained by more efficient factor markets?

Appendix 7.1. *Poor-relief payments: Adding relief payments to farm laborers' wages*

County	(1) Annual wage income (£)	(2) 1831 Population (000)	(3) Increase in laborers' income due to poor relief (£)	(4) Annual income (£)
Bedford	25.50	95	2.22	27.72
Berkshire	27.30	147	2.73	30.03
Buckingham	26.95	147	2.88	29.83
Cambridge	26.18	144	2.21	28.39
Essex	26.48	318	2.42	28.90
Hertford	28.39	143	2.18	30.57
Huntington	29.36	53	2.30	31.66
Kent	32.26	399	3.36	35.62
Norfolk	28.27	390	2.83	31.10
Northampton	24.96	179	2.89	27.85
Oxford	25.03	154	2.85	27.88
Hampshire	26.95	314	3.12	30.07
Suffolk	26.00	296	2.82	28.82
Sussex	28.73	273	3.63	32.36
Wiltshire	22.25	237	2.69	24.94
Weighted average	27.27	3,289	2.86	30.13

Average % Increase, 15 Speenhamland counties 10.5%
Average % Increase, All Southern counties 7.1%
Average % Increase, All of England 4.4%

Source: The basic data in cols. (1) and (3) are from Boyer (1985), Table 1, assuming his 33% share. Col. (2) is from Mitchell and Deane (1962, p. 20). The average for the South of England also uses 1831 population weights. Surrey and Middlesex are assumed to behave like the 15 counties in the table above, while all other southern counties have their poor-relief "increase" set at one quarter of the 10.5%. The North of England "increase" is set at zero.

Appendix 7.2. Modeling the general equilibrium effects of factor-market failure

The general equilibrium model used in Section 7.7 has two versions, one in which capital is mobile between sectors but with a wedge driving a gap between rates of return in agriculture and elsewhere, and one in which capital is completely immobile between agriculture and elsewhere. The second is only an extension of the first, and thus this Appendix will dwell only on the first. Both are variants of a parent model that has been used elsewhere to analyze the impact of the French wars (Williamson, 1984), the determinants of inequality across the British Kuznets Curve (Williamson, 1985a), and the impact of the Irish on British labor markets (Chapter 6).

As before, the model has five domestic factors of production:

farmland (J), excluding improvements other than initial clearing for cultivation and pasture;
capital (K), consisting of all reproducible capital in the public and private sectors, excluding dwellings;
unskilled labor (L), or total manhours compensated at the unskilled wage rate, including family labor time utilized on farms and in nonfarm proprietorships;
skills (S), or all attributes of labor inputs generating earnings in excess of the unskilled wage; and
intermediate resource inputs (B), used directly in the manufacturing sector or indirectly in the urban sectors facilitating manufacturing production.

In addition, the model introduces one imported intermediate input:

imported raw material inputs (F), processed by manufacturing and unavailable at home.

As with all comparative static models, factor endowments are given, so the first four in the list are determined exogenously. Intermediate inputs (F and B), however, are determined endogenously in response to supply and demand, domestic and foreign.

These factor inputs are used in the production of four sectoral outputs:

agriculture (A), or all national income originating in agriculture, forestry, and fisheries;
manufacturing (M), or all national income originating in manufacturing, building, and construction;
the tertiary sector (C), or all national income originating in finance, trade, gas, electricity and water, private services, local and national government, transport, and communications; and
intermediate resources (B), or all national income originating in mining and quarrying.

The model is open to trade, and it conforms to the reality that Britain was a net importer of agricultural goods and a net exporter of manufactured goods. The small-country assumption has prices of all tradables determined exogenously by commercial policy (the Corn Laws) and by world markets. That is, demands for exportables and supplies of importables are taken to be highly price elastic. The home-produced intermediate good B cannot be traded internationally (for example, coal) and the foreign-produced intermediate good F cannot be produced at home (for example, cotton). Tertiary outputs (home services) cannot be traded.

Production relationships can be summarized as follows:

$$A = A(L,K,J),$$
$$M = M(L,K,S,B,F),$$
$$C = C(L,K,S,B),$$
$$B = B(L,K).$$

Capital and unskilled labor are assumed to move freely among all sectors, except that a gap is driven between wages and rates of return in agriculture and elsewhere, thus accommodating the labor and capital market failure discussed in the text; skilled labor is mobile between the tertiary and manufacturing sectors to which its use is restricted; land is specific to agricultural production; the imported intermediate resource (cotton) is an input to manufacturing only; and the home-produced intermediate resource (coal) is used in manufacturing and the service sector.

By the small-country assumption, P_A, P_M, and P_F are taken as exogenous. The remaining eight prices are determined endogenously:

d	=	rent earned on an acre of cleared farmland under crop or pasturage;
r_A	=	rent (or rate of return) earned on reproducible capital in agriculture:
r_I	=	rent (or rate of return) earned on reproducible capital in all nonagricultural sectors, and where the ratio of nonagricultural to agricultural rates of return is determined exogenously;
w_A	=	the wage rate (or annual earnings) for unskilled farm labor;
w_I	=	the wage rate (or annual earnings) for common labor in all nonagricultural sectors, and where the ratio of nonagricultural to agricultural unskilled wages is determined exogenously;
q	=	the wage (or annual earnings) for skills;
P_C	=	the price of tertiary services; and
P_B	=	the price of home-produced resources.

The first six of these prices are factor rents. Thus, the distribution of income can be explored by the behavior of farm rents and profits ($dJ + r_A K_A$), profits in nonagriculture ($r_I K_I$), the earnings of skills (qS), and the wages of unskilled labor ($w_A L_A + w_I L_I$).

The model also predicts the following seven quantities:

A	=	home-produced agricultural goods;
M	=	home-produced manufactured goods;

C = home-produced tertiary services;
B = home-produced resources;
A_M = imported agricultural goods;
M_X = exported manufactured goods;
F = imported intermediate goods.

Final product demands are exogenous, where demands are a function of per capita income, relative prices and population. National income is defined as:

$$Y = P_A A + P_M M + P_C C + D$$

where resource output, $P_B B$, is excluded since it is an intermediate good, and D is the net trade deficit in nominal terms. A final equation insures that the trade account is in balance:

$$P_A A_M + P_F F = P_M M_X + D.$$

The model can easily be converted into rates of change, and the experiments reported in the text exploit the fact.

In private correspondence and discussion, Peter Solar and Miles Kimball have pointed out some inconsistencies among the parameters used in earlier versions of this model. The listing which follows gives (c1821) empirical content to the model used here, and it includes a revision of those values which troubled Solar and Kimball:

Technology. Elasticities of substitution in production (σ_{ij}^k) are revised from my book (Williamson, 1985a, p. 242), in part to make them consistent at the value-added level, but still retaining capital-skill relative complementarity:

$$\sigma_{KL}^A = \sigma_{KJ}^A = \sigma_{JK}^A = \sigma_{LJ}^A = 1 \qquad \text{(Cobb Douglas)}$$
$$\sigma_{KL}^M = \sigma_{LS}^M = 1.4059, \ \sigma_{KS}^M = .7029 \qquad \text{(CES)}$$
$$\sigma_{KL}^C = \sigma_{LS}^C = 1.0102, \ \sigma_{KS}^C = .5051 \qquad \text{(CES)}$$
$$\sigma_{KL}^B = 1 \qquad \text{(Cobb Douglas)}$$

Demand. Based on "stylized facts of demand," the price elasticity of demand (ϵ_j) for manufactures is assumed elastic, for agriculture inelastic, and for services unit elastic, with no changes from my book (Williamson, 1985a, p. 242). In addition, Engel Effects are captured by assumptions on income elasticities (η_j) – high for manufactures and low for agriculture, with only little change from my 1985 book. Thus:

$$\epsilon_A = -.6, \ \epsilon_M = -1.3, \ \epsilon_C = -1.0$$
$$\eta_A = .6, \ \eta_M = 1.35, \ \eta_C = 1.11$$

The cross-price elasticities (ϵ_{ij}) are implied by adding-up conditions (Williamson, 1985a, p. 242):

$$\epsilon_{AM} = .0896, \ \epsilon_{AC} = -.0896, \ \epsilon_{MC} = .1080$$
$$\epsilon_{MA} = -.1580, \ \epsilon_{CA} = -.2712, \ \epsilon_{CM} = .1612$$

Input Mix in 1821. The initial sectoral distribution of labor, capital, skills, and intermediates are unchanged from my earlier book (Williamson, 1985a, pp. 243–4), and thus they are not repeated here.

Demand and Output Mix in 1821. The distribution of output and final demand by sector is revised only slightly from my earlier book (Williamson, 1985a, pp. 243–4) so they are not repeated here.

Factor Shares in 1821. The share of factor payments in total value added by sector (θ_{ij}) has been revised from my earlier book (Williamson, 1985a, p. 241), primarily to reflect wage and rate of return differentials now introduced in the model as factor market distortions. Thus:

$$
\begin{aligned}
\theta_{JA} &= .32559 & \theta_{KM} &= .26206 & \theta_{KC} &= .40571 & \theta_{KB} &= .31520 \\
\theta_{KA} &= .35778 & \theta_{LM} &= .36456 & \theta_{LC} &= .36943 & \theta_{LB} &= .68480 \\
\theta_{LA} &= .31663 & \theta_{SM} &= .10551 & \theta_{SC} &= .21474 \\
& & \theta_{BM} &= .03899 & \theta_{BC} &= .01011 \\
& & \theta_{FM} &= .22888
\end{aligned}
$$

8. Did Britain's cities grow too fast?

8.1 Setting the stage

Was city growth too fast or too slow during the First Industrial Revolution? Such questions are rarely posed of British historical experience, even though implicit judgments are being made all the time. Answers hinge on an assessment of the behavior of private labor and capital markets, on the one hand, and the provision of public social overhead, on the other.

Most historians have taken the view that fast city growth was a Good Thing. After all, Britain underwent the industrial revolution first and was also more urbanized than her competitors. That historical correlation implies for most historians that Britain's fast-city-growth regime must have been optimal, that slower city growth would have been a mistake, and that faster city growth would have been infeasible.

Anthony Wohl (1983) takes the contrary view. He argues that British authorities were unprepared for and surprised by the rapid city growth that carried the industrial revolution, with disastrous results. City governments didn't plan for the event, public-health officials were unprepared for the event, and city social overhead technologies were too backward to deal with the event. Furthermore, entrepreneurial and technological failure in the public sector, and rising land scarcity in the private sector, both served to breed levels of crowding, density, mortality, morbidity, and disamenities that were high even by the standards of the poorest Third World cities. Britain was simply unable or unwilling to house itself properly during the First Industrial Revolution. So much so that the 1830s and 1840s are seen by Michael Flinn (1965, p. 14) as a Malthusian retribution by disease. Furthermore, her cities were full of pauperism and poverty, a sure sign to some historians that there were too many migrants in Britain's cities. Based on quality-of-life indicators, the critics argue that either city growth was too fast, or investment in urban social overhead too low, or both.

219

Earlier chapters in this book have noted that city growth debates have been equally intense in the Third World. Here too pessimists have documented pauperism and poverty. They have also stressed the city's inability to cope with the social overhead and housing requirements of rapid growth, arguing that city growth has been too fast, requiring public intervention in "failing" private-factor markets. As a United Nations' survey in 1978 showed, this view was certainly the dominant one among government authorities in the developing countries: "Among the 116 developing countries that responded to the United Nations' 'Fourth Population Inquiry Among Governments' . . . [on] the desirability of current rates of rural-urban migration . . . 76 [wished] to slow it down and 14 to reverse it" (Preston, 1979, p. 195). Things had not changed when a similar survey was taken in 1983. In short, the pessimists tend to view Third World city growth as another example of failure in private markets, in this case an example in which a collective resource, the urban commons, is overused. Based on Manchester slums in the 1830s, interventionists like James Kay (1832), Frederick Engels (1845), and the social reformers would certainly have agreed.

In contrast, laissez-faire optimists view city growth as the central force raising average living standards. Indeed, the optimists tend to attribute any overuse of the urban commons to government-induced price distortions and an urban bias rather than to failure in private markets (Lipton, 1976).

Although the optimists favor an open, laissez-faire approach to city growth, the pessimists search for efficient legislative devices to close them down. Like the Victorian Reformers, Third World city planners think city growth has been too fast, and many social scientists would appear to agree (Shaw, 1978; Simmons, 1979; Preston, 1979; UN, 1980, chp. 9).

So, did cities grow too fast during the First Industrial Revolution? The development and economic history literature rarely makes it clear exactly what evidence is required to answer that question, so Section 8.3 dwells at length on defining optimal migration and city growth. Indeed, the traditional literature from the 1830s to the 1980s typically cites evidence irrelevant to debates over city growth, as Section 8.2 makes clear. Having cleared away this important methodological underbrush, the chapter will then offer an answer based on what we have reported in this book so far; namely, that cities grew too slowly, not too fast. With that issue settled, the next two chapters move on to what I feel is the more pertinent question: Did Britain underinvest in city social overhead, thus following an ugly-city regime which had much nastier mortality and morbidity implications than was optimal?

8.2   Dealing with some important irrelevancies

It is, of course, true that cities were crowded with impecunious common labor, and that ugly urban disamenities were graphically apparent. Such evidence suggested to Victorian observers that cities were growing too fast. However, although the Victorian critics were quick to cite conditions in the cities themselves to prove their point, the more relevant question might have been whether Britain as a whole, not just the cities, would have been better off had city growth been slower.

Was city growth fast?

Although England's peak city growth rates in the early nineteenth century were certainly impressive by eighteenth-century standards (Chapter 1), they were no different from those achieved by the rest of Europe in the late nineteenth century at their peak rates of city growth, and they were quite modest when compared with the contemporary Third World. The rate of urban population growth in the Third World was 4.35 percent per annum in the 1960s and 1970s (Todaro, 1984, p. 13), almost double the 2.35 percent per annum rate reached in England 1811 to 1846 (Table 2.4). On the other hand, although English city growth rates were about half of those recorded in the contemporary Third World, city immigration rates were quite similar, ranging between 1.10 and 1.91 in England 1776–1806 (Table 2.5) and averaging 1.79 in the Third World (Kelley and Williamson, 1984). Given that England's rate of city growth was only half that of the Third World, her city immigration rates were really quite spectacular.

It appears that England's cities relied more heavily on immigration than has the Third World. Although immigration accounted for about 46 percent of city population growth in England between 1811 and 1846, it accounted for only about 39 percent in the Third World in the 1960s and 1970s. The relative importance of immigration to English city growth was even greater in the early years of the First Industrial Revolution: Between 1776 and 1811 immigration accounted for nearly 60 percent of city growth.

Does this imply that city immigration in England was excessive? Not necessarily. In an arithmetic sense, high immigration rates were necessary to accommodate the reality that crude death rates were so high in the cities. Crude death rate differentials between city and countryside declined some after 1841 (Chapters 2 and 9), but they were still pronounced in 1866. They continued to decline during the remainder of the nineteenth century, but the switch to a mortality environment in which cities had the lower death rates did not take place until around World War I. The impact of public-health and sanitation reform in making the city a relatively benign mortality environment, even in the Third World, is a twentieth-century phenomenon. In nineteenth-century England, the cities were killers.

In the contemporary Third World, crude rates of natural increase are about the same in urban and rural areas (22.5 versus 22.4 per thousand: Rogers, 1984, p. 288), while in England they were considerably higher in the countryside even as late as 1841 (15.0 versus 11.9 per thousand: Table 2.1), and the differential was probably far higher in the late eighteenth century. The higher rate of natural increase in the countryside clearly placed great stress on rural-urban labor markets as booming labor demands in the cities were distant from booming labor supplies in the countryside.

Compared with the Third World, Britain did not undergo exceptionally rapid rates of city growth during the industrial revolution. Yet, the Third World has not had to cope with the poor match between excess city labor demands and excess rural labor supplies, which was Britain's burden. This is the key reason why city immigration rates were so high in England even though the rates of industrialization and city growth were relatively modest by Third World standards. We should remember this finding when confronted with the argument by Victorian interventionists that immigration to Britain's cities was too fast, and that the rapid immigration was a symptom of "overurbanization."

Were the cities faced with demographic surprises?

In contrast with the alarmist comments of contemporaries in the 1830s and Wohl's assertion that municipal planners were unprepared for rapid city growth in the early nineteenth century, England's urbanization experience during the First Industrial Revolution was remarkably stable (Table 2.4). Although there is some evidence of a quickening in city growth rates between 1811 and 1846 which coincides with an acceleration of industrialization after the French wars, and while they were very fast in some cities in the North (e.g., in the 1820s Manchester, 3.9 percent per annum, Bradford, 5.9 percent per annum, and West Bromwich, 4.8 percent per annum), the surge in city growth on average was really quite modest. The average rate of city growth over the thirty-five years of most rapid growth (1811–46) was 2.35 percent per annum, not very much greater than the 2.1 per annum rate achieved before and the 2.2 rate achieved after. Based on such evidence, one can hardly argue that municipal planners in general, exceptions aside, were taken unawares by an unexpected acceleration of city growth in the 1820s, 1830s, and 1840s since similar growth rates had been experienced over the previous six decades.

If the housing and municipal public sectors failed in the early nineteenth century, the explanation did not lie with demographic "surprises." The failure may have had its source, of course, with the limits on social overhead accumulation imposed by capital-market austerity during the French wars (Ashton, 1959, chp. 4; Williamson, 1984a). As we shall argue in the next two chapters, the crowding-out effects of the massive increase in war debt appears to have had its biggest impact on housing and social overhead investment. This wartime postponement of housing and social overhead investment eventually became an environmentally nasty peacetime legacy that helped precipitate the Reform Debates of the 1830s. Demographic "surprises," however, cannot be used to support an overurbanization argument.

Did the cities suffer dependency burdens?

Some historians and development economists argue that displaced rural migrants flocked to the cities in search of relief, contributing to overurbanization. No doubt some did, including the Irish, but the demographic evidence certainly fails to support the general premise.

Chapter 2 confirmed that migration to Britain's cities was highly selective of young adults. Almost 63 percent of the city immigrants in the 1850s were aged 15 to 29 (Table 2.12) whereas only a little more than a quarter of the national population fell into that group. This young-adult-selectivity bias among the migrants (including the Irish: Table 6.4) served to twist the age distribution in the cities, heaping the city population in the young adult ages and shrinking the number of very young and very old dependents. This had two very important implications.

In the first place, the inflow of young adults implied a human capital transfer from countryside to city. Indeed, Chapter 3 estimated that the human capital – in the form of rearing costs – embodied in the city's immigrants were from 15 to 18 percent of city investment in 1850. This human capital transfer must have served to take the pressure off conventional capital markets in financing accumulation requirements in England's cities. Such evidence rejects the view that cities were full of migrants who were a drain on city resources, contributing to overurbanization.

In the second place, by lowering the dependency rate, cities had far lower relief burdens. England's cities had lower pauper rates than the countryside, and Chapter 2 argued that the lower dependency rates might well have accounted for all of the difference in pauper rates. As a result of these favorable demographic features, the cities should have had higher saving and accumulation rates. This follows directly from the life-cycle and dependency hypotheses. These hypotheses argue that high dependency rates increase consumption requirements at the expense of saving. The dependency effect may have been manifested by a direct influence on household saving behavior, or, perhaps more likely, indirectly through the impact of dependency rates on poor relief, the tax burden, and thus on disposable incomes of potential savers. In any case, the inference seems to be that the young adult bias must have served to favor saving and accumulation rates in England's cities during the industrial revolution.

There is no dependency burden or pauperism evidence to support the overurbanization thesis. On the contrary, compared with the countryside the cities had low dependency and pauperism rates, and a very strong young-adult-migrant-selectivity bias accounts for that result. Not only did these demographic forces favor the cities, but city migrants suffered no greater unemployment than did nonmigrants (Chapter 5), and employed labor in the cities had earnings far higher than in the English and Irish countryside (Chapter 7).

Did Britain overurbanize in the Hoselitz sense?

As Chapter 4 pointed out, Bert Hoselitz (1955, 1957) was the first to coin the term overurbanization. Although his primary focus was on Asian experience in the 1950s, it became a stylized fact of Third World development until Samuel Preston (1979) and the United Nations (1980) gave it more careful attention. The thesis seemed persuasive. Hoselitz assumed that manufacturing was the key export staple that drove urban employment. If the manufacturing sector employed a small share of the total urban labor force by historical standards, then it could be inferred that the Third World was overurbanizing. The mechanism is initiated by rural push, either from Malthusian pressure on the land or by labor-saving technological events in agriculture. As the glut of rural immigrants floods the city, it spills over into low-wage service sectors, unemployment, and pauperism. Overurbanization ensues.

The evidence from the First Industrial Revolution has not been kind to this hypothesis. Urbanization did not outrun industrialization in any dramatic way over the century following 1760. Indeed, during the period of most rapid urbanization between 1811 and 1841, industrialization was leading urbanization. The evidence simply does not support the view that the cities were being glutted with a flood of migrants pushed off the land. Instead, they were being pulled into the city by rapid job creation in industry.

Was private migrant behavior inconsistent with socially optimal migration?

Although there is no evidence that rates of pauperism and poor relief were higher in Britain's cities, what about unemployment and underemployment? And if we could find such evidence, how would we account for the apparent irrationality of rural immigrants rushing to the city in the face of unemployment and underemployment? Michael Todaro (1969) offered an answer about two decades ago, which some economic historians think applies to Victorian Britain as well (Pollard, 1978, 1981; Matthews et al., 1982, pp. 82–3).

The Todaro model takes expected earnings as the critical force motivating migration behavior, fortunate migrants being selected for the good jobs (primarily in manufacturing) and unfortunate migrants making do with low-wage service-sector jobs and unemployment. Todaro stresses the role of the low-wage service sector and unemployment as holding areas for the reserve army of immigrants who have come to the city in anticipation of getting those high-wage modern-sector jobs. If one supports Todaro's "irrational migrant" view of city immigration during the First Industrial Revolution, then it implies that city growth was too fast. After all, it would have been socially more productive if migrants had waited for those good city jobs in rural areas, where they would have been more fully employed, although at low wages, than waiting in the city unemployed or underemployed.

The Todaro model makes some testable assertions about how urban labor markets operate and how immigrants are absorbed into those markets. As Chapter 5 points out, the admittedly incomplete evidence from the 1851 Census seems to be inconsistent with the model: Migrants did not respond to expected future high earnings, suffering unemployment and underemployment while they waited for the better jobs. Rather, they appear to have been motivated by current job prospects, and those prospects appear to have been confirmed.

It appears that British cities did not grow too fast due to Todaro-irrational migration. City growth was not driven by a flood of overoptimistic migrants.

8.3   Were there too many migrants in Britain's cities? The relevant evidence

Wage gaps and private factor-market failure

Chapter 7 documented large rural-urban wage gaps in England during the 1830s, when the Reform Debates were heating up and Britain was said to be having its greatest difficulties coping with city growth. Wage gaps and rural labor surpluses imply insufficient migration and labor-market failure. They also imply that urban labor was too expensive, that urban employment was choked off, and thus that city growth was too slow. Private labor-market failure therefore implies that there were too few migrants in Britain's cities, not too many. In addition, private capital markets failed. Evidence on rates of return to invested capital confirm that the cities had excess demands for capital while excess supplies prevailed in the countryside, also serving to choke off city growth.

Given such evidence, how could anyone possibly argue that Britain's cities were too large and too many?

First, was there an urban bias?

Because we infer from wage differentials that the marginal product of urban labor exceeded that in the countryside, does it not follow that labor transfer would have augmented Britain's national income? Maybe yes, maybe no. After all, those marginal productivities were conditioned by prevailing policy, and that policy may itself have distorted relative marginal productivities. This argument has always been popular in Third World debates. Exchange rate policy, tariffs, subsidies, the manipulation of the domestic terms of trade, and cheap finance for favored sectors have typically tended to favor the cities, protecting city industry at agriculture's expense. Furthermore, government social overhead expenditures are tilted heavily to favor the cities. These attributes of Third World development strategy – an output price twist favoring cities, an input price twist favoring cities, and social-overhead expenditures favoring cities – have been labeled the urban bias by such commentators as Michael Lipton (1976). Since they serve to raise artificially the marginal product of urban labor and capital, perhaps those wage and rate-of-return gaps favoring the cities are spurious. Perhaps in their absence, marginal productivity differentials would favor the countryside.

Although this argument certainly has much to support it in the Third World, Chapter 4 showed that it has little to support it in early Victorian Britain, just as Lipton himself argued (p. 99). Tariffs did not serve to protect industry. Not only were there negative effective rates of protection facing British manufacturing (McCloskey, 1980), but the Corn Laws strongly favored British agriculture, at least prior to Repeal. Indeed, elsewhere I have estimated that the Corn Laws may have made the agricultural labor force some 20 percent bigger than it would have been under free trade (Williamson, 1986c). In addition, Chapter 10 will show that the cities were not favored by, but rather may have been starved for, government social overhead, in sharp contrast with the Third World, where "the most wasteful and unfair parts of the city's allocation are in infrastructure" (Lipton, 1976, p. 60).

Although the "urban bias" may be an important fact of life in the contemporary Third World, it was not an attribute of early Victorian England. Government allocative distortions favoring the cities is not an issue that need trouble us in assessing whether Britain's city growth was too fast. If anything, these distortions reinforce the view that British city growth was too slow.

Second, do wage gaps grossly overstate the benefits to additional migration?

The calculations reported in Chapter 7 are made under some strong assumptions. They assume that city dwellers had perfect information on mortality environments, that mortality environments were exogenous, and that there were no externalities associated with disease (e.g., disease was not communicable). To the extent that these assumptions did not hold, then we have overstated the benefits to additional migration, and we have overstated the case for city growth having been too slow.

Because workers presumably place some positive value on the good life, employers in the ugly towns must have been forced to pay higher wages to attract and hold their labor force. Higher wages were, of course, necessary to cover higher rents in the crowded cities, but they were also required to compensate workers for the forgone good life. The higher city wages should have had two effects: They should have choked off employment and city growth, and they should have encouraged firms to migrate to cheaper labor in the countryside, where wages were not inflated by the city-ugliness bribe and scarce housing. As we have seen in Chapter 7, city employers did pay higher wages, a part of which was a bribe to attract and hold workers in the ugly cities. A part of those higher city wages also appears to have reflected disequilibrium in the rural-urban labor market. We exploited a general equilibrium model to estimate the impact on city growth had rural emigration increased sufficiently to eliminate the disequilibrium. The numbers were big, suggesting that city growth was much slower than what would have been optimal.

The calculations in Chapter 7 may, however, seriously understate the marginal social cost of city growth and seriously overstate the amount of added rural emigration necessary to eliminate the wage gap. As we pointed out above, it assumes that the city mortality and disamenity environment was exogenous. It was not. As Chapter 9 will show, greater density and crowding bred higher mortality rates and disamenity levels. If rural emigrants had been more responsive to real-wage gaps, city growth would have been faster, crowding and density would have been greater, and city mortality rates would have been higher. Although the supply price of labor would surely have fallen with the entrance of additional migrants from the countryside, it would have fallen far less if added crowding had raised city rents and mortality even higher. In short, when city mortality and rents are allowed to rise with density, the number of immigrants necessary to eliminate the real-wage gap between city and countryside is less. The same argument holds if externalities prevailed: to the extent that diseases were communicable, then the social costs of an added migrant exceeded his private costs, and the former may have even increased more than the latter; and to the extent that the added migrant created social tensions, violence and political instability, his social cost exceeded his private costs on that score too. On the other hand, the calculations ignore the possible existence of agglomeration economies in the cities. Although these economies are often invoked by the optimists in city growth debates, the evidence supporting the view even on twentieth-century economies is very slim (Sveikauskas, 1975; Segal, 1976; Henderson, 1984; Shukla, 1984).

There are other reasons for suspecting that the calculations in Chapter 7 overstate the case that city growth was too slow. The calculations assume that city dwellers had perfect knowledge of the mortality and disamenity environment. If instead immigrants from environmentally more benign rural areas understated city mortality risk, then their revealed wage-disamenity trade-off understates the social cost of city growth. This seems especially likely to have been the case prior to the 1840s, when the Victorian reformers' propaganda reached a fever pitch and pamphlets could be purchased for a penny.

On all of the above counts, it follows that Chapter 7 has overstated the extent to which city growth was too slow during the First Industrial Revolution. However, it does not follow that city growth was too fast.

8.4   The planners' dilemma: Who gains and who loses from migration?

It is never quite clear whose objective function is being considered in the too-many-city-immigrants argument, whether one is reading Chadwick's *Sanitary Report* in 1842 or the results of the United Nations' 1983 questionnaire. One can appreciate the planners' dilemma of dealing with what appears to be an overwhelming rush to the cities, or their complaints that the quality of urban services newly created rapidly deteriorates as they get stretched across an ever increasing set of users, but what about the urban and, indeed, the national residents who the planning bureaucracy serves?

Oddly enough, there is almost no attention in the development literature of the 1980s and the Victorian reformist literature of the 1830s and 1840s to the issue of who gains and who loses from an influx of unskilled labor to the city. The relative silence in this literature on the distributional impact of urban immigration is odd indeed since so much seems to hinge on it.

Who gains and who loses from city immigration of unskilled labor seems clear enough. Unskilled labor that stays behind in the countryside should gain, to the extent that increased labor scarcity tends to raise their earnings. Agricultural land rents should fall, as the amount of farm labor available to work with the same acres declines (and in the absence of offsetting terms of trade effects). The recent city immigrants gain, having moved to higher paying jobs. However, unskilled city-born laborers and previous immigrants who are crowded out by the competition from the new immigrants lose as the urban labor market becomes glutted with more unskilled labor. Urban skilled labor gains as the now-swollen unskilled labor supply augments city output and drives up the demand for skills. Certainly capitalists gain for identical cheap labor reasons. And, finally, to the extent that the middle class and the rich tend to consume heavily the personal services offered by the urban unskilled, they get an additional cost-of-living gain.

Thus, while urban planners may push for restrictions on immigration, making their job of coping with city growth easier, one can hardly imagine any other class of city residents pushing for restrictions in the contemporary Third World, especially given that older immigrants have very little political power. It is hardly surprising, therefore, that immigration restrictions have hardly been tried, and have often failed when tried (Shaw, 1978; Simmons, 1979; Stark, 1980; Laquian, 1981). Their failure stems from two sources: The evidence in support of the too-many-city-immigrants view is much too weak to motivate policy makers to do more; and the urban political forces that matter come from classes who clearly gain from the city immigration. What has been true of the contemporary Third World was also true of Victorian Britain.

8.5   Death and the marginal social costs of city growth

When we look at migration and labor markets alone, it is difficult to establish a case that British cities grew too fast. In fact, the opposite appears to have been true.

How do we reconcile this conclusion with the fact that the cities were ugly, crowded, and, most important, killers? Chapter 9 will confirm that crowding and density were critical ingredients of the ghastly mortality environment of the cities. Since immigration contributed much to the crowding, doesn't this imply that the marginal social costs of migration were excessive during the First Industrial Revolution? In Chapter 9, I will try to show that it does not. I suspect, however, that this may be the wrong question. We pose a different one, therefore, in Chapter 10: Did Britain invest too little in her cities?

9. City housing, density, disamenities, and death

9.1 The perils of nineteenth-century city life

The quality of urban life has always played a key role in debates over the British industrial revolution. It certainly attracted the attention of Chadwick, Kay, and other social reformers in the 1830s and 1840s, but for hot rhetoric it is hard to beat Frederick Engels, who viewed the migration of rural labor to British cities as "social murder." High density and resulting environmental decay both contributed to high city mortality and morbidity rates, and immigrants entered that environment at their peril. The early Victorian perception persists in academic debate even today, and the "pessimists" in the standard-of-living debate have made much of the issue. Although even the most ardent pessimist would acknowledge the dreary environment of rural England at this time,[1] urban disamenities have, nonetheless, been viewed as seriously lowering working class living standards up to the 1840s and beyond. Not only was this true of old urban residents – whose cities, it was alleged, deteriorated in quality over time, but it was true of the new urban immigrants – who left more benign rural environments for employment in the ugly cities.

What did the common laborer forego by leaving some Sweet Auburn[2] for some ugly urban Sheffield during the First Industrial Revolution? Are quantitative answers to such questions possible? A. J. Taylor (1975, p. liv) certainly didn't think so when surveying the standard-of-living debate more than a decade ago: "How . . . can a just comparison be made between [that] which removal from a rural to urban environment entailed, and the social amenities which town and factory, however squalid, offered . . . ?"

This chapter will show that answers can be found by applying methods

---

1 See, for example, the classic survey by Buer (1926, pp. 249–252).
2 "Sweet Auburn, loveliest village of the plain," a poetic image coined in 1770 by Goldsmith, refers to a deserted village. In contrast with Engels, Marx had a more pragmatic view of "Sweet Auburn." Marx, in *Das Kapital*, stated that the industrial revolution eliminated the "idiocy of rural life."

231

suggested by recent research in twentieth-century urbanization and economic growth. Application of those methods to assess the perils of city life in the early nineteenth century is especially attractive because it makes it possible for the workers themselves to reveal their preferences. And it's about time! For more than a century, our perceptions have been colored by the more verbal Victorian middle-class observer who wrote books and pamphlets which, as it turns out, reveal far stronger preferences for urban amenities than did the workers themselves who placed higher priority on better-paying jobs.

This debate over the economic significance of city disamenities during the First Industrial Revolution has its contemporary analogies. Planners in the contemporary Third World think their industrializing countries have overurbanized and many think the solution is to close the cities down to new immigrants. And twentieth-century pessimists and neo-Malthusians have spent the past two decades attacking the optimists' premise that economic growth is a Good Thing even in the industrialized countries. These modern pessimists – Ehrlich, Meadows, Forrester, and the Club of Rome – prodded the modern optimists to action. Among the first economists to respond, William Nordhaus and James Tobin (1972, pp. 49 and 50) rose to the challenge in *Is Growth Obsolete?* "The disamenities of urban life come to mind: pollution, litter, congestion, noise, [and] insecurity . . . Failure to allow for these consumption items overstates not only the level but very possibly the growth of consumption. The fraction of the population exposed to these disamenities has increased, and the disamenities themselves may have worsened." How did they propose to estimate these disamenities? Pay has always tended to be higher in cities – certainly that was true of England in the 1830s (Chapter 7), and this fact suggested to Nordhaus and Tobin a path to measurement:

> some portion of the higher earnings of urban residents may simply be compensation for the disamenities of urban life and work. If so we should not count as a gain in welfare the full increments of NNP that result from moving a man from farm or small town to city. The persistent association of higher wages with higher population densities offers one method of estimating the costs of urban life as they are valued by people making residential and occupational decisions.[3]

3 Nordhaus and Tobin (1972, p. 13). For more elaborate, recent extensions of urban disamenities measurement see the following: Hoch (1976, 1977), Tolley (1974), Smith (1978), Getz and Huang (1978), Izraeli (1979) and Rosen (1979). The list could easily be extended into the 1980s, but what would still be missing are studies of Third World cities in which the disamenities are more pronounced.

In short, Nordhaus and Tobin suggested that we ignore the subjective environmental pleas of the pessimists and ask the workers who were involved in the urbanization process to speak. But how is the voice of the nineteenth-century British worker to be heard? Most were silent. Most lacked the right to vote. But all of them could vote with their feet. And vote they did, their response having left its mark on rates of pay, high wages compensating workers in locations with high density and thus ghastly environments, disamenities, and high mortality.

But we have run ahead too far. Although this chapter will offer estimates of the value of city disamenities in early nineteenth-century England, first we need to explore the causes of the high city densities that helped breed those high mortality and ugly city environments. That is, land scarcity, dwelling scarcity, and high rents.

9.2   The high cost of urban housing

The issues: Early nineteenth-century Britain and the Third World

As Chapter 1 pointed out, analysts and policymakers are sharply divided on the city growth problem. Pessimists cite the Third World's inability to cope with the social overhead and housing requirements of rapid urban growth, treating environmental decay and inadequate housing as evidence of private-market failure. Third World city growth is viewed as another example of overuse of a collective resource. In contrast, optimists view city growth as the central force raising average living standards. For them, city problems reflect greedy interest groups, poor economic planning and inappropriate prices. Policy debate remains intense, the optimists favoring an open-city approach, the pessimists searching for ways to close the cities down. The debate is hardly new, and can be found as early as the 1830s in the *Parliamentary Papers*, health surveys and reformist pamphlets. Then as now, crowding, slums, substandard housing, and nonexistent social services take center stage in the debate.[4]

> To the extent that urban disamenities have mortality implications, as they certainly did in early nineteenth-century England, the economic assessment should be extended to life expectancy. Dan Usher (1973) has offered such an extension, and I recently applied it to the British experience between 1781 and 1931 (Williamson, 1984b).

4 This paragraph and the one to follow draw on Kelley and Williamson, 1984, pp. 3–4 and 44–5.

In the United Nations' *Global Review of Human Settlements* (UN, 1976, p. 11), we are told that squatter settlements "generally refer to areas where groups of housing units have been constructed on land to which the occupants have no legal claim. In many instances housing units located in squatter settlements are shelters or structures built of waste materials without a predetermined plan. Squatter settlements are usually found . . . at the peripheries of the principal cities." According to the same source, these squatter settlements are by no means a small share of total urban dwellings, but account for the bulk of the growth in cities throughout the Third World (Mohan, 1979, chp. 1; Linn, 1979, Table II-7). With regards to numbers, Manchester wasn't much different in the early nineteenth-century because there too the "bulk" of the population was inadequately housed. But nineteenth-century Manchester slums differed from contemporary Manila slums (the "Tondo") in two fundamental ways: common labor was located in the central city, not on the periphery; and common labor was housed in even worse slums.

There is no shortage of graphic description of urban housing in England's cities in the early nineteenth century. In his *Moral and Physical Condition of the Working Class* (pp. 27–8), James Kay reported the findings of the district boards of health who, when visiting Manchester's slums in the early 1830s, found them

> of very recent origin; and . . . untraversed by common sewers. The houses are [noisy], often ill ventilated, unprovided with privies, and, in consequence, the streets which are narrow, unpaved, and worn into deep ruts, become the common receptacles of mud, refuse, and disgusting ordure . . . Predisposition to contagious disease is encouraged by every thing which depresses the physical energies, amongst the principal of which agencies may be enumerated imperfect nutrition; exposure to cold and moisture, whether from inadequate shelter, or from want of clothing and fuel, or from dampness of the habitation; uncleanliness of the person, the street, and the abode; an atmosphere contaminated, whether from the want of ventilation, or from impure effluvia . . .

In Michael Flinn's (1965, p. 14) words "the population of this country was beginning to exceed its capacity – or willingness – to house itself healthily." Chapter 10 will try to disentangle "willingness" from "capacity," but for the moment we simply note that

> the pressure on housing was possibly at its most acute just at the moment when Chadwick and his poor law colleagues focused their attention on it.

One symptom of increasing housing density . . . in the early nineteenth century, which conduced to ill-health, was the spread of back-to-
back housing, an innovation of the late eighteenth century, as a regular
practice rather than an exception. By the third and fourth decades of the
nineteenth century, back-to-back houses were very common in many
towns. In 1840 between 7,000 and 8,000 of Nottingham's 11,000
houses were reported to be back-to-back. As early as 1797 it was estimated that 9,000 of Liverpool's population of 63,000 lived in back-to-
back houses. There was a similar extension to cellar dwellings, even
more injurious to human health . . . Out of 175,000 persons in Liverpool in 1841, 38,000 lived in cellars (Flinn, 1965, p. 6).

Flinn then concludes with a challenge, one which the next section will
take up:

This sort of population pressure on housing must certainly have been
reflected in trends of rents, and one of the more frustrating *lacunae* in
the study of nineteenth-century economic and social history is the absence of any statistical study of house rents (Flinn, 1965, p. 6).

The rising cost of housing

High density and crowding in England's cities in the early nineteenth
century were clearly a response to scarcity and high price. Rents were
relatively high in the cities in part due to land scarcity, those scarcities made
all the more pronounced by the absence of efficient intra-urban transportation thus forcing workers to crowd in close to areas of employment
(Rimmer, 1960; Royal Commission on the State of Large Towns, 1844). In
addition, rents were driven higher by the fact that high nominal wages in the
city building trades (Chapter 7) tended to inflate construction costs. The
prices of building materials served to have the same effect. Baltic and
American timber soared in price, as did the price of bricks, partly due to war
duties and partly due to the fact that all resource-intensive commodities
increased in relative price. Furthermore, the long period of war from the
1760s to Waterloo, financed by enormous government debt issue, tended to
crowd out conventional capital accumulation, especially dwelling construction (Aston, 1955, 1959; Williamson, 1984a). With increasing urban immigration, excess demand for the urban dwelling stock increased, and the
dwelling stock became of increasingly older vintage. As urbanization quick-
ened after the 1810s and 1820s, urban land got even scarcer and labor- and
resource-intensive products like dwellings rose in relative cost (especially
in the absence of significant productivity advance in the building trades).

Table 9.1. *Trends in city rents, 1790 to 1900 (percentage per annum growth)*

	Period		
Early nineteenth century	1790–1839/42	1790–1839/42	1800–1840
Black Country town rents			1.7
Leeds rents			
Demand-side estimate	2.0		
Supply-side estimate	3.6		
Average	2.8		
Trentham (Staffs) rents		2.9	
Cost of living	0.3	0.3	−0.9
Rents relative to cost of living	2.5	2.6	2.6
	Period		
Late nineteenth century	1850–1900	1850–1897	1873–1910
Black Country town rents	0.8		
Trentham (Staffs) rents		0.7	
England and Wales, urban			0.5
Cost of living	−0.2	−0.4	1.0
Rents relative to cost of living	1.0	1.1	1.5

Source: The Black Country figure is based on rents in Dudley, Walsall, Warley, West Bromwich, Wolverhampton, Stourbridge, and Halesowen: Barnsby (1971), Appendix II, p. 236. The Leeds figures are constructed from Rimmer (1960), where the "demand-side" estimates are from his rent quotations (pp. 186–9) and the "supply-side" estimates are constructed from his dwelling cost figures (pp. 190–2). The Trentham figure is for Lord Stafford's cottages adjusted for changing quality: Williamson (1985a), p. 214, based on calculations by Peter Lindert. The cost-of-living index is taken from Lindert and Williamson (1985), p. 148 up to 1850 and from Williamson (1985a), p. 220 after 1850. The England and Wales urban figure is from Feinstein (1987, Table A.1) a revision of Singer (1941).

Because urban housing was in relatively inelastic supply, and because demand was shifting to the right at an accelerating rate, a rise in its relative scarcity across the industrial revolution was guaranteed.

Evidence in support of this view is offered in Table 9.1. Three city-rent series are presented in the table for the early nineteenth century: for some Black Country towns, for Leeds, and for Trentham in Staffs. On average, city rents increased at an annual rate of about 2.5 percent between the 1790s and the 1840s, a rate far in excess of the overall cost-of-living index.[5] Rising land scarcities could easily explain a third of this rise. In

5 Of course, the relative price of rents rises even more dramatically when it is compared with the cost of living excluding rents.

Leeds, for example, the site value of urban land "appreciated tenfold" (Rimmer, 1960, p. 190) between 1770 and 1820. Because site values may have been as much as 20 percent of total cottage costs, the tenfold appreciation implies a rise in housing costs, and thus rents, of about .9 percent per annum (4.7 percent per annum times .2).

This very rapid annual increase in city rents is confirmed by other evidence as well. We know that the share of rents in town workers' budgets rose sharply over the period, from something like 5 percent in 1790 to between 10 and 20 percent in 1840 (Tucker, 1936; Rimmer, 1960; Barnett, 1969; Gauldie, 1974). Define the expenditure share devoted to rents as $s = rH/Y$, where s is the share, r is the rent per unit of housing, H is the quality-adjusted housing stock consumed by the worker, and Y is his income. In per annum rates of change, this expression can be written as

$$\overset{*}{s} = \overset{*}{H} + \overset{*}{r} - \overset{*}{Y}.$$

We know that nominal wages among unskilled city workers rose at about .75 percent per annum between 1797 and 1835 (Williamson, 1985, Table 2.5, p. 14), and we know that s increased at least from 5 to 10 percent over roughly the same period ($\overset{*}{s} = 1.84$ percent per annum). If the housing stock did not deteriorate in quality, then it follows that rents increased at 2.6 percent per annum, almost exactly the figure reported in Table 9.1. Of course, if the expenditure share on rents was more like 20 percent in 1840, then rents increased even more rapidly than the already fast rate of 2.6 percent per annum estimated.

Real rents – that is, those deflated by a cost-of-living index – increased by about the same as nominal rents, for a whopping 30 percent each decade. This rent explosion must have encouraged workers to economize on dwelling expenditures by moving to lower quality housing in more unpleasant districts as well as by greater crowding within all districts, thus creating greater disamenities and mortality risk. To the extent that they did, it implies that the rise in rents is understated because the quality of the dwelling units must have declined. Certainly many distinguished economic historians think that was the case (Mantoux, 1928, pp. 441–2; Ashton, 1954, pp. 50–1; Hammond and Hammond, 1947, pp. 50–1), although they don't suggest by how much housing quality deteriorated. If it deteriorated by as much as 0.5 percent per annum, then the expression above suggests that rents rose at 3.1 rather than 2.6 percent per annum.

Table 9.1 also confirms Flinn's (1965, p. 6) hunch that the "pressure on housing was possibly at its most acute just at the moment when Chadwick and his colleagues focused their attention on it." Although real rents increased at about 2.6 percent per annum up to 1840, their growth fell to almost a third of that rate after 1850, to 1 or 1.1 percent per annum. However, Table 9.1 may overstate Flinn's case because the rise in the relative cost of urban housing seems to have been most dramatic during the French wars and the decade or so thereafter. Based on the Trentham series, rents rose relative to the overall cost of living at the following rate:

1790–1812   3.2% per annum

1812–1830   3.6

1830–1850   1.5

Nonetheless, it appears either that the demand for housing slowed down or that housing supply made some progress catching up with past excess demand or both as England emerged from its most dramatic rate of urbanization and immigration after mid-century, or even earlier, after the 1820s.

Inelastic city labor supplies and limits to city growth?

These rising housing scarcities and city densities may have played an important role in placing limits on urbanization during the First Industrial Revolution. Certainly the relatively rapid rate of urban job creation was the central force driving city growth (Chapter 4), but that relatively rapid rate was itself conditioned by two forces – first, accumulation, which pushed the derived demand for city labor rightwards at a rapid rate; second, the cost of city labor, which if kept cheap implied more jobs.

As W. Arthur Lewis (1954) pointed out some time ago, the urban transition can be choked off if inelastic urban labor supplies drive up the nominal cost of labor facing urban firms. In the Lewis model of labor surplus, the price of foodstuffs conditions nominal wages in the city. If farm emigration causes food production to contract, the rise in food prices tends to twist the terms of trade in favor of the countryside, thus driving up the cost of labor in the city. As labor's rising supply price tends to choke off employment in the city, growth slows down there, and immigration slacks off. Although the ability of agriculture to deliver foodstuffs to the growing city is the key "limit to urban growth" in conventional models of development, most economic historians agree that England was not constrained by that limit (Crafts, 1980).

Table 9.1 offers another possible "limit to urban growth," one which was city specific and in inelastic supply. As we have seen, housing was hardly a trivial component of city budgets – ranging between 10 and 20 percent of the urban worker's expenditures in the 1840s – so high city rents could have had a significant impact on the nominal cost of labor in the city. Furthermore, that impact must have risen over time because rents were rising, and so too was the share of the worker's budget devoted to housing. Between 1790 and 1840, the rise in rents by itself may have served to push up nominal wages in the city by almost .6 percent per annum (2.8 percent per annum nominal rent increase times a budget share of .2).

And what about other city-specific costs that could have served to drive up nominal wages and thus to limit city growth? Inelastic land supplies helped drive up urban rents, but they also encouraged greater crowding and density. To the extent that crowding implied a reduction in the quality of housing, then trends in city rents understate this limit to urban growth. And to the extent that crowding also contributed to the very high city mortality rates, and to the extent that workers placed some positive value on health and longevity, then the health disamenities induced by crowding must have been compensated by a city wage premium. With the rise in crowding and density, housing quality could have fallen, disamenities would have been exacerbated, and thus the wage premium would have risen. In short, the critical limits to urban growth during the First Industrial Revolution may have been inelastic housing and amenity supplies.

This position does not necessarily imply that the housing industry failed, even if the Hammonds (1947) thought so. They felt that the failure lay with the greed of speculators and with local building firms whose monopoly supply of housing was jerry-built and inadequate. Ashton (1954) also thought that housing market failure was a partial explanation of crowding, but subsequent research has suggested instead that local building industries were very competitive, especially those involved in low-cost housing construction (Rimmer, 1960; Johnson and Pooley, 1982). Nor does it imply that urban land markets failed. The alleged failure of urban land markets was the banner under which Henry George led his reformers on both sides of the Atlantic well into the early twentieth century, and for them the source of the failure was aristocratic urban estates and the English leasehold system. It was alleged that the aristocratic urban estate owners were unresponsive to competitive forces, thus implying inefficient land use and a less than optimal allocation to low-cost housing, and that the leasehold system failed to encourage optimal quality and dwelling improvements. Cannadine (1980) and others suggest the contrary. It appears that tenure arrangements in England were little different from those in America, which English reformers wished to emulate. There is also little evidence supporting the view that large estates were unresponsive to market signals. Furthermore, there is little evidence that English towns dominated by urban estates revealed significantly different low-cost housing attributes than those dominated by small freehold plots. Fortunately, we do not need land or housing market failure to explain rising rents, crowding, and disamenities in English cities across the industrial revolution.

By how much did urban rents exceed rural rents?

It turns out that we have very good information documenting the rent differential between urban and rural areas. In the early 1830s, the Manchester Statistical Society, distressed by the crowding and disamenities around them, initiated a set of housing surveys that were quite remarkable. The first of these involved 4,102 families in a working-class district of Manchester (1834, covering the police divisions of St. Michael's and New Cross). To augment their sample and to make comparative judgments possible, the Society then surveyed rural districts outside of Dudley, followed by similar surveys of Rutland and Northumberland. By the 1840s, statistical societies in London, Bristol, Leeds and elsewhere were replicating the work of the Manchester group. Each of these studies was surprisingly detailed, including information on the size and quality of the dwellings surveyed as well as of the districts in which they were located – for example, the number of families per privy, quality of drainage, distance to water supply and its quality, persons per room, and so on. The information on the quality of these dwellings is sufficiently detailed that the rents quoted in Table 9.2 can be viewed as applying to fairly homogeneous housing between cities and towns. However, because most of the rural rents are for dwellings that include small gardens, pig sties, and other perquisites, Table 9.2 probably understates the size of the urban-rural rent differential. The Manchester Society thought so, and Chadwick

Table 9.2. *Urban and rural dwelling rents, 1834 to 1851*

Region	Annual rent (£)	Date	Source and notes
London	*9.42*		Unweighted average of the following:
St. George's, Hannover Sq., Inner Ward	11.06	1843	*JSSL*, 6(1843): 1,465 families of the "poorest localities" of the Ward.
St. George's, East End	9.32	1845	*JSSL*, 11(1848): 1,954 working-class families.
St. Margaret's and St. John's, Westminster	7.89	1840	*JSSL*, 3(1840–41): 5,366 working-class families.
Northern Towns	*7.01*		Weighted average (using 1841 population) of the following:
Manchester	7.58	1834	*BAAS*, 9(1839): 4,102 working-class families in police division of St. Michael's and New Cross.
Black Country towns	7.80	1815–1850	Barnsby (1971), p. 236, covering the period 1815–1850.
Leeds	6.67	1838/39	*JSSL*, 2(1839–1840): 61,212 working-class persons in eight wards.
Macclesfield	6.06	1842	"Local Reports," p. 246: 8,902 tenements or cottages
Stockport	6.65	1842	"Local Reports," p. 246: 14,925 tenements or cottages
Newcastle	4.78	1842	"Local Reports," p. 246: 2,888 tenements or cottages
Stoke-upon-Trent	5.55	1842	"Local Reports," p. 246: 8,737 tenements or cottages
Rural North	*3.13*		Weighted average (using 1841 population) of the following:
Rural North Midlands	3.11	1839–1851	"Local Reports," pp. 133–7, 153, 186–90, 250 and Caird (1967), p. 474: Lincs, Staffs, Derby, Notts.
Rural North	3.00	1851	Caird (1967), p. 474: Northumb.
Rural Northwest	3.15	1839–1851	"Local Reports," pp. 186–90; 227–8 and Caird (1967), p. 474: Cumb., Ches., Salop, Lancs.
Rural South	*4.03*		Weighted average (using 1841 population) of the following:
Rural East	3.74	1839–1851	"Local Reports," pp. 133–7 and Caird (1967), p. 474: Norfolk, Suffolk, Camb., Essex, Hunts.

Table 9.2. *(cont.)*

Region	Annual rent (£)	Date	Source and notes
Rural West	3.69	1839–1851	"Local Reports," p. 15 and Caird (1967), p. 474: Cornwall, Worc., Devon, Wilts., Hereford.
Rural Home Counties	3.37	1851	Caird (1967), p. 474: Surrey, Bucks, Berk.
Rural Southeast	5.43	1839–1851	"Local Reports," pp. 36–40 and Caird (1967), p. 474: Sussex, Hampshire, Kent.
Rural South Midlands	3.68	1839–1851	"Local Reports," pp. 96–137, 153 and Caird (1967), p. 474: Leic., Northamp., Rutland, Glouc.

Notes: These attempt to control for dwelling quality. They are "average" in quality and space, although the rural dwellings normally included a garden and/or pig sty, thus implying an understatement of the true cost of housing in the city, which did not have such perquisites. *JSSL* refers to the *Journal of the Statistical Society of London; BAAS* to the *British Association for the Advancement of Science;* and "Local Reports" to *Local Reports on the Sanitary Condition of the Labouring Population in England* (July 1842).

exploited their expertise in the 1842 *Sanitary Report*, in which he says, with typical exaggeration, "the dimensions of [rural] houses are double those in large towns, with comforts and conveniences which the latter never can possess" (p. 156).[6]

High city rents in the 1830s and 1840s are certainly confirmed by the evidence in Table 9.2. London rents for the working class were about two and a half times those prevailing in the rural South, and the same was true of Manchester compared with the rural North. Furthermore, there was considerable variance between cities, rents higher the bigger and more dense the city. The variance seems to have been far less between rural

---

6 It might be argued that city rents are understated for another reason – disamenities. High rents reflect land scarcity, land scarcity breeds crowding, and crowding tends to create pollution, crime, and other environmental "bads." Shouldn't house rents at some urban "bad" location reflect these disamenities in the form of lower rents? Classical urban economics suggests this is so, and although the urban surveys summarized in Table 9.2 seem to have tried to control for environmental factors, they made no effort to do so for the rural-urban comparisons.

Table 9.3. *Infant-mortality rates in England: 1841, 1871, and 1906 (deaths per 1,000)*

Region	1906	1871	1841
North			
Sweet Auburn	145.3	156.1	114.8
Sheffield	148.8	212.1	174.5
Difference	+3.5	+56.0	+59.7
York			
Sweet Auburn	138.9	163.5	138.3
Sheffield	149.5	189.4	171.7
Difference	+10.6	+25.9	+33.4
Lancs-Cheshire			
Sweet Auburn	143.4	172.3	154.7
Sheffield	164.1	195.6	198.2
Difference	+20.7	+23.3	+43.5
Midlands			
Sweet Auburn	116.8	124.9	137.0
Sheffield	145.4	193.2	190.2
Difference	+28.6	+68.3	+53.2
East & South			
Sweet Auburn	110.5	154.3	129.8
Sheffield	133.0	170.9	173.2
Difference	+22.5	+16.6	+43.3

Sources and Notes: All data calculated from various issues of the *Annual Reports of the Registrar General,* "Births, Deaths and Marriages." The aggregations used to calculate "Sweet Auburn" and "Sheffield" are given in Appendix 9.4. See Williamson (1982), Table 1, p. 227.

locations, suggesting that it was city land scarcity and nominal-wage costs in the city building trades that determined the structure of dwelling rents across England.

9.3   Crowding, disamenities, and mortality in the cities

That there was wide variance in mortality rates across cities, towns, and villages in nineteenth-century England cannot be denied. We saw it in Chapter 2 and we see it again in Table 9.3. The table presents infant-mortality rates – agreed by all to be the best mortality indicator across locations – back as far as the earliest *Annual Reports* of the Registrar General. Not only were infant-mortality rates higher in the 1840s than in the 1900s, but the cities had very high rates. Thus, the difference in mortality experience, and thus in the quality of life, between what I shall call "Sweet Auburn" and "Sheffield" was far greater in 1841 than in 1906. As Appendix 9.4 indicates, Sheffield is an aggregation of thirty-eight cities and towns and Sweet Auburn is the rural residual after these towns are subtracted from the county totals. Thus, for example, in York Sweet Auburn consists of the three counties minus eight Sheffields, the latter composed of Keighley, Bradford, Leeds, Halifax, Huddersfield, Hull, York, and Sheffield itself. In 1841, Sheffield had an infant-mortality rate of 171.7 per thousand and Sweet Auburn had 138.3, a difference of 33.4 per thousand. Similar differentials existed for the other regions, the biggest appearing in the North and in the Midlands. These differentials persisted over the next seven decades, but they were smaller by 1906. By the 1920s, these differentials had disappeared, reflecting a new twentieth-century regime, during which cities became relatively benign mortality environments, a regime that prevails today even in the Third World. But for nineteenth-century England, the cities were indeed the killers advertised by Engels' rhetoric.

What role did density, crowding, city size, and industrialization play in accounting for the wide variance in mortality rates? Table 9.4 explores the determinants of infant-mortality rates (INFM) in 109 urban parishes surveyed in the 1834 *Poor Law Report* and 72 cities and towns included in a 1905 survey taken by the Board of Trade. Because we deal with relatively homogeneous occupations in our data (urban common labor), we can finesse Ratcliffe's (1850) important work of a century ago, which emphasized occupations as one key determinant of variance in mortality and morbidity. In addition, weather variables may have affected infant-mortality rates, although such variables were hardly urban-specific; thus, the inclusion of temperature (TEMP)[7] in Table 9.4. We also add city size (POP) and density (DEN) to the regression because these variables surely served as proxies for the difficulty facing municipal authorities in maintaining the social overhead expenditures necessary to offset the population pressure on the urban environment. In addition, we include a "dark satanic mill" index (SATMIL) – measuring the share employed in manufacturing, mining and other nonservice/nonagricultural occupations – to capture the alleged effects of factory work environment and industrial pollution on the mortality environment. Finally, even before Edwin

---

7 The temperature variable (TEMP) works far better than sunshine (SUN) in the infant-mortality regressions.

Table 9.4. *Explaining infant-mortality rates (INFM): 1834 Poor Law commissioners' urban parishes and 1905 Board of Trade towns compared*

Variable: log-linear regression	1834 Poor Law parishes		1905 Board of Trade towns	
	β	t-statistic	β	t-statistic
CONSTANT	6.8509	1.2313***	14.432	3.830*
DEN	.0280	1.7024*	.068	2.413*
POP	.0726	3.6174*	.043	2.218*
SATMIL	.0382	1.1744***	.043	1.212
TEMP	−.5007	.3520	−2.670	2.759*
CROWD	–	–	.061	2.430*
North	.1902	1.3887**	.086	.580
York	.2728	2.1258*	.161	1.132
Lancs-Cheshire	.2191	2.0424*	.325	2.430*
Midlands	.3129	2.8812*	.259	1.888*
East	.2850	2.1555*	.352	2.375*
South	.1438	1.4455**	.269	1.915*
Wales	.0923	.6793	.294	2.000*
R^2	.449		.508	
N	109		72	
Mean INFM	200.997		144.569	

Sources and notes: All variables are defined in Appendixes 9.1 and 9.2. The 1834 sample here of 109 parishes is larger than that used in Table 9.5, since the POOREX variable is unavailable for the remainder. In addition, the CROWD variable is unavailable for the 1834 sample. Results taken from Williamson (1982), Table 3, p. 233.
*   Denotes 5% significance levels.
**   Denotes 10% significance levels.
*** Denotes 20% significance levels.

Chadwick's 1842 *Sanitary Report*, it was felt that crowded housing conditions were central contributors to high urban mortality rates, especially among infants. Thus, the inclusion of CROWD in the 1905 regression in Table 9.4. Indeed, crowded housing and poor health were the hypothesized correlates that motivated the 1908 Board of Trade inquiry in the first place. Unfortunately, neither the *Poor Law Report* nor the Registrar General's *Annual Reports* supplies the necessary data to compute a crowded living conditions variable for 1834. We shall have to infer the effect of crowding in the 1830s by reference to the 1905 results.

Table 9.4 reports our attempt to explain the variance in infant mortality across urban locations in both the 1830s as well as in 1905. The results are very similar, but with some notable differences. City density (DEN) and size (POP) both play a consistent and significant role, confirming the conventional wisdom that urbanization bred high mortality in the nineteenth century. Municipal social overhead expenditures simply could not or did not keep up with the requirements that population density and size generated, thus implying a deterioration in mortality environment. In contrast, the dark satanic mill index (SATMIL) only barely plays a significant role early in the century and it plays no significant role at all in 1905. It was not industrialization that generated the disamenities associated with high infant-mortality rates, but rather urbanization.[8] It also appears that the South of England and Wales were regions of very high quality of life in 1834, even after controlling for regional urban and industrial attributes. By 1905, Wales and the South of England had lost that advantage. The really nasty regions stay nasty over the seven decades – Lancashire, Cheshire, Yorkshire, the Midlands, and the eastern counties. Thus, while there are some changes in the relative ranking of regional disamenity levels between 1834 and 1905, these are less notable than is the remarkable consistency in the determinants of INFM over these seven decades. Finally, we note that crowding – thought to be an index of low housing quality and unhealthy conditions by the Board of Trade and others since Kay's work on Manchester[9] – does indeed have a significant impact on infant-mortality rates in the 1905 regression.

In summary, almost all of the predicted infant-mortality variance within regions can be explained by two forces: crowding within dwellings, and density and size of the urban environments within which those dwellings were located.

9.4   Urban disamenities and the wage bribe

Increasing land scarcity, rising labor costs, lagging productivity advance, more expensive resource-intensive building materials, and forgone dwelling investment during the French wars all served to generate a spectacular increase in city rents from the 1790s to the 1840s. Workers responded by economizing on dwelling space and quality. Crowding resulted. Perhaps

---

8 This finding is consistent with the conventional wisdom that most of the evils associated with industrialization are really attributable to urban density and crowding.

9 J. P. Kay-Shuttleworth (1832). Engels leans very heavily on Kay – indeed, plagiarizes him – in describing "social murder" in the great towns of early nineteenth-century England.

for some of the same reasons, municipal planners found it difficult to maintain the necessary social overhead capital to serve the environmental needs of a rapidly expanding city population. City environments may have deteriorated as a result. Both of these forces kept disamenity levels, morbidity rates, and mortality rates high in the cities.

Now then, how is this growth regime to be assessed? In Taylor's (1975) words, can we place a value on the urban disamenities that workers accepted when migrating from rural towns to city employment? Nordhaus and Tobin (1972) suggested an answer. What follows is an application of their idea to seventy-two British towns in 1905 and sixty-six urban parishes in 1834.

British towns in 1905

Relying on the Board of Trade (1908) inquiry into seventy-two British towns in 1905, I was able to show in two earlier papers (Williamson, 1981, 1982) that the pessimists have greatly exaggerated the role of urban disamenities, at least as the workers assessed them. The conclusion was reached in three steps.

First, 1905 town data (Appendix 9.1) were used to estimate hedonic wage regressions of the following sort (reported here in linear form for convenience):

$$W_j = BO + B1DEN_j + B2POP_j + B3INFM_j + B4SUN_j + e_j \quad (9.1)$$

where W_j is the average nominal weekly wage of unskilled labor in the building trades deflated by the jth town's cost-of-living index, DEN, is the town's density, POP_j is the town's size, $INFM_j$ is the town's average infant-mortality rate, and SUN_j is a "sunshine" amenities variable. Regional dummy variables were also introduced into the estimation.

The results of the exercise can be found in Table 9.5. The key findings for 1905 can be quickly summarized. First, our proxy for disamenities, the infant-mortality rate,[10] has a highly significant impact on the real wage.

---

10 As we shall see below, mortality rates appear to be excellent proxies for urban disamenities, a result consistent with William Farr's rule that two persons were seriously ill for each that died (R. Wall, 1974, p. iv). Furthermore, the infant-mortality rate is a far more effective index than the overall mortality rate, a point well appreciated by the Registrar General long ago: "the death rate in any district is dependent not only on the sanitary conditions of the locality, but also on the proportions of the sexes and the population at different ages ... The infant

Thus, a 10 percent change in the infant-mortality rate implied a 2 percent change in the real wage across the seventy-two Board of Trade towns. It does indeed appear that urban disamenities, at least in the form of infant-mortality rates, did require a pecuniary bribe to induce the low-wage worker to locate in the cities with the lowest quality of life. The opposite was true of SUN; it appears that towns in sunny regions were able to pay lower wages.[11] Second, DEN and POP did not have a consistent, statistically significant impact on real wages.[12] If real wages rose with city size, then it must have been the association of INFM (disamenities) and/or the quality of labor that produced the relationship. Density and population size did not have any other independent, statistically significant influence. Third, regions did not matter. For unskilled common labor, regional influences, independent of the influences already identified that may be correlated with region, did not play a statistically significant role in accounting for the variance in wages across towns. This clearly suggests that British city labor markets were quite well integrated by the turn of the century, and real wages (where nonpecuniary rewards are included) tended to equate themselves across towns.[13]

The second step involved the selection of some small market towns with low density and high quality of life, after which we then asked by how much workers had to be "bribed" to move into the large, crowded towns with low quality of life. Thirty-two towns were selected which fell at least one standard deviation away from mean values of the explanatory vari-

mortality rate is free from this source of error" (Board of Trade, 1908, p. lii). While Farr, Buer, and other students of the problem concur with the view that INFM is an excellent proxy for the quality of nineteenth-century urban life, INFM had far higher rural-urban variance than did death rates at other ages. In *Health, Wealth and Population*, Buer tells us that between 1813 and 1830, INFM in the six great towns (London, Manchester, Liverpool, Birmingham, Bristol, and Leeds) was 1.73 times the average for England and Wales. Over all ages, the figure for the six great towns was only 1.39 times that for England and Wales. The difference is explained by the young-adult bias discussed at length in Chapter 2. In any case, the relative sensitivity of infant-mortality rates to environmental conditions has already been established in Section 9.3, and it confirms the work on the early twentieth century by Titmuss (1943) and the 39th Annual Report of the Local Government Board (House of Commons, Accounts and Papers, 1910).

11 These regressions were also run using rainfall and temperature as explanatory weather variables. The sunshine variable was most successful.

12 Because town density and size were thought to be highly correlated, the wage regressions were all recomputed eliminating first density and then population size. The results varied but little because the density-size correlation was quite imperfect.

13 Rural-urban wage gaps are another matter entirely, as we have seen in Chapter 7.

Table 9.5. *Explaining real wages: 1834 Poor Law commissioners' laborers in urban parishes and 1905 Board of Trade town laborers compared*

Variable: linear regression	1834 Poor Law parishes			1905 Board of Trade towns		
	β	t-statistic	Elasticity (at mean)	β	t-statistic	Elasticity (at mean)
CONSTANT	12.8960	2.4380*	–	1.0327	3.5360*	–
DEN	−.0098	1.0164	−.0176	−.0006	.8303	−.0129
POP	$-.0162/10^5$	1.2817***	−.0012	−.0000	.2812	−.0032
INFM	.0160	1.9696*	.2771	.0015	3.1223*	.2149
SUN	.0750	.0676	–	.0355	1.4388***	–
POOREX	−.0980	1.2392***	–	–	–	–
PIRISH	4.2091	.4461	–	–	–	–
North	−2.1157	.9807	–	−.1276	.4585	–
York	−1.9243	.8821	–	−.0868	.3193	–
Lancs-Cheshire	−1.1774	.5425	–	−.0855	.3130	–
Midlands	−3.5794	1.8542*	–	−.0146	.0535	–
East	.2638	.1141	–	−.1486	.5312	–
South	−2.8761	1.4535**	–	−.1418	.5152	–
Wales	−2.7834	1.0738***	–	−.1331	.4798	–
R^2	.296			.559		
N	66			72		

Sources and notes: All regressions use OLS. Dependent variable for the 1834 sample is the parish unskilled weekly wage in shillings, deflated by regional cost-of-living indexes, the latter constructed primarily from parish union records on food purchases in the early 1840s. Mean real wage RWAGEC = 12.016. See Appendix 9.2 for data documentation. Dependent variable for the 1905 sample is the town unskilled weekly wage, deflated by town cost of living, relative to London. Mean real wage RWAGEC = 1.009. See Williamson (1982), Table 2, p. 229, and Table 9.4 for definition of significance levels. The 1834 estimates reported here are somewhat different from those reported in the 1982 paper since we have improved the cost-of-living estimates.

ables. As in Section 9.3, the towns with high quality of life were called Sweet Auburn and the towns with low quality of life were called Sheffield. The difference (D) between Sweet Auburn and Sheffield was then calculated for town density, town size, and infant mortality. Given the estimated coefficients in equation (9.1), I then calculated the cost of the marginal urban disamenities package as

$$COST = B1DDEN + B2DPOP + B3DINFM. \qquad (9.2)$$

This estimate of COST was then taken as a share of the predicted unskilled wage in Sweet Auburn. The result is an estimate of the percentage premium offered to potential migrants considering the move from Sweet Auburn to Sheffield.

The results of this calculation compared with 1905 nominal-wage differentials were as follows (Williamson, 1982, p. 225):

Intraregional migration within	1905 urban disamenities wage premium (%)	1905 actual nominal wage differential (%)
North	+ 3.12	+18.83
York	+ 2.79	− .71
Lancs-Cheshire	+ 5.09	− 7.57
Midlands	+ 7.00	+12.36
East	−12.13	+22.23
South	− 9.50	+ 8.58

Note the contrast between North and South. In the northern counties, the worker required a 3 to 7 percent bribe over his current wage to induce him to move from Sweet Auburn to Sheffield. No such bribe was required to move an unskilled worker from the rural southern and eastern counties to London.

The final step used these estimates to test the pessimists' hypothesis regarding trends in the standard of living up to 1850. Suppose the disamenities bribe prevailing everywhere in England in the 1830s and 1840s was pretty much like that estimated for the North of England in 1905. (Presumably, it was the higher disamenity bribes up north that are most relevant, because nineteenth-century industrialization was centered on those regions.) So, what difference would the 3 to 7 percent disamenities correction make to our estimates of common labor's standard of living gains up to 1850? Even inflating the correction up to 15 percent made little difference. I concluded that the pessimist's stress on the worker's declining quality of life was misplaced.

Urban Poor Law parishes in the 1830s

What is the relevance of a 1905 disamenities calculation to the early nineteenth century, the battleground for the standard-of-living debate and the epoch of migration and city growth, which is the central focus of this book?

The most important contrast between the 1830s and 1905 must surely lie with the disamenity indexes themselves, influenced as they were by the late nineteenth-century commitment to social overhead investment, which helped clean up Britain's cities (Chapter 10). The mortality evidence in Table 9.3 suggests that quality-of-life differences between Sweet Auburn and Sheffield were far greater early in the nineteenth century than late, perhaps reaching a peak in the 1830s and 1840s. The issue is not that British quality of life was lower a century before 1905. Surely that was so. Rather, the issue is the extent to which quality-of-life differentials between small market towns and large industrial cities changed over the nineteenth century. The largest and nastiest cities underwent enormous improvements in sanitation and housing after the 1840s, suggesting that 1905 rural-urban differences in infant mortality seriously understate the differences in the 1840s. Table 9.3 certainly confirms that view, suggesting that we have indeed understated the disamenities premium facing potential rural-urban migrants in the early nineteenth century by using 1905 intratown differences in INFM to make that inference.

Sidney Pollard (1981) and other critics also complained that the worker in the 1830s may have had quite different attitudes toward urban disamenities, presumably placing a higher value on the good life they left behind in Sweet Auburn, thereby requiring a larger bribe to incur urban disamenities than his grandchildren who, in 1905, were hardened to Sheffield's ghastly urban environment and were not aware of the world they had lost. The argument seems highly plausible. On the other hand, environmental amenities may be a relative luxury thus implying that workers with low incomes early in the century would place lower value on it. Which of these plausible forces dominated? Did urban workers in the 1830s, with lower standards of life, attach higher or lower premia to the ghastly disamenities in which they lived and worked than did their grandchildren in 1905?

Although the data are more fragile than those supplied by the 1908 Board of Trade inquiry, the 1834 *Poor Law Report* did include the kind of information necessary to repeat the 1905 regressions, and thus to test Pollard's hypothesis that the worker's earnings/disamenities elasticity fell over time. Appendix 9.2 supplies the details, but we might note here that the 1834 *Report* published "Answers to Town Questions," which included average wages of urban laborers (in "normal" weeks), town parish expenditures on poor relief, parish area, and parish population. When this information is augmented by 1831 Census data and the Registrar General's early estimates on mortality rates in urban districts, we have all the information we need to estimate the earnings equation in Table 9.5, except cost of living in the towns. This is clearly a tougher task, but with the help of the estimates in Chapter 7, we are at least able to apply regional price deflators to the parish nominal wage estimates. In a world of primitive transportation, wide cost-of-living differentials are to be expected and thus regional deflators are unlikely to capture parish-price variance completely, but what we have here is good enough to supply an effective test of the central hypothesis.

Table 9.5 presents the results based on sixty-six urban parishes that supplied the necessary data. These parishes are sprinkled all over England and Wales, and were located in very small industrial villages and market towns as well as in the biggest cities, London and Liverpool. The range on infant mortality is also extensive, from 344 and 304 per thousand in Oldham and Toxteth Park (Liverpool), to 110 and 125 in Totnes and Townstall, both in rural Devon. Thus, the sample is well represented by Sweet Auburns and Sheffields, the latter including Oldham, Huddersfield, Preston, Sheffield, Wakefield, Toxteth Park, South Shields, Stockport, the City of London, and nine others from the London Metropolitan area. The nominal wage varied considerably in the 1834 sample: six parishes reported six to eight shillings per week and four reported wages in excess of fifteen shillings per week. Finally, it should be emphasized that data supplied by parish should please critics like Sidney Pollard (1981, p. 903), who rightly point out that the 1905 town averages for infant mortality "offer but a poor guide [to disamenities], since they hide the enormous intraurban dispersion."[14] As Appendix 9.2 points out, the infant-mortality data for the 1830s analysis are given at the district level.

The 1834 and 1905 regressions estimated in Table 9.5 differ. The 1834 version contains two additional variables reflecting a social and demographic environment unique to early nineteenth-century labor markets. The first of these reflects the potential influence of the Old Poor Laws, where POOREX measures the impact of parish poor-relief expenditures per capita on market wages. The second reflects the alleged attributes of labor-market segmentation and/or short-run disequilibrium. Pollard (1959) and others have argued that the Irish immigrants served as

---

14 Pollard (1959, p. 99) offers the following example from Sheffield's urban districts (infant-mortality rates per 1,000 births, 1867–87):

Sheffield West	204	Brightside	172
Sheffield	199	Heeley-Nether Hallam	161
Sheffield South	188	Ecclesall	155
Sheffield Park	185	Upper Hallam	113
Attercliffe	173		

the industrial revolution's shock troops, flooding urban labor markets and depressing wages. Although Chapter 6 did not find these forces to be very important economy-wide, they may have been bigger in the northwestern cities, where the Irish concentrated. If disamenities were highest in the industrial towns in which the Irish clustered, then our regressions would understate the disamenity premium British in-migrants demanded to suffer the nasty life of the worst towns. The PIRISH variable (percentage born in Ireland among those above age 20) should help confront Pollard's Irish shock-troops thesis.

Table 9.5 makes it quite apparent that we have been somewhat less successful in explaining real-wage variance in the 1830s than in 1905.[15] No doubt, one key reason for the difference is our inability to secure parish-level cost-of-living data, and we already know that the cost of living was one of the prime determinants of nominal wage variance across urban locations in 1905. But the 1834 results are quite suggestive even if the t-statistics are low.

First, high poor-relief expenditures per capita (POOREX) are associated with low market wages, a result that certainly fails to support the view that relief tended to cause a contraction in labor supply, creating local labor scarcity. Rather, poor-relief expenditures were a safety net needed most in low-wage areas. Second, the evidence fails to support Pollard's Irish shock-troops thesis, a result consistent with Chapter 6. Not only is the estimated coefficient on PIRISH statistically insignificant, but the sign is positive. Either Irish immigrants were more discriminating than British immigrants in making location decisions, or, equally absurd, the British were the minority suffering from labor-market segmentation. I believe the explanation is simpler: The Irish had the good fortune to locate closest (in terms of migration costs) to the source of the British industrial expansion and thus could best exploit the relative labor scarcity and high wages prevailing there. Third, there is the interesting suggestion that town (as opposed to farm) wages were not lower in the "depressed" East of England, once cost-of-living and disamenity adjustments are performed. Furthermore, the North becomes a low-wage region (even compared with the East) when disamenity and cost-of-living deflators are applied.

More to the point, however, is that INFM was a highly significant determinant of nominal wages in 1834, repeating the 1905 finding. Fur-

---

15   In both cases, the linear specification reported here does as well or better than
      the log linear.

thermore, Pollard is right. Although significance tests suggest that the conclusion should not be pushed too hard, it does appear that the elasticity of real wages with respect to the infant-mortality rate was higher in the 1830s, .215 for 1905 and .277 for 1834. Thus, workers in the 1830s did seem to place a higher value on the good life they left behind in Sweet Auburn than their grandchildren did in 1905.

Do the higher urban disamenity elasticities for 1834 matter much in accounting for wage differentials between Sheffield and Sweet Auburn? The pessimists' stress on urban disamenities gains support from two sources: we have already seen in section 9.3 that the large, dense and nasty towns were, compared to Sweet Auburn, more ghastly in 1841 than in 1905 (the DXj effect in equation 9.2); and we now find that workers placed higher weight on disamenity differentials in the 1830s than in 1905 (the Bj effect in equation 9.2). Both served to make the urban disamenities wage premium considerably higher in the 1830s than at the turn of the century.

However, before we report the results, it should be noted that our estimates can be revised in two ways. First, ordinary least squares may be inappropriate in estimating the hedonic equations because one of the key disamenity proxies, the infant-mortality rate, may itself be a function of the real wage. If so, then instrumental variables may be a better econometric device to apply to the data. As Table 9.6 shows, the two estimating procedures yield much the same results, but the elasticity of the real wage to INFM in the ordinary least squares regression is about half that of the elasticity implied by the instrumental variables regression. In what follows, therefore, I will report both the ordinary least squares and the instrumental variables estimates, thus offering a range of disamenity effects. Second, the marginal disamenities package may have been misspecified. The cost of the package was calculated before as

$$COST = B1DDEN + B2DPOP + B3DINFM$$

where DDEN refers to the difference in density between some typical rural village and large city, DPOP refers to the difference in population size, and DINFM refers to the difference in infant mortality. The Bj are weights that emerge from the hedonic regression. COST was then expressed as a percentage of the village unskilled wage. It could be argued, however, that COST should include the influence of DINFM only, because density is simply another, and poorer, proxy for urban disamenities

Table 9.6. *Explaining real wages: 1834 Poor Law commissioners' laborers in urban parishes, the OLS vs. instrumental variables approach*

Variable	OLS		Instrumental variables	
	β	t-statistic	β	t-statistic
CONSTANT	12.8960	2.4380*	6.5686	.9288
DEN	−.0098	1.0164	−.0113	1.0838***
POP	−.0162/10⁵	1.2817***	−.0163/10⁵	1.1959***
INFM	.0160	1.9696*	.0393	2.2136*
SUN	.0750	.0676	.6339	.5066
POOREX	−.0980	1.2392***	−.1264	1.4491**
PIRISH	4.2091	.4461	−5.4430	.4534
North	−2.1157	.9807	−1.7605	.7543
York	−1.9243	.8821	−2.0574	.8756
Lancs-Cheshire	−1.1774	.5425	−1.0277	.4395
Midlands	−3.5794	1.8542*	−3.8622	1.8530*
East	.2638	.1141	.0768	.0308
South	−2.8761	1.4535**	−3.0529	1.4312**
Wales	−2.7834	1.0738***	−2.3279	.8295
R²	.296		.185	
N	66		66	

Notes: Dependent variable is the parish unskilled weekly wage in shillings, deflated by regional cost-of-living indexes, the latter taken from Table 7.4, cols. (3) and (4), those bracketed. OLS estimates are taken directly from Table 9.5. "Instrumental variables" result takes as instrumental variables CONSTANT, SUN, DEN, POP, POOREX, PIRISH, TEMP, and the regional dummies.

   * Denotes 5% significance levels.
  ** Denotes 10% significance levels.
*** Denotes 15% significance levels.

and because population size is simply an index of city living costs. If so, the disamenity package should be calculated as COST = B1DINFM. These two revisions both serve to raise the estimated urban disamenity wage premium, offering an upper bound to be added to what appears to be a lower bound reported in my earlier work.

Table 9.7 reports the disamenities premium as a percent of rural real wages. The premium was higher in the North of England (ranging between 12 and 30 percent)[16] than in the South of England (ranging be-

16 A recent paper by John Brown (forthcoming) applies this technique to power loom weavers in the mid-1830s living in Lancashire's most unhealthy cities. He finds an average disamenities premia of 24.8 percent, a value which falls about midway in our 12 to 30 percent range for the North of England. The more dense and crowded urban areas in his sample had, of course, higher disamenities.

Table 9.7. *Calculating the urban disamenities premium for the 1830s*

Item	North	South	Notes
Average rural wage (w)	12.114sh	13.699sh.	Weekly wage in 11 southern rural parishes and 6 northern rural parishes underlying the 66 parishes in the regressions reported in Table 9.6, weighted by population size, and deflated by cost of living.
ΔINFM	92.34	69.19	Difference in infant mortality rate per 1,000 between rural parishes noted above and 10 southern urban parishes plus 6 northern urban parishes underlying the regression reported in Table 9.6, weighted by population size.
$COST_1 = \hat{\beta}_1 \Delta INFM$	1.480sh	1.107sh.	The estimate $\hat{\beta}_1 = .0160$ is from Table 9.6, OLS, and we take it to be the same in both regions.
$COST_2 = \hat{\beta}_2 \Delta INFM$	3.630sh	2.720sh.	The estimate $\hat{\beta}_2 = .0393$ is from Table 9.6, instrumental variables, and we take it to be the same in both regions.
$PREMIUM_1 = (COST_1 \div w) \times 100$	12.22%	8.08%	The average for all England is 9.7%, using 1841 population weights.
$PREMIUM_2 = (COST_2 \div w) \times 100$	29.97%	19.86%	The average for all England is 23.9%, using 1841 population weights.

Source: See text for a description of the method.

tween 8 and 20 percent). The larger nominal wage gaps down South cannot be explained by larger urban disamenities in London, because the northern towns were environmentally worse. For England as a whole, the urban disamenities premium ranged between 10 and 24 percent.

Whether infant-mortality rates served as a proxy for all urban disamenities or whether they were a key component of the total disamenity package, the fact remains that INFM had a very important impact on the location decisions of low-wage workers. Density and population, on the other hand, appear to have added no direct influence either in 1905 or in 1834. Instead, the influence was indirect. As we have seen in section 9.3, high density, crowding, and city size all had an influence on the quality of city life, especially on the mortality environment. Land scarcity fostered high rents. Workers adjusted as best they could by crowding into low quality housing, economizing on rents at the cost of higher mortality and

disamenities. High city density and size also made it difficult for municipal planners to maintain the necessary expenditures to clean up the city
environment. Facing financial constraints and public-health ignorance,
rarely could municipal planners mount an adequate defense of their city
environments against the attack of rapid immigration and population
growth, let alone find the resources to improve those environments.

   Crowding and high city density both tended to create a high mortality
environment, and the workers appear to have demanded some compensation for it.

9.5   Was the industrial revolution worth it? The workers'
         view

Our estimates suggest that the urban disamenities premium in the 1830s
and 1840s ranged from 12 to 30 percent in the North of England. These
are only tentative estimates, to be sure, but would a large error matter in
forming inferences for the standard-of-living debate? Would such disamenities seriously deflate the measured real-wage gains of the British worker
after the Napoleonic Wars? Because so much of those wage gains hinged
on the migration response of rural workers to high-wage city job creation,
the question is clearly important.

   Suppose, for example, that the "true" disamenities premium was 30
percent in all of Britain during the decades prior to 1850, an upper-bound
estimate. Suppose further that the relative shift of employment from
Sweet Auburn to Sheffield was at the same rate as the measured decline
in the agricultural employment share, that is, from 36 to 22 percent of the
labor force between 1801 and 1851 (Deane and Cole, 1962, Table 30, p.
142). These figures would imply that the average wage of common labor
would have increased by about 4 percent over the full half-century due
solely to the premium paid for urban disamenities (for example, $[.36 -
.22] \times [.30] = .042$). Alternatively, consider the rise in the population
urbanized. Based on Table 2.12, the share living in urban places rose
from 33.8 to 54 percent between 1801 and 1851, implying that the average wage of common labor would have increased by about 6 percent due
solely to the premium paid for urban disamenities (for example, $[.54 -
.338] \times [.30] = .061$). Either calculation implies a trivial downward adjust-
ment in the measured improvement in the standard of life. Based on

recent estimates of the real-wage gains accruing to urban common labor (Lindert and Williamson, 1983), real-wage improvements over the 1810 to 1851 period might be reduced from the measured increase of 94 percent to an adjusted increase of 88 percent, a modest disamenities correction indeed.

The pessimists' hypothesis has not yet been fully tested, however, because they have raised two disamenity issues, not just one: (1) that the process of urbanization involved a move into ghastly towns, a move implying a spurious rise in nominal wages measured by the size of the disamenities premium; and (2) that there was a steady deterioration in the quality of urban life in all cities and towns over time, implying a spurious rise in nominal wages due to an increase in the disamenity premium everywhere in British urban life. The first effect has been found to be trivial. What about the second?

Was there a steady deterioration in the quality of urban life from the late eighteenth century up to 1848 and the Public Reform Era? E. P. Thompson (1975, pp. 149–50) would surely have us believe so: "This deterioration of the urban environment strikes us today . . . as one of the most disastrous of the consequences of the Industrial Revolution." Statements such as these are certainly consistent with the rise in city rents – breeding crowding and shifts to low-quality housing – that took place over the same period, but how can we reconcile such statements with the evidence, admittedly weak, of improved mortality conditions in Britain, especially in the cities?

Wrigley and Schofield (1981, Table A3.1, pp. 528–9) report a decline in the crude death rate nationwide from 28.83 per thousand in 1781 to 22.80 per thousand in 1851, while life expectancy at birth rose by five years, from 34.7 to 39.5. Furthermore, adult male heights, an index of health, were higher for cohorts born in 1840 than for cohorts born in 1810 (Fogel, 1986, p. 496). Because rapid urban immigration implied movement into locations of high mortality, a nationwide decline in the death rate is consistent with an even greater decline in urban mortality, unless, of course, there was a spectacular, but unlikely, decline in rural mortality.

Indeed, what limited pre-Registrar General evidence we do have does suggest that death rates fell most precipitously in the cities throughout the late eighteenth century up to the early 1820s,[17] and especially in London

17 A number of city mortality time series have been constructed covering the period 1780 to 1850: Carlisle (Armstrong, 1981, pp. 99–102); Leeds, Manchester, Birmingham, Bristol, and Liverpool (Griffith, 1926, p. 186); York (Armstrong,

(Farr, 1885, p. 195; Buer, 1926, pp. 33–4; Landers, 1987). True, Wrigley and Schofield tell us that the nationwide death rate ceased its secular fall after the 1820s, but given the much higher mortality rates in the towns, and given the rapid rate of urbanization between 1830 and 1850, it is hard to avoid the inference that urban mortality rates either stabilized or continued to decline before the Public Reform Era, an inference reached long ago by Bateman, Farr, Buer, and other analysts of nineteenth-century urban life (Buer, 1926, pp. 225–6).

Inference is one thing, evidence another, and the urban mortality data are much too crude to confirm a rise in the quality of city life up to 1850. Barbara Hammond (1928, p. 428) was quite right when she stated: "A close examination of the figures for Manchester does not lead to confidence in statistical proof of *improved* urban conditions in the early nineteenth century." But *improvement* is not the issue. The issue is whether the evidence supports the view of urban *deterioration*, and Hammond, a pessimist, agrees that it does not. Furthermore, many observers sympathetic to the condition of the working class, and who were caught up in the great public debates of the 1830s and 1840s, cautioned members of the House of Commons from inferring trends in the quality of urban life from a single town inquiry. The first such inquiry was James Kay-Shuttleworth's graphic description of Manchester's ghastly environment in his *Moral and Physical Conditions of the Working Classes*, used later by Engels with such great effect. Although an accurate account of Manchester in 1832, his work fails to point out that things may well have been worse previously. Speaking before a House of Commons committee, Francis Place noted: "I believe that what he [Kay] says is correct; but he gives the matter as it now stands, knowing nothing of former times; his picture is a very deplorable one [but] many Manchester operatives . . . inform me . . . that the condition of a vast number of the people was as bad some years ago, as he describes the worst portion of them to be now."[18] Obviously, Kay, Chad-

1974, p. 110); Glasgow and Edinburgh (Flinn, 1977, pp. 377, 379, and 383); and London (Landers, 1987, pp. 63–8). See Figure A2.1 in Appendix 2.1.

18 The reference is to Francis Place's appearance before the House of Commons (Accounts and Papers, 1835, p. 868), where he was asked to comment on James P. Kay-Shuttleworth's *The Moral and Physical Condition of the Working Class* (1832). The qualitative evidence on urban water supply, pollution, and sanitation does not unambiguously support the deterioration thesis, at least within cities. In addition to Buer's work, Dorothy George (1930) and Kitson Clark (1962) found conditions in the eighteenth century as bad or worse than those documented in the sanitary, municipal, and mortality reports of the 1830s and 1840s.

wick, and their followers were not interested in writing accurate history; they were intent on developing the best possible case for reform. Perhaps the pessimists have had their perception of the First Industrial Revolution distorted ever since.

As a final concession to the urban-quality-of-life-deterioration thesis, however, suppose that the infant-mortality rate rose by as much as a third in all British cities and towns between 1790 and 1850. Although the evidence does not appear to support such a premise, what would it imply for trends in the real standard of living of the working class? Using the 1834 elasticity of real wages to INFM (Table 9.5, .2771), a 33 percent rise in INFM implies a 9 percent fall in the quality of life for urban workers. But only 44.3 percent of the population was living in "urban places" in 1831. Thus, the impact of the hypothetical deterioration in the quality of urban life would have been to lower the standard of living of the British working class by 4 percent (for example, $[.33 \times .2771] \times .443 = .0405$), a trivial amount.

So much for the pessimist's view that early nineteenth-century urbanization produced an environmental deterioration so great that workers' standard of living was significantly diminished. Certainly the workers did not see it that way. They placed a far higher weight on high-wage city jobs than they did on low-quality city environments. It could be argued, of course, that their living standards might have risen by more if, in addition, the cities had been cleaned up earlier in the nineteenth century.

9.6   Trading off environment for commodities

None of the above confronts the question: What should have been? Was Britain's environmental ugliness the most efficient path to industrialization? Could the discounted value of the workers' stream of annual living standards have been improved with an earlier victory by the reformists?

Because the British tax system appears to have been highly regressive at this time, and certainly prior to Peel's tax reforms of 1842, the working class would have borne most of the cost of cleaning up the cities and improving housing earlier in the nineteenth century. To the extent that the incidence would have fallen on the working class through indirect taxation of necessities and rising rents on now-greater-taxed urban property, then their real-consumption levels might well have been eroded. Efforts to legislate higher residential health standards and lower levels of tenement crowding would also have inflated rents. So too would have space-intensive municipal urban renewal schemes. If the reader believes the contrary, and that urban landlords, merchants, and capitalists would have absorbed the tax burden, how would they have responded? Surely they would have responded in part by diminished saving as their disposable incomes contracted by the rise in taxes. If some productive accumulation and capacity creation would have been foregone as a consequence, some future urban jobs would also have been foregone. Fewer urban jobs imply a lower absorption of low-wage rural workers into high-wage city employment. Thus, workers' nominal incomes would have diminished on that score too. The trade-off between commodities and environment was very real and the Reform Debate much more subtle than first meets the eye.

So far, neither the pessimists nor the optimists have confronted these issues. Chapter 10 will explore these themes further in an attempt to assess whether Britain underinvested in her cities, thus generating mortality and environmental decay that was "too high."

Appendix 9.1. Data for the 1905 hedonic regressions

The sources of the data utilized for the analysis of the 1905 Board of Trade towns are as follows:

Wages. Average weekly wages for unskilled workers in the building trades (common laborers), taken from the October 1905 inquiry. Town wages are expressed relative to London (= 100). Source: Board of Trade (1908, pp. xxxiv–xxxv).

Cost of living. The cost-of-living index includes rents, the latter carefully adjusted to standardize by quality. The house rent index was constructed in three steps. The inquiry first identified housing types most frequently rented in the town, grouped by number of rooms. Then the inquiry computed rents relative to London (= 100) for each of the housing types. A simple average of these percentages yielded the town rent index. The commodity price information was gathered by surveying shopkeepers who, in October 1905, were asked what prices they charged for a standard basket of commodities (e.g., tea, sugar, bacon, eggs, cheese, butter, potatoes, flour, bread, milk, meat, and coal). A working class family budget was used to generate the aggregate index, the same fixed weights applied to all towns. Source: Board of Trade (1908, Table A, pp. xliv–xlv), London = 100, column labeled "rents and prices combined."

Population (POP). 1901 Census figures in thousands reported in Board of Trade (1908, Table B, pp. xlvi).

Density (DEN). Population (in thousands) divided by acres (in thousands). Town acreage was taken from the 1911 census.

Infant mortality rate (INFM). Infant mortality per 1000 births, averaged over the period 1902–6. Source: Board of Trade (1908), various pages.

Occupational index (SATMIL). The "dark satanic mill" index is constructed as the percent of males, ten and older, who were employed in the following occupational categories:

IX	Mines and Quarries,
X	Metals, etc.,
XIII	Woodworking, etc.,
XIV	Brick, etc.,
XV	Chemicals, etc.,
XVI	Skins and Hides, etc.,
XVIII	Textiles,
XXII	Mechanics and Laborers, not accounted for elsewhere.

1901 Census data were used to construct the above.

Regional code. The following code is used:
0–London,
1–Northern Counties and Cleveland (NORTH),
2–Yorkshire, except Cleveland (YORK),

3–Lancashire and Cheshire (LANCS-CHESHIRE),
4–Midlands (MIDLANDS),
5–Eastern Counties (EAST),
6–Southern Counties (SOUTH),
7–Wales and Monmouth (WALES).

Weather data (TEMP and SUN). Observations on two climate variables, temperature (TEMP) and sunshine (SUN), were obtained from *The Book of Normals 1881–1915* (1919). TEMP records mean annual temperature in degrees Farenheit to the nearest 0.1°. Sunshine normals refer to duration of bright sunshine observed by the Campbell-Stokes sunshine-recorder, annual mean. While the Meteorological Office had weather stations dispersed all over the British Islands, many of the seventy-two Board of Trade cities had no weather stations. In such cases, representative stations were chosen to reflect the climate characteristics of each city: its latitude, elevation, and distance from the sea. In most cases it was possible to choose a weather station within a few miles of the actual town or city. Proximity to large urban centers, said to affect both temperature and sunshine, was also considered.

Crowded living conditions (CROWD). The "percentage of population living in overcrowded tenements in 1901" (i.e., greater than 2 per room) reported by the Board of Trade was used as an index of crowded living conditions and housing quality. Source: Board of Trade (1908, pp. xlvii–xlviii).

Appendix 9.2. Data for the 1834 hedonic regressions

The source of the data utilized for the analysis of the 1834 Poor Law urban districts are as follows:

Wages and earnings. The 1834 *Report from the Commissioners for the Inquiry into the Administration and Practical Operation of the Poor Laws*, XXX–XXXVI, Appendix B2, "Answers to Town Questions," includes a number of parish responses with earnings and/or weekly wage data (in shillings) for laborers in various nonfarm occupations. Some of the parishes are aggregated in the analysis in the text (e.g., there are 12 parishes underlying our City of London observation, 4 underlying York, 3 underlying Shrewsbury, etc.), but most are sole parish observations. The sample has also been augmented by seven urban observations supplied by A. L. Bowley (1900a, p. 60 and 1900b, pp. 297–315). These are for "labourers in the building trades": Manchester (1834), Kidderminster (1836), Newcastle (1840), Macclesfield (1832), Bath (1831), Worcester (1839), and Bedfont (1830).

Density (DEN). Population (in thousands) of the parish divided by acres (in thousands).

Population (POP). Population size (in thousands) of the town (or city) in the 1831 Census of which the parish was a part, or to which the parish was contiguous, or of the parish itself, whichever was bigger. All figures taken from the 1831 census.

Infant-mortality rate (INFM). Infant-mortality rate per 1000 births, averaged over the period 1838–1844. These are district-level figures. Source: Appendix to the *Ninth Annual Report of the Registrar-General* (1849).

Weather data (TEMP and SUN). Observations on these two climate variables were taken from *The Book of Normals* as in Appendix 9.1 for 1905. See Appendix 9.1 also for a description of the assignment of weather stations to, in this case, parish locations.

Poor relief (POOREX). Total annual parish poor relief expenditures (in shillings) per capita in 1831, also contained in the 1834 *Report*.

Cost of living. The cost-of-living data are *not* available by parish, but they are available by regions in Table 7.4. Each of the 66 urban parishes is assigned the cost-of-living index of one of the ten regions: e.g., London, Northern Industrial, North Midlands, South Midlands, North, North West, East, West, Home Counties, and South East.

Occupational index (SATMIL). The "dark satanic mill" index is constructed as the share of adult males who were employed in the following occupational categories:

(i)   those employed in manufacturing or in making machines;
(ii)   all other (common) labor, nonagricultural.

1831 parish-level census data were used to construct the index.

The Irish (PIRISH). Number of persons greater than twenty years of age born in Ireland as a percentage of all persons greater than twenty in the registration district of which the urban parish was a part.

Appendix 9.3. "Sweet Auburn" and "Sheffield" for the migration experiment

In calculating the percent wage premium associated with migration between the various locations listed in Section 9.4, the following towns compose "Sweet Auburn" and "Sheffield":

Region	Towns composing "Sweet Auburn"	Towns composing "Sheffield"
North	Carlisle	Gateshead
		Middlesbrough
		Newcastle-on-Tyne
York	York	Bradford
		Castleford
		Leeds
		Sheffield
Lancs-Cheshire	Barrow-in-Furness	Burnley
	Chester	Liverpool
		Macclesfield
		Preston
		Stockport
		Wigan
Midlands	Burton-on-Trent	Birmingham
	Gloucester	Hanley
East	Bedford	London
	Ipswich	
	Luton	
	Peterborough	
South	Croydon	London
	Dover	
	Reading	
	Southampton	
	Taunton	

Appendix 9.4. "Sweet Auburn" and "Sheffield" for infant-mortality rates

In constructing the regional infant-mortality rates for "Sweet Auburn" and "Sheffield" in Table 9.3, the following aggregations were applied (using population weights):

Region	Area composing "Sweet Auburn"	Towns composing "Sheffield"	
North	All four counties *minus* five "Sheffields"	Gateshead Newcastle-on-Tyne Stockton-on-Tees	South Shields Sunderland
York	All three counties *minus* eight "Sheffields"	Keighley Bradford Leeds Halifax	Huddersfield Hull York Sheffield
Lancs-Cheshire	Both counties *minus* fourteen "Sheffields"	Burnley Blackburn Preston Wigan Warrington Macclesfield Birkenhead	Rochdale Bolton Oldham Stockport Manchester & Salford Liverpool & Bootle Chester
Midlands	All thirteen counties *minus* ten "Sheffields"	Nottingham Derby Burton-on-Trent Stoke-on-Trent	Leicester Northampton Birmingham Bristol Walsall Wolverhampton
East & South	All nineteen counties *plus* city of London *minus* London	London metropolis	

10. Did Britain underinvest in its cities?

10.1 Optimal versus actual investment behavior

Were investment requirements really "modest" during the industrial revolution?

By the standards of the contemporary Third World and the late nineteenth century, Britain recorded very modest investment shares in national income (Williamson, 1984a). That fact has generated a long and active debate centered around the question: Was the investment share low because investment requirements were modest, or was the investment share low because of a savings constraint? The first argues that investment demand in the private sector was the critical force driving accumulation during Britain's industrial revolution, low rates of technical progress and an absence of a capital-using bias both serving to minimize private-sector investment requirements. The second argues that Britain's growth was savings-constrained. Until very recently, the first view dominated the literature.

This dominant view sees early nineteenth-century Britain as so labor-intensive that investment requirements to equip new workers could be easily fulfilled by modest amounts of domestic savings, so easily in fact that domestic savings had to look for outlets overseas. Thus, David Landes (1969, pp. 78–9) brushes problems of accumulation aside with one magisterial sweep, leaving him free to deal with technology and private-sector entrepreneurship in the remaining 550 pages of *The Unbound Prometheus:*

> however justified this concern with saving and capital may be in this age of costly equipment and facilities [in] abysmally poor would-be industrial economies, it is less relevant to the British experience . . . the capital requirements of these early innovations were small . . . these critical innovations were [also] concentrated at first in a small sector of the economy, and their appetite for capital was correspondingly limited . . . Under these circumstances, it is not surprising to learn that the aggre-

gate volume of investment was a relatively small proportion of national income in those early decades of the Industrial Revolution, and that it was only later, when a more elaborate technology required large out-lays . . . that the proportion rose to the level that economists [look] upon as a characteristic of industrialization.

Phyllis Deane and W. A. Cole (1962, p. 277) use similar language in *British Economic Growth:*

the amount of new fixed capital required was quite small in relation to the output it would generate. By working factory labour long hours and on shift systems throughout the night, capital and buildings could be, and were, used relatively more intensively in the first quarter of the nineteenth century than ever before.

Peter Mathias (1972, p. viii) also supports this modest investment-requirements view:

The modesty of rates of capital accumulation . . . emphasizes the very profound differences between the context within which industrialization was proceeding in eighteenth-century England and that of many poor countries in our own day. The initial capital requirements for entering even the most capital intensive industries were astonishingly small; tech-nology was simple; many devices were employed for economizing in fixed capital . . .

According to Deane, Cole, Landes, and Mathias, the explanation for the modest investment requirements during the industrial revolution lies with simple labor-intensive technologies, capital-saving innovations, capital-stretching, and intelligent exploitation of excess capacity.[1] Contemporary World Bank analysts would find this interpretation attractive because they could use it to support their critique of Third World economies which, it is argued, often adopt inefficient capital-intensive development strategies during their ongoing industrial revolutions.

Where does this benign modest-investment-requirements view come from? François Crouzet (1972) tells us in his superb introduction to his *Capital Formation in the Industrial Revolution.* The tradition starts in the 1930s with two very influential papers by Michael Postan (1935) and Herbert Heaton (1937), the latter the source of the statement that the initial capital requirements during the industrial revolution were "mod-

---

1 Although the excess capacity was, presumably, a purely fortuitous historical leg-acy, one wonders about the capital-stretching, because that sounds suspiciously like a conventional response to capital scarcity and savings constraints.

est." It turns out, however, that Postan and Heaton restricted their attention to the direct investment requirements of factory production. They ignored the indirect public-sector infrastructure requirements, city social overhead in particular. This very narrow window on the industrial revolution tends to blur their vision, as we shall see.

The investment-requirements-were-modest view was briefly displaced by the capital-was-a-prime-mover view in the 1950s. It was led by two important developments in economics at that time: first, by the flowering of neoclassical growth models like those pioneered by Roy Harrod, Evsey Domar, and Robert Solow; and second, by the thinking of development economists like W. Arthur Lewis. Lewis stated the saving-constrained view of development with uninhibited assertiveness (1954, p. 155):

> The central problem in the theory of development is to understand the process by which a community which was previously saving and investing 4 or 5 per cent of its national income or less, converts itself into an economy where voluntary saving is running at about 12 to 15 per cent of national income or more. This is the central problem because the central fact of economic development is rapid capital accumulation . . . We cannot explain any 'industrial revolution' . . . until we can explain why saving increased relatively to national income.

It followed for Walt Rostow (1956, 1960) to apply this proposition to various historical cases. The British historical evidence from the industrial revolution, which was eventually brought to bear on the debate in the 1960s, was not very kind to the capital-was-a-prime-mover view. Little evidence could be found to support the Lewis-Rostow revolutionary doubling in the investment rate (Williamson, 1987), the evidence appeared to support the view that industry was labor-intensive in the early nineteenth century, and technological progress became the prime mover (McCloskey, 1981). Written at about this time, the Deane, Cole, Landes, and Mathias positions reflect the state of the accumulation debate.

In the fifty years since Postan wrote his paper, there have been some amazingly consistent limitations to the debate from which this chapter will try to escape. First, rarely do we hear any mention of housing, infrastructure, and social overhead. This is surely a puzzling attribute of the accumulation debate because there is another strand of historical literature that stresses crowding in the cities, a deteriorating urban environment, and lack of public investment in infrastructure (sewers, water supplies, street paving, lighting, refuse removal, and so on). It is also puzzling because we have come to learn just how large such investments loom in typical industrial revolutions, the Third World included. Indeed, many development economists and historians have argued that such investments are essential complements to the plant and equipment set in place in modern industry. Without them, rates of return in the modern private sector may sag and industrialization can be choked off. Dirty and unhealthy cities can serve to drive up the effective price of labor to urban firms either by producing sick workers or by requiring large nominal wage bribes to get reluctant workers to enter the dirty cities. Both would serve to raise the effective cost of labor and choke off industrial profits. Thus, slow rates of accumulation in industry may be induced, in part, by low rates of investment in complementary public infrastructure and private housing.

Second, and more important, the literature has confused what actually was with what should have been. It may be a mistake to conclude that Britain's labor-intensive growth strategy was a good thing. Heaton's "modest" investment requirements may reflect an attempt to achieve an industrial revolution on the cheap. If so, the strategy may have turned out to be more expensive in the longer run.

Scarce investment in city social overhead: A smoking gun?

If investment requirements during the First Industrial Revolution were really modest, it should have been reflected in relatively low capital-output ratios. Here we have an advantage over Deane, Cole, Landes, and Mathias since Charles Feinstein's careful estimates were published somewhat later.[2]

Table 10.1 collects the evidence for Britain 1800–60 and for a number of industrial revolutions that have followed in the wake of the First. Feinstein supplies the ingredients necessary to calculate both average capital-output ratios (ACOR) and incremental capital-output ratios (ICOR), but the late nineteenth- and twentieth-century estimates are limited to ICORs only. Furthermore, all of the figures in Table 10.1 are for fixed capital.

Panel A offers provisional support for the modest-investment-requirements view: Britain's ACOR underwent a spectacular drop from 5.21 in 1800 to 3.55 in 1860, the biggest fall by far taking place in the

---

2 What follows uses Feinstein's 1978 estimates of capital stock and investment because his 1988 estimates appeared too late to exploit them. Any further revisions of the evidence presented here also ought to rely more heavily on recent output estimates that appear to be displacing Deane and Cole. We use the latter in this chapter, however.

Table 10.1. *Average (ACOR) and incremental (ICOR) capital–output ratios: Britain 1800 to 1860 compared with other industrial revolutions*

PANEL A

Britain: ACOR	1800	1830	1860
Total	5.21	3.81	3.55
Agriculture	5.93	4.69	3.72
Industry, commerce & transport	3.27	2.58	3.29
Total *less* agriculture	4.87	3.54	3.52
Total *less* agriculture, housing & public works	2.15	1.90	2.47
Britain: ICOR	1800–1830	1830–1860	1800–1860
Total	2.65	3.32	3.10
Industry, commerce & transport	2.19	3.86	3.30
Total *less* agriculture, housing & public works	1.74	2.94	2.54

PANEL B

20th century: ICOR	1950s	1885/9–1914/18
Total: Ten countries	4.1	
Total: Low-income countries	3.4	
Total: Japan		2.9

PANEL C

Late 19th century: ICOR	Period	ICOR
Germany	1851/5–1911/13	7.4
Italy	1861–1914/16	9.6
Denmark	1870–1914	3.9
Norway	1865–1910/19	6.3
Sweden	1861–1911/20	4.1
Unweighted average		6.3
UK	1851/61–1905/14	4.1

Source: Panel A: gross stock of domestic reproducible fixed capital (£m. 1851–1860 prices) from Feinstein (1978, Table 8, p. 42); real GDP (£m. 1851–1860 prices) from Feinstein (1978, Table 25, p. 84), allocated by sector using the shares reported in Deane and Cole (1962, Table 37, p. 166). Panel B: Kuznets (1960, Table 15, p. 64, classes V and VI) and Kuznets (1961, Table 5, p. 17). Panel C: Kuznets (1961, Table 5, p. 17).

first three decades of the nineteenth century. No diminishing returns to capital, it appears. Or, if there was diminishing returns, it was dominated by capital-saving technical change (von Tunzlemann, 1981, pp. 160–1). At the margin, therefore, Britain's investment requirements during the industrial revolution were far below eighteenth-century averages. Indeed, the economy-wide ICOR up to 1830 was only 2.65, far below

Simon Kuznets' ten-country average for the 1950s (Panel B), and even below that for low-income countries in the 1950s and Meiji Japan (the latter viewed by most analysts to have been the classic example of capital-saving development).

The margin that mattered during the First Industrial Revolution lay, of course, outside agriculture. As it turns out, agriculture had a far higher ACOR in 1800 than did industry, commerce, and transport combined, 5.93 versus 3.27. François Crouzet (1972, p. 29) is quite right, therefore, in stressing that "a large proportion of the new developments were taking place in industries with a relatively low ratio of capital to income." Furthermore, Britain's relatively modest investment requirements at the margin persists into the late nineteenth century: Compared with five continental European countries, Britain's ICOR stays low (4.1 versus 6.3; Panel C).

In this sense, Deane, Cole, Landes, and Mathias are correct: Britain's investment requirements on the margin were modest during the industrial revolution, and they stay modest until late into the century. However, I believe the inferences which they draw from that observation are incorrect.

First, the case for Britain's unique "modesty" of investment requirements has been overdrawn. Britain's ICOR during the first half of the nineteenth century was 3.1 (Panel A, total, 1800–60), above the 2.9 figure for Meiji Japan and not far below the 3.4 figure for low-income countries in the 1950s (Panel B). Furthermore, there is no evidence that Britain's ICOR in manufacturing was any different from that of the contemporary developing countries cited by Simon Kuznets (1960). Although Britain's ICOR was low, to describe her investment requirements as "astonishingly small" (Mathias, 1972, p. viii) and concern with saving and capital "less relevant" (Landes, 1969, p. 78) compared to many poor developing countries today is, to say the least, overstating the case.

Second, one of the key reasons why investment requirements during the First Industrial Revolution were so modest is that Britain failed to commit resources to those urban investment activities which, in Landes' (1969, p. 78) words, make industrialization such a costly venture today, and which, in W. Arthur Lewis' words (1977, p. 29), make contemporary Third World cities so capital-intensive. Investment in housing and public works simply failed to keep pace with the rest of Britain's economy in the first half of the nineteenth century. One can see this very clearly in Panel A of Table 10.1. Although the total ACOR drops precipitously between 1800 and 1860, the ACOR for the total economy less agriculture, housing and public works actually *rises* over the same period. Although the ACOR

Table 10.2. *Capital stock growth per capita by use: 1760 to 1860 (percentage per annum)*

Use	1760–1800	1800–1830	1830–1860	1800–1860
Social overhead capital	−0.13	0.10	0.39	0.24
Dwellings	−0.13	0.12	0.27	0.19
Public works and buildings	−0.10	−0.09	1.43	0.67
All other fixed capital	0.44	0.27	1.43	0.85
Total fixed capital	0.21	0.21	1.09	0.65

Source: Feinstein, 1978, Table 8, p. 42 (gross stock of reproducible fixed capital, 1851–1860 prices) divided by population (p. 84).

outside of agriculture does fall, implying low ICORs and modest investment requirements at the margin, the reason for it is that capital-intensive housing and public works were given short shrift.

To repeat: Deane, Cole, Crouzet, Landes, and Mathias are all correct in stressing the "modest" investment requirements at the margin during the First Industrial Revolution. They were misled, however, by failing to note that those low investment requirements reflect a growth strategy which starved housing, public works and other urban social overhead investment.

Another way of illustrating this point is to examine the behavior of capital stock growth in what we shall call social overhead – residential housing plus public works and public buildings. Based on Feinstein's data, Table 10.2 documents per annum growth rates in capital stocks per capita (1851–60 prices). The table's message is clear. Investment requirements during the late eighteenth century were kept modest by allowing the stock of social overhead per capita to fall, contributing, presumably, to a deterioration in the quality of life, an item usually excluded from conventional measures of output. This growth strategy continued for the first three decades of the nineteenth century, although not with quite the same intensity. Per capita stocks in public works continued to decline, but dwelling stocks per capita began to rise. The latter did not rise enough, however, to regain the levels of 1760.

By 1830, therefore, Britain had accumulated an enormous deficit in her social overhead stocks by pursuing seventy years of industrialization on the cheap. It cost her dearly, as the social reformers were about to point out. Between 1830 and 1860, there is some evidence of catching up in public works, in part a response to the goading of the social reformers, but the gap in growth rates between dwelling stocks and all other fixed capital per capita increased.

All of this suggests that while actual investment requirements may have been modest during the First Industrial Revolution, they would not have been so modest had investment in social overhead kept pace. In fact, had social overhead investment kept up with all other investment after 1800 – let alone making good on accumulated past deficits – the ICOR over the first half of the nineteenth century would have been in excess of 4, not the "modest" 3.1 actually achieved.

The argument could be sharpened if we could identify which of Feinstein's investment and capital stock estimates were city-specific. Then we could talk more explicitly in terms of underinvestment in city social overhead. With some plausible assumptions, it appears that we can. Before the evidence from the First Industrial Revolution is explored, consider twentieth-century industrial revolutions. W. Arthur Lewis writes on this issue with authority: "Urbanisation is decisive because it is so expensive. The difference between the cost of urban and rural development does not turn on comparing the capital required for factories and that required for farms. Each of these is a small part of total investment, and the difference per head is not always in favor of industry. The difference turns on infrastructure" (Lewis, 1977, p. 29). Indeed, when social overhead (including dwellings) is added to direct capital requirements, the capital-labor ratio in India's cities is about 4.5 times that of her rural areas (Becker, Williamson, and Mills, forthcoming, Table 3.1). Similar findings are reported by Lipton (1976, Table 7.1, pp. 442–3), who finds urban capital-labor ratios, relative to rural, to be: Argentina (1955), 2.3; Colombia (1953), 3.3; India (1950), 7.7; Mexico (1950), 16.7; and Yugoslavia (1953), 12.5.

Although the Third World cities are very capital-intensive, Table 10.3 shows that Britain's cities in the early nineteenth century were not. Three estimates of the capital-labor ratio are reported in the table. The first is limited to direct fixed capital only. Capital-labor ratios were generally lower in nonagriculture in the first three decades of the nineteenth century, and they began to exceed agriculture only after the 1830s. Even in the 1850s, however, capital-labor ratios were not much higher in nonagriculture. The second adds housing to direct fixed capital, and here I had some problems. Housing stock values are not available by urban-rural breakdown, so some crude allocation rules had to be used. As the notes to Table 10.3 indicate, I was not happy with the result and prefer the alternative estimates in parentheses. The third adds the remaining social overhead. In sharp contrast to Lewis's characterization of the Third World,

Table 10.3. *Were Britain's cities labor-intensive? Capital–labor ratios, 1800 to 1860*

Year	(1)	(2)	(3)	(4)	(5)	(6)	(7)	(8)	(9)
	Direct fixed capital			Direct fixed capital plus housing			Total fixed capital		
	Agriculture £	Nonagriculture £	Ratio (2)/(1)	Agriculture £	Nonagriculture £	Ratio (5)/(4)	Rural £	Urban £	Ratio (8)/(7)
1800	63.5	67.7	1.07	108.4 (91.7)	81.7 (95.9)	.75 (1.05)			
1810	66.1	65.9	.99	113.7 (93.9)	80.5 (93.7)	.71 (1.00)			
1820	72.8	60.9	.84	128.6 (101.7)	75.9 (89.8)	.59 (.88)			
1830	76.1	65.5	.86	145.3 (108.9)	82.7 (98.3)	.57 (.90)			
1840	76.8	82.1	1.07	157.2 (107.3)	102.2 (112.5)	.65 (1.05)	172.5 (126.2)	94.0 (122.5)	.54 (.97)
1850	77.6	98.9	1.27	151.4 (110.6)	117.9 (131.9)	.78 (1.19)	178.4 (140.4)	106.5 (150.5)	.60 (1.07)
1860	90.0	110.4	1.23	179.7 (123.7)	128.4 (144.1)	.71 (1.16)	211.3 (159.8)	117.0 (166.7)	.55 (1.04)

Sources and notes. Net capital is taken from Feinstein's recent revisions (Feinstein, 1987, Table XIII), and it is in 1851–60 prices. The labor-force estimates are from Deane and Cole (1962, p. 143), and labor in "domestic and personal" occupations is excluded throughout. Direct fixed capital excludes housing. Total fixed capital includes housing and an allocation of total transport capital (and labor) based on the percentage of railroad revenues coming from agricultural freight and rural passenger revenues. Dwelling values were first allocated by using census estimates of houses per person for urban and rural areas, and the share of population urban. The resulting percentage was then used to allocate Feinstein's total dwelling stock. Direct fixed capital plus housing simply adds "rural" housing estimates to direct agricultural fixed capital and "urban" housing to direct nonagricultural fixed capital, and thus is not exactly a rural/urban breakdown. The result of this housing capital allocation yields implausibly high rural housing capital per laborer compared to urban (e.g., a ratio of 4:1 in 1840). As an alternative, we simply assumed that the housing capital per laborer was the same in rural and urban areas. These are reported in parentheses. There are no entries under total fixed capital for 1800–30 since Deane and Cole do not supply the labor-force breakdown required.

when social overhead is included Britain's cities look no more capital-intensive compared with the countryside than when the social overhead is excluded. While urban capital-labor ratios are about 4.5 times rural in India, they were about the same or less in mid nineteenth-century Britain. The data underlying both estimates are, of course, very fragile, but it would take an enormous error to reverse that finding.

Cities are very capital-intensive in the contemporary Third World. Cities were relatively labor-intensive during the First Industrial Revolution. The difference appears to be explained in large part by a remarkably weak commitment to city social overhead in Britain.

Circumstantial evidence? The problem of proof

City social overhead was low during the First Industrial Revolution. It lowered investment requirements, perhaps freeing up resources for consumption of foodstuffs and other essential commodities. But it had its price: The cities became ugly, crowded, and polluted, breeding high mortality and morbidity, trends that, according to Eric Jones and M. E. Faulkus (1979), were absent up to 1780. In sharp contrast with the contemporary Third World, Britain's cities were killers: In 1841, city mortality rates were 5.6 per thousand higher than in the countryside (Table 2.1); in 1960, Third World cities had mortality rates that were 6.3 per thousand lower than the countryside (Rogers, 1984, p. 288). We simply do not know how much of this stark demographic contrast between 1841 Britain and the contemporary Third World is due to Britain's low investment in city social overhead. Nor are we certain what contribution low investment in city social overhead made to the observed lag of life expectancy behind GNP gains (Fogel, 1986). But surely it mattered.

Evidence such as this invites the inference that more and earlier investment in city social overhead would have lowered mortality and morbidity, while raising the quality of life. But what would it have cost? Would it have been a good thing? Was low investment in city social overhead necessarily evidence of underinvestment? Let me restate the question in a different way. By focusing on low investment in city social overhead, we have so far only sharpened the debate over British accumulation during the industrial revolution. The low investment could have been due to any one of the following forces, and they have quite different implications: Investment demand for city social overhead may have been low because public-health technologies were primitive, or because urban poverty bred low demand for housing; investment demand for city social overhead may have been low because of some capital market failure; investment demand for city social overhead may have been low because of some public-sector failure; and investment in city social overhead may have been low due to savings constraints and crowding-out by other projects, including those abroad.

It isn't obvious which of these forces accounts for Britain's low investment commitment to city social overhead. Presumably, Deane, Cole, Crouzet, Landes, and Mathias could all argue that the low commitment to city social overhead was consistent with low returns to such investments. They could argue that the demand for city housing was constrained by poverty and that city social overhead was much too primitive in the early nineteenth century to make bigger investment in them profitable. Perhaps. But apologist explanations such as these would have to deal with equally plausible saving-constrained, capital-market-failure, and public-sector-failure explanations.

Although no mono-causal hypothesis is likely to be sufficient by itself, consider the saving-constrained and crowding-out hypothesis. Writing after the French wars had ended, but in the face of an immense war debt, John Stuart Mill saw crowding-out as an important cause of relatively slow accumulation in Britain (Mill, 1909, vol. 2, p. 481). T. S. Ashton agreed, and in Chapter 4 ("Building and Construction") of his *Economic Fluctuations in England* he made the case that it was building and construction – housing and public works – that was most heavily hit (Ashton, 1959, p. 65). Not too long ago, I followed these leads and became persuaded that war debt crowding-out could explain much of Britain's sluggish accumulation experience up to about 1820 (Williamson, 1984a: but note the disagreement registered by Heim and Mirowski, 1987, and Mokyr, 1987). The especially severe crowding-out of city social overhead (including housing) makes sense in this saving-constrained explanation:

> As for investment in transport and public utilities, the minimum scale of initial expenditure was high, the gestation period was long, and interest charges on borrowed capital an important element in the annual costs. Building was also heavily dependent upon credit for mortgages, and mortgage rates moved in harmony with the going rate of interest on government stock. So the timing of projects in those sectors was undoubtedly affected by the shifts in the rate of interest . . . Investment [in building] was badly hit by wars, during which heavy government borrowing . . . drove up rates of interest. On the other hand, investment in manufacturing industry was little affected by interest rate movements. (Crouzet, 1972, p. 31).

In short, total private savings were a constraint on investment, government war debt served to diminish the residual savings available for accumulation, and city social overhead was likely to have suffered the most.

This kind of reasoning helps to account for the low investment in city social overhead during the industrial revolution up to about 1820, but what about afterward? The same crowding-out argument could be invoked, but this time it's the railroads doing the work. Table 10.4 offers evidence on the distribution of nonagricultural investment for the first half of the nineteenth century. Social overhead investment declined very sharply from 42.3 percent of nonagricultural investment in the 1820s to 24 percent in the 1840s, while investment in transportation and communication soared from 17.6 percent to 44.8 percent over the same period. Social overhead investment wasn't the only activity crowded out by railroad construction, since the industry and commerce investment share declined from 40.1 to 31.2 percent, but it absorbed the biggest adjustment by far, and all of it was in dwelling construction.[3] If there was ever evidence of crowding-out and savings constraints, this is surely it, even though there is the puzzling evidence that the share of investment in public works and buildings does not decline during the same period. Furthermore, these inverse long swings continuue throughout the nineteenth century. Indeed, it could be argued that social overhead in Britain's cities (with high social returns but low private returns) continued to be crowded out by railroad investment overseas (with high private returns), but that these crowding-out effects only eased off as returns on foreign past investments began to match new capital exports, so that potential savings available for domestic investment increased as a share of national income.[4] Thus, investment in public works continued to rise

3 Cairncross and Weber (1956) noted the slump in house-building in the 1840s and rejected crowding-out as a source: "It is conceivable that the slump in house-building in the 1840s reflected a squeeze executed by railway-building on the capital market and on the finance of house-building; but . . . this is not a very plausible explanation" (p. 295). Although the authors did not pursue the issue, they assert that investment "demand was dominated by demographic factors." This is a puzzling statement, because it is a decline in house-building per capita that is at issue, not simply house-building itself.

4 The long swing literature of the 1950s and 1960s is relevant here, of course. It has been long appreciated that British home and foreign investment varied inversely in the nineteenth century. However, investment demand was stressed to reconcile the evidence. I suspect it would be of some value to return to that literature while exploring the savings and crowding-out connections, following some of the leads offered in Michael Edelstein's 1982 book.

Table 10.4. *Distribution of nonagricultural gross fixed capital formation (in %): Great Britain 1801 to 1860, and United Kingdom, 1851 to 1910*

A. Great Britain 1801–1860

Use	1810–1810	1811–1820	1821–1830	1831–1840	1841–1850	1851–1860
Social overhead	40.4	44.3	42.3	36.9	24.0	29.7
Dwellings	32.4	35.6	34.7	29.2	15.7	18.8
Public works & buildings	8.0	8.7	7.6	7.7	8.3	10.9
Transportation & communications	26.1	21.4	17.6	26.2	44.8	35.3
Industry & commerce	33.5	34.3	40.1	36.9	31.2	35.0
Total nonagriculture	100.0	100.0	100.0	100.0	100.0	100.0

B. United Kingdom 1851–1910

Use	1851–1860	1861–1870	1871–1880	1881–1890	1891–1900	1901–1910
Social overhead	29.6	30.7	37.5	34.4	36.5	34.0
Dwellings	18.5	20.0	24.9	22.0	21.1	18.7
Public works & buildings	11.1	10.7	12.6	12.4	15.4	15.3
Transportation & communications	35.2	38.3	30.5	36.9	31.0	29.6
Industry & commerce	35.2	31.0	32.0	28.7	32.5	36.4
Total nonagriculture	100.0	100.0	100.0	100.0	100.0	100.0

Source: Based on decade averages, from Feinstein, 1987, Table IX. "Nonagricultural" investment is total investment less that in agriculture, but rural dwellings are retained. Investment in "Public works & buildings" includes gas, water, electricity, public services, and social services. "Industry & commerce" includes mining. Panel A: In 1851–1860 prices. Panel B: In 1900 prices.

across the nineteenth century, so that its share by the turn of the century, more than 15 percent, was double that of the 1830s, between 7 and 8 percent. By the standards of the late Victorian era, there was certainly underinvestment in public works in the first half of the nineteenth century.

Thus, we have no shortage of explanations for the low commitment to city social overhead investment during the First Industrial Revolution. As we have argued, it could be explained by crowding-out and savings constraints. But it could also be explained by low returns to such investment, or by some capital-market failure which made it difficult for municipal authorities to secure long-term financing at fair rates. And, of course, it could be explained by a wide gap between "private" and social rates of return on investment in city social overhead. If it is the latter, however, how do we account for public authorities' unresponsiveness to, presumably, high social rates of return? Ignorance? A political mismatch between those who stood to gain from the social overhead investments and those who would have carried the tax burden?

If Britain underinvested in city social overhead, then we should see it in the form of high social rates of return to such investment. That's easy enough to say, but implementing the calculation would be an enormous task. We would need to know the quantitative impact of additional social overhead investment on improving longevity and reducing sickness. We would need some way of assessing the value of those mortality and morbidity gains. And we would need to know just who would have gained and who would have borne the tax burden. This chapter's goal is more modest. All that is attempted here is to set up the research agenda in a coherent way. Section 10.2 turns to public-health investment and the Great Sanitation Debate. The quantitative impact of public-health investment on mortality and morbidity is unresolved even today, but that didn't stop the social reformers from offering benefit-cost ratios which favored city sanitation and other public-health investment projects. The social reformers made no effort to calculate anything approximating a social rate of return, but rather simply tried to show that investment in public health would pay by lowering the pauper burden. There are good political reasons for their reluctance to offer social rate-of-return calculations, but some guesses on the likely magnitude of the social rate-of-return to public-health investments are offered in Section 10.2 just the same. They turn out to be very large. Section 10.3 estimates "overcrowding" in urban housing across the nineteenth century, and then assesses the cost of a decrowding policy had it been introduced in the 1840s. The costs of decrowding are difficult to estimate (investment costs being the least important), and the returns even more difficult, so even illustrative social rate-of-return calculations are impossible, at least at this time.

The key issue throughout is: Who would have paid for more social overhead investment sooner? I believe the answer tells us much about Britain's choice of the ugly-city and industrialization-on-the-cheap development strategy.

10.2 Should Britain have introduced sanitary reform faster and sooner?

The Great Sanitation Debate

In early July 1842, during a summer of high unemployment and social protest in the cities, Edwin Chadwick, secretary to the Poor Law Commission, presented his *Report on the Sanitary Conditions of the Labouring Population of Great Britain* to the House of Lords.[5] His *Report* has been viewed as a turning point in sanitary reform ever since. Part of a flood of public documents which were directed toward social reform in the 1830s and 1840s, Chadwick's *Report* is far and away the best. As a piece of pure legislative and social protest rhetoric, it is superb. The *Report* also contains an extraordinary amount of empirical documentation on the economic condition of the urban labor force – disease, mortality, morbidity, housing, and, most important, the state of city sanitation or what we would now call the quality of public-health infrastructure. It also offers engineering and cost details on sewage and water systems. The *Report* even goes so far as to compute benefit/cost assessments of various sanitation projects. It also contains explicit administrative and legislative proposals on how the sanitary reform could best be implemented. Although an outstanding social document, the *Report* also represented a turning point in another way. It reflected the fact that the public-health movement now had a leader in Chadwick, who gave the movement a well-defined legislative focus.

It is said that the *Sanitary Report* awakened middle-class and upper-class sensibilities to the ghastly environment of Britain's urban poor, an environment that most nonpoor Victorians had failed to appreciate (Cartwright, 1977, p. 103). Most Victorians with political influence were located at a safe distance from the worst part of that environment, and their pride in Britain's economic success was based on the manifest evidence of booming industrialization, accumulation, and world trade. The *Report* served to inform them of the ugly underside of urbanization and industrialization, and it appealed to their humanitarian instincts to make an investment in cleaning up the cities and thus improve the sanitary and economic condition of the laboring poor. Chadwick spared no effort in distributing

5 Flinn (1965), p. 1. Michael Flinn's piece on *The Sanitary Condition* is the classic on this topic and I have drawn on it extensively in this section.

the *Report*, abridging it to manageable size and mailing it to all who might be persuaded to join the sanitary reform movement. It was a smash hit, and Chadwick claimed that some 20,000 copies were sold. Indeed, as Sir John Simon (1890) was to point out a half-century later, even the Metropolitan Working Classes' Association followed Chadwick's propaganda lead, producing a *Manual of Public Health and Domestic Economy* (1847) five years later, and selling a whole series of working-class pamphlets on health, public sanitation, clean water, and the environment, each costing only a penny.

Yet, we can easily make too much of the 1842 *Sanitary Report*. Remarkable as the document and Chadwick may have been, the fact remains that the *Report* was preceded by at least a century of accumulated understanding and public-health experimentation. If we fail to appreciate that fact, then we will be left with the mistaken impression that a far greater commitment to cleaner cities through social overhead investment was impossible prior to 1842. We will also make the far greater error of assuming that a major commitment of public resources to sanitation reform took place in the decades immediately following. Neither of those statements is true.

Although the *Report* devoted some attention to the crowding tuberculosis connection (an air-borne disease), the vast majority of its pages are devoted to diarrheal diseases, to typhoid and to cholera (water-borne diseases). It is, after all, a document whose focus is on drainage, sewage, and water supply. Furthermore, although the epidemiological theory underlying these diseases was not well understood, the empirical correlates of these diseases certainly were. Tuberculosis (for example, consumption) seemed to be highly correlated with poor nutrition and crowded dwellings, and was specific to family circumstances. Typhoid, cholera, and the other diarrheal diseases seemed to be highly correlated with location and the quality of the public-health infrastructure. In other words, mortality was less class-specific in the early nineteenth century than it was to become in the early twentieth century after the sanitary reformers had made significant progress in eradicating the water-borne diseases (Titmuss, 1943, chp. IV). Because the water-borne diseases touched closer to the lives of the rich, especially cholera epidemics, they were more likely to pay attention to sanitary reform than to cries for decrowding (Flinn, 1965, p. 10). The standard explanation for these water-borne diseases was, ironically, "miasma," or germs infecting the atmosphere generated by exposed garbage and animal waste. Indeed, one can see the miasma theory in the imagery which William Farr selects in the *Tenth Annual*

Report of the Registrar General (1847, p. xvii): "This disease-mist, arising from the breath of two millions of people, from open sewers and cess-pools, graves and slaughterhouses, is continual . . . in one season it is pervaded by cholera . . . at another it carries fever on its wings. Like an angel of death it has hovered for centuries over London. But it may be driven away by legislation."

It was not until the second cholera epidemic that John Snow demonstrated unambiguously in 1849 that cholera was a water-borne disease, and the bacteriological causation of disease was not established until the 1870s and 1880s (Flinn, 1965, pp. 62–3). Fortunately, the wrong theory and the right theory implied the same action – improved sanitation through drains, sewers, and clean water. But these urban environmental commitments had a tradition that stretched back a century or more.

With the quickening of urbanization in the late eighteenth century, medical opinion had reached the conclusion that infectious disease could be explained by crowding and the lack of sanitation, long before the 1842 *Report* (Flinn, 1965, pp. 15–16, 18–25). There were also quantitative precedents to the *Report*, and medical writers had produced an impressive number of local studies on the mortality-crowding-sanitation connection. The best known of these was James Kay's study of Manchester slums in 1832, which attracted attention in House of Commons hearings and was used by Frederick Engels in *The Condition of the Working Class in England* a decade or so later. Not only were there many precedents to Kay's study, but English towns had introduced active public-health measures long before the onset of the First Industrial Revolution (Flinn, 1965, p. 17). James Riley (1986, 1987) has recently traced those interventionist public-health policies back into the late seventeenth and early eighteenth century:

> In the latter decades of the seventeenth and early decades of the eighteenth century, a number of internationally renowned physicians, including Thomas Sydenham in England . . . , formulated specific measures of intervention. Relying on Hippocratic tradition, specifically, on its suggestion that endemic and epidemic diseases are caused by forces in the environment, and influenced by Renaissance efforts at urban sanitation, these . . . environmentalist physicians proposed to drain swamps, bogs, moats, and other sites of standing water; to introduce hydraulic devices that would circulate water in canals and cisterns; to flush refuse from areas of human habitation; to ventilate living quarters and meeting places . . . or apply other insecticidal measures in houses, prisons, meeting halls, and ships; to inter corpses outside the city; and by other measures, including refuse burial, to detach humankind from organic

waste. Theory became practice in the 1740s and thereafter as a growing body of physicians and public health authorities persuaded local and central government officials . . . to introduce the reforms they recommended (Riley, 1986, pp. 838–9).

In fact, Eric Jones and M. E. Faulkus (1979) have presented a persuasive case supporting the view that English urban environments improved up to the mid-late eighteenth century as a result of activist public-health infrastructure policy. Things had certainly changed by the 1830s. Furthermore, as we shall see below, French commitment to public-health infrastructure seems to have been more extensive at that time than in England.

Britain's cities were ugly and public commitment to sanitation and health infrastructure shockingly modest at the time of Chadwick's 1842 *Report*. One can hardly argue that this condition was attributable to ignorance or even that infrastructure technology was too primitive. There was plenty of scope for applying the efforts introduced long before in both England and in France. It didn't happen. Even with the 1835 Municipal Corporation Act, the 1848 Public Health Act, and all the subsequent Acts in place, the fact remains that it was almost a half century before a significant commitment of resources was to be made and notable progress on mortality and morbidity in the cities could be reported.

The impact of public-health investment on mortality

The *Sanitary Report* and subsequent reformist arguments certainly made the case that the cities were crowded and filthy, and that sickness and death were highly correlated with city ugliness, but to clinch the case for public intervention the reformers had to show clearly that public-health investment would yield favorable returns as well as to show which projects should have been favored first. The reformers could not show this in 1842 and modern historians have difficulty showing it today. Indeed, we are not even sure what was driving mortality trends across the nineteenth century, including the contribution of sanitary reform to those trends.

To paraphrase Flinn (1965, p. 8), the demographic history of Britain's cities in the first half of the nineteenth century is a history of tuberculosis, cholera, and typhus (the latter called a poor man's disease even as early as 1832: Flinn, 1965, p. 10). According to Thomas McKeown (McKeown and Record, 1962; McKeown, 1976), these three diseases accounted for the vast majority of the decline in nineteenth-century British mortality, and the same was true of late nineteenth-century America (Meeker, 1972; Condran and Crimmins-Gardner, 1978). The first of these is an air-borne disease, where crowding and nutrition play a critical role. The water-borne diseases, such as cholera, were the target of the *Sanitary Report*. McKeown guessed that public-health investments introduced by the sanitary reformers accounted for about a quarter of the mortality decline in the second half of the nineteenth century, but even that brilliant guess has been challenged in subsequent debate.

Before we engage that debate, we need to clarify its relevance to the task at hand. Suppose we split cause of death into three parts, that due to diarrheal diseases, typhoid and cholera (c), tuberculosis (tb), and all other (z)

$$D = D_c + D_{tb} + D_z.$$

The simplest decomposition of the mortality decline can then be written as

$$dD = b_c dX_c + b_{tb} dX_{tb} + b_z dX_z,$$

where dD is the observed decline in death rates, dX_c denotes those sanitary investments that served to lower death from diarrheal diseases, typhoid and cholera, b_c (a coefficient with negative sign) denotes the marginal impact of those investments on mortality from those three sources, dX_{tb} denotes the investment in decrowding and nutrition, which served to lower death from tuberculosis, b_{tb} (a coefficient with negative sign) denotes the marginal impact of those investments on mortality from tuberculosis, and $b_z dX_z$ denotes the decline in the death rate from other causes (includ-ing diarrheal diseases, typhoid, cholera, and tuberculosis directly unre-lated to public health, decrowding, and nutrition). In this simple state-ment, we ignore for the moment the reality that morbidity intervenes before death. It also ignores the reality that nutritional status may influ-ence the size of b_c and b_z, or that city sanitation may influence the size of b_{tb} and b_z. That is, "diseases of filth . . . are likely to be found simultaneously in given individuals, and these diseases . . . influence one another" (Riley, 1986, p. 849).

When McKeown guessed that one quarter of the decline in mortality across the late nineteenth century was attributable to sanitary investment, his judgment was guided by the ratio of the decline in water-borne disease deaths to dD. That is, he inferred the impact of public-health investment by simply exploring the trends in the cause of death. Edward Meeker (1972) did the same for America. But the decline in water-borne disease deaths can be influenced by increases in dX_c–due to investment in sanitation, by increases in b_c–due to improved nutrition and diminished crowding, or by other forces captured in $b_z dX_z$. Nowhere does McKeown, or any other participant in the debate for that matter, offer any firm estimate of b_c, although assertions, of course, abound. Nor does McKeown offer any estimate of the impact of sanitation investment on what Robert Fogel (1986) calls "nutritional status" and thus the spillover effects on the incidence of death from tuberculosis, $b_{tb} dX_{tb}$, and other diseases, $b_z dX_z$.

Without the estimate of b_c, we cannot explore the counterfactuals that really matter. We cannot ask, for example, what would have been the improvement in mortality had the expenditure on sanitary investment been twice as high in the 1830s than it was; that is, if the public-health share had been at 1900 levels in the 1830s. The debate can inform us about changes in the cause of death which were actually driving the mortality decline across the nineteenth century, and it can suggest the likely sources of those changes (for example, improved nutrition, sanitary investments, decrowding), but it cannot help us assess the likely impact of alternative policies. Unfortunately, those alternative policies are precisely the issues that guided reformist debates in the nineteenth century and should guide today our historical assessment of the magnitude of Britain's public-sector failure in her cities. We must keep all this in mind when confronting debates over the great mortality decline.

McKeown's work has set standards for the debate over the past three decades. In a series of publications starting in 1955, McKeown changed our thinking about the sources of the great mortality decline since 1700 (McKeown, 1976, 1978, 1983; McKeown and Brown, 1955; McKeown and Record, 1962; McKeown, Record, and Turner, 1975). As Fogel (1986, Table 9.1, p. 440) has recently shown, the British standardized death rate declined by 21 points between 1700 and 1980, from 28 per thousand to 7 per thousand, about half of which took place before 1911, and a third in the six decades following 1850. In the place of medical technology, McKeown argued that improved nutrition and sanitation investment were the principal factors accounting for the decline, especially the former. In fact, McKeown and Record (1962, p. 120) suggested that in the second half of the nineteenth century investment in public health accounted for about a quarter of the decline and the rise in nutrition accounted for about half.[6] Decrowding explained none of the decline, because it failed to take place (Section 10.3).

McKeown's stress on the rise of nutrition and the modest contribution of investment in public health found some early support from American evidence. Robert Higgs (1973, p. 189), for example, thought that the decline in American rural mortality before 1920 was due to rising nutrition and living standards. Even more damning to the reformers' position were the findings by Gretchen Condran and Eileen Crimmins-Gardner (1978) that expenditures on sewers and waterworks in American cities had a relatively modest effect on mortality in 1900.[7] However, Celeste Gaspari and Arthur Woolf (1985) found just the opposite for American cities in 1910; by that time, those that had invested in sewer systems had the lower mortality rates. One possible explanation for these ambiguous and incompatible results may lie with causality. If "dirty" cities with high-mortality incidence were the first to introduce sanitary investment (perhaps prodded to action by the reformers), then the data would reveal low and even positive values for b_c because high mortality would be associated with more active public-health commitment (Condran and Crimmins-Gardner, 1978, pp. 40–1; Meeker, 1972, pp. 369–70). The estimate of b_c would tell us more about how mortality influenced the demand for public health rather than about how the supply of public health influenced mortality. Furthermore, these demand-side forces may have dominated the mortality–public-health investment relationship during the transition phase as public health began to be diffused across cities in the late nineteenth century. As Flinn pointed out some time ago, the same would certainly have been true in the second quarter of the nineteenth century in England, when the deterioration of urban public-health conditions created a sanitation response by some local authorities (Flinn, 1965, p. 16).

6 It is important to point out that although Robert Fogel (1986) also stresses nutrition in accounting for the mortality decline, his hypothesis is far less precise. By nutrition, Fogel means nutritional status, and the latter is the "balance between the intake of nutrients and the claims against it." Those claims include crowding, disease environment, public-health investment, and other forces. Fogel's documentation of a high correlation between death rates and nutritional status (or its surrogate, height), does not resolve the debate between intake and claims. McKeown, in contrast, comes down hard in favor of intake.

7 Robert Higgs and David Booth (1979) used 675 wards in seventeen American cities in 1890 and found quite different results than did Condran and Crimmins-Gardner. However, Higgs and Booth used the typhoid fever death rate as an index of "the general sanitary conditions of a city, and of its public water supply in particular" (p. 365). The procedure seems to assume what they set out to prove.

When most cities had some public-health investment in place, say, by 1910, it seems likely that the estimate of b_c would reflect mostly the supply-side effects and thus would be less biased against the favorable case for public-health investment programs.

In any case, we need to know whether the long delay in the nineteenth-century decline in water-borne diseases was driven by low investment in public health (a small dX_c) or by a weak health impact of money spent on any given public-health project (a small b_c). The evidence just cited cannot tell us.[8]

To repeat, because the debate has focused on $b_c dX_c$, rarely are these two components decomposed. If the impact of public-health investment was modest, was it due to inadequate investment, or to a weak impact of public-health investment on mortality, or both? As Section 10.1 reveals, I favor the first hypothesis, especially because it helps account for the fact that Britain appears to be an exceptional case. That conclusion is based in part on the evidence that eighteenth-century public-health environmental efforts had recorded considerable success in reducing English mortality. The conclusion is also based in part on Michael Flinn's (1965, p. 52) observation that reformers thought that French public-health practice was in advance of the British at the time of the *Sanitary Report*, and it may have influenced Chadwick's thinking. Perhaps more to the point, as with Riley's (1986) eighteenth-century English evidence, work by Samuel Preston and Etienne van de Walle (1978) suggests that water and sewage improvements played an important role in nineteenth-century French urban-mortality declines. These were concentrated among the water-borne diseases, but they think that cleaning up French cities may have lowered death rates by air-borne disease too because sanitation invest-ments improved nutritional status (Preston and van de Walle, 1978, p. 288). Thus, they conclude that "water support rather than food support systems are the key to understanding trends in urban French mortality" (Preston and van de Walle, 1978, p. 284), quite in contrast with McKeown's characterization of nineteenth-century Britain. In another

8 Although Simon Szreter (1986) may argue with great vigor that McKeown has understated the impact of public health investment in Britain after 1850, and while he himself may believe that "the decline in mortality, which began to be noticeable in the national aggregate statistics in the 1870s, was due more to the eventual successes of the politically negotiated movement for public health than to any other positively identifiable factor" (Szreter, 1986, p. 27), the fact remains that Szreter offers little evidence to substantiate what may otherwise appear to be a very plausible position.

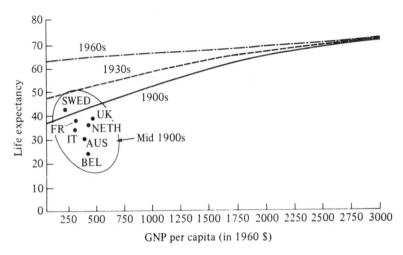

Figure 10.1   The life-expectancy and living-standards correlation through time

paper, Preston and Verne Nelson have shown that the mortality changes in late nineteenth-century Britain were quite unusual based on the "normal" cause of death patterns among forty-eight nations between 1861 and 1964, the high share attributed to tuberculosis in particular (Preston and Nelson, 1974, p. 24).

In 1985, Preston offered one more piece of evidence that suggests that McKeown has exaggerated the role of nutritional intake and living standards, and, by inference, understated the potential impact of public health. Preston estimated the relationship between per capita income and life expectancy for the 1960s and the 1930s, comparing each with limited observations on the 1900s. Across the twentieth century at least, income per capita (standard of living or nutrition intake) improvements can explain at most a quarter of the rise in life expectancy, encouraging the view that omitted variables – like the rise in public-health investment – can account for at least three quarters. Figure 10.1 reproduces Preston's exercise for what I believe is an improved data set, and one which is augmented with mid nineteenth-century observations as well. The upward drift in the relationship is fully consistent with Preston's findings; namely, a much larger share of the rise in life expectancy from the mid nineteenth century onward is due to factors uncorrelated with per capita income, among them, of course, the rise in public health.

If we wish to assess the optimality of Britain's ugly-city strategy and whether sanitary reform should have come sooner, we need to know b_c as well as dX_c, not simply $b_c dX_c$. We do not have that information. This fact has not, however, moderated the enthusiasm of some who have offered counterfactual assessments of more activist public-health investment policies. This includes both the contemporary historian and the sanitary reformer, as we shall see below.

The social rate of return to investment in public health

Edward Meeker (1974) published an important paper that has failed to get the attention it deserves. Meeker used conventional benefit/cost analysis and impressive archival research to estimate the social rate of return to investment in public health in American cities between 1880 and 1910. The calculation is relevant if we have no evidence to support the view that returns to investment in British cities at the time of the *Sanitary Report* were significantly lower than they were in American cities around the turn of the century. In any case, it is the only such calculation of which I am aware for either of these two nineteenth-century economies, and it is exactly what we need to assess public-sector "failure."

Meeker estimates the social rate of return in the United States as follows. Calculate the decline in absenteeism that came as a result of the reduced incidence of the three disease groups that can be associated with public-health activities. These disease groups are: diarrheal diseases, cholera, and typhoid (from improved water supplies and sewage systems); smallpox (from the enforcement of smallpox vaccination ordinances); and malaria, an important cause of mortality in America, but not in nineteenth-century Britain[9] (from improved drainage resulting from the installed sewers). Calculate the decline in mortality from the same three sources. Place a value on the total person-weeks gained by the fall in absenteeism and mortality. This value is calculated in two ways. First, the benefits are calculated in terms of market wages forgone. This serves to understate the social rate of return. It places no value on the mortality and morbidity experience of those out of the labor force, including children, the elderly and married women working at home. It also ignores the fact that individuals might be willing to pay far more than their market wage to improve their morbidity and mortality experience, a portion of their nonlabor income, for

---

9 Although malaria may not have been an important disease in Britain in the nineteenth century, recent evidence suggests that it was in the eighteenth century and earlier. Malaria is not simply a tropical disease (Riley, 1986, pp. 846–9).

example. Second, the benefits are calculated in terms of per capita income. This may serve to overstate the social rate of return because the poor had a higher incidence of these three diseases than did the rich (Titmuss, 1943), and wages are a better measure of the poor's value than is income per capita. Yet, the second calculation at least places some value on those who were not employed at market work, and, in addition, admits the possibility that individuals might be willing to pay more than their current market wage to improve their mortality and morbidity experience. Finally, assume that all of the longevity gains associated with these three diseases were attributable to public-health measures while none of the gains in absentee-ism were. Both assumptions are based on Meeker's comparison of rural mortality and morbidity trends – areas where public health had little impact – with urban mortality and morbidity trends – areas that were the center of public-health reform.

Given estimates of the costs of public health (capital and current operat-ing costs), Meeker emerges with what he calls an upper and lower bound on the social rate of return to investment in public health – 6 and 16 percent. Both of these social rates of return exceed private market rates: 4.2 percent on railroad bonds, 4.4 percent on common stocks, and 5.3 percent on industrial stocks. Meeker concludes that investment in public health was sound. What he fails to stress, however, is that these high rates of return imply that there was gross underinvestment in public health.

There is reason to believe that both of these estimates are conservative. After all, they ignore the fact that sick workers are less productive even if they are not sick enough to be absent from work. The same is true for women, children, and the elderly who normally perform valuable nonmar-ket home-work activities. It also ignores the fact that clean cities had amenity value over and above the morbidity and mortality implications. In short, the underinvestment was even bigger than the already high 6 to 16 percent social rates of return imply.

The social reformers' benefit/cost analysis

If the social rate of return to public-health investment was so high, why did almost a half century elapse between the appearance of the *Sanitary Report* and a truly active public commitment to such investment? Indeed, why didn't the social reformers make greater use of such calculations during the debates in the 1830s and 1840s? The answer does not lie with evidence – Chadwick had pretty much the same evidence at hand in the

1840s as Meeker had in 1974.[10] Nor does the answer lie with the evolution of economic sophistication. As we shall see, the social reformers understood the notion of human capital and were quite adept at applying elementary benefit/cost analysis. I believe that the reformers made very little of social rate-of-return calculations for quite another reason: they were politically sophisticated activists and it never occurred to them that such calculations would persuade anyone who controlled the size of the public sector. The next section will pursue that point, but first let me try to establish exactly what sort of benefit/cost calculations the reformers did find useful in their political rhetoric.

Benefit/cost arguments for sanitary reforms can be found in the 1842 *Sanitary Report*, in the First and Second *Reports of the Parliamentary Commissioners of Inquiry into the State of Large Towns and Populous Districts* (1844 and 1845), and in the Registrar General's *Annual Reports* (from 1838 onward). The first of these is pure Chadwick, while the last is William Farr. These documents contain three kinds of arguments for the adoption of sanitary reform, that is, for investment in drains, sewers, and water supplies: First, sanitary reform would be worth it to the rich; second, sanitary reform would be worth it to the poor; third, sanitary reform would be worth it to the city and the nation.

All three arguments suffer from partial equilibrium assumptions; that is, they all fail to take account of the fact that declines in mortality and morbidity would augment the labor supply and thus drive wages down below current levels. They can be forgiven on this score, especially if the augmented labor force would have simply crowded out new Irish or rural British immigrants. All three arguments are also based on very strong

---

10 I do not mean to imply, of course, that Chadwick had the same understanding of epidemiology that we have today. But he certainly had plenty of evidence on the correlations between disease, crowding, and lack of sanitation. The point is simply this: Chadwick had enough evidence in the 1840s to make pretty much the same social rate-of-return calculation that Meeker did for 1880–1910. Indeed, Chadwick in 1842 and Meeker in 1974 made the same very strong assumption about the impact of public-health investment on mortality. Meeker, the reader will recall, assumed that the difference between rural and urban mortality trends could be accounted for entirely by the rise in urban public-health investment. Chadwick (and Farr) assumed that the difference in mortality between "good" and "bad" towns could also be accounted for by the absence of sanitary investment in the latter. Thus, they were both prepared to assume that sanitation investment lowered diarrheal diseases, cholera, and typhoid, and by the amounts actually observed. A strong assumption indeed, though it may be correct.

assumptions about the precise effects of the sanitary reforms on health (see footnote 9). Finally, when the reformers offered explicit estimates of the costs of a city social overhead project, they turn out to be underestimates based on subsequent experience. In spite of these flaws, the arguments certainly gave focus to the debate then, and they also serve to guide any historical assessment today.

Sanitary reform would be worth it to the rich. The argument here takes two forms. First, quoting the *Second Report of the Commissioners* (1845, p. 4), "the pecuniary saving from ... the inevitable result of a large outlay for improvements [justifies] the interference of the Legislature," where that saving would be attributable to a decline in Poor Law expenditures. The latter was calculated from evidence from Preston (p. 52) and Glasgow (p. 272), which showed that the reduction in mortality and morbidity would reduce the burdens on the Poor Law unions from diminished sickness, unemployment, fewer widows and orphans. The reformers thought the evidence showed that the reduction in Poor Law expenditures would, in fact, more than offset the increase in sanitary investment. Second, there were important externalities to consider, the most important of which was a check to the spread of disease to the rich. Again, from the *Second Report*:

> The presence of such emanations, whether they be derived from stagnant ditches, open cesspools, or from accumulations of decaying refuse, is a great cause of disease and death, not confined to the immediate district in which they occur, but extending their influence to neighbouring, and even to distant places (p. 2).

> these reservoirs of contagion ... may suddenly overflow their usual boundaries, and devastate neighbourhoods, the inhabitants of which are now unconscious of their proximity to such danger (p. 54).

In the *First Annual Report* (1838), William Farr tells us: "the poor-rates would be reduced: but all classes of the community are directly interested in their adoption, for the epidemics ... which arise in the east end of the town [London] do not stay there; they travel to the west end, and prove fatal ..." (p. 168). In subsequent publications, the reformers stressed this point again and again: that sanitary reform would be worth it to the rich. Although they also appealed to the humanitarian instincts of the rich, they made far less use of their arguments that sanitary reform would be worth it to the poor or to the nation.

Sanitary reform would be worth it to the poor. Chadwick devotes an entire section of the 1842 *Report* to this issue. He computes the cost of water,

water closets, and drainage, and estimates the annual cost of such invest-ments if paid over thirty years at 5 percent interest. The stream of benefits include the reduction in sick days by one half, augmenting annual earn-ings, and a similar reduction in doctors' bills. He concludes that the benefits would have exceeded the costs (p. 291).

Why, then, didn't the urban poor willingly pay for the improved sanitary conditions? First, they were not well informed about the poor sanitation and mortality connection. Second, there was the free-rider problem. Third, drainage and water supply required the cooperation of the whole neighborhood, because the social overhead project obeyed classic dimin-ishing marginal costs. Fourth, the initial cost of "laying on the water" was considered the tenant's responsibility. High mobility, rapid turnover, and short tenancy made the renter reluctant to make an investment he could not fully internalize. Fifth, the urban poor faced liquidity constraints and imperfect capital markets, making even "sound" self-improvement proj-ects beyond their reach. All of these, of course, are classic arguments for public intervention to overcome "failure" in private markets.

Sanitary reform would be worth it to the nation. At this stage of the argu-ment, Chadwick and Farr exhibit their most sophisticated human-capital economics, although they minimized its use in public debate. Using McCulloch's estimates of the value of productive workers, the 1842 *Report* (p. 274) concludes that the saving in human life would have far exceeded the cost of sanitation investment. The most elaborate social benefit/cost calculation, however, can be found in the *Second Report* (1845) in which a Reverend Clay reports a calculation for Preston, reproduced in Table 10.5. The benefit/cost ratio is enormous, 5.4 (the ratio of "total annual saving per individual" to "total annual expenditure per head").

The critical issue: Who paid and what failed?

If the social rate of return on investment in city social overhead was so high in the 1830s and 1840s, why was the level of investment so low? I have been persuaded by Anthony Wohl's marvelous book, *Endangered Lives*, that the explanation lies with failure of two kinds – capital-market failure and public-sector failure.

The capital-market-failure hypothesis is motivated by the evidence that until the passage of various municipal acts over the three decades follow-ing 1835, most cities in England found it difficult if not impossible to secure long-term finance for social overhead investments. However, the fact that cities were investing so little in social overhead is not enough evidence to support the capital-market-failure hypothesis, because low demand may have been the source. We need more cross-sectional evidence at the local level to assess whether capital-market failure was really an important quantitative source of underinvestment in sanitation.

The public-sector-failure hypothesis is even more appealing, and it is developed with great skill in chapter 7 of Wohl's book (1983, especially pp. 166–75). What follows draws heavily on his evidence, although it should be noted that recent work on German late nineteenth-century experience with sanitation investment tends to support Wohl's view (Brown, 1988a, 1988b).

In the second half of the century, there were over 1,000 sanitary districts in England and Wales, but neither the 1835 Municipal Corporations Act nor the 1848 Public Health Act had a significant impact on the local groups responsible for health matters. Municipal franchise was based on ratable values, so the electorate was very narrow. In 1861, only 3 percent of the population of Birmingham could vote for members of the town council (and thus influence sanitary-investment decisions), while the figure for Leeds was 13 percent. A survey taken in 1886 of about a fifth of the sanitary districts revealed that those administering the public-health acts were mainly shopkeepers (30.8 percent of local sanitary officials), followed by manufacturers (17.5 percent), gentlemen (11.8 percent), merchants (8.6 percent), farmers (7.7 percent), and builders (7.6 percent). Most of these, especially shopkeepers and polluting manufacturers, stood to gain from low rates, and this was the main source of town revenues.

Although the greatest opposition to the sanitary reforms marched under the banner of "economy," the word was clearly misplaced. "Opposition to Unfair Taxes" would have been a more accurate banner. In 1866, James Hole, a Leeds radical, characterized local sanitary groups in precisely that way:

> They and those who elect them, are the lower middle class, the owners, generally speaking, of the very property which requires improvement. To ask them to close the cellar dwellings is to ask them to forfeit a portion of their incomes. Every pound they vote for drainage, or other sanitary improvement, is something taken out of their own pocket . . . (Wohl, 1983, p. 170).

The public failure, therefore, lay with an inefficient and unjust tax system. Taxes were assessed on the rental value of property, and "thus a man

Table 10.5. *The Reverend Clay's calculation of social benefits and costs to investment in sanitation in Preston, taken from the Second Report (1845)*

I. – Proximate estimate of expenditure

	Total number of houses	A. Cost per house for capital			B. Rent per house		C. Total outlay	D. Total increased rental required defraying by annual instalments of principal and interest of 20 years for house-cleansing and water apparatus, and 30 years for sewers and drains		
		£	s.	d.	s.	d.	£	£	s.	d.
1. In want of water	5,000	0	10	0	0	6	2,500	200	15	0
2. " main sewer	10,000	0	5	0	0	2	2,500	162	12	6
3. " secondary ditto	7,919	2	9	6	2	6	19,599	1,274	18	9
4. " house-drains	10,000	0	15	0	0	9	7,500	487	17	9
4. " water-closets	10,000	2	0	0	2	0	20,000	1,606	1	0
5. " ventilation	10,000	0	15	0	0	9	7,500	602	4	6
6. " street-sweeping	10,000	.	.		9	3	.	4,625	0	0

	£	s.	d.
Total immediate expenditure of capital required for the improvement of the town	59,599	0	0
Total increased rental (including the annual expense of street sweeping)	8,959	9	8
Immediate expenditure for each house	5	19	3
Total increased annual rent for each house	0	15	11
Immediate expenditure per head of the population	1	3	9
Annual expenditure per head of the population	0	3	6½

II. – Proximate estimate of pecuniary and other saving from sanatory improvements in Preston

(1)	(2)	(3)	(4)	(5)	(6)	(7)	(8)
Saving by one-third of the actual number of deaths. The expense of each being estimated at 10£	Saving in the excess of births beyond 1 in 44 of the population; the expense of each birth being taken at 1£	Saving in days' labour from sickness, estimating one-third of the cases out of the expense. 16,710 cases	Reduction by one-half of the existing expenses of widowhood and orphanage, the amount taken from the actual expenditure	Saving in the expense of insurance, by keeping the water on night and day, so as to be in readiness at one minute's notice. Estimated on half the number of houses at 6s. per house	Saving of productive manure estimated at 10s. per head on the whole population. All liquid and solid manure and street sweepings being carried out of town by the sewers	Saving in washing, &c. consequent on the burning of factory smoke. Estimated at 1d. per head per week of the population	Saving of outside painting of shops and houses; estimating the cost per house at 25s., and the saving at one-fourth of the sum.
£ 1,240	£ 827	£ 7,047	£ 501	£ 1,500	£ 25,000	£ 10,450	£ 1,250

	£.	s.	d.
Total annual saving to the town	47,815	0	0
Total annual saving to each house	4	15	7
Total annual saving to each individual	0	19	1

whose sole income was derived from rents paid much higher rates in proportion to his total income than others" (Wohl, 1983, p. 171). No wonder "the economists" were hostile to sanitary improvements. No wonder there was underinvestment in city social overhead.

Two important developments began to overcome this impasse in the 1860s, although a three-decade lag implied enormous social losses due to the public-sector failures. The first was general economic growth in the cities, which served to augment the local tax base and thus lower the effective tax rate. The second was more interventionist and the result of central-government action; subsidized terms on loans for town improvements from the central government. It appears that "the opportunity to borrow money at a lower-than-market rate of interest over a long repayment period proved too tempting to resist, and did much to stimulate local activity and to silence the objections of the 'economists' " (Wohl, 1983, p. 174). What we need to know, of course, is the size of the subsidy, and exactly how significant these subsidized loans were in accounting for the rise in social overhead investment in the late nineteenth century. In the absence of tax reform at the local level, what the central-government loan subsidies served to do was to distribute the tax burden more equally. It served, therefore, to create a better match between those who gained from cleaning up Britain's cities and those who paid.

10.3   Decrowding city housing: What would it have cost?

The social reformers' views on crowding

From the social reform debates of the 1830s and 1840s to the early twentieth century, overcrowding in Britain's cities has received much attention. The pessimists in the standard-of-living debate felt certain that overcrowding in tenements and cottages was at the heart of high morbidity and mortality in the cities, and that things had gotten worse from the 1790s to the 1840s. Most observers felt that "What mattered from the point of view of health was housing densities – the number of houses per acre, and the number of people per house – and the supply of the basic amenities, water, sanitation, paving and street cleansing" (Flinn, 1965, p. 4). The issue was sufficiently important that overcrowding was highlighted in the 1842 *Sanitary Report* and in the 1844 *Report of Large Towns*. It was also central to the 1885 *Royal Commission on the Housing of the*

Working Classes, indicating that little progress had been made on the problem over the four decades from the 1840s to the 1880s. Nor had the problem disappeared by 1904, when the *Glasgow Municipal Commission on the Housing of the Poor* appeared, or in 1917, when the results of the *Royal Commission on the Housing of the Industrial Population in Scotland* were published. Indeed, the immense empirical inquiry of the Board of Trade into town cost of living in 1905 was motivated primarily by rents, housing scarcity, and crowding. In short, qualitative reports such as these suggest that Britain had made little or no progress on decrowding in her cities from the French wars to World War I.

But the term "over" in overcrowding implies a departure from social optimality, and such a departure implies some market failure. If it were simply crowding at issue, then the concern would be more clearly centered on poverty and a more just distribution. If it was "over" crowding at issue, then which factor markets failed? What were the causes of overcrowding and why did they persist?

Measuring overcrowding

How many were overcrowded? The question is simple enough: the answers come hard: "historians cannot yet determine – and may never be able to determine precisely – what proportion of the population at any point of the eighteenth or nineteenth centuries lived under housing conditions that were conducive to good, or bad health" (Flinn, 1965, p. 4). Indeed, we are not even sure that urban crowding was on the rise during the period of most rapid city growth after the French wars, from the 1820s to the 1840s. The census commissioners thought they had such an index with their reported number of people per inhabited house, which behaved as follows: 1801, 5.6; 1811, 5.6; 1821, 5.7; 1831, 5.6; and 1841, 5.4. In fact, the decline in the number of people per inhabited house across the 1830s was taken as evidence of decrowding, until Chadwick pointed out that the evidence was spurious because the commissioners had changed the definition of "house" between 1831 and 1841 (Flinn, 1965, p. 5). In any case, it was changes in crowding among the urban working class that was at issue, and the economy-wide averages shed no light on that target group.

To make any progress at all, we need first to agree on what constitutes crowding. However imperfect and arbitrary, the standard used throughout the debate, from the *Sanitary Report* to World War I, was "more than two

Table 10.6. *Crowding as a percentage of total urban England and Wales, 1841 to 1911*

| Year | Predicted, based on | | Actual |
	1891 parameters	1901 parameters	
1841	14.0	12.3	
1851	16.5	14.8	
1861	16.5	14.7	
1871	15.2	12.9	
1881	15.1	12.8	
1891	14.3	11.9	14.7
1901	14.1	11.7	10.4
1911	13.3	10.9	10.7

Source: Appendix Table 10.2, Panel C, and Appendix 10.1.

persons per room." As Appendix 10.1 points out, starting with 1891 the censuses report crowding by this standard at the city and even district level within cities. Prior to 1891, the censuses report only number of people per house, although at the same locational detail. However, Appendix 10.1 shows how we can "backcast" crowding from predictive equations estimated on 1891 and 1901 evidence. The results of this exercise are summarized in Table 10.6.

Based on Table 10.6, McKeown is right; namely, that levels of urban crowding changed hardly at all between 1841 and 1901 (McKeown and Record, 1962, p. 114). Crowding in the cities rose sharply in the 1840s (when housing construction activity was so low), and fell in the 1860s, the 1880s, and the 1900s. Yet the share of the urban population crowded was about the same in 1901 as it was in 1841.

The costs of decrowding

What would it have cost to decrowd the poor in England's cities in 1851? There are two components of that cost, the augmented dwelling stock and the site value of land on which that augmented dwelling stock would have been placed.

The site value of urban land is calculated in Table 10.7 under various assumptions about the elasticity of urban land supplies. A perfectly elastic land-supply assumption simply assumes that the average cost of urban land in 1851 would have applied to the augmented dwelling stock in the counterfactual. This assumption sets a lower bound on the costs of

Table 10.7. *The cost of decrowding England's cities in 1851*

A. *Site value of urban land, assuming land supply elasticity equal to:*

% Crowded	.4	.8	1.0	1.5	2.5	α
16.5	£37.30m	£31.84m	£30.76m	£29.30m	£28.14m	£26.40m
14.8	32.44	28.06	27.18	26.02	25.08	23.68

B. *Cost of augmenting dwelling stock, assuming various per dwelling costs equal to:*

% Crowded	Average economy- wide	Average urban	Average urban slum
16.5	£30.94m	£15.69m	£6.73m
14.8	27.75	14.07	6.04

C. *Total costs of decrowding, assuming average urban per dwelling costs and a low land supply elasticity = .4:*

% Crowded	Total Costs
16.5	£52.99m
14.8	46.51

Notes. The percent crowded estimates are taken from Table 10.6. The site value of land to decrowd the poorest urban workers is calculated as

Site value = (% increase in land required)(value of urban land stock in 1851)(price of new land/price of land in 1851)

= $(\%\Delta J)(JP_J)(1 + \%\Delta P_J)$

where $JP_J = £160m$ (1861: Feinstein, 1978, p. 71), $\%\Delta J$ = percent crowded, and $(1 + \%\Delta P_J)$ is generated by land-supply-elasticity assumptions. The cost of augmenting the dwelling stock is calculated as

Cost = (% increase in dwelling stock required)(gross value of urban dwellings in 1851)(deflator)

= $(\%\Delta H)(HP_H)(d)$

where $HP_H = £187.5m$ (based on data underlying Table 10.3), $\%\Delta H$ = percent crowded, and d equals (Feinstein, 1978, p. 45, Table 10)

urban slum = £30/£138 = .2174
average urban = £70/£138 = .5072
average economy-wide = £138/£138 = 1.0.

The total costs in Panel C favor assumptions that place an upper bound on the estimate, namely I believe the supply of land elasticity to have been very low (.4), and that the decrowded would have been moved into higher quality housing (e.g., "average urban").

decrowding; it is clearly unrealistic because land supplies were obviously very inelastic in the center of England's cities where jobs were located. An elasticity of .4 sets an upper bound on the costs of decrowding; I believe it is far more realistic because it reflects the fact that land prices would have been pressed upward sharply by any decrowding policy. The cost of the augmented counterfactual dwelling stock is reported under three assumptions: at average economy-wide 1851 per dwelling costs; at average urban 1851 per dwelling costs; and at average (low quality) slum 1851 per dwelling costs. The high economy-wide figure is clearly irrelevant since our interest is in city crowding only. The slum figure is also likely to be irrelevant because those decrowded would have moved out of the slums into more "average" urban housing. Thus, the average urban per dwelling costs appears to be the best assumption.

The total costs of decrowding in England's cities in 1851, under the low land-supply-elasticity assumption, would have been between 46.5 and 53 million pounds, about 70 percent of which would have been land costs. These are hardly trivial numbers, even when distributed evenly across the 1840s, rather than having decrowding take place in a single year, 1851. On average, it implies about 5 million pounds per annum across the 1840s, a decade when railroad investment was 14.11 million per annum and total gross fixed investment was 49.43 million (in 1850–61 prices: Feinstein, 1978, p. 40). A decrowding policy spread across the 1840s would have raised Britain's investment requirements by about 10 percent per year. The total costs of decrowding would have been more than 10 percent of Britain's yearly GDP (450 million: Feinstein, 1978, Table 28, p. 91), or considerably more than a fifth of her urban GDP (or 2 percent of urban GDP if the decrowding costs are spread over the decade). If the decrowding were financed by raising urban land rates, the lump-sum tax would have been 3 percent per annum (5/160, the denominator equal to total 1861 urban land values in millions of pounds, from Feinstein, 1978, p. 73). If the decrowding were financed by raising urban rates on wealth in dwellings and land combined, the lump-sum tax would have been 1.4 percent per annum (5/160+187.5, the added term in the denominator equal to the 1851 gross value of urban dwellings in millions of pounds, from Table 10.7 "notes"). Both of these tax rates are high enough to suggest that taxpayers would have strongly resisted the decrowding policy.

Furthermore, there is reason to believe that this already large cost of decrowding is a gross understatement. That is, I believe that a low urban land elasticity assumption of .4 is still too high. It assumes that space would have been found for the decrowded poor near their places of employment. Since building technologies limited the height of low-cost tenements (iron and steel struts and beams were an innovation of the future), where were the decrowded to be located? Obviously, out at the periphery, e.g., the suburbs. However, we must remember that this was an era prior to the introduction of cheap and fast intraurban transportation, and shelter was required within walking distance of work (Rimmer, 1960; Royal Commission on the State of Large Towns, 1844), for otherwise commuting time would have cut sharply into available time for employment.

Suppose that the urban land elasticity of .4 was possible only if workers moved to the suburbs. Suppose the commuting time for the decrowded would have been an added two hours per day, one to employment in the central city and one back to the suburbs. Suppose further we take the average work day to have been twelve hours, so that the ratio of lost wages from commuting to the potential twelve-hour day was .167. Given what we know about urban wages, the commuting cost of the decrowding would have been about .7 percent of GDP, or more than 1.4 percent of urban GDP.[11] When this is added to the investment and land costs of the decrowding, we get something like 3.4 percent of urban GDP in each year across the decade of the 1840s, implying that we should almost double all of the figures in the preceding paragraph (and the added commuting costs would have persisted after 1851). In addition, it is not clear how the commuting costs would have been financed by the worker. After all, the worker was forced to work the twelve-hour day, and we know that little energy remained for long commuting walks thereafter. Perhaps it would have required the legislation of a ten-hour day. But even then, would the worker have preferred the decrowded environment with lost wages? I doubt it, because it represented almost 17 percent of the wages of workers affected. Alternatively, if somehow employers were made to bear the commuting cost of decrowding, it would have raised their wage costs by about 2.8 percent

11 Commuting costs as a share of GDP are estimated by the product of the following four ratios: lost wages from commuting as a share of potential wages; urban commuters as a share of urban workers; urban wages as a share of the total wage bill; and the total wage bill in GDP. Thus, $(.167)(.140)(.7939)(.3867) = .0072$, or .72 percent of 1841 GDP. The share in urban GDP is taken to be about twice that figure because about half of the population was urban at that time. The first figure, .167, is defended in the text. The second, .14, is the estimated percent crowded in the cities, where, to be conservative, the 1841 figure is used. The third and fourth, .7939 and .3867, are derived from Deane and Cole (1962, Tables 37 and 43, pp. 152 and 166).

(16.7 percent rise in wages of decrowded times 16.5 percent decrowded), eroding the exporter's edge in world markets and eating into his profits for accumulation. Following Bowley (1919, p. 45), if profits were about a third of value added in manufacturing, then the added commuting costs would have lowered profits by more than 5 percent.

These costs seem high to me, and the stream of social returns would have had to have been implausibly large to suggest that there was signifi-cant underinvestment in housing in Britain's cities. These high costs also suggest why crowding persisted for so long even as the real incomes of urban common labor rose throughout the nineteenth century. In this sense, there was nothing "over" about overcrowding. There was no obvi-ous market failure, there were just poor urban workers making rational choices given the available technologies and prices. A redistributive policy to eliminate crowding would certainly have been a welcome event for the poor, but it would not have come cheap. And new space-augmenting technologies – cheap, fast, and efficient intraurban transport, and higher tenements – would have reduced crowding in the 1840s, but they were technologies of the future.

Perhaps we have reached this conclusion with too much haste. After all, wasn't there one more option? Why didn't employers move their capital to the suburbs so that workers could decrowd at little cost? No doubt employ-ers did move to exploit the cheaper and more elastic land on the periphery (the move certainly would have been inexpensive for new plant, although not for old), but did they move anywhere near fast enough? I don't know the answer to this question, but it seems to be central in any search for failure, the discovery of which would help confirm the "over" in overcrowding.

10.4   The agenda

Modern revisionists have shown that it is simply not enough to point to various manifestations of poverty in making assessments of Britain's treat-ment of her poor. Nor is it enough to point to rapid industrialization to conclude that Britain was a country to emulate. Rapid industrialization may have been either too rapid or not rapid enough. To prove the case that Britain failed, we have to show that things could have been better with more intelligent policy and more efficient institutions.

The same holds for Britain's cities during the industrial revolution. It is not enough to document high city mortality, morbidity, ugliness, pollution, and crowding. We have to show that things would have been better had Britain pursued more intelligent policy and developed more efficient institutions. Although our intuition may support the view that Britain underinvested in her cities, finding the evidence of failure is a tougher task. This chapter certainly had no difficulty showing that Britain invested very little in urban social overhead, but would more investment of that sort have been better? In the case of housing, I think the answer is no. In the case of city infrastructure and sanitation, I think the answer is yes. But the evidence brought to bear on either question is insufficient. What we have done here, I hope, is to establish a plausible hypothesis and a research agenda. To do more is another book.

Appendix 10.1. Estimating urban crowding in the nineteenth century

Despite the rhetoric that surrounded the housing of the poor, useful data on urban crowding did not appear until the late nineteenth century. For previous years, we have only information on people per house, a measure that Chadwick himself considered useless as an indicator of crowding. The problem, then, is to construct a close proxy for the relevant crowding variable (the proportion of urban population living more than two people per room) from the available data (the average number of people per house). Our proxy of choice is an estimate of crowding generated by applying regression parameters from the abundant turn-of-the-century data to the sparser evidence for the mid-nineteenth century.

Explicit and extensive data on urban crowding were first published in the 1891 census, which provided matched data on household size and rooms per household for large cities. These data reveal that the average number of people per household and its square, along with a regional dummy variable for northern cities (which supports the view that crowding was significantly higher up North), predict the level of crowding quite well. In other words, Chadwick was wrong, and the 1901 data on crowding confirm this conclusion. Appendix Table 10.1 presents these results, as well as the coefficient estimates produced by 1911 data. (The crowding variable for 1911 was slightly different from the definition used for earlier census years; we report the 1911 results for comparison, although they are not used in constructing the nineteenth-century crowding estimates.)

With these coefficients in hand, we can predict the extent of crowding for earlier census data. We first look for those cities from the 1901 sample (which was

Appendix Table 10.1. *Predicting overcrowding 1891–1911*

	1891	1901	1911
Constant	.537	.603	.170
	(.341)	(.153)	(.141)
People/house	−.219	−.240*	−.092
	(.111)	(.051)	(.049)
(People/house)^2	.023*	.025*	.013*
	(.009)	(.004)	(.004)
North	.102*	.054*	.058*
(= 1 if North)	(.026)	(.010)	(.009)
Adjusted R^2	.61	.71	.62
SER	.062	.041	.042
F	17.47	66.50	53.48
n	33	80	98

Notes: Standard errors in parentheses, * = significant at 5 percent. Unit of observation = city. Dependent variable for 1891 and 1901 is the number crowded in housing units of four or fewer rooms, as a proportion of total population. For 1911, the dependent variable is the number crowded in housing units of any size as a proportion of total population.

broader than the 1891 sample) that have data on population and the number of houses (approximately equal to households). This determines our sample of urban areas. After applying the regression coefficients from 1891 and 1901 to this sample, we emerge with two sets of city-by-city estimates of the proportion of the population which was crowded; by implication, we also have two sets of estimates of the number crowded in each city, and thus of the total number crowded in our urban sample. All that is left is to convert this urban sample into a measure of crowding in the urban population as a whole.

To do this, we simply multiply the number crowded in our sample by the ratio of total urban to sample urban population to get an estimate of the total number crowded. Rather than doing this for the national urban population in the aggregate, however, we compute total/sample urban ratios for North and South separately, multiply each by its respective number crowded, and then sum the two regions to get a national total. In this way, we allow for the different crowding experience in the two regions. Finally, we convert the national number crowded into our bottom line: the predicted proportion of the urban population living under crowded conditions. Appendix Table 10.2 reports the predicted crowding according to both sets of regression coefficients, 1891 and 1901; we also report "actual" crowding based on the censuses of those years. (Note, however, that "actual" crowding still rests on inflating sample crowding, as reported in the census, by the ratio of total to sample urban population.)

Data Sources
All data on population, households and crowding come from the census returns published in *Parliamentary Papers:*
1841: 1843, vol. 22, County Summaries. London's figures are from 1847–48, vol. 25, p. cxi.
1851, 1861: 1862, vol. 50, Table IX.
1871: 1873, vol. 77 (2), Tables 32 and 32a.
1881, 1891: 1893–94, vol. 104, Tables III, IV, and VI (population and houses); 1893–94, vol. 106, Table 30 (crowding);
1901: 1903, vol. 84, Table XI (population, houses); 1904, vol. 108, Table 42 (crowding).
1911: 1913, vol. 77, Table 3 (population, crowding); 1912–13, vol. 113, Table 2 (houses).

To inflate our sample urban populations and numbers crowded into national urban totals, we used the following estimates of urban population and its distribution:
National urban population: Law (1967), p. 141.
Regional population shares: 1841–61, based on Chapter 2, Table 2.3;
1871–1901, *Parliamentary Papers.* 1871: 1873, vol. 71 (2), Table 34.
1881: interpolated from 1871 and 1891 figures. 1891: 1893–94, vol. 105, Table IV. 1901: 1912–13, vol. 111, Table 7.

Appendix Table 10.2.   Estimating urban overcrowding, 1841–1901

A. Ratio of total urban to sample urban populations

Year	(1) Northern sample	(2) Northern total	(3) 2/1	(4) Southern sample	(5) Southern total	(6) 5/4
1841	1,606,851	3,409,593	2.12	2,554,012	4,283,533	1.68
1851	2,852,101	4,466,134	1.57	3,200,868	5,211,793	1.63
1861	3,551,844	5,472,516	1.54	3,783,098	6,311,540	1.67
1871	4,111,980	8,440,157	2.05	4,564,440	6,361,943	1.39
1881	5,343,208	10,511,744	1.97	5,341,224	7,668,373	1.44
1891						
(a) n = 33	4,666,944	12,660,353	2.71	5,396,256	8,938,499	1.66
(b) n = 77	6,165,596	12,660,353	2.05	6,078,408	8,938,499	1.47
1901						
(a) n = 80	7,218,285	14,837,457	2.06	7,450,738	10,534,392	1.41
(b) n = 98	7,542,619	14,837,457	1.97	7,853,781	10,534,392	1.34

Notes: *For 1891 and 1901, populations in (a) refer to the regression sample; in (b), they refer to the observations included in the predictions of crowding. The size of the regression samples is constrained by the availability of actual crowding data.

B: *Estimating regional crowding in the cities*

Year	(1) Northern sample crowding	(2) Northern total/ sample population	(3) Northern crowding (= 1×2)	(4) Southern sample crowding	(5) Southern total/ sample population	(6) Southern crowding (= 4×5)
1841						
1891	225,045	2.12	477,545	358,105	1.68	600,542
1901	151,902	2.12	322,336	371,025	1.68	622,209
1851						
1891	444,573	1.57	696,201	551,892	1.63	900,136
1901	315,464	1.57	494,017	573,232	1.63	934,941
1861						
1891	518,721	1.54	799,349	682,704	1.67	1,138,750
1901	358,377	1.54	552,259	709,698	1.67	1,183,776
1871						
1891	566,238	2.05	1,162,487	778,038	1.39	1,084,585
1901	381,786	2.05	783,807	808,387	1.39	1,126,891
1881						
1891	710,944	1.97	1,398,427	940,272	1.44	1,350,231
1901	468,260	1.97	921,067	977,592	1.44	1,403,822
1891						
1891	820,546	2.05	1,684,581	953,688	1.47	1,402,875

B: *Estimating regional crowding in the cities (cont.)*

Year	(1) Northern sample crowding	(2) Northern total/ sample population	(3) Northern crowding (= 1×2)	(4) Southern sample crowding	(5) Southern total/ sample population	(6) Southern crowding (= 4×5)
1901	543,356	2.05	1,115,510	991,128	1.47	1,457,949
Actual	614,016	2.71	1,665,825	908,955	1.66	1,505,229
1901						
1891	1,010,257	1.97	1,987,176	1,179,594	1.34	1,581,836
1901	675,668	1.97	1,329,039	1,229,124	1.34	1,648,255
Actual	694,314	2.06	1,427,510	854,224	1.41	1,207,873

Notes: "1891" refers to crowding predicted by 1891 regression coefficients; "1901" refers to crowding predicted by 1901 coefficients; "Actual" refers to census-reported crowding.

C: *Estimating national urban crowding*

Year	National crowding (North & South)	National urban population	Proportion crowded (= 1/2)
1841			
1891	1,078,087	7,693,126	0.140
1901	944,545	7,693,126	0.123
1851			
1891	1,596,337	9,687,927	0.165
1901	1,428,958	9,687,927	0.148
1861			
1891	1,938,099	11,784,056	0.164
1901	1,736,035	11,784,056	0.147
1871			
1891	2,247,072	14,802,100	0.152
1901	1,910,698	14,802,100	0.129
1881			
1891	2,748,657	18,180,117	0.151
1901	2,324,890	18,180,117	0.128
1891			
1891	3,087,456	21,601,012	0.143
1901	2,573,459	21,601,012	0.119
Actual	3,171,055	21,010,012	0.147
1901			
1891	3,569,011	25,371,849	0.141
1901	2,977,294	25,371,849	0.117
Actual	2,635,382	25,371,849	0.104

Sources: See text.

References

W. F. Adams, *Ireland and Irish Emigration to the New World from 1815 to the Famine* (New Haven, Conn.: Yale University Press, 1932).

M. Anderson, *Family Structure in Nineteenth Century Lancashire* (Cambridge: Cambridge University Press, 1971).

M. Anderson, B. Collins, and J. C. Stott, *Preparation and Analysis of a Machine-Readable National Sample from the Enumerators Books of the 1851 Census of Great Britain* (Edinburgh: University of Edinburgh, 1980).

A. Armstrong, *Stability and Change in an English Country Town: A Social Study of York, 1801–1851* (Cambridge: Cambridge University Press, 1974).

W. A. Armstrong, "The Trend of Mortality in Carlisle Between the 1790s and the 1840's: A Demographic Contribution to the Standard of Living Debate," *Economic History Review*, 2nd Series, 34, 1 (February 1981), pp. 94–114.

E. Asher, "Industrial Efficiency and Biassed Technical Change in American and British Manufacturing: The Case of Textiles in the Nineteenth Century," *Journal of Economic History*, 32, 2 (June 1972), pp. 431–42.

T. S. Ashton, "The Treatment of Capitalism by Historians," in F. A. Hayek (ed.), *Capitalism and the Historian* (London: Routledge & Kegan Paul, 1954).

An Economic History of England: The 18th Century (London: Methuen & Co., 1955).

Economic Fluctuations in England, 1700–1800 (Oxford: Oxford University Press [Clarendon Press], 1959).

J. Atack and F. Bateman, *To Their Own Soil: Agriculture in the Antebellum North* (Ames, Iowa: Iowa State University Press, 1987).

W. O. Atwater and A. P. Bryant, *American Foodstuffs* USDA Bulletin No. 28, revised edition (Washington, D.C.: 1899).

D. Baines, *Migration in a Mature Economy: Emigration and Internal Migration in England and Wales 1861–1900* (Cambridge: Cambridge University Press, 1985).

B. Bairoch and G. Goertz, "Factors of Urbanisation in the Nineteenth Century Developed Countries: A Descriptive and Economic Analysis," *Urban Studies* 23 (1986), pp. 285–305.

G. J. Barnsby, "The Standard of Living in the Black Country During the Nineteenth Century," *Economic History Review*, 2nd Series, 24, 2 (1971), pp. 200–39.

J. R. Bellerby, "Distribution of Farm Income in the United Kingdom 1867–1938," *Journal of the Proceedings of the Agricultural Economics Society* 10, 2 (1953), pp. 127–38.

Agriculture and Industry Relative Income (London: Macmillan, 1956).

C. M. Becker, J. G. Williamson, and E. S. Mills, *Indian Urbanization and Economic Growth: Modeling the Past, the Present and the Future* (Baltimore: Johns Hopkins University Press, forthcoming).

A. Berry and R. H. Sabot, "Labour Market Performance in Developing Countries: A Survey," *World Development* 6, 9/10 (1978), pp. 1199–242.

B. J. L. Berry and F. E. Horton, *Geographic Perspective in Urban Systems* (Englewood Cliffs, N.J.: Prentice-Hall, 1970).

R. E. Bilsborrow, "Dependency Rates and Aggregate Savings Rates Revisited," in J. L. Simon and J. DaVanzo (eds.), *Research in Population Economics* vol. 2, pt. 1 (Greenwich, Conn.: Johnson Associates, 1980), pp. 183–204.

N. Birdsall, "Fertility and Economic Change in Eighteenth and Nineteenth Century Europe: A Comment," *Population and Development Review* 9, 1 (March 1983), pp. 111–23.

M. Blaugh, "The Myth of the Old Poor Law and the Making of the New," *Journal of Economic History* 23, 2 (June 1963), pp. 151–84.

R. C. Blitz, "A Benefit-Cost Analysis of Foreign Workers in Germany, 1957–1973," *Kyklos* 30, fasc. 3 (1977), p. 479–502.

The Book of Normals, 1881–1915 (London: Meteorological Office, 1919).

G. J. Borjas, "The Impact of Assimilation on the Earnings of Immigrants: A Re-examination of the Evidence," *NBER Working Paper* No. 1515, Cambridge, Mass. (December 1984).

A. L. Bowley, *Wages in the United Kingdom in the Nineteenth Century* (Cambridge: Cambridge University Press, 1900a).

"The Statistics of Wages in the United Kingdom During the Last Hundred Years," *Journal of the Royal Statistical Society* 63 (1900b), pp. 297–314.

The Division of the Product of Industry (Oxford: Oxford University Press [Clarendon Press], 1919).

G. R. Boyer, "An Economic Model of the English Poor Law, c1780–1834," *Explorations in Economic History* 22, 2 (April 1985), pp. 129–67.

"Malthus Was Right After All: Poor Relief and Birth Rates in Southwestern England," School of Industrial and Labor Relations, Cornell University, mimeo (April 1986a).

"The Poor Law, Migration, and Economic Growth in England," *Journal of Economic History* 46, 2 (June 1986b), pp. 419–30.

G. R. Boyer and J. G. Williamson, "A Quantitative Assessment of the Fertility Transition in England, 1851–1911," *HIER Discussion Paper* No. 1302, Harvard University (March 1986).

P. P. Boyle and C. Ó Grada, "Fertility Trends, Excess Mortality and the Great Irish Famine," mimeo (May 1984).

British Association for the Advancement of Science, 9 (1839).

J. C. Brown, "Coping with Crisis: The Diffusion of Waterworks in Late Nineteenth-Century German Towns," *Journal of Economic History* 48, 2 (June 1988a), pp. 307–18.

"Public Health Crises and Public Response: The Role of Investments in Sanitary Infrastructure in German Cities 1871–1910," paper presented to the Social Science History Association Meetings (October, 1988b).

"The Quality of Life and the Standard of Living: The Case of the Cotton Textile Industry in Northwest England 1806–1850," *Journal of Economic History* (forthcoming).

M. C. Buer, *Health, Wealth and Population in the Early Days of the Industrial Revolution* (London: Routledge and Sons, 1926).

J. Burnett, *A History of the Cost of Living* (Harmondsworth, England: Penguin Books, 1969).

P. J. Cain and A. G. Hopkins, "Gentlemanly Capitalism and British Expansion Overseas II: New Imperialism, 1850–1945," *Economic History Review*, 2nd Series, 40, 1 (February 1987), pp. 1–27.

J. Caird, *English Agriculture in 1850–51.* 2nd edition, first published in 1852. (Fairfield, N.J.: Augustus Kelley, 1967).

A. K. Cairncross, "Internal Migration in Victorian England," *The Manchester School of Economic and Social Studies*, 2nd Series, 9, 1 (January 1949), pp. 67–85.

Home and Foreign Investment 1870–1913 (Cambridge: Cambridge University Press, 1953).

A. K. Cairncross and B. Weber, "Fluctuations in Building in Great Britain, 1785–1849," *Economic History Review* 1X, 2 (December 1956), pp. 283–97.

J. E. Cairnes, *Some Leading Principles of Political Economy Newly Expounded* (London: Macmillan, 1874).

D. Cannadine, "Urban Development in England and America in the Nineteenth Century: Some Comparisons and Contrasts," *Economic History Review*, 2nd Series, 33, 3 (August 1980), pp. 309–25.

F. Capie, "Tariff Protection and Economic Performance in the Nineteenth Century," in J. Black and L. A. Winters (eds.), *Policy and Performance in International Trade* (London: Macmillan, 1983).

F. F. Cartwright, *A Social History of Medicine* (London: Longman Group, 1977).

H. B. Chenery and W. J. Raduchel, "Substitution in Planning Models," in H. B. Chenery (ed.), *Studies in Development Planning* (Cambridge, Mass.: Harvard University Press, 1971).

H. B. Chenery, S. Robinson, and M. Syrquin, *Industrialization and Growth* (London: Oxford University Press, 1986).

H. B. Chenery and M. Syrquin, *Patterns of Development, 1950–1970* (Oxford: Oxford University Press [Clarendon Press], 1975).

B. Chiswick, "The Economic Progress of Immigrants: Some Apparently Universal Patterns," in W. Fellner (ed.), *Contemporary Economic Patterns, 1979* (Washington, D.C.: American Enterprise Institute, 1979).

"Human Capital and the Labor Market Adjustment of Immigrants: Testing Alternate Hypotheses," in O. Stark (ed.), *Research in Human Capital and Development*, vol. 4 (Greenwich, Conn.: JAI Press, 1986).

J. H. Clapham, *An Economic History of Modern Britain, Vol. I. The Early Railway Age* (Cambridge: Cambridge University Press, 1930).

"Irish Immigration into Great Britain in the Nineteenth Century," *Bulletin of the International Committee of Historical Sciences* 20, 5, pt. 3 (July 1933), pp. 596–604.

C. Clark, *The Conditions of Economic Progress* (London: Macmillan, 1957), 3rd edition.

G. Clark, "Why Isn't the Whole World Developed? Lessons from the Cotton Mills," *Journal of Economic History* 47, 1 (March 1987), pp. 141–73.

K. Clark, *The Making of Victorian England* (London: Methuen & Co., 1962).

J. Cleland, *Enumeration of the Inhabitants of the City of Glasgow and its Connected Suburbs* (Glasgow: 1820).

Enumeration of the Inhabitants of the City of Glasgow and the County of Lanark (Glasgow: 1832).

The Former and Present State of Glasgow (Glasgow: 1840).

W. R. Cline, "Distribution and Development: A Survey Article," *Journal of Development Economics* 2, 1 (February 1975), pp. 359–400.

A. J. Coale and E. M. Hoover, *Population Growth and Economic Development in Low-Income Countries* (Princeton, N.J.: Princeton University Press, 1958).

W. E. Cole and R. D. Sanders, "Internal Migration and Urbanization in the Third World," *American Economic Review* 75, 3 (June 1985), pp. 481–94.

B. Collins, "Irish Emigration to Dundee and Paisley During the First Half of the Nineteenth Century," in J. Goldstrom and L. Clarkson (eds.), *Irish Population, Economy and Society: Essays in the Honor of the Late K. H. Connell* (Oxford: Oxford University Press [Clarendon Press], 1981).

Committee of the Statistical Society of London, "Report on the State of the Working Classes in the Parishes of St. Margaret and St. John, Westminster," *Journal of the Statistical Society of London* 3 (1840–1), pp. 14–24.

"Investigation into the State of the Poorer Classes in St. George's in the East," *Quarterly Journal of the Statistical Society of London* 11 (1848), pp. 193–249.

G. A. Condran and E. Crimmins-Gardner, "Public Health Measures and Mortality in U.S. Cities in the Late Nineteenth Century," *Human Ecology* 6 (1978), pp. 27–54.

W. Corden and R. Findlay, "Urban Unemployment: Intersectoral Capital Mobility and Development Policy," *Economica* 42 (February 1975) pp. 59–78.

N. F. R. Crafts, "Income Elasticities of Demand and the Release of Labor," *Journal of European Economic Hstory* 9 (Spring 1980), pp. 59–78.

"Regional Price Variations in England in 1843: An Aspect of the Standard-of-Living Debate," *Explorations in Economic History* 19, 1 (January 1982), pp. 51–70.

British Economic Growth During the Industrial Revolution (Oxford: Oxford University Press [Clarendon Press], 1985).

"British Economic Growth, 1700–1850; Some Difficulties of Interpretation," *Explorations in Economic History* 24, 3 (July 1987), pp. 245–68.

F. Crouzet, "Capital Formation in Great Britain During the Industrial Revolution," in *The Proceedings of the Second International Conference of Economic History* (The Hague: 1965). Reprinted in F. Crouzet (ed.), *Capital Formation in the Industrial Revolution* (London: Methuen & Co., 1972).

"Introduction," in F. Crouzet (ed.), *Capital Formation in the Industrial Revolution* (London: Methuen & Co., 1972).

P. A. David, *Technical Choice, Innovation and Economic Growth* (Cambridge: Cambridge University Press, 1975).

"Invention and Accumulation in America's Economic Growth: A Nineteenth-Century Parable," in K. Brunner and A. Meltzer (eds.), *International Organization, National Policies and Economic Development* (Amsterdam: North Holland, 1977), pp. 179–228.

K. Davis, "The Urbanization of the Human Population," *Scientific American* 213, 3 (March 1965), pp. 41–53.

P. Deane and W. A. Cole, *British Economic Growth 1688–1959* (Cambridge: Cambridge University Press, 1962).

L. del Panta, "Italy" in W. R. Lee (ed.), *European Demography and Economic Growth* (New York: St. Martin's, 1979).

P. Demeny, "Demographic Aspects of Saving, Investment, Employment and Productivity," *World Population Conference, 1965* (New York: United Nations, 1967).

H. Dendy, "The Industrial Residuum," *Economic Journal* (1893), pp. 606–16.

E. F. Denison, *Why Growth Rates Differ: Postwar Experience in Nine Western Countries* (Washington, D.C.: The Brookings Institution, 1967).

Accounting for United States Economic Growth, 1929–1969 (Washington, D.C.: The Brookings Institution, 1974).

E. F. Denison and W. K. Chung, *How Japan's Economy Grew So Fast* (Washington, D.C.: The Brookings Institution, 1976).

T. Dillon, "The Irish in Leeds, 1851–1861," *Publications of the Thoresby Society* 64, 119, pt. 1 (1973), pp. 1–28.

A. Dixit, "Models of Dual Economies," in J. A. Mirrlees and N. H. Stern (eds.), *Models of Economic Growth* (New York: Wiley, 1973).

C. Dougherty and M. Selowsky, "Measuring the Effects of the Misallocation of Labor," *Review of Economics and Statistics* 55, 3 (1973), pp. 386–90.

J. D. Durand, *The Labour Force in Economic Development* (Princeton, N.J.: Princeton University Press, 1975).

R. S. Eckaus, "The Factor Proportions Problem in Underdeveloped Areas," *American Economic Review* 45, 4 (September 1955), pp. 539–65.

M. Edelstein, *Overseas Investment in the Age of High Imperialism* (New York: Columbia University Press, 1982).

Sir F. M. Eden, *The State of the Poor*, vol. 3 (London: 1797).

M. Ellman, "Did the Agricultural Surplus Provide the Resources for the Increase in Investment in the U.S.S.R. During the First Five Year Plan?" *Economic Journal* 83 (December 1975), pp. 844–64.

E. Engel, *Der Werth des Menschen, Part I: Der Kostenwerth des Menschen* (Berlin: 1883).

F. Engels, *The Condition of the Working Class in England.* Edited and translated by W. O. Henderson and W. H. Chaloner. 2nd edition. (Oxford: Basil Blackwell, 1971).

C. Erickson, "Emigration from the British Isles to the U.S.A. in 1831," *Population Studies* 35, 2 (July 1981), pp. 175–97.

S. Fairlee, "The Corn Laws and British Wheat Production, 1829–1876," *Economic History Review*, 2nd Series, 22, 1 (February 1969), pp. 88–116.

W. Farr, *Vital Statistics* (London: Sanitary Institute, 1885).

J. C. H. Fei and G. Ranis, *Development of the Labor Surplus Economy: Theory and Policy* (Homewood, Ill.: Richard D. Irwin, 1964).

C. H. Feinstein, "Capital Formation in Great Britain," in P. Mathias and M. M. Postan (eds.), *The Cambridge Economic History of Europe: Volume VII: The Industrial Economies: Capital, Labour and Enterprise* Part 1 (Cambridge: Cambridge University Press, 1978).

"National Statistics, 1760–1920," in C. H. Feinstein and S. Pollard (eds.), *Studies in Capital Formation in the United Kingdom 1750–1920* (Oxford: Oxford University Press [Clarendon Press], 1988).

A. Fishlow and P. A. David, "Optimal Resource Allocation in an Imperfect Market Setting," *Journal of Political Economy* 69, 6 (1961), pp. 529–46.

D. Fitzpatrick, *Irish Emigration, 1800–1921* (Dublin: 1984).

M. Flinn, "Introduction" to E. Chadwick, *Report on the Sanitary Condition of the Labouring Population of Great Britain*, 1842, ed. by M. W. Flinn (Edinburgh: Edinburgh University Press, 1965).

(ed.)., *Scottish Population History from the 17th Century to the 1930's* (Cambridge: Cambridge University Press, 1977).

R. Floud and D. McCloskey (eds.), *The Economic History of Britain Since 1700, Volume I: 1700–1860* (Cambridge: Cambridge University Press, 1981).

R. W. Fogel, "Nutrition and the Decline in Mortality Since 1700: Some Preliminary Findings," in S. L. Engerman and R. E. Gallman (eds.) *Long-Term Factors in American Economic Growth*, NBER Studies in Income and Wealth, vol. 51 (Chicago: Chicago University Press, 1986).

T. W. Freeman, *Pre-Famine Ireland: A Study in Historical Geography* (New York: Barnes and Noble, 1957).

D. Friedlander, "Demographic Responses and Population Change," *Demography* 6, 4 (November 1969), pp. 359–81.

R. E. Gallman, "Gross National Product in the United States, 1834–1909," in *Output, Employment, and Productivity in the United States After 1800* (New York: Columbia University Press, 1966), pp. 3–76.

C. Gaspari and A. G. Woolf, "Income, Public Works, and Mortality in Early Twentieth-Century American Cities," *Journal of Economic History*, 45, 2 (June 1985), pp. 355–61.

E. Gauldie, *Cruel Habitations: A History of Working-Class Housing 1780–1918* (London: Allen & Unwin, 1974).

D. George, *London Life in the 18th Century* (London: Kegan Paul, 1930).

N. Georgescu-Roegen, "Process in Farming Versus Process in Manufacturing: A Problem of Balanced Development," in V. Papi and C. Numm (eds.), *Economic Problems in Agriculture in Industrial Societies* (London: Macmillan, 1969), pp. 497–528.

M. Getz and Y. Huang, "Consumer Revealed Preference for Environmental Goods," *Review of Economics and Statistics* 60 (1978), pp. 449–58.

C. Goldin and K. Sokoloff, "Women and Children and Industrialization in the Early Republic," *Journal of Economic History* 42, 4 (December 1982), pp. 741–75.

P. A. Graham, *The Rural Exodus* (London: Methuen & Co., 1892).

M. Gray, "Migration in the Rural Lowlands of Scotland, 1750–1850," in L. M. Cullen and T. C. Smout (eds.), *Comparative Aspects of Scottish and Irish Economic and Social History 1600–1900* (Edinburgh: John Donald, 1977).

D. R. Green, "Street Trading in London: A Case Study of Casual Labour 1830–60," in J. Johnson and C. Pooley (eds.), *The Structure of Nineteenth Century Cities* (London: Croom Helm, 1982).

M. J. Greenwood and L. B. Thomas, "Geographic Labor Mobility in Nineteenth Century England and Wales," *Annals of Regional Science* 7, 2 (1973), pp. 90–105.

W. R. Greg, "Report on the State of the Working Classes in Part of Rutlandshire," *British Association for the Advancement of Science* 9 (1839), pp. 112–14.

G. T. Griffith, *Population Problems of the Age of Malthus* (Cambridge: Cambridge University Press, 1926).

J. B. Grossman, "The Substitutability of Natives and Immigrants in Production," *Review of Economics and Statistics* 64 (November 1982), pp. 596–603.

M. R. Haines, "Poverty, Economic Stress, and the Family Life Cycle in a Late Nineteenth Century American City: Whites in Philadelphia, 1880," in T. Hershberg (ed.), *Philadelphia: Work, Space, Family and Group Experience in the Nineteenth Century* (New York: Oxford University Press, 1981), pp. 240–76.

"The Life Cycle, Savings, and Demographic Adaptation: Some Historical Evidence for the United States and Europe," in A. S. Rossi (ed.), *Gender and the Life Course* (Hawthorne, N.Y.: Aldine, 1985), pp. 43–63.

D. S. Hammermesh and J. Grant, "Econometric Studies of Labor – Labor Substitution and their Implications for Policy," *Journal of Human Resources* 14, 4 (1979), pp. 518–42.

B. Hammond, "Urban Death-Rates in the Early Nineteenth Century," *Economic History* 3 (January 1928).

J. L. Hammond and B. Hammond, *The Bleak Age* (New York: Longmans, Green and Co., 1947).

J. E. Handley, *The Irish in Modern Scotland* (Oxford: B. H. Blackwell, 1947).

C. K. Harley, "British Industrialization Before 1841: Evidence of Slower Growth During the Industrial Revolution," *Journal of Economic History* 42, 2 (June 1982), pp. 267–89.

J. R. Harris and M. Todaro, "Migration, Unemployment, and Development: A Two-Sector Analysis," *American Economic Review* 60, 1 (March 1970), pp. 126–42.

T. J. Hatton and J. G. Williamson, "Wage Gaps Between Farm and City: Testing the Todaro Model with American Evidence, 1890–1941," paper presented to the Second World Congress of Cliometrics, Santander, Spain (June 24–7, 1989).

Y. Hayami and V. Ruttan, *Agricultural Development: An International Perspective* (Baltimore: Johns Hopkins University Press, 1971).

H. Heaton, "Financing the Industrial Revolution," *Bulletin of the Business Historical Society* XI, 1 (February 1937), pp. 1–10.

C. E. Heim and P. Mirowski, "Interest Rates and Crowding-Out During Britain's Industrial Revolution," *Journal of Economic History* 47, 1 (March 1987), pp. 117–39.

J. V. Henderson, "Industrialization and Urbanization: International Experience," Department of Economics, Brown University (October 1984).

R. Higgs, "Mortality in Rural America, 1870–1920: Estimates and Conjectures," *Explorations in Economic History* 10, 2 (Winter 1973), pp. 177–95.

R. Higgs and D. Booth, "Mortality Differences Within Large American Cities in 1890," *Human Ecology* 7, 4 (December 1979), pp. 353–70.

I. Hoch, "Climate, Wages, and Quality of Life," in L. Wingo and A. Evans (eds.), *Public Economics and the Quality of Life* (Baltimore: Johns Hopkins University Press, 1977).

B. F. Hoselitz, "Generative and Parasitic Cities," *Economic Development and Cultural Change* 3 (April 1955), pp. 278–94.

"Urbanization and Economic Growth in Asia," *Economic Development and Cultural Change* 5 (October, 1957), pp. 42–54.

House of Commons, *Parliamentary Papers* 1822, vol. 15.

"The First Report of the Factories Inquiry Commission," *Parliamentary Papers* 1833, vol. 20.

"Report from the Commissioners for the Inquiry into the Administration and Practical Operation of the Poor Laws," *Parliamentary Papers* 1834, vols. 30–6.

Parliamentary Papers 1835, vol. 7.

"The First Annual Report of the Poor Commission," *Parliamentary Papers* 1835, vol. 35.

"Report on the State of the Irish Poor in Great Britain," *Parliamentary Papers* 1836, vol. 34 (Poor Inquiry [Ireland], Appendix G.)

"Local Reports on the Sanitary Conditions of the Labouring Population of England," *Parliamentary Papers* 1842.

"Report from the Poor Law Commissioners on an Inquiry into the Sanitary Condition of the Labouring Population of Great Britain," *Parliamentary Papers* 1842.

Parliamentary Papers 1842, vol. 6.

Parliamentary Papers 1843, vols. 22 and 25.

"Report of the Commissioners Appointed to Take the Census of Ireland for the Year 1841," *Parliamentary Papers* 1843, vol. 24.

Parliamentary Papers 1843, vol. 45.

"Report of the Commission for Inquiry into the State of Large Towns and Populous Districts," *Parliamentary Papers* 1844, vol. 17.

"Second Report of the Commission for Inquiry into the State of Large Towns and Populous Districts," *Parliamentary Papers* 1845, vol. 18.

Parliamentary Papers 1847–8, vol. 25.

"Ninth Annual Report of the Registrar General: Appendix," *Parliamentary Papers* 1849, vol. 21.

"Tenth Annual Report of the Registrar General," *Parliamentary Papers* 1849, vol. 21.

Parliamentary Papers 1852–3, vols. 8 and 88.

"1851 Census," *Parliamentary Papers* 1852–3, vol. 83, pt. 1.

"Report on the 1851 Census of Great Britain," *Parliamentary Papers* 1852–3, vol. 85.

Parliamentary Papers 1862, vols. 17 and 50.

Parliamentary Papers 1863, vol. 53, pt. 1.

Parliamentary Papers 1865, vol. 13.

Parliamentary Papers 1872, vol. 17.

"1871 Census of Scotland," *Parliamentary Papers* 1873, vol. 73.

Parliamentary Papers 1873, vols. 71 and 77.

Parliamentary Papers 1875, vol. 18.

Parliamentary Papers 1887, vol. 89.

"Report of the Royal Commission on Labour," *Parliamentary Papers* 1893–4, vol. 37, pt. 2.

Parliamentary Papers 1893–4, vols. 104–106.

Parliamentary Papers 1898, vol. 83.

Parliamentary Papers 1903, vol. 84.

Parliamentary Papers 1904, vol. 108.

"Cost of Living of the Working Class," Board of Trade, *Parliamentary Papers* 1908, vol. 107.

"Report by the Medical Officer on Infant and Child Mortality," 39th Annual Report of the Local Government Board, *Parliamentary Papers* 1910, vol. 39.

Parliamentary Papers 1912–13, vols. 111 and 113.

Parliamentary Papers 1913, vol. 77.

E. H. Hunt, *Regional Wage Variations in Britain 1850–1914* (Oxford: Oxford University Press [Clarendon Press], 1973).

K. Hvidt, *Flight to America: The Social Background of 300,000 Danish Emigrants* (New York: Academic Press, 1975).

S. Ishikawa, *Economic Development in Asian Perspective* (Tokyo: Kinokuniya Bookstore, 1967).

O. Izraeli, "Externalities and Intercity Wage and Price Differentials," in G. Tolley (ed.), *Urban Growth Policy in a Market Economy* (New York: Academic Press, 1979).

J. A. Jackson, *The Irish in Britain* (London: Routledge and Paul, 1963).

J. A. James and J. S. Skinner, "The Resolution of the Labor-Scarcity Paradox," *Journal of Economic History* 45, 3 (September 1985), pp. 513–90.

J. Johnson and C. Pooley (eds.), *The Structure of Nineteenth Century Cities* (London: Croom Helm, 1982).

E. L. Jones, "The Agricultural Labour Market in England, 1793–1872," *Economic History Review*, 2nd Series, 17, 2 (December 1964), pp. 322–38.

E. L. Jones and M. E. Falkus, "Urban Improvement and the English Economy in the Seventeenth and Eighteenth Centuries," *Research in Economic History* 4 (1979), pp. 193–233.

G. S. Jones, *Outcast London* (Oxford: Oxford University Press, 1971).

Journal of the Statistical Society of London, 6 (1843).

Journal of the Statistical Society of London, 11 (1848).

Journal of the Statistical Society of London, 2 (1839–40).

Journal of the Statistical Society of London, 3 (1840–1).

J. P. Kay-Shuttleworth, *The Moral and Physical Condition of the Working Class Employed in the Cotton Manufactures in Manchester* (London: Ridgeway, 1832).

A. C. Kelley and J. G. Williamson, *What Drives Third World City Growth? A Dynamic General Equilibrium Approach* (Princeton, N.J.: Princeton University Press, 1984).

N. Keyfitz, "Do Cities Grow by Natural Increase or by Migration?," *Geographical Analysis* 12 (April 1980), pp. 142–56.

J. B. Knight, "Rural–Urban Income Comparisons and Migration in Ghana," *Bulletin of Oxford University Institute of Economics and Statistics* 34, 2 (1972), pp. 199–228.

N. Koffsky, "Farm and Urban Purchasing Power," *Studies in Income and Wealth* vol. 11, (New York: National Bureau of Economic Research, 1949).

S. Kuznets, "Quantitative Aspects of the Economic Growth of Nations: V: Capital Formation Proportions: International Comparisons for Recent Years," *Economic Development and Cultural Change* III, 4, pt. 2 (July 1960).

"Quantitative Aspects of the Economic Growth of Nations: VI: Long-Term Trends in Capital Formation Proportions," *Economic Development and Cultural Change* IX, 4, pt. 2 (July 1961).

Modern Economic Growth (New Haven, Conn.: Yale University Press, 1966).

Economic Growth of Nations (Cambridge, Mass.: Belknap, 1971).

J. Landers, "Mortality and Metropolis: The Case of London 1675–1825," *Population Studies* 41 (March 1987), pp. 59–76.

D. Landes, *The Unbound Prometheus* (Cambridge: Cambridge University Press, 1969).

A. Laquian, "Review and Evaluation of Urban Accommodationist Policies in Population Redistribution," in *Population Distribution Policies in Development Planning* (New York: United Nations, Department of International Economic and Social Affairs, 1981).

C. M. Law, "The Growth of Urban Population in England and Wales, 1801–1911," *Institute of British Geographers Transactions* 41 (June 1967), pp. 125–43.

"Some Notes on the Urban Population of England and Wales in the Eighteenth Century," *The Local Historian* 10, 1 (February 1972), pp. 13–26.

R. Lawton, "Irish Immigration to England and Wales in the Mid-Nineteenth Century," *Irish Geography* 4, 1 (1959), pp. 35–54.

S. Lebergott, *Manpower in Economic Growth* (New York: McGraw Hill, 1964).

J. Ledent, "Rural–Urban Migration, Urbanization, and Economic Development," *Economic Development and Cultural Change* 30, 3 (April 1982), pp. 507–38.

T. H. Lee, *Intersectoral Capital Flows in the Economic Development of Taiwan, 1895–1960* (Ithaca, N.Y.: Cornell University Press, 1971).

L. H. Lees, "Patterns of Lower-Class Life: Irish Slum Communities in

Nineteenth-Century London," in S. Thernstrom and R. Sennett (eds.), *Nineteenth-Century Cities: Essays in the New Urban Histories* (New Haven, Conn.: Yale University Press, 1969).

Exiles of Erin: Irish Migrants in Victorian London (Ithaca, N.Y.: Cornell University Press, 1979).

N. Leff, "Dependency Rates and Savings Rates," *American Economic Review* 69, 5 (December 1969), pp. 886–95.

H. Leibenstein, "The Theory of Underemployment in Backward Economies," *Journal of Political Economy* 65 (1957), pp.91–103.

F. D. Lewis, "Fertility and Savings in the U.S.: 1830–1900," *Journal of Political Economy* 91 (October 1983), pp. 825–40.

W. A. Lewis, "Economic Development with Unlimited Supplies of Labour," *Manchester School of Economic and Social Studies* 22 (May 1954), pp. 139–91.

"The Evolution of the International Economic Order," Discussion Paper No. 74, Woodrow Wilson School, Research Program in Development Studies, Princeton University (1977).

P. H. Lindert, *Fertility and Scarcity in America* (Princeton, N.J.: Princeton University Press, 1978).

"English Occupations, 1670–1811," *Journal of Economic History* 40, 4 (December 1980), pp. 685–712.

"English Living Standards, Population Growth, and Wrigley-Schofield," *Explorations in Economic History* 20 (1983), pp. 131–55.

"Lucrens Angliae: The Distribution of English Private Wealth Since 1670," Working Paper Series No. 18, Agricultural History Center, University of California, Davis (February 1985).

P. H. Lindert and J. G. Williamson, "English Workers' Living Standards During the Industrial Revolution: A New Look," Economic History Discussion Paper Series, Graduate Program in Economic History, University of Wisconsin (September 1980).

"Revising England's Social Tables 1688–1812," *Explorations in Economic History* 19 (1982), pp. 385–408.

"English Workers' Living Standards During the Industrial Revolution: A New Look," *Economic History Review*, 2nd Series, 36, 1 (February 1983), pp. 1–25.

"English Workers' Real Wages: A Reply to Crafts," *Journal of Economic History*, 45, 1, (March 1985), pp. 145–53.

J. Linn, "Policies for Efficient and Equitable Growth of Cities in Developing Countries," Staff Working Paper No. 342 (Washington, D.C.: World Bank, 1979).

M. Lipton, *Why Poor People Stay Poor: Urban Bias in World Development* (Cambridge: Cambridge University Press, 1976).

H. J. Little, "The Agricultural Labourer," *Journal of the Royal Agricultural Society* 2nd Series, 14 (1878), pp. 499–536.

R. E. B. Lucas and O. Stark, "Motivations to Remit: Evidence from Botswana," *Journal of Political Economy* 93 (October 1985), pp. 901–18.

J. S. Lyons, "Family Response to Economic Decline: English Cotton Handloom Weavers in the Nineteenth Century," paper presented to the Conference of Europeanists, Washington, D.C. (March 19–31, 1979).

D. F. Macdonald, *Scotland's Shifting Population, 1770–1850* (Glasgow: Jackson, Son and Co., 1937).

W. A. Mackenzie, "Changes in the Standard of Living in the United Kingdom, 1860–1914," *Economica* 1, 3 (1921), pp. 211–30.

P. Mantoux, *The Industrial Revolution in the Eighteenth Century* revised edition, T. S. Ashton, ed. (London: Jonathan Cape, 1961).

S. A. Marglin, *Growth, Distribution and Prices* (Cambridge, Mass: Harvard University Press, 1984).

K. Marx, *Capital* Vol. I (New York: International Publishers, 1947). Originally published in 1848.

P. Mathias, "Preface" in F. Crouzet (ed.), *Capital Formation in the Industrial Revolution* (London: Methuen & Co., 1972).

R. C. O. Matthews, C. H. Feinstein, and J. C. Odling-Smee, *British Economic Growth 1856–1973* (Stanford, Calif.: Stanford University Press, 1982).

H. Matzerath, "The Influence of Industrialization on Urban Growth in Prussia (1815–1914)," in H. Schmal (ed.), *Patterns of European Urbanization Since 1500* (London: Croom Helm, 1981).

H. Mayhew, *London Labour and the London Poor*, vols. I–IV (London: Griffin Bohn, 1861).

D. Mazumdar, "Labour Supply in Early Industrialization: The Case of the Bombay Textile Industry," *Economic History Review* 26, 3 (1973), pp. 477–96.

"The Urban Informal Sector," *World Development* 4, 8 (1976), pp. 655–79.

D. N. McCloskey, "New Perspectives on the Old Poor Law," *Explorations in Economic History* 10, 4 (Summer 1973), pp. 419–36.

"Magnanimous Albion: Free Trade and British National Income, 1841–1881," *Explorations in Economic History* 17, 3 (1980), pp. 303–20.

"The Industrial Revolution: A Survey," in R. Floud and D. N. McCloskey (eds.), *The Economic History of Britain Since 1700, Volume I: 1700–1860* (Cambridge: Cambridge University Press, 1981).

T. McKeown, *The Modern Rise of Population* (New York: Academic Press, 1976).

"Fertility, Mortality and Causes of Death: An Examination of Issues Related to the Modern Rise of Population," *Population Studies* 32 (1978), pp. 535–42.

"Food, Infection, and Population," *Journal of Interdisciplinary History* 14 (1983), pp. 227–47.

T. McKeown and R. G. Brown, "Medical Evidence Related to English Population Changes in the Eighteenth Century," *Population Studies* 9 (1955), pp. 119–41.

"Reasons for the Decline of Mortality in England and Wales During the Nineteenth Century," *Population Studies* 16, pt. 2 (November 1962), pp. 94–122.

T. McKeown, R. G. Record, and R. D. Turner, "An Interpretation of the Decline of Mortality in England and Wales During the Twentieth Century," *Population Studies* 29, 3 (November 1975), pp. 391–422.

R. McKinnon, *Money and Capital in Economic Development* (Washington, D.C.: The Brookings Institution, 1973).

E. Meeker, "The Improving Health of the United States, 1850–1915," *Explorations in Economic History* 9, 4 (Summer 1972), pp. 354–73.

"The Social Rate of Return on Investment in Public Health, 1880–1910," *Journal of Economic History* 34, 2 (June 1974), pp. 392–421.

T. W. Merrick, "Employment and Earnings in the Informal Sector in Brazil," *The Journal of Developing Areas* 10, 3 (1978), pp. 337–54.

Metropolitan Working Classes' Association, *Manual of Public Health and Domestic Economy* (London: John Churchill, 1847).

J. S. Mill, *Principles of Political Economy* 3rd edition (London: J. W. Parker, 1852). *Principles of Political Economy* 5th edition (New York: D. Appleton, 1909).

K. Miller, *Emigrants and Exiles: Ireland and the Irish Exodus to North America* (New York: Oxford University Press, 1985).

B. R. Mitchell, *European Historical Statistics 1750–1970* (New York: Columbia University Press, 1978).

B. R. Mitchell and P. Deane, *Abstract of British Historical Statistics* (Cambridge: Cambridge University Press, 1962).

R. Mohan, *Urban Economic and Planning Models* (Baltimore: Johns Hopkins University Press, 1979).

"The People of Bogotá: Who They Are, What They Earn, Where They Live," *Bank Staff Working Paper* No. 390 (Washington, D.C.: The World Bank, 1980).

J. Mokyr, *Industrialization in the Low Countries, 1795–1850* (New Haven, Conn.: Yale University Press, 1976).

Why Ireland Starved: A Quantitative and Analytical History of the Irish Economy, 1800–1850 (London: Allen & Unwin, 1983; 2nd edition, 1985a).

"The Industrial Revolution and the New Economic History," in J. Mokyr (ed.), *The Economics of the Industrial Revolution* (Totowa, N.J.: Rowman and Allanhead, 1985).

"Has the Industrial Revolution Been Crowded Out? Some Reflections on Crafts and Williamson," *Explorations in Economic History* 24, 3 (July 1987), pp. 293–325.

J. Mokyr and C. Ó Grada, "Emigration and Poverty in Prefamine Ireland," *Explorations in Economic History* 19 (October 1982), pp. 360–84.

"New Developments in Irish Population History, 1700–1850," *Economic History Review*, 2d Series, 37, 4 (November 1984), pp. 473–88.

D. Morawetz, "Employment Implications of Industrialization in Developing Countries: A Survey," *Economic Journal* 84 (September 1974), pp. 491–542.

S. Morley, *Labor Markets and Inequitable Growth: The Core of Authoritarian Capitalism in Brazil* (Cambridge: Cambridge University Press, 1982).

E. Mueller, "The Economic Value of Children in Peasant Agriculture," in R. G. Ridker (ed.), *Population and Development* (Baltimore: Johns Hopkins University Press, 1976).

L. Neal and P. Uselding, "Immigration: A Neglected Source of American Economic Growth, 1790 to 1917," *Oxford Economic Papers* 24, 7 (1972), pp. 66–88.

S. Nicholas and P. R. Shergold, "Internal Migration in England," Working Paper No. 39, The Australian National University, Canberra, Australia (1985a).

"Intercounty Labour Mobility During the Industrial Revolution", Working Paper No. 43, The Australian National University, Canberra, Australia (1985b).

"Human Capital and the Pre-Famine Irish Emigration to England," *Explorations in Economic History* 24 (April 1987), pp. 158–77.

W. Nordhaus and J. Tobin, "Is Growth Obsolete?" in National Bureau of Economic Research, *Economic Growth: Fiftieth Anniversary Colloquium V* (New York: Columbia University Press, 1972).

D. C. North, "The United States Balance of Payments, 1790–1860," in *Trends in the American Economy in the Nineteenth Century*, Studies in Income and Wealth, vol. 24 (New York: National Bureau for Economic Research, 1960), pp. 573–627.

G. O'Brien, *An Economic History of Ireland from the Union to the Famine* (London: Longmans, Green and Co., 1921).

C. Ó Grada, "A Note on Nineteenth-Century Irish Emigration Statistics," *Population Studies* 29, 1 (March 1975), pp. 143–9.

"Some Aspects of Nineteenth-Century Irish Emigration," in L. M. Cullen and T. C. Smout (eds.), *Comparative Aspects of Scottish and Irish Economic and Social History 1600–1900* (Edinburgh: John Donald, 1977).

"Across the Briny Ocean: Some Thoughts on Irish Emigration to America, 1800–1850," in T. Devine and D. Dickson (eds.), *Ireland and Scotland: Essays in Comparative Economic and Social History* (Edinburgh: John Donald, 1983).

"Technical Change in the Mid-Nineteenth Century British Cotton Industry: A Note," *Journal of European Economic History* 13 (Fall 1984), pp. 345–53.

M. Ó Tauthaigh, "The Irish in Nineteenth-Century Britain: Problems of Integration," *Transactions of the Royal Historical Society* 5th Series, 31 (1981), pp. 149–73.

W. H. Phillips, "Induced Innovation and Economic Performance in Late Victorian British Industry," *Journal of Economic History* 42, 1 (March 1982), pp. 97–103.

I. Pinchbeck, *Women Workers and the Industrial Revolution 1750–1850.* 3d Edition. (London: Virago, 1981).

S. Pollard, *A History of Labour in Sheffield* (Liverpool: Liverpool University Press, 1959).

"Labour in Great Britain," in P. Mathias and M. M. Postan (eds.), *The Cambridge Economic History of Europe: Volume VII: The Industrial Economies: Capital, Labour, and Enterprise* (Cambridge: Cambridge University Press, 1978).

"Sheffield and Sweet Auburn – Amenities and Living Standards in the British Industrial Revolution: A Comment," *Journal of Economic History* 41, 4 (December 1981), pp. 902–4.

K. Polyani, *The Great Transformation* (New York: 1944).

Poor Law Commission, *Local Reports on the Sanitary Condition of the Labouring Population of England* (July 1842).

M. M. Postan, "Recent Trends in the Accumulation of Capital," *Economic History Review* 6, 1 (October 1935), pp. 1–12. Reprinted in F. Crouzet (ed.), *Capital Formation in the Industrial Revolution* (London: Methuen, 1972).

S. J. Prais and H. S. Houthakker, *The Analysis of Family Budgets* (Cambridge: Cambridge University Press, 1955).

S. H. Preston, "Urban Growth in Developing Nations: A Demographic Reappraisal," *Population and Development Review* 5 (June 1979), pp. 195–215.

"The Changing Relation Between Mortality and Level of Economic Development," *Population Studies* 29, 2 (July 1985), pp. 231–48.

S. H. Preston and V. E. Nelson, "Structure and Change in Causes of Death: An International Summary," *Population Studies* 28, 1 (March 1974), pp. 19–51.

S. H. Preston and E. Van de Walle, "Urban French Mortality in the Nineteenth Century," *Population Studies,* 32, 2 (July 1978), pp. 275–97.

F. Purdy, "On the Earnings of Agricultural Laborers," *Journal of the Statistical Society of London* 24 (1861), pp. 328–73.

R. Ransom and R. Sutch, "Domestic Saving as an Active Constraint on Capital Formation in the American Economy, 1839–1928: A Provisional Theory," Department of Economics, University of California, Berkeley, mimeo (November 1983).

H. Ratcliffe, *Observations on the Rate of Mortality and Sickness* (Manchester: George Falkner, 1850).

E. G. Ravenstein, "The Laws of Migration," *Journal of the Statistical Society* 48 (1885), pp. 167–227.

"The Laws of Migration," *Journal of the Statistical Society* 52 (1889), pp. 214–301.

M. W. Reder, "The Economic Consequences of Increased Immigration," *Review of Economics and Statistics* 45, 3 (August 1963), pp. 221–30.

A. Redford, *Labour Migration in England, 1800–1850* (Manchester: Manchester University Press, 1926).

H. Remple and R. A. Lobdell, "The Role of Urban-to-Rural Remittances in Rural Development," *Journal of Development Studies* 14, 3 (April 1978), pp. 324–41.

C. Richardson, "Irish Settlement in Mid-Nineteenth Century Bradford," *Yorkshire Bulletin of Economic and Social Research* 20, 1 (May 1968), pp. 40–57.

T. L. Richardson, "The Standard of Living Controversy, 1790–1840," Ph.D. thesis, University of Hull, 1977.

J. C. Riley, "Insects and the European Mortality Decline," *American Historical Review* 91, 4 (Occtober 1986), pp. 833–58.

The Eighteenth Century Campaign to Avoid Disease (London: Macmillan, 1987)

W. G. Rimmer, "Working Men's Cottages in Leeds, 1770–1840," *Publications of the Thoresby Society* 46, 108, pt. 2 (1960), pp. 165–99.

A. Rogers, "Migration, Urbanization, Resources, and Development," in H. McMains and L. Wilcox (eds.), *Alternatives for Growth: The Engineering and Economics of Natural Resource Development* (Cambridge, Mass.: Ballinger, 1978).

Migration, Urbanization and Spatial Population Dynamics (Boulder, Colo.: Westview, 1984).

A. Rogers and J. G. Williamson, "Migration, Urbanization, and Third World Development: An Overview," *Economic Development and Cultural Change* (April 1982), pp. 463–82.

S. Rosen, "Wage-Based Indexes of Urban Quality of Life," in P. Miewzkowski and M. Straszheim (eds.), *Current Issues in Urban Economics* (Baltimore: Johns Hopkins University Press, 1979).

W. W. Rostow, "The Take-off into Self-Sustained Growth," *Economic Journal* LXVI, 261 (March 1956), pp. 25–48.

The Stages of Economic Growth (Cambridge: Cambridge University Press, 1960).

B. S. Rowntree, *Poverty: A Study of Town Life* (London: Macmillan, 1901).

L. Sanberg, "Movements in the Quality of British Cotton Textile Exports, 1815–1913," *Journal of Economic History*, 28 (March 1968), pp. 1–27.

J. Saville, *Rural Depopulation in England and Wales 1851–1951* (London: Routledge & Kegan Paul, 1957).

T. P. Schultz, *Economics of Population* (Reading, Mass.: Addison-Wesley, 1981).

D. Segal, "Are There Returns to Scale in City Size?," *Review of Economics and Statistics* 48 (1976).

A. K. Sen, "Peasants and Dualism With or Without Surplus Labor," *Journal of Political Economy* 74 (October 1966), pp. 425–50.

H. A. Shannon and E. Grebenik, *The Population of Bristol* (Cambridge: Cambridge University Press, 1943).

R. P. Shaw, "On Modifying Metropolitan Migration," *Economic Development and Cultural Change* 26 (July 1978), pp. 677–92.

J. B. Shoven and J. Whalley, "Applied General-Equilibrium Models of Taxation and International Trade," *Journal of Economic Literature* 22, 3 (1984), pp. 1007–51.

V. Shukla, "The Productivity of Indian Cities and Some Implications for Development Policy," Ph.D. thesis, Princeton University (1984).

A. B. Simmons, "Slowing Metropolitan City Growth in Asia: Policies, Programs and Results," *Population and Development Review* 5 (March 1979), pp. 87–104.

J. Simon, *English Sanitary Institutions* (London: Cassell, 1890).

M. Simon, "The United States Balance of Payments, 1861–1900," in *Trends in the American Economy in the Nineteenth Century*, Studies in Income and Wealth, vol. 24 (New York: National Bureau for Economic Research, 1960), pp. 629–715.

H. W. Singer, "An Index of Urban Land Rents and House Rents in England and Wales, 1845–1913," *Econometrica* 9 (April 1941), pp. 221–30.

N. J. Smelser, *Social Change in the Industrial Revolution* (Chicago: University of Chicago Press, 1959).

B. Smith, "Measuring the Value of Urban Amenities," *Journal of Urban Economics* 5 (1978), pp. 370–87.

P. A. Sorokin, C. C. Zimmerman, and C. J. Galpin, *A Systematic Source Book in Rural Sociology*, vol. 3 (Minneapolis: The University of Minnesota Press, 1932).

L. Squire, *Employment Policy in Developing Countries* (Oxford: Oxford University Press, 1981).

O. Stark, "On Slowing Metropolitan City Growth," *Population and Development Review* 6 (March 1980), pp. 95–102.

"On the Role of Urban-to-Rural Remittances in Rural Development," *Journal of Development Studies* 16, 3 (April 1980), pp. 369–74.

"The Asset Demand for Children During Agricultural Modernization," *Population and Development Review* 7, 4 (December 1981), pp. 671–5.

O. Stark and E. Katz, "On Fertility, Migration and Remittances in LDCs," Migration and Developmental Program Discussion Paper, Harvard University (September 1985).

Statistical Committee of the Town Council, "Report upon the Condition of the Town of Leeds and of its Inhabitants," *Journal of the Statistical Society of London* 2, (1839–40), pp. 397–424.

R. Stavins, "A Model of English Demographic Change: 1573–1873," Department of Economics, Harvard University, mimeo (January 1986).

E. D. Steele, "The Irish Presence in the North of England, 1850–1914," *Northern History* 12 (1976), pp. 220–41.

J. Stiglitz, "Wage Determination and Unemployment in LDCs," *Quarterly Journal of Economics* 88, 2 (May 1974), pp. 194–227.

L. Sveikauskas, "The Productivity of Cities," *Quarterly Journal of Economics* 89 (1975).

E. Sydenstricker and W. I. King, "The Measurement of the Relative Economic Status of Families," *Quarterly Publication of the American Statistical Association* 17, 135 (September 1921), pp. 842–57.

S. Szreter, "The Importance of Social Intervention in Britain's Mortality Decline c. 1850–1914: A Re-Interpretation," Discussion Paper No. 121, Centre for Economic Policy Research, London (July 1986).

A. J. Taylor, "Editor's Introduction," in A. J. Taylor (ed.), *The Standard of Living in Britain in the Industrial Revolution* (London: Methuen & Co., 1975).

L. Taylor, E. L. Bacha, E. A. Cardoso, and F. J. Lysy, *Models of Growth and Distribution for Brazil* (New York: Oxford University Press, 1980).

M. S. Teitelbaum, *The British Fertility Decline* (Princeton, N.J.: Princeton University Press, 1984).

V. Thomas, "Spatial Differences in the Cost of Living," *Journal of Urban Economics* 8 (1980), pp. 108–22.

E. P. Thompson, *The Making of the English Working Class* (New York: Pantheon, 1963).

"The Making of the Working Class," in A. J. Taylor (ed.), *The Standard of Living in Britain in the Industrial Revolution* (London: Methuen & Co., 1975).

F. M. L. Thompson, *English Landed Society in the Nineteenth Century* (London: Routledge and Kegan Paul, 1963).

D. Thomson, "The Decline of Social Welfare: Falling State Support for the Elderly Since Early Victorian Times," *Aging and Society* 4, 4 (December 1984), pp. 451–82.

R. M. Titmuss, *Birth, Poverty, and Wealth: A Study of Infant Mortality* (London: Hamish Hamilton Medical Books, 1943).

M. P. Todaro, "A Model of Labor Migration and Urban Unemployment in Less Developed Countries," *American Economic Review* 59, 1 (March 1969), pp. 138–48.

"Urbanization in Developing Nations: Trends, Prospects, and Policies," in P. K. Ghosh (ed.), *Urban Development in the Third World* (Westport, Conn.: Greenwood, 1984).

G. Tolley, "The Welfare Economics of City Bigness," *Journal of Urban Economics* 1 (July 1974), pp. 324–45.

R. S. Tucker, "Real Wages of Artisans in London, 1729–1933," *Journal of the American Statistical Association* 31 (March 1936), pp. 73–84.

C. Tuttle, "The Role of Children in the Industrial Revolution," Ph.D. thesis, Northwestern University (September 1985).

United Nations, *Global Review of Human Settlements: A Support for Habitat*, 2 vols. (Oxford: Pergamon Press, 1976).

Patterns of Urban and Rural Population Growth (New York: United Nations Department of International Economic and Social Affairs, 1980).

"Age and Sex Structure of Urban and Rural Populations, 1970–2000: The 1980 Assessment," United Nations Department of International Economic and Social Affairs, Population Division, Working Paper No. 81 (New York: December 8, 1982).

U. S. Department of Commerce, Bureau of the Census, *Historical Statistics of the United States*, Part 1 (Washington, D.C.: USGPO, 1975).

D. Usher, "An Imputation to the Measure of Economic Growth for Changes in Life Expectancy," in M. Ross (ed.), *The Measurement of Economic and Social Performance* (New York: Columbia University Press, 1973).

R. Vedder and D. Cooper, "Nineteenth Century English and Welsh Geographic Labor Mobility: Some Further Evidence," *Annals of Regional Science* 8 (1974).

G. N. von Tunzelmann, "Technical Progress During the Industrial Revolution," in R. Floud and D. N. McCloskey (eds.), *The Economic History of Britain Since 1700, Volume 1: 1700–1860* (Cambridge: Cambridge University Press, 1981).

R. Wall, *Mortality in Mid 19th Century Britain* (London: Greggs International, 1974).

A. F. Weber, *The Growth of Cities in the Nineteenth Century* (New York: Macmillan, 1899).

C. R. Weld, "On the Condition of the Working Classes in the Inner Ward of St. George's Parish, Hanover Square," *Journal of the Statistical Society of London* 6 (1843), pp. 17–23.

T. A. Welton, "Note on Urban and Rural Variations According to the English Census of (1911), *Journal of the Royal Statistical Society* 76 (February 1913), pp. 304–17.

J. M. Werly, "The Irish in Manchester, 1832–49," *Irish Historical Studies* 18, 71 (March 1973), pp. 345–58.

F. M. Williams and C. C. Zimmerman, *Studies of Family Living in the United States and Other Countries*, USDA Miscellaneous Publication No. 223 (Washington, D.C.: 1935).

J. G. Williamson, "Inequality, Accumulation, and Technological Imbalance: A Growth-Equity Conflict in Economic History?" *Economic Development and Cultural Change* 27, 2 (January 1979), pp. 231–54.

"Urban Disamenities, Dark Satanic Mills, and the British Standard of Living Debate," *Journal of Economic History* 41, 1 (March 1981), pp. 75–83.

"Was the Industrial Revolution Worth It? Disamenities and Death in 19th Century British Towns," *Explorations in Economic History* 19, 3 (July 1982), pp. 221–45.

"Why Was British Growth So Slow During the Industrial Revolution?" *Journal of Economic History* 44, 3 (September 1984a), pp. 687–712.

"British Mortality and the Value of Life: 1781–1931," *Population Studies* 38 (March 1984b), pp. 157–72.

Did British Capitalism Breed Inequality? (Winchester, Mass.: Allen & Unwin, 1985a).

"The Urban Transition During the First Industrial Revolution: England 1776–1871," HIER Discussion Paper No. 1146, Harvard University (April 1985b).

"City Immigration, Selectivity Bias and Human Capital Transfers During the British Industrial Revolution," HIER Discussion Paper No. 1146, Harvard University (July 1985c).

"Migrant Earnings in Britain's Cities in 1851: Testing Competing Views of Urban Labor Market Absorption," HIER Discussion Paper No. 1176, Harvard University (August 1985d).

"Did Rising Emigration Cause Fertility to Decline in 19th Century Rural England? Child Costs, Old-Age Pensions and Child Default," paper presented to the University of California Tenth Conference in Economic History, Laguna Beach, California (May 1986a).

"The Impact of the Irish on British Labor Markets During the Industrial Revolution," *Journal of Economic History* 46, 3 (September 1986b), pp. 693–720.

"The Impact of the Corn Laws Just Prior to Repeal," HIER Discussion Paper No. 1279, Harvard University (November 1986c).

"Debating the British Industrial Revolution," *Explorations in Economic History* 24, 3 (July 1987) pp. 269–92.

"Migration and Urbanization," in H. B. Chenery and T. N. Srinivasan (eds.), *Handbook of Development Economics* (Amsterdam: North Holland, 1988).

J. G. Williamson and P. H. Lindert, *American Inequality: A Macroeconomic History* (New York: Academic Press, 1980).

A. S. Wohl, *Endangered Lives: Public Health in Victorian Britain* (Cambridge, Mass.: Harvard University Press, 1983).

G. H. Wood, *The History of Wages in the Cotton Trade During the Past Hundred Years* (London: Sherratt and Hughes, 1910).

E. A. Wrigley and R. S. Schofield, *The Population History of England, 1541–1871: A Reconstruction* (Cambridge: Cambridge University Press, 1981).

L. Yap, "The Attraction of Cities: A Review of the Migration Literature," *Journal of Development Studies* 4 (1977), pp. 239–64.

W. Zelinsky, "The Hypothesis of the Mobility Transition," *Geographical Review* 61 (1971), pp. 219–49.

Index

331